Preparing for the Multistate Bar Examination

Volume III: An Outline of Every MBE Topic and Subtopic

Nelson P. Miller

Preparing for the Multistate Bar Examination: Volume III: an outline of every MBE topic and subtopic.

Miller, Nelson P.

Published by:

Crown Management LLC – March 2017

1527 Pineridge Drive
Grand Haven, MI 49417
USA

ISBN: 978-0-9980601-5-6

Table of Contents

The Parts I and II introductory text to this Volume III is substantially the same as the Parts I and II introductory text to Volumes I and II.
Volume III differs in its Part III outline.

The Parts I and II introductory text to this Volume III is substantially the same as the Parts I and II introductory text to Volumes I and II. Volume III differs in its Part III outline.

Part I: The Multistate Bar Examination

A.   Overview

The Multistate Bar Examination is a six-hour, 200-question multiple-choice test scoring 175 of the 200 questions. The examiners use the other 25 unscored questions as pre-test questions. The Multistate Bar Examination appears on the bar exams of all states other than Louisiana and U.S. territories other than Puerto Rico. The District of Columbia's bar exam also includes the Multistate Bar Examination. The Multistate Bar Examination is the same in every state.

The Multistate Bar Examination is a one-day, all-day examination, given on the same day in every location. Examinees take 100 questions in a morning three-hour block and, after a two-hour lunch break, the second 100 questions in an afternoon three-hour block. State bar exams also include an essay portion (often the Multistate Essay Examination) and may include a performance portion (often the Multistate Performance Test). Examiners administer other bar-exam components on a second, and in some cases a third, day.

You are very likely to have to do well on the Multistate Bar Examination in order to pass a bar exam and receive a law license. States typically weight the Multistate Bar Examination at up to fifty percent of the exam's total score. Indeed, the Uniform Bar Examination used in half of the states weights the Multistate Bar Examination at fifty percent of the exam's total score.

The Multistate Bar Examination tests the seven subjects of civil procedure, constitutional law, contracts, criminal law and procedure, evidence, real property, and torts. Plan early to do well on these subjects. Take these courses in law school whether your curriculum requires that you do so or not. Learning a subject in a short bar-review course just before the bar exam is not ideal. Refreshing yourself on a subject that you have already learned in a law school course is far better than learning the subject for the first time in your bar-review course.

The National Conference of Bar Examiners drafts the Multistate Bar Examination. Its website provides a five-page outline showing the tested topics and sub-topics in each of the seven subject areas. The five-page outline also indicates the proportion of questions asked on various topics. Examining the outline should convince you of the need to study these topics while also serving as a focus, reminder, and guide during your studies.

B.   Time

The Multistate Bar Examination gives you 1.8 minutes for each of its 200 multiple-choice questions, in two three-hour sessions of 100 multiple-choice questions each. That time of just less than two minutes means that you must complete 33 to 34 questions every hour to keep on pace to finish all multiple-choice questions.

Time may be the single most-important condition with which you must deal effectively to do well on the Multistate Bar Examination. When you are practicing multiple-choice questions, you should know the amount of time that you must answer each question and should gage how you are doing. Develop the skill to answer within the time that the Multistate Bar Examination allows. You do yourself little good to confirm the comprehensive knowledge base and analytical skill that multiple-choice questions require unless you can apply the knowledge and exercise the skill quickly enough to finish the Multistate Bar Examination.

Time management is thus a critical success strategy for the Multistate Bar Examination. You must learn to use your time strategically. If you rush through leaving too much extra time at the end for review, then you will have compromised your ability to answer correctly the first time through. If, on the other hand, you drag through failing to finish timely, then you will get zero credit for unanswered questions and only random credit for answers that you guess when you have no time to read the question.

Falling behind and rushing through final questions is also not a sensible option because of the errors that rushing creates. Time stress reduces concentration, resulting in reduced performance. Practice under the allotted time constraint until you no longer feel rushed. Accustom yourself thoroughly to the time constraint until the clock no longer affects your concentration. Habituation to exam conditions is an important practice to ensure maximal performance.

As you navigate the exam's time pressure, remain fully in the moment. You cannot answer all questions at once. Looking ahead to answering 100 questions in three hours may unnerve you. Don't look ahead. Answer one question at a time while periodically checking your progress.

As soon as you finish one question, forget it, and move on to the next question. Ruminating over a prior answer while you attempt to answer the next question will not improve the prior answer but will instead delay you in completing the next answer. Don't let tough questions sap your confidence. Instead, let easy questions boost your confidence.

C. Tracking Time

Given that the Multistate Bar Examination requires that you answer 200 questions total in two three-hour sessions of 100 questions each, working out to 1.8 minutes per question or 33 to 34 questions every hour, how do you track that time?

A simple and accurate way of tracking time is to figure that you must complete a little more than one question every two minutes. At 30 minutes, you should have completed about 17 questions, while at one hour you should have completed about 34 questions. Halfway through at the hour-and-a-half mark, you should have completed 50 questions. Two hours into the exam, you should have completed about 67 questions. At two-and-a-half hours, you should have completed 84 questions, to complete 100 questions by the end of the third hour. The sequence for every half hour is thus 17, 34, 50, 67, 84, and 100 questions. Note these numbers when the exam begins, and use them to track your time.

With effective bar-exam preparation, you should find yourself quickly ahead of time, enough so that you can pace yourself. If you can build a small cushion of time, getting five minutes ahead early, then that cushion can relieve time pressure, which should make you even more efficient at reading, reflecting, and answering.

Do *not* stick on questions. If you don't know the answer to one question, then mark whatever answer seems best, moving promptly on because the next question and each question after it will have just as much value. Remember that twenty-five questions are pre-test questions that the National Conference of Bar Examiners will not even count against your score. The question that you could not answer may be a defective pre-test question. Otherwise, every question has equal weight. Keep moving.

D. Finishing Early

Following the above approaches, and with effective study and substantial practice, you may well finish each of the two three-hour Multistate Bar Examination multiple-choice sessions with ten or twenty minutes or more to spare. If in your practice sessions you find yourself finishing way too early, then slow down your approach.

Finishing ahead of time can nonetheless provide good benefit in that you have time to go back to check and confirm or change answers. Don't hesitate to do so. Make good use of extra time to confirm or correct answers.

You may recall the frustration of getting an answer correct the first time but changing it to a wrong answer when re-reading the question and second-guessing your analysis. Research shows that examinees typically *benefit* from changing answers. The reason that second-guessing can seem hazardous is that examinees find it hard to forget the times when changing answers led to a wrong answer. We remember our losses and regrets much more than our successes.

Avoid reading too much into a question. Examiners expect you to figure out the answer from a single reading. However, if upon review a different answer seems like the better choice, then odds favor that changing to the new choice will improve your score. If you finish early, then by all means, reread your answers and change wrong answers.

E. Scoring

Learn how your state's bar examiners will score your bar exam. Scoring practices including the weight given to each section and minimum passing scores vary from state to state, particularly within states that do not follow Uniform Bar Examination format. The National Conference of Bar Examiners maintains individual state scoring information on its website, which would also be available directly from the state's bar examiners.

While you expect to perform at your best no matter how the examiners score your effort, scoring can matter in how you allocate your preparation time and effort. The bar exam tends to reward comprehensive rather than peculiar performance. You should not generally plan to overcome poor performance on one section of the bar exam with stellar performance on another. Instead, plan to perform with at least minimal competence on all parts of the exam, even if your state bar weighs all parts of the exam equally.

You may feel that the strength of your skill in one area will offset weakness in another, but you may instead find that remediating the weakness with a little more bar preparation pays greater scoring dividends than honing your strength. After all, low scores leave more room for improvement than do high scores. Olympic performers can only achieve tiny gains no matter how hard or long they struggle because they are already near optimal athletic performance.

In the same way, given that you have only limited time, you don't want to invest all your efforts into achieving a tiny gain in one area that will have an inconsequential effect on your overall performance. For the same investment of time and energy, you may have a huge leap in overall ability if you focus on your weak spots. You always want to find the areas that offer you the greatest potential for improving performance. The incremental gain that your studies achieve may be greater in your poorer performance areas than in your better areas.

Moreover, a few state bars require that you reach a minimum score in one or more parts of the bar exam no matter how high the rest of your bar-exam score is. If you do decide to ignore a difficult area of the law that you just cannot seem to master after at least some diligent study, then be sure that it is a *small subtopic* that you are ignoring, one unlikely to be on the exam or if on the exam likely to be only a very small part of it.

F. Scaling

Do not worry unduly about your bar exam being especially difficult compared to prior exams. The National Conference of Bar Examiners *scales* Multistate Bar Examination scores. The examiners add a certain number of points, usually in the range of 10 to 15 points, to your raw score in order to equate the exam's difficulty to the difficulty of prior exams. If your exam turned out to be more difficult than prior exams, then you will receive additional scaled points to ensure that the exam's difficulty does not affect your results.

If your raw scores on practice exams are just below your state's required passing score, then scaling may help you pass. Scaling improves your Multistate Bar Examination raw score, although you will not know until after the exam by how much. Read more about scaling on the National Conference of Bar Examiners website. While the National Conference of Bar Examiners scales the Multistate Bar Examination, state bars may or may not scale scores on their state-specific essay or performance tests. Investigate your state bar examiners' scaling and scoring practices until you know approximately what score you must obtain for your practice and assessment purposes, and are confident that the examiners will treat you fairly.

G. Subjects

Knowing the content of your bar exam, meaning the law that the exam actually tests, is critical to your preparation. Law is vast. Fortunately, the bar exam tests only a slice of that vast amount of law. Even more fortunately, bar examiners disclose in advance the subject areas that they will test. Not only do they disclose the law fields that will be on the exam, but for certain tests, in particular the Multistate Bar Examination, they also disclose the testable topics and subtopics within those fields. Only a fool or glutton for punishment would disregard these disclosures and attempt to study all fields and all topics within those fields.

Beyond the advantage of disclosure of fields, topics, and subtopics, you may also locate resources, particularly but not exclusively commercial bar-preparation-course resources, that summarize topic-testing patterns. For instance, to teach a free state-specific bar-preparation essay workshop at the authors' law school, one of the authors studies and summarizes the testing pattern of the subject for the past ten-plus years.

You can thus see how knowing the fields and their topics and subtopics, and then adding to it some sense of the most-frequently tested topics within fields, can give you both confidence and a genuine advantage. Research field, topic, and subtopic coverage as you prepare for the bar exam.

Every examinee understands that to perform well on the bar exam, you need a certain minimum level of knowledge. What you might not appreciate is that some evidence suggests that reaching a much higher level of knowledge than the minimum that the bar exam requires does not necessarily give you an advantage. Bar examiners possess a requisite level of knowledge. They also expect examinees, most of whom are very recent law school graduates, to possess a certain level of knowledge, certainly one that demonstrate competence but not necessarily one that demonstrates deep subject mastery. The questions are, after all, fairly rudimentary in their nature simply because of the bar exam's limited time and restrictive format.

Examiners can't do too much with a multiple-choice question, given the time and format limitations, not to mention the limitations imposed by relatively objective evaluation and scoring. Given these time-and-format limitations and the examiners' tempered expectations, you may find yourself doing better on practice questions in areas where your level of knowledge is good but not necessarily outstanding, masterful, or excellent.

You may, in other words, not be doing yourself any favors by applying the superior knowledge that you have in one or more topics or subtopics, gained for instance through a research paper, teaching-assistant role, or clerkship. Sometimes you need to fly at 1,000 feet rather than 100 feet, meaning that sometimes you need to think at a simpler level than at the most-complex level of which you are capable. Some things you need to simplify and clarify, even while you hope to demonstrate your overall mastery of any subject. You can know too much, just as you can know too little. Next consider some special problems that the Multistate Bar Examination subjects present.

1. Civil Procedure

Procedure questions present two distinct challenges when compared to substantive-law (doctrinal) questions. First, examiners often interweave procedural questions with substantive law, making issue spotting more complex. After all, procedural issues arise out of substantive-law claims.

For example, the process for entering a judgment requires that a certain party, perhaps a creditor, have a certain kind of claim, perhaps an unpaid debt, on which to enter the judgment. Your challenge is to see the procedural question rather than allow the substantive law to distract you. Don't, for instance, turn a plain question on the procedure for entry of judgment into a complex question over the validity of an obligation or of creditor or debtor rights.

Second, the procedural issues may be harder to identify. With substantive-law questions, rights, obligations, charges, claims, and defenses are the core issues. For substantive-law questions, you must be sure that you know the law, meaning the concepts, rules, elements, conditions, and definitions. Thus, substantive-law subjects like torts, crimes, and contracts often lend themselves well to orderly outlines where one law construct bears clear relationship to other law constructs, so that your law knowledge builds from one concept to another. If you can recall a little, you can often recall a lot.

By contrast, civil-procedure questions tend to present problems in the context of the adversary system, where the parties and court are required to react to strategies as they unfold. Civil procedure's content structure involves process knowledge—actions, reactions, and decision standards—rather than a hierarchical outline of descending claims. You must recall rules, procedures, and standards associated with interests, objectives, actions, options, responses, and decisions. You must also be sure that you understand the parties' competing strategic interests.

The three major civil-procedure topics of *personal jurisdiction*, *subject-matter jurisdiction*, and *venue* are examples. While you must know the rules, standards, and definitions associated with each of those topics, the jurisdiction and venue issues will arise when a party with one set of interests and objectives strategically sues another party in a certain court and location, to which the second party must respond, perhaps requiring a court's ruling. Whatever procedural rules you apply, perhaps involving pleading, joinder, discovery, summary judgment, trial, post-trial proceedings, or appeal, you must do so cognizant of the parties' strategic interests and options, and the standards the law requires the court to apply.

In some questions, particularly where summary judgment is involved, you may have to deploy this process knowledge in the context of substantive claims. You may have to know a little about the law's substance in order to make a right judgment about the available procedures. For example, evaluating a summary-judgment motion that tests the sufficiency of the evidence of proof of breach in a negligence action requires that you know at least a little about the tort law of negligence and its element breach. Don't get lost in the substantive law. Know the civil procedure. But build and trust your knowledge of the substantive law so that you have a firm foundation for applying the procedure. See the Multistate Bar Examination topic and subtopic outline for more detail.

2. Constitutional Law

Constitutional law has a unique content structure that requires an exam approach unlike other subjects. Constitutional-law questions are commonly *whether a certain action, particularly the enactment of a certain statute, is constitutional*. When the answer is unclear and unpredictable, the examiners often ask you to select the best argument on which to uphold or challenge the statute. Making that analysis often requires two steps, first to determine whether the government had the power to take the questioned action and second whether the Constitution limits that power.

First determine from the given facts whether the statute is a federal or state enactment. If federal, then consider whether the enactment falls is necessary and proper to carry out one of Congress's enumerated powers. Those enumerated powers include, among other things, taxing and spending for the general welfare, national defense and addressing foreign affairs, regulating interstate commerce, defining citizenship, eminent domain, civil rights, congressional elections, and admiralty. Legislating beyond enumerated powers, such as exercising a general police power that only the states hold, violates the Tenth Amendment.

While acts of Congress must fall within Congress's enumerated powers, acts of the President must fall within the President's enumerated powers or powers appropriately delegated by Congress. You must know those federal enumerations and delegations of limited power to answer constitutional-law questions correctly, while recognizing that states retain expansive police powers.

If the questioned enactment is state rather than federal, then recall that states have broad police powers to regulate public health, safety, welfare, and morals. Congress's commerce-clause power, though, is one major limitation on state police power. The state must not place an undue burden on interstate commerce. Legitimate state interests must outweigh any burden, which also must not discriminate against other states' interests unless the enactment is the only way to protect health and safety.

Thus constitutional-law questions often require that you recognize and address an underlying federalism or separation of powers issue, limiting state authority or the authority of a federal-government branch. For example, examiners often test whether Congress has impermissibly reserved a legislative veto over delegated executive authority, violating the bicameral-passage or presentation clauses. While these limitations depend on clauses within the Constitution and its amendments, you must often recall and apply the Supreme Court's standard or multi-part test for that constitutional construct, as just illustrated with the commerce clause.

Yet you must also know the individual rights that limit those enumerated, delegated, and retained powers. Limits on power include the individual rights guaranteed in the Bill of Rights, some rights that the Constitution does not enumerate, and more generally what due process or equal protection require. Distinguishing an equal-protection challenge from a due-process challenge is one key to success. Equal-protection challenges depend first on identifying state action and then the action's classification, if any. The classification tells you the level of scrutiny to apply, whether strict scrutiny for a suspect classification (particularly race), intermediate scrutiny for semi-suspect classes (particularly gender and legitimacy), or the easily satisfied rational-relation test for non-suspect classes.

Be especially on the lookout for due-process challenges. Again, first identify the government action. Then consider whether the problem is procedural, in which case notice and opportunity for hearing are the concerns, or substantive, in which case the question is whether the government action substantially interferes with a fundamental right, in which case strict scrutiny applies. Fundamental rights include First Amendment rights, privacy rights (contraception, procreation, abortion, and marriage), and rights of interstate travel.

First Amendment issues can be significantly more complex than other issues, in part because freedom of expression includes not only free speech but also freedom of the press, assembly, and association. Regulations must be narrow and definite to avoid overbreadth and vagueness challenges. Laws addressing commercial speech, defamation, obscenity, fighting words, and clear-and-present dangers, or constituting prior restraints, have their own peculiar constitutional tests. The First Amendment's religion clauses, involving the balancing of free-exercise and disestablishment clauses, further complicate the subject.

Standing and jurisdiction are other subtle constitutional issues that may lurk just beneath the obvious features of a fact pattern. Parties must generally advocate their own substantial interests rather than the interests of others. As to jurisdiction, constitutional clauses and doctrine prohibit the federal courts from addressing political questions and issuing advisory opinions or opinions on issues that are moot or not yet ripe.

Recognizing the specific constitutional issue, recalling the specific provision and associated Supreme Court test, and analyzing any associated due process or equal protection issues do not quite complete your challenge, though. The actors and actions themselves vary widely. A constitutional-law fact pattern may involve the President exercising war, appointment, or veto powers, Congress authorizing federal regulation of commerce, a federal agency promulgating those regulations, a state legislature enacting legislation affecting interstate commerce, a state agency regulating speech or association, or a private person or entity acting in violation of law, rule, or regulation.

Indeed, because constitutional-law outcomes often depend on close Supreme Court rulings on nuanced issues, knowing the outcome of major Supreme Court cases can be highly helpful. Examiners can face a challenge in crafting predictable outcomes. One sure way that they meet that challenge is to draw relatively close parallels to cases that the Supreme Court has already decided. Watch for fact patterns that align to already-decided Supreme Court cases, and then use those cases to guide your answer.

In short, you must have not only clear knowledge of the basic constitutional-law constructs but also fluency in their application, a process that one scholar likens to peeling an onion very quickly so as to avoid painful eyes and tears running down your cheeks. Prepare earnestly to develop that fluency and facility. See the Multistate Bar Examination topic and subtopic outline for more detail.

3. Contract Law

Contract-law questions tend to have lots of facts, such as a series of written or oral communications, dates, quantities, terms, and conditions. While contract-formation law (offer, acceptance, and consideration) is relatively straightforward, examiners often have to give you extra facts in order to reach and test that law. Fact patterns grow even longer and more complex when they involve employees or agents acting for a corporate party or the interests of third-party beneficiaries, often the case for contract-law questions.

Complex fact patterns require more time and effort. You have to get the facts straight. Complex facts invite error in assembling the facts into a meaningful scenario. Reading the question's call before reading the full fact pattern can help you extract and organize relevant facts. Quickly outlining the facts or drawing a picture of them can be another helpful tactic.

Contracts questions can also lend themselves readily to multiple sub-parts or to a final twist or turn as to the outcome. This characteristic means that you can be forming ideas as you read the question, only to find by the end of the question that the examiner wants you to think about something else altogether. This feature is another reason that reading the call of the question first can be a good idea. Know the law, but be sure to read and understand the facts, just as much in contracts questions as elsewhere.

As to the law itself, contract law has its own overarching order to it. That order first involves which law applies, the U.C.C. governing the sale of goods or the common law wherever the U.C.C. does not apply. The distinction can be important. For example, the common law requires consideration to modify a contract, while the U.C.C. requires only good faith. For another example, the common law requires consideration for an irrevocable offer (an option), while the U.C.C. requires of a merchant only a signed writing indicating that the offer is irrevocable for a period of up to three months and no longer.

You may then have to consider first whether the parties formed a contract, then whether a party breached the contract, whether that party has defenses, or whether the non-breaching party should have certain breach remedies. The sub-question of contract formation also has an overarching order to it involving offer, acceptance, consideration, and terms.

Examiners frequently test consideration issues. Consideration relates closely to the question of whether the parties bargained. Is one party getting something in return for what the party promised? If not, then the promise is only an offer to make a gift and not generally enforceable. Consideration, though, can include not just a monetary exchange for the promised good or service (the performance or action). Consideration can also include foregoing a legal right or relinquishing a legal claim, if the reasonable person could believe that the claim is well founded and could pursue it in good faith. The consideration substitute of promissory estoppel, where a promise without consideration induces the promisee's reliance, can lead to the not-quite-a-contract claim of

unjust enrichment, where the promisor benefits from the promisee's reliance.

Conditions are another examiner favorite. Conditions can be expressed in the agreement, in which case they require strict compliance, or implied by the circumstances, in which case substantial performance will suffice. Conditions can also be precedent, meaning that the condition must occur before the party has an obligation to perform, or concurrent, meaning that each party has an obligation to perform without which the other party need not return performance.

The statute of frauds is another examiner favorite. Contracts within the statute must ordinarily be in a writing signed by the charged party for other party to enforce the agreement. Suretyships (to guarantee the debt of another), contracts relating to interests in land, contracts that a party cannot perform within one year, and (under the U.C.C.) contracts for the sale of goods worth more than $500, fall within the statute of frauds. As to the latter goods transactions, part performance (delivery and acceptance of the goods) satisfies the statute, as would judicial admission of the obligation.

Third-party beneficiaries, assignment and delegation, and integration and parol evidence are other popular exam subjects. These larger frameworks remain important even if your sharply analytic mind wants to seize upon one of contract law's many minor rules and address only that rule. Be cautious of falling into the trap of deciding or addressing a question on a subsidiary contracts rule when following the larger frameworks may show you other more-important issues.

A good approach as soon as your recognize that a question addresses a contract-law issue is thus to decide first whether the question involves a transaction in goods to which the U.C.C. applies. Next, determine whether the parties' interaction forms a contract (offer, acceptance, and consideration or substitute). Lean toward contract formation. If you don't find a contract, then consider the reliance, promissory estoppel, and unjust-enrichment theory. Watch for seemingly insignificant detail. That detail, such as implying whether one of the parties is a merchant or not, is instead probably significant. Distinguish third-party beneficiaries from assignees or a non-party to whom a party delegates contract performance. See the Multistate Bar Examination topic and subtopic outline for more detail.

4. Criminal Law and Procedure

In criminal law and procedure, examiners obviously test your knowledge of specific crimes and their elements. Especially know the types of homicide from murder to manslaughter, misdemeanor manslaughter, and negligent homicide, distinguished largely by the required state of mind. Do not miss that intent to kill is not the only way to satisfy murder's malice element. Intent to cause serious injury, felony murder, and depraved-heart disregard of an unreasonably high risk of serious harm, also suffice. Reasonable provocation without cooling off reduces the crime to manslaughter, while unintentional killing may satisfy negligent homicide and death in the course of a misdemeanor may satisfy misdemeanor manslaughter.

Other crimes against persons, such as assault and battery, and property crimes like larceny, robbery, and burglary, make other significant exam topics. Know, for instance, that common-law larceny is the trespassory taking and carrying away of the personal property of another with the intent to permanently deprive, and distinguish it from robbery adding the element of force or fear, and burglary involving the breaking and entering of a dwelling at night with the intent to commit a felony inside. Because these crimes are not particularly hard to spot and define, especially watch for subtle variations that create causation or intent issues. Examiners often have the hypothetical actors making mistakes that negate the intent element of the crimes.

Criminal-law questions can also be different in that they may quote or paraphrase portions of a statute that you must apply to determine whether the suspect has committed a crime. In that respect, criminal-law questions can involve relatively routine and straight-forward application of black-letter law to clear and often compelling facts.

In applying a given criminal-code statute, though, you may have to recall and apply key common-law or criminal-code definitions for traditional terms of art. Recalling and applying unstated definitions adds a manageable challenge. You need only have studied those definitions to the point of achieving fluency in spotting their factual triggers, recalling the actual definition, and applying it swiftly and surely in your analysis.

Defenses to specific crimes are also popular but manageable test subjects. Once again, you need only have studied those defenses to the point of achieving fluency in spotting their factual triggers, recalling the defense's conditions, and applying those conditions swiftly and surely in your analysis. Remember, though, that a victim forgiving or condoning a crime does not negate the perpetrator's culpability.

As is especially true for homicide charges (as shown above), the special challenge that criminal-law questions often present has to do with the suspect's state of mind. You must often read the presented statute or summary very carefully to discern the wrongdoer's state of mind to see if that state of mind satisfies what the statute requires for conviction. You must read and construe scant facts very carefully for state-of-mind evidence. Do not miss that evidence.

While state of mind presents its own peculiar examination issue, the examiner may use other elements of the charge, such as entry or possession, to test your treatment of a close-call issue. Multiple-choice questions are too short to test much more than one element. Indeed, the Multistate Bar Examination designs fact patterns and question calls to isolate and test one rule of law rather than several rules or elements. Focus your reading of criminal-law questions to identify the tested element of the charge.

In contrast to criminal-law questions, focusing on discrete elements of the charge, criminal-procedure questions usually test narrow constitutional-law constructs. For example, the constitutional construct may in the context of a criminal search be *reasonable expectation of privacy*, or in the arrest context *probable cause*, or in the Miranda context *custodial interrogation*. Focus your reading of criminal-procedure questions to identify the tested constitutional-law construct.

In search questions, first determine the circumstances of the search, whether with probable cause or not, under a warrant or not, or incident to an arrest or not. Then confirm the purpose of the search, whether for safety or evidence. Beware of the hidden issue of a person's standing to object to a search. For instance, watch for detail on whether the objecting person was the owner of the searched home or vehicle, or renter of the searched apartment.

In these criminal-procedure questions, you must often know and recall the Supreme Court's latest iteration of these and other constitutional-law constructs. The Supreme Court articulates those constructs in the precarious balance between effective police investigation versus the individual rights of the criminally charged. Pay particular attention to recent Supreme Court decisions and hot topics relating to criminal procedure. See the Multistate Bar Examination topic and subtopic outline for more detail.

5. Evidence

Among all bar-tested subjects, evidence questions may be the most discrete and peculiar, qualities that can surprise and mislead you. You may feel that evidence relates closely to civil procedure and criminal procedure, and even to criminal law, torts, contracts, property, and any other subject frequently involving litigation. Yet while other subjects may often implicate the existence or sufficiency of evidence, with the exception of criminal procedure they do not typically address the *admissibility* of that evidence, which is the core evidence subject. The rules of evidence are a world unto themselves.

For example, criminal procedure considers the admissibility of evidence in the peculiar context of constitutional rights and protections. Criminal-procedure questions address evidence admissibility under the confrontation clause, privilege against self-incrimination, and exclusionary rule for evidence obtained in violation of Fourth Amendment rights, all special criminal-procedure rules rather than ordinary rules of evidence.

Similarly, civil-procedure questions can involve summary-judgment rules as to the sufficiency of evidence and the form, by affidavits or otherwise, in which a party presents evidence. Summary-judgment questions involve civil-procedure rules, not evidence rules. Evidence questions have their own complex set of rules. Distinguish evidence questions from procedure questions and questions having to do with the substance of contracts, torts, and property claims.

Because of the discrete and technical nature of admissibility questions, you must know the evidence rules in their detail. Trying to reason your way to conclusions based on broad principles, such as you might do in a constitutional-law question, will usually not work for an evidence question. You must know the detail of the evidence rules. The evidence rules are sensible and based on broad principle, but you will not have the time under exam circumstances to apply those principles reliably. You must be able to recall and apply the rule detail fluently, just as you would when rising to object to an opposing counsel's direct or cross-examination question in court.

As an example, when studying for the evidence questions, pay particular attention to the rules on consistent and inconsistent prior statements, and prior statements of identification. To make these prior statements admissible as falling outside of the hearsay rule or within a hearsay exception, the out-of-court declarant of these statements must be the presently testifying witness through whom a party seeks to introduce the out-of-court statement. In other words, you need first to determine whether the declarant or someone else is testifying to the statement. On the other hand, a prior inconsistent statement remains available to impeach a testifying witness or rehabilitate an impeached witness, even when not available to prove what the statement asserts. Know these technical ins and outs, or you will struggle with evidence questions.

Evidence questions have to do with more than just testimony. They also address the admissibility of demonstrations, compilations, summaries, exhibits, and copies of exhibits. The best-evidence rule, requiring the original document or an innocent explanation for its absence when the parties dispute the material terms of a writing, is a common evidence topic. Authentication of exhibits is another common exam topic, particularly because anyone, whether an expert or recordkeeper or not, observing the matter can authenticate the item such as a photograph or account record.

Qualifying witnesses, whether expert or lay witnesses, is another common evidence topic. Witness competence may be an issue, whether due to very young age, bias or interest, or lack of first-hand knowledge. Note that the competence rules are broad, generally barring only those witnesses who do not understand and affirm the need to tell the truth, or who lack any direct knowledge of the matter on which they testify. Bias and interest are not disqualifying grounds.

Expert testimony generally applies scientific and other technical matters on which the testimony could help the jury. Experts must have a factual basis for their opinions, but an expert may easily satisfy that requirement based on personal observation or facts presented in or outside of the trial, even inadmissible facts. Experts also need a scientific basis for their opinions, generally meaning one that the science generally accepts

because sound, peer reviewed, published, and testable under an error rate. Yet not every technical-looking issue needs an expert. For example, signatures do not need an expert's verification if the authenticating witness knows the person's signature.

The fact patterns in evidence questions are often short. Your challenge is not so much in reconstructing the parties' strategic interests, which are instead often obvious. The party offering the evidence wants it in, while the objecting party wants it out. You can usually quickly discern why one party wants the evidence in and the other party wants it out. Be sure to do so.

Your bigger challenge with evidence questions is instead to recognize that parties may offer evidence for two or more different purposes, some of which the rules countenance and others of which the rules do not. For example, a party may offer certain evidence either to prove character consistent with conduct, on the one hand, or to attack credibility, on the other hand. Different rules determine the admissibility of each form of evidence, either character evidence or credibility evidence. To answer an evidence question correctly, you often have to distinguish for which of two or more purposes the proponent offers the evidence.

As this point suggests again, your major challenge is in knowing the evidence rules. If you must analyze quickly and clearly several layered issues to see which evidence rule answers the specific question, then you must be fluent in the evidence rules.

Relevance and undue prejudice, requiring discerning probative value versus prejudicial effect, are frequent issues in evidence questions. But do not let relevance and prejudice issues distract you when the fact pattern and question call proceed promptly to hearsay or privilege issues. Similarly, while a fact pattern may implicate hearsay or privilege, ignore those issues of the question call directs you to witness foundation, document authentication, or the best-evidence rule. In other words, be ready to relinquish your first thought as soon as the fact pattern and question call direct you to another evidence issue.

These features of evidence questions make skill at issue spotting, accuracy of rule recall, facility in rule application, and fluency in written analysis all key evidence-question skills. Most of all, you need precise knowledge of the rules. Examiners often test not the major rule but its minor exception or peculiar balancing test.

To simplify the considerable issue-spotting challenges, consider focusing first on *what* the proponent offers, meaning whether testimony, tangible evidence (an exhibit to authenticate), or demonstrative evidence. If the proponent offers testimony, then consider whether the testimony describes what the witness *saw* (foundation issues around personal knowledge), *heard* (hearsay issues), *happened in the past* (character evidence), or *reviewed* (expert testimony). See the Multistate Bar Examination topic and subtopic outline for more detail.

6. Real Property

Property-law questions can challenge you with complex fact patterns involving multiple parties, transactions, events, and dates. Be sure to take the extra bit of time to note and even diagram those facts to get them straight. You may know and like the technical clarity of property law. Yet if you consistently get the facts wrong, you will answer property-law questions incorrectly.

The difficulty of real-property fact patterns often arises out of the multiple layers of relationships. The patterns typically begin with a landowner who may have an existing relationship with an easement holder, joint tenant, renting tenant, option holder, or family members expecting to inherit. The complexity arises when the fact pattern introduces a competing interest holder such as a buyer, adverse possessor, subtenant, competing family member, or assignee of the interest. Three-way and even four-way disputes are

relatively common in real-property questions. Quickly chart fact patterns to ensure that you keep them straight as you analyze the question.

While property-law facts are often complex, property law itself is complex. Property law is just foreign and unfamiliar enough for many examinees, to present significant recall and fluency challenges. The various joint, present, and future interests of property owners, the rights of others arising by covenant, use, or zoning, peculiar concerns over conveying real property, mortgaging real property, and ways in which property law treats title transfer and recording, are all technical issues with which examinees may have no practical or clinical experience. Preparing exhaustively will meet those challenges. You may, in other words, be relying here solely on classroom instruction. Take that instruction in earnest.

Property law also has specific doctrines that can give examinees special difficulty. The Rule Against Perpetuities is the bane of many examinees, as can also be the related treatment of future interests. Indeed, these subjects can be so difficult as to cause some examinees to question whether mastery of the subjects is worth the time and effort. If you choose to spend less time on especially difficult rules, then be sure to spend adequate time on the rest of the property-law subject.

Another example of a common, frequently tested topic of some difficulty is the doctrine of marketable title and related consequences of merger. Real covenants and equitable servitudes are another common challenging topic, as are the race, notice, and race-notice recording statutes. You are not alone if you find these topics a special challenge, but preparing for questions on these topics must be part of your study.

Do not dismiss property law as unmanageable. Practice property-law questions with a special eye toward eliminating wrong answers rather than seizing upon what appears to be the first correct answer, particularly if you are unsure of the topic. Real-property-law questions are especially difficult because of the examiner's ease in introducing attractive distractors.

You may love property law, or you may not, but in either case, you can master enough of the subject to achieve the score that you need. See the Multistate Bar Examination topic and subtopic outline for more detail.

7. Torts

The subject of torts has a straight-forward content structure often making it a favorite of examinees. You must generally recall and name the tort claim. You must then recall the claim's elements or, if it doesn't have elements, its definition, conditions, or factors. You must then apply that law to the facts.

Tort law can present a moderate challenge in recalling the many claims and their elements. Invasion of privacy, for example, may come in any one of the four different forms of intrusion, appropriation, public disclosure, and false light, depending on the jurisdiction. The numerous elements of misrepresentation (a false material representation made knowingly to induce reliance causing loss) and, separately, defamation (false words published of and concerning the plaintiff that together with extrinsic facts lower the plaintiff's reputation causing special damages other than in the case of an exception to special damages) are each subtle. Elements of a claim may also overlap, making them read more like meandering definitions.

One event may also give rise simultaneously to multiple different tort claims. While as you read a fact pattern you should promptly note any claims that may apply, resist jumping to conclusions as to which of several tort claims the question addresses, until you have read the question call. Be ready to consider a tort other than the one that first occurred to you, when the question call sends you in that new direction.

Many examinees feel that they know tort law's claims well enough to recall their elements, definitions, and conditions. Tort law's challenge is often instead in the breadth of its application. Torts can arise anywhere persons act creating foreseeable risks of harm. Law recall may not be your torts challenge. Applying tort law in the widest variety of factual contexts may instead be your challenge.

You may get tort questions in contexts that you know, such as driving motor vehicles. Or you may get tort questions in contexts that you don't know, such as engineering a building, marketing a drug, or manufacturing a product. Don't let unfamiliar context disarm you. Trust that the examiners will give you the facts that you need to know. Apply the law rigorously, even when you don't fully get the facts in an unfamiliar context.

Beyond knowing tort claims and being able to apply them in unfamiliar settings, you also need to know tort defenses. One tort claim such as negligence may implicate several defenses such as a limitations period, immunity of one form or another, contributory or comparative negligence, or assumption of the risk. Maintain a familiar mental checklist of defenses.

While recalling claims and elements, and recalling and applying defenses, present straightforward challenges, a greater challenge can be in the examiner's decision to test any number of special torts rules. Those rules can include subtopics like: the First Amendment's effect on defamation of public officials and figures adding an actual-malice element; the expert-witness requirement to establish the professional's standard of care in malpractice cases other than for obvious malpractice; and the three forms of design, manufacturing, and warning defect in products-liability cases, including the seven factors of the Second Restatement's risk-utility test to determine when a product is in a defective condition unreasonably dangerous.

In that respect, be sure to separate defamation claims from invasion of privacy claims, and strict liability claims for abnormally dangerous activities on land from strict *products* liability claims for defective and unreasonably dangerous products. Defamation has a different definition from invasion of privacy and different privilege defenses and constitutional considerations. Strict liability for activities on land has different factors from the conditions and factors that courts apply to strict products liability.

The liability of one party for the misconduct of another party, such as a retailer's strict products liability for a manufacturer's defective product, or an employer's vicarious liability for an employee's negligence, make other significant tort-law exam topics. Indeed, questions on multiple defendant parties can raise peculiarly challenging issues around joint-and-several liability, allocation of fault, and settlement and release.

Causation issues may also involve multiple actors or events, requiring that you apply not only the logical but-for construct but also the substantial-factor test, or shift the proof burden on causation. Don't miss that more than one actor's fault may be a cause in fact of the loss or injury. You may also face the dreaded proximate-cause question, although you can simplify those questions into applying the traditional direct-sequence test or modern foreseeability test, or examining intervening causes to see if they are so extraordinary as to supersede and cut off liability for the prior negligence. Remember that you need both cause in fact (usually the but-for type but maybe the alternative substantial factor) and proximate cause.

A significant percentage of torts questions, though, may address the core fault issue of negligence claims. You may get a significant percentage of questions correct simply by knowing that negligence involves failing to use the reasonable care that the reasonably prudent person would use under similar circumstances, creating a foreseeable risk of harm that caused the claimant's loss or injury. If proving negligence is the issue, then the key may be in recalling that proof may consist of direct or circumstantial evidence but also that law may draw proof from the destruction of evidence or from circumstances under the defendant's exclusive control that speak of negligence (res ipsa loquitur).

While considering torts a straightforward and manageable subject, do not underestimate its subtlety and complexity. See the Multistate Bar Examination topic and subtopic outline for more detail.

Part II: Multiple-Choice Strategies

A.   Multiple Choice Matters

Your performance on the Multistate Bar Examination's multiple-choice questions is as important an ingredient to your success as any other thing that you can do to pass the bar exam. You have no way around it: you must do reasonably well on the bar exam's multiple-choice questions.

You may feel, as many examinees do, that you are better at essays or perhaps will be better at a performance test if your bar exam has one. You may believe that as a strong writer, you will do well enough on the essay section of the test to bring up your multiple-choice score to an overall passing level. You may even feel that you have just *never been good* at multiple-choice questions, as if being good at multiple-choice questions is an attribute with which one is born or not born.

If these statements sound like you, then put aside all such thinking now. You can and will improve your multiple-choice skills and scores with appropriate resources and concerted, believing, and discerning effort. Multiple-choice questions require certain skills that you can and must learn, hone, and practice. Make your goal to do well enough on multiple-choice questions not to have to have your other work carry you through. Commit to making multiple-choice questions your strong suit, not weak suit.

B.   Design

As any law graduate knows perfectly well, multiple-choice questions begin with a fact pattern that examiners call the *root* or *stimulus*. Questions then provide enough procedural context to support the call of the question that examiners call the *stem*. Questions in the Multistate Bar Examination style then offer four answer choices that examiners call the *options*.

The National Conference of Bar Examiners gives other helpful clues to how examiners design Multistate Bar Examination questions. First, examiners design questions so that you should be able to answer *without reading the options*. Of course, you should read *every* option because you must choose the best one. One option should supply you with a definitively correct answer. But depending on how effective your bar preparation has been, you should nonetheless have a good sense of what the correct answer is even before reading the options.

That design means that you should be reading the options primarily to *confirm* an answer you have already discerned. Answer options do not, for instance, supply additional facts for you to process to choose the best answer. This benefit of developing an answer before finding one among the options is another reason why it was important to practice your fluency in law concepts. You want to force yourself into confirming a choice before looking at the possibilities.

Second, examiners design questions to test only one rule. Answer options may present several alternative rationales, each reflecting a different rule, but the fact pattern and question should require knowledge of only the one rule that the correct answer reflects.

Third, fact patterns have the minimum number of actors necessary to support the question. You won't find extra figures whose roles and actions have no bearing on the question.

Fourth, fact patterns use roles (baker, plumber, employer, etc.) rather than proper nouns (Bill, Mary, Gerry, etc.). You shouldn't be confusing actors and actions.

Trust that the National Conference of Bar Examiners drafts sound and fair questions. If you see practice multiple-choice questions that do not follow these conventions, then you are looking at old, not newer, released questions, or questions that someone other than the National Conference of Bar Examiners drafted.

C.   Signals and Triggers

Because of the large number of questions and thus necessarily small number of facts in each question, and because the examiners are testing subtle rules, every word of the facts can be consequential. Even more so than in the case of essay questions, examiners use words and short phrases as signposts and signals.

Certain words like *contractor* and *subcontractor* or *lender* and *borrower* will construct and highlight the parties' relationship. Watch for words that define the critical relationship.

Other words usually having some law content, like *owner, title, claim,* or *charge,* must trigger your recognition of the tested law issue. Watch for words that highlight the law issue.

Other words, often adverbs like *carefully* or *unintentionally,* or prepositional phrases like *without knowledge*, must rule out other possible issues so that you focus only on the tested issue. Don't miss these rule-out markers.

In its few remaining words, the fact pattern must also give you the data, such as dates or perhaps clues to an actor's state of mind, to answer the question. Recognize that relevant data. Practicing many multiple-choice questions, where you promptly review answers and explanations, has the effect of honing your skill at recognizing and relying on signals, signposts, and triggers.

D.   Question Call

For strong multiple-choice performance, you must pay particular attention to the call of the question or *stem*. Obviously, if you read and construe the question call incorrectly, then you are very likely to choose the wrong option. Your law recall and analytic skill may be perfect, but you will have answered the wrong question.

The calls of Multistate Bar Examination questions are usually sound in their construction. For example, the committees drafting and approving the questions, and the psychometric expert guiding the drafters, generally eschew the too-easy-to-confuse negative question calls such as, "Which of the four defendants would *not* be liable?" or "Which of the following outcomes is *least* likely?" If you see a rare negative question call, be especially careful to follow it closely rather than mistakenly read its negative request in the positive.

The question calls can, though, have awkwardly formal, cautious constructions, as in "Which of the following would be the most likely basis for the court's ruling granting the motion?" or "On what rationale would the court most likely award judgment against the homeowner?" Read awkward question calls in their more-direct and shorter meaning, such as, "Why grant the motion?" or "Why would the homeowner lose?" Your mind will naturally want to do so. Encourage it, indeed train it.

When necessary or helpful, quickly translate the question call into something firmer and more obvious to guide your selection of the one right option. When you see questions that include phrases like "the most likely basis," "most likely rule," or "most likely award," the examiners are acknowledging that more than one option may be plausible, which will not generally aid in your analysis because you are still looking for the one correct answer. Simply ask *why*, expecting that one answer will be clearly correct even if other answers appear possible or even plausible. Make your best effort to recall the rule that clearly justifies the one correct option.

E.   Options

One of the distinct features that examinees observe in multiple-choice answer options is that they often pair a conclusion such as *yes* or *no*, or *granted* or *denied*, with a justification. Often, the justification begins with *because* before reciting a law, rule, or principle, as in *yes because summary judgment is appropriate in the absence of a genuine issue of material fact* paired with other options like *no because summary judgment is inappropriate when the evidence raises a genuine issue of material fact.* Indeed, two options are often *yes because* or *granted because* while the other two options are *no because* or *denied because.*

The construct of two options beginning with the same conclusion *yes, yes,* and then *no, no,* or *granted, granted,* and then *denied, denied,* require you to both reach the correct conclusion and also know the justifying rationale or dispositive rule. It is often not enough, in other words, to reach the correct conclusion without also knowing the supporting law, rule, or rationale. In many questions, examiners balance the conclusions equally in pairs of two as just shown, in which case the examinee must know the rationale (or be able to rule out a false rationale) no matter which conclusion the examinee draws.

In other questions, examiners supply three options each of which draws one conclusion, but with different rationales, and only one option with the opposite conclusion. Do not prefer either conclusion simply because one conclusion has more or fewer options among which to choose. In other words, a single *no* option may be correct even if the other three options are all *yes.* Strategies of that type mislead. Use your law knowledge, not game strategy.

F.   Qualifiers

As just indicated, *because* is a common unconditional qualifier to distinguish among options that draw the same conclusion. *Because* is not the only qualifier. Examiners also use *if, unless, provided that* or *as long as,* and other conditional qualifiers when the fact pattern has a latent ambiguity. Conditional qualifiers test your logic skills, the kind of skills that should be fully familiar to you insofar as they enabled you to get a qualifying LSAT score to get into law school.

Most obviously, the law, rule, principle, or statement following the unconditional qualifier *because* implies a straightforward logical justification connecting the fact pattern to the conclusion, as in *this option answers the question because the following rule logically compels that answer.* Examiners may occasionally substitute the modifiers *since* and *as* for *because,* each meaning the same thing that the rationale compels the conclusion.

By contrast, conditional qualifiers *if, unless,* and *provided* serve a slightly different function. The law, rule, or principle that follows a conditional qualifier like *if* may clarify which law the undisclosed and imaginary jurisdiction follows, for instance a majority or minority rule. Multistate questions can often involve non-uniform law in which the examinee may know the law subject but have legitimate question over which of two or more rules apply in the imaginary jurisdiction. Conditional qualifiers like *if, unless,* and *provided* will often confirm for the examinee that the question expects the examinee to apply a specific rule among several possible options, as in the following examples:

- *Yes, if following the traditional premises-liability classifications.*
- *No, provided that the modern foreseeability test applies.*
- *Granted, unless in a contributory-negligence jurisdiction.*
- *Denied, as long as the rules permit pleading amendment.*

Conditional qualifiers like *if, unless,* and *provided,* can also clarify or confirm different reasonable interpretations of the facts. The short fact patterns of a multiple-choice question cannot possibly resolve every possible interpretation into one. The fact pattern may leave you leaning toward one interpretation but uncertain that you have inferred as the examiners expected. The justification following conditional qualifiers can confirm that you are drawing the intended inference, as in the following examples:

- *Yes, if the man's status is that of a trespasser.*
- *No, provided that the explosion was reasonably foreseeable.*
- *Granted, unless the owner's actions constituted consent.*
- *Denied, as long as the conspiracy evidence is plausible.*

G. Distractors

Another feature of Multistate Bar Examination questions is that all three incorrect answers will be credibly attractive options. Conventional wisdom suggests that one or two options will be obvious throwaways, while the other options will present deliberately close calls as to which answer is the best option. Conventional wisdom is wrong. The National Conference of Bar Examiners intends that the correct answer be clearly correct and clearly the best answer but also that *all three remaining options* be credible distractors. You certainly won't find any humorously wrong options intended to entertain you along the way.

Credible distractors are often correct but irrelevant statements of law that simply do not apply to resolve the call of the question and support that answer option. Distractors can also be incorrect but plausible-sounding rule statements including such things as a minority rule where a majority rule applies, a rule where an exception to the rule applies, or an exception where the rule applies. Distractors can also be incomplete statements that do not go far enough to resolve the question. Distractors can also misrepresent or misconstrue the facts that the fact pattern just gave you. They can also deliberately but subtly swap roles, for instance perpetrator for victim, movant for non-movant, or proponent of the proffered evidence for opponent of the evidence.

Because all three incorrect options will be credible distractors, you should make more effort to answer the question as you read it *before reading the options*. Reading the options before you make any effort to discern the answer may mislead you to seize upon and incorrectly rationalize an attractive distractor. Also, because all four options will be credible but only one option correct, and the three wrong options credibly attractive distractors, you should train yourself to read all four options even when you are confident that you know and have located the correct answer. You may instead have chosen an attractively credible distractor.

H. Procedural Context

Question design, though, is not quite as simple as facts (root), question call (stem), and answers (options). After or in the middle of the fact pattern, questions must also supply the *procedural or practice context*, meaning the judge-lawyer-client-and-opposing-party part that creates the strategic tension.

Examiners deliberately vary the procedural and practice contexts for the calls of the questions. Each call of the question is not as simple as a straightforward evaluation like "Does plaintiff have a claim?" or "Do the parties have a contract?" Rather, examiners include many different procedural and practice contexts. Those practice contexts may involve client intake and interview, factual investigation, pleading, discovery, pretrial motions, alternative dispute resolution, trial events, post-judgment proceedings, appeals, office practice, meetings, and transactions. Here are a few of many possible examples:

- "How should the trial judge rule on the objection?"
- "Which would be the best method of discovery?"
- "Would an appeal be available to the employer?"
- "What is the effect of the officer's testimony?"

- "Which is the best advice regarding the claim?"
- "How would the creditor best enforce the judgment?"

Getting the context right is its own skill, requiring special concentration. You may know the law and understand the facts but misread and misunderstand your particular procedural stance or practice role. Don't rush through the procedural and practice context.

I.   Approach

While the approach may seem unnatural and forced, practice reading the call of the question first before going back and reading the full question. You may also find it helpful to scan the answer options quickly before reading the fact pattern.

Here is why you should consider first reading the call of the question and scanning the answer options *before* reading the fact pattern. The examiner designs the fact pattern of a multiple-choice question to trigger your law recall. Read any fact pattern, and you should notice legal issues that spur law recall. When you read the call of the question first, you learn the procedural context and, along with it, confirm the law subject area, especially if you also scan the answer options and those options confirm the subject area.

When you then return to the top to read the full facts, those facts should be triggering relevant rather than irrelevant law recall. By reading the call of the question first and scanning the options so that you already know the law subject, the facts will trigger relevant law, while you ignore false triggers of irrelevant law. For example, you can read a criminal-procedure fact pattern more quickly and confidently knowing in advance that the question is on criminal procedure than you would if you mistakenly guessed that it was a fact pattern and question having to do with evidence, property law, or some other subject area.

Once you have quickly read the call of the question and maybe scanned the options to get a sense of the law subject, and then read the full fact pattern carefully, recognizing the issue and recalling and applying the law as you do so, you should be able to answer the call of the question without even looking at the options. Allow and indeed encourage yourself to do so. Preserve and amplify in the back of your mind, rather than squelch and silence, those tenuous hypotheses that your mind generates as you read the fact pattern. Then formulate an answer as you finish reading the call of the question and before reading the options. The best option should then jump out at you, free of the attractive but incorrect distractors.

Also, read and answer every multiple-choice question in order. Unlike some multiple-choice exams, with the Multistate Bar Examination *you face no penalty for wrong answers.* Thus, *answer every question in order, even if you must guess.*

Some examinees adopt a practice of skipping hard questions, expecting to return to them after completing the rest of the exam. Skipping questions introduces the stress and hazards of not having time to return, losing track of which questions the examinee did not answer, and starting to answer questions out of order so that the examinee records multiple wrong, unintended answers.

Rather than skip a hard question, choose the best answer but mark the question to return to it later if you have the time. While you may mark as many as a dozen or even two dozen questions, many examinees finish with thirty minutes or more of extra time, giving them time to return to every one of those questions marked as difficult.

J.   IRAC

The IRAC method of reasoning is not only for essay questions but has its own application to multiple-choice questions. The above sections of this chapter should already have shown you how important the skills of spotting the issue, recalling and applying the law, and concluding are to answering multiple-choice questions. Multiple-choice questions are not some peculiar matching game divorced from legal reasoning. They are instead routine and highly structured tests of exactly what lawyers do day to day in analyzing law questions. Recognizing that you are using IRAC skills to answer multiple-choice questions can go a long way toward reinforcing the same skills that you will need for both essay and multiple-choice questions.

IRAC analysis is also a primary way in which you can diagnose and improve your multiple-choice performance. When you miss a multiple-choice question, take yourself back through your thoughts on that question, asking first whether you spotted the issue, then recalled the rule, then applied the rule correctly, and finally drew the correct conclusion. Use the answer explanation in conjunction with the IRAC method to discern whether you are missing answers because you failed to spot the issue, failed to recall the rule, failed to apply the rule, or drew illogical conclusions.

Using IRAC to diagnose your performance issues can help you strengthen the weaker aspects of your performance. You may need to practice issue spotting, or learn more law, or sharpen your analytic skill, or simply be more logical about your conclusions. IRAC is king here as elsewhere.

K.   Wrong Options

Obviously, you will not immediately know the answer to every question. Many questions will involve choosing between two or three options that each appear to you to be plausible. In those situations where two answers both look correct, your challenge is not so much to choose the correct option as to reject the *incorrect* option. Multistate Bar Examination success has much to do with rejecting subtly incorrect options in favor of choosing wholly correct options. Indeed, even when you know that you have identified the correct option, you should confirm that the other options are incorrect.

To identify an incorrect option, first recognize that to be a correct answer an option must be *entirely correct*, not just correct in part. Usually, in these close-call questions, you are not looking for an option that is *entirely* incorrect but only *partly* incorrect.

So how are Multistate Bar Examination options incorrect? Some options misrepresent the facts just given. When the facts in the question's root say one thing and an option says anything different about the facts, rule out that option. An option cannot correctly contradict the facts. Nor can a correct option over-extend the facts or decide a fact issue that the root leaves open. Examiners deliberately write incorrect options that go too far with the facts including in resolving factual disputes.

Next, rule out options that state incorrect law. Examiners will write incorrect options using outdated law, overruled law, law overstating or understating actual requirements, and simply nonsensical statements that sound like law.

Then, rule out options the conclusion of which or rationale for which sounds incorrect. Options are sometimes wrong because they have the correct conclusion along with a correct rule but the rule does not compel the conclusion. These options present non-sequiturs, often attempting to use, say, a tort rule to justify a contract conclusion. The rule is right but the application wrong. The option's rule must match the rule that decides the issue. Don't choose a negligence-concept option when the fact pattern and question call raise an intentional-tort issue. Match option rule to fact-pattern rule.

Options are also sometimes wrong because their rationale is overbroad, especially when they include absolutes like *never* and *always*. Options are also sometimes wrong because another option is somewhat more clear and precise in the way that the rationale compels the conclusion. Choose the more-precise option over the one that leaves ambiguity.

L.   Errors

Examinee errors on multiple-choice questions fall into familiar patterns. As you practice multiple-choice questions, diagnose your error pattern for missing answers. Correct common mistakes that you discover in your practice answers.

For example, some examinees fail to assemble in their minds the fact scenario as the examiner wrote it. Sometimes this error is the result of the examinee knowing too much about similar fact patterns, for instance from having worked in that non-law field or having had a similar event happen. If the fact pattern seems familiar to you, then don't let your experience mislead you to add facts that are not present or change facts that are present. Go with what the facts tell you, not with what you think would or should have happened.

Other examinees fail to construct the procedural and practice context, and construe the call of the question, as the examiner wrote it. For instance they may frequently swap roles, mistakenly assuming that the *employer* filed the motion when instead the *employee* filed the motion, or misreading *sustain* to mean *overrule* in the context of an evidentiary offer. Read procedural and practice context, and the question call, very carefully.

Other examinees just don't know the law well enough to avoid attractive correct-but-inapplicable law distractors. Be sure to bring your full substantive law knowledge to bear on multiple-choice questions. Law practice is for lawyers who know law. Learn the details, not simply the broad concepts.

Other examinees fail to reason logically and analytically. They do not spot the issue, recall the rule, and apply law to facts to decide whether the scenario satisfies elements, factors, and conditions. Don't forget your analytic skill on multiple-choice questions. Work carefully through multiple-choice questions as you would essay questions.

M.   Guessing

When you don't know the law and thus do not know the answer, no simple strategy like always choosing option C, or always choosing the longest option, shortest option, or only option deciding the question the other way, will save you. The National Conference of Bar Examiners uses psychometric experts to ensure that examinees cannot game the Multistate Bar Examination.

Yet even when you do not know the one single correct option, you may know just enough to influence positively your probability of choosing more rather than fewer correct options. Out of a 200-question exam, you are likely to be unsure of a good number of answers, enough answers that making better choices on uncertain answers will improve your score, even if only slightly. Slight improvement may be all that you need to pass the bar exam.

If you must guess because you cannot recall the applicable law and no answer clearly appears to be the correct answer, then choose an option strategically. Your strongest strategy then is to rule out incorrect options in the manner that a paragraph above describes.

Do not grow too frustrated at only being able to narrow the number of attractive options. Narrowing your guess to just two options substantially increases your chance of a correct answer. Increased probabilities matter. Use every bit of your knowledge, even when and indeed especially when your knowledge is incomplete. Your knowledge will also be incomplete at times in practice. Following reasoned hunches can be a helpful exam strategy, even if in practice you would instead do the research.

When all else fails, and you have nothing to distinguish two or more options, then avoid options that simply repeat results without supporting logic or rationale, such as a conclusion that a homeowner should prevail because he owns the home, or a contractor should prevail because he had a contract. The Multistate Bar Examination tests applying law to facts. Choose options that do so.

Then move on to the next question with a fresh attitude. Whether the prior question was hard or easy has nothing to do with how you should answer the next question. The Multistate Bar Examination makes every question independent of every other question. If you miss one question, then you will not necessarily miss the next question or a later question. Every new question is a new opportunity for success or error.

Part III: Multistate Bar Examination Outline

Instructions on Use

Use the following outline to confirm, review, and improve your knowledge of the seven Multistate Bar Examination subjects and each of their topics and subtopics. The outline duplicates the Multistate Bar Examination topics and subtopics list just as the National Conference of Bar Examiners publishes it. The following outline divides itself into the seven Multistate Bar Examination subjects. Each of the seven subject sections then treats each of the subject's listed topics and subtopics in exactly the order and way in which the Multistate Bar Examination topics-and-subtopics list presents it.

For example, the topics-and-subtopics list for the tort-law subject begins with the heading *Intentional Torts* followed by a subheading listing the personal-harm intentional torts *assault, battery, false imprisonment,* and *infliction of mental distress,* followed by the property-harm intentional torts *trespass to land, trespass to chattels,* and *conversion.* The outline repeats each heading and subheading in boldface type, followed by text elaborating the rules that you should know in order to do well on those topics and subtopics. The outline repeats each topic and subtopic in exactly the order and way in which the list states them.

The following outline intentionally gives you wide margins on which to write. The more that you engage the reading, the better your recall should be. Yet do not simply highlight, underline, paraphrase, or use other linear reading techniques. Instead use analytic reading techniques like generating hypothetical examples and near non-examples, noting relevant experiences and current events, and noting supporting or competing policies. Also, elaborate the knowledge into acronyms or mnemonics, diagrams, tables, lists, and flow charts. Active, analytic, and elaborative reading aids memorization and recall.

Civil Procedure

A. Civil Procedure

NOTE: Approximately two-thirds of the Civil Procedure questions on the MBE will be based on categories I, III, and V, and approximately one-third will be based on the remaining categories II, IV, VI, and VII.

The Multistate Bar Examination emphasizes certain civil-procedure topics. Two thirds of the civil-procedure questions address **jurisdiction and venue, pretrial procedures**, and **motions**. Focus your studies on these three subjects having to do with initiating a proper proceeding and engaging in discovery and motion practice making up so much of civil litigation. Only one third of civil-procedure questions address the other four categories of law applied by federal courts, jury trials, verdicts and judgments, and appealability and review. All references to rules in this section are to the Federal Rules of Civil Procedure.

I. Jurisdiction and venue

Jurisdiction involves a court's authority to bind parties. A party pursuing a civil case must first choose a court having the authority to bind the party's opponents. If a plaintiff files a complaint in a court that has no jurisdiction over the defendant, then the decision of that court does not bind the defendant. Jurisdiction takes two forms. **Personal jurisdiction** involves the power of a court *over a person*, requiring some relationship of the person to the court's forum state. Thus, a defendant who had no relationship with the court's forum state would challenge the court's personal jurisdiction. **Subject-matter jurisdiction** involves the court's power to decide the *type of matter* that the parties dispute, based on the constitutional or legislative provision that created the court or authorized it to hear the particular matter. Thus, a defendant whose business dispute a family or probate court attempts to address would challenge the court's subject-matter jurisdiction.

Venue involves choosing a proper and reasonably convenient forum, relating not to the court's power but to its location. Venue questions presume that the court has personal jurisdiction over the defendant and subject-matter jurisdiction over the claims. Statutes, rules, and doctrines on venue answer questions about **where to litigate** a civil case, when multiple locations are available within the same state or federal district, or different states or federal districts. Venue is not a constitutional question of a court's permissible reach but instead a statutory and common-law question of which is an appropriate or more-convenient forum. Rule 12(b) authorizes a defendant to move to dismiss for lack of personal and subject-matter jurisdiction, and the propriety of venue.

A. Federal subject matter jurisdiction...

Civil Procedure

Federal subject-matter jurisdiction involves the question of whether Congress has authorized the federal court to hear the case, within limited constitutional authority. The court must be **competent** to hear the matter, not meaning skilled but instead meaning having authority over the matter's subject. The Constitution creates a United States Supreme Court but does not expressly create federal district courts. The Constitution instead enumerates the limited potential powers of federal district courts if Congress chooses to create them. When creating the federal district courts, Congress limited their subject-matter jurisdiction to less than the Constitution permitted. Congress authorized **federal-question**, **diversity-of-citizenship**, and **supplemental** jurisdiction. The federal courts have **concurrent jurisdiction** with the state courts unless Congress provides otherwise. For example, Congress restricted to the federal courts jurisdiction over admiralty, bankruptcy, and antitrust cases, while prohibiting the federal courts from hearing state tax-collection cases.

...(federal question...

The federal courts have **federal-question** jurisdiction over all civil actions *arising under* the **Constitution**, **federal laws**, and **treaties**. For example, when a plaintiff sues under a federal statute creating a private cause of action, such as the federal civil-rights statutes, the plaintiff may file that case in federal district court under its federal-question jurisdiction. Federal-question jurisdiction does *not* require a minimum amount in controversy or depend on the parties' diversity of citizenship. While the action arising under federal law is sufficient for federal-question jurisdiction, if the federal law simply **refers to** state or local customs for the substantive rights, then the federal court will *not* have federal-question jurisdiction. On the other hand, if the state law merely provides the means for enforcing a **federal substantive right**, then the federal courts have federal-question jurisdiction.

The plaintiff's **pleadings** initially determine whether the case arises under federal law. The federal question must arise out of the plaintiff's **well-pled complaint**, not from the defendant's affirmative defenses or counterclaim, and not from a complaint artfully drafted to anticipate a federal defense. Similarly, when a plaintiff settles and dismisses a federal case enforcing a federal right, the plaintiff has recourse only to state, not federal, court to enforce the settlement agreement because enforcement is a question of state contract law. Federal courts have federal-question jurisdiction to enforce federal-court judgments but not to enforce private settlement agreements. In close cases of whether the matter arises under federal law, the federal courts consider the **federal elements** of the claim, **federal interest**, and **impact** of federal judicial resolution.

A federal district court hearing a **declaratory-judgment action** under federal law authorizing that form of action must still involve enforcement of an underlying federal right for the federal court to hear the case. Similarly, a plaintiff bringing a state tort claim that relies on **federal standards** to establish the defendant's standard of care must file in state rather than federal court for lack of federal-question jurisdiction. Yet federal elements and interests may still be sufficiently substantial for the plaintiff's state claim to

Civil Procedure

arise under federal law for purposes of federal-question jurisdiction, even if federal law does not explicitly create the right of action. For example, the federal government has sufficient interest in uniform enforcement of federal tax obligations for the federal courts to hear a state-law dispute to quiet title in lands seized for federal tax-lien enforcement.

Rule 12 authorizes a defendant to move to challenge subject-matter jurisdiction. A party may challenge federal subject-matter jurisdiction **at any time**, even after it has lost the case. The federal court may also raise the issue of subject-matter jurisdiction **on its own**. Parties have **no ability to waive** subject-matter-jurisdiction objections. A judgment, though, binds parties who appear, challenge subject-matter jurisdiction, and lose, or when they appear, fail to challenge jurisdiction, lose, and then attempt a collateral attack in another court.

...diversity...

Federal courts also have subject-matter jurisdiction in suits between **citizens of different states**, whose matter in controversy exceeds **$75,000**. **Diversity-of-citizenship jurisdiction** insulates non-resident parties from local bias in state courts. Every plaintiff must have different citizenship from every defendant, requiring **complete diversity** between the sides, although not among the parties on only one side. Two or more plaintiffs may be citizens of the same state, or two or more defendants, as long as no plaintiff is a citizen of the same state as any defendant.

Citizenship depends on **domicile** for individuals, meaning the one location where the individual resides principally intending to remain indefinitely. Corporations are citizens of their state of **incorporation** and **principal place of business**, meaning that corporations can be citizens of two states. Federal courts follow the **nerve-center test** for where a corporation has its principal place of business, referring to control of corporate functions. Citizenship of a partnership, limited-liability company, or unincorporated association depends on the citizenship of each of its individual members. Citizenship of a representative of an estate, minor, or incompetent is the citizenship of the person or estate represented. An alien permanent resident is a citizen of the alien's state of domicile. Under the **time-of-filing rule**, the courts determine domicile as of the complaint's filing date, not a later date after a party's domicile changes.

Congress alters diversity-of-citizenship requirements for certain kinds of cases, often substituting **minimal diversity** for complete diversity. A **class action** has a federal forum if the claims total more than $5 million and at least one plaintiff is a citizen of a different state than at least one defendant. **Interpleader** actions also have a federal forum with only minimal rather than complete diversity and lower the jurisdictional minimum to just $500. **Mass-tort cases** have a federal forum if at least seventy-five persons died in the tort in one location, and the case presents certain diversity aspects.

When, though, the case requires complete diversity, the federal court must dismiss a case having only minimal diversity, unless it is able to dismiss non-diverse parties in order to preserve diversity jurisdiction over the case. Under the **master-of-the-complaint** rule, plaintiffs ordinarily determine

Civil Procedure

whether a case presents complete diversity, by naming diverse or non-diverse parties in the complaint. Yet a federal court may in the unusual case disregard non-diverse parties whom the court determines are only **nominal parties**, whom the plaintiff may have joined in an attempt to defeat federal removal. Federal law also prohibits **collusive joinder** attempting to create diversity jurisdiction. Diversity jurisdiction does not authorize divorce, child-custody, child-support, or other family-law cases, or probate cases, even when the parties have diverse citizenship.

The plaintiff has leeway to allege the minimum $75,000 **amount in controversy** in good faith, no matter the ultimate recovery. The claim must appear to a certainty less than the jurisdictional amount to justify dismissal. A single plaintiff may aggregate multiple smaller claims against a single defendant into an amount that meets the jurisdictional minimum, just as a plaintiff who has a single claim against the defendant worth more than the jurisdictional minimum may in the same case maintain a claim against the same defendant worth less than the jurisdictional minimum. On the other hand, a single plaintiff may not aggregate claims against multiple defendants, and multiple plaintiffs may not aggregate claims, to satisfy the jurisdictional minimum. Plaintiffs who have a common and undivided interest to enforce a single right may consider the aggregate value of that interest. A plaintiff with an injunctive rather than damage remedy may plead the injunction's value to satisfy the minimum. Diversity jurisdiction remains when events after the plaintiff files suit reduce the recoverable amount to below the $75,000 minimum. A cost-shifting provision creates accountability for the plaintiff who alleges an amount in controversy but recovers less than the jurisdictional minimum.

...supplemental...

Federal courts also have **supplemental jurisdiction** over state claims that, if brought alone, would not qualify for federal subject-matter jurisdiction but that do qualify because of their close relationship to a federal claim satisfying federal-question jurisdiction. For supplemental jurisdiction to arise, the non-qualifying state claims must arise out of the **same case or controversy** as the federal claim that qualifies for federal-question jurisdiction. The law defines the *same case or controversy* as involving a **common nucleus of operative fact** with the qualifying federal claim. Thus, while a federal court would not have subject-matter jurisdiction over a state civil-rights claim between non-diverse parties, if the plaintiff files a federal civil-rights claim to which the plaintiff joins the state claim arising out of the same facts, then the federal court would have supplemental jurisdiction over the state claim.

A plaintiff who pleads a federal claim in federal court can also gain supplemental jurisdiction not only over a state claim but also over a **third party** whom the defendant adds on a contribution or indemnity theory. A plaintiff cannot, though, gain supplemental jurisdiction over a third party when the plaintiff's claim against the defendant depends on diversity-of-citizenship jurisdiction rather than federal-question jurisdiction. Supplemental jurisdiction also permits class-action members whose

Civil Procedure

individual claims are for less than diversity's $75,000 jurisdictional minimum to maintain claims if at least one class member's claim exceeds $75,000. Congress separately provides for federal subject-matter jurisdiction over class-action claims aggregating over $5 million even if none of the claims have a value of more than $75,000.

The federal courts have supplemental jurisdiction over a defendant's **counterclaim** that arises out of the same case or controversy (the same common nucleus of operative fact) as the plaintiff's qualifying claim. Nonetheless, the federal courts retain **discretion to decline** supplemental jurisdiction for claims raising a novel or complex state-law issue. The courts may also decline supplemental jurisdiction when the state claim predominates over the claim qualifying the case for federal jurisdiction, when the court dismisses the qualifying claim, or for other compelling reasons to decline jurisdiction.

...and removal)

When a plaintiff files in state court a case that would qualify for federal subject-matter jurisdiction, defendants in the case may under certain circumstances **remove** the case from state to federal court. The defendant's right to remove depends on the face of the **well-pled complaint**. For example, a defendant may ordinarily remove a complaint that pleads a federal claim that would qualify for federal subject-matter jurisdiction, or a case that would qualify for federal diversity-of-citizenship jurisdiction. Under the **home-state defendant rule**, though, if any defendant is a citizen of the state in which the plaintiff filed the action, then defendants may remove only if federal-question jurisdiction provides the removal basis, not diversity of citizenship.

A **federal defense** to the action or **federal counterclaim** does *not* qualify for removal an otherwise non-removeable case. On the other hand, if a plaintiff omits a complaint's federal-removal basis from an artfully drafted complaint, then the defendant may remove by demonstrating the omitted federal basis. Non-removable additional claims do not affect removal of qualifying claims. If the plaintiff amends after removal to eliminate the basis for federal jurisdiction, the federal district court retains removal jurisdiction. Beyond the general removal statute, other statutes provide for removal of cases involving federal civil-rights claims, interstate class actions, and federal-officer defendants.

A defendant who wishes to remove a case need simply file a **notice of removal** in the federal court for the district and division where the plaintiff filed the state action. A federal court may construe defendant's answering or otherwise defending in state court before seeking removal as consent to state-court jurisdiction and waiver of right to remove. Defendants have **thirty days** from the complaint's service within which to remove or, if the case only later becomes removable (for instance, when the plaintiff amends the complaint to add a federal claim), then thirty days from that event. Yet a defendant removing based on diversity jurisdiction must also do so within **one year** of the original filing of the case, even if the basis for removal, such as the dismissal of a non-diverse defendant, occurs later.

Civil Procedure

Plaintiffs who wish to challenge removal and obtain a remand to state court must do so within thirty days of removal if the grounds are the removal's untimeliness. Plaintiff may have the costs and attorney's fees incurred in obtaining remand, when the defendant has removed without reasonable basis. Federal law permits removal of state securities-law claims and then authorizes dismissal in federal court of those claims, effectively preempting state securities law.

B. Personal jurisdiction

To obtain an enforceable judgment, a plaintiff must choose a court of a forum state that has **personal jurisdiction** over the defendant. Personal jurisdiction must satisfy constitutional **due process** involving notice and opportunity for hearing. The defendant must have had **minimum contacts** with the **forum state** such that jurisdiction would be reasonable. To judge reasonableness, courts must look to the plaintiff's interest, defendant's burden, the forum state's interest, and shared state interests, and efficient resolution. While ensuring that cases satisfy constitutional due process, courts must also give **full faith and credit** to the judgments of other courts.

Personal jurisdiction takes different forms. **Specific jurisdiction** depends on (1) **purposeful acts** giving rise to the litigation that the defendant took toward the forum state, out of which the defendant **purposefully avails** the defendant of the privilege of relations with the forum state, (2) the dispute arising out of those purposeful forum-related acts, and (3) that personal jurisdiction must also be reasonable. For example, if a mother and father dispute child custody in a state in which they have raised the children together, then the courts of that state would have specific jurisdiction over the dispute, both parties having purposefully acted in that state as to the children's custody. Yet if the mother moves across country with the children to sue the father for child custody in a state where the father had taken no action as to the children, then the courts of that state would not have specific jurisdiction.

The test for **general jurisdiction** depends on whether the defendant is an individual or corporation. An individual **residing** in a state establishes general jurisdiction, as does a corporation **incorporating** or having its **principal place of business** in the state. For example, a corporation having its principal place of business in one state may dispute a joint venture in another state with another corporation having its principal place of business in a third state. Either corporation may sue the other in the state of their principal place of business, notwithstanding that the joint venture took place in another state, because both corporations would be at home in their state of principal place of business. A plaintiff may only in exceptionally rare circumstances obtain general jurisdiction over a defendant corporation not incorporated or having its principal place of business in the state, when the corporation's affiliation through continuous and systematic activities make the corporation essentially **at home** in the state.

Transient jurisdiction involves serving the defendant with process in the forum state, even if the defendant had neither purposefully acted toward the forum state nor maintained continuous, systematic, and substantial contacts with the forum state. For example, an individual client and

Civil Procedure

consultant may have engaged in a disputed transaction in a state where both maintain their offices and residences, and where a court would have both specific and general jurisdiction over either of them. Yet if one of them retains counsel in another state to file an action arising out of the dispute in that other state, and counsel is able to personally serve the defendant as the defendant happens to pass through that state, then the court of that state has transient jurisdiction. Presence in the state at the time of personal service, alone without other forum contacts, ordinarily establishes personal jurisdiction, although tricking a person to enter a state for service, or serving a defendant whom subpoena has compelled to enter a state, may be constitutionally insufficient.

Parties may also **consent** to personal jurisdiction. Corporations appointing a **resident agent** for service of process in another state may have consented to personal jurisdiction in that state particularly if they then do at least some business in that state, although some authority holds that mere registration to do business may be insufficient contacts. An individual defendant, who accepts service of process, authorizes defense counsel to make a **general appearance** in the case, and answers or otherwise defends without raising lack of personal jurisdiction as a defense, also consents to personal jurisdiction. By contrast, the defendant making only a **special appearance** solely to contest personal jurisdiction does not consent, although that party must comply with discovery as to jurisdiction issues.

Parties may also contract in advance to consent to jurisdiction. For example, if a corporation in one state leases equipment to a farmer in another state under written agreement in which the farmer designated an agent in the corporation's state for service of process, consenting to that state's personal jurisdiction, then the courts of that state may subject the farmer to personal jurisdiction in a dispute arising out of the lease. A **forum-selection clause** in a contract designates the forum in which the parties agree to resolve disputes arising out of the contract. Forum-selection clauses must be **fundamentally fair** for the selected forum to exercise of personal jurisdiction. For example, if a cruise line includes in passenger contracts a forum-selection clause for the cruise line's home state, then the clause is likely enforceable given the foreseeability of passengers having to litigate in that state and the benefit to passengers in reduced fares. Yet if the clause chose a distant and anomalous forum bearing no relationship to expectations or costs, simply to frustrate passenger suits, then the clause may be unfair and unenforceable.

Personal jurisdiction also depends on the court's **statutory authority** to exercise personal jurisdiction. **State courts** depend on **long-arm statutes** for that statutory authority. A long-arm statute defines the jurisdictional reach of the state's courts over non-resident defendants. Long-arm statutes vary from state to state. One type enumerates specific acts subjecting a non-resident defendant to personal jurisdiction. If the defendant does not so act, then the state's courts must not exercise personal jurisdiction over the defendant even if due process permits it. Another type of long-arm statute ties jurisdiction to its constitutional limit. Watch for these statutory issues when addressing personal jurisdiction.

Federal rule and statutes establish the personal-jurisdiction reach of the **federal courts**, within constitutional limits. Some federal statutes grant

Civil Procedure

nationwide or even **worldwide** personal jurisdiction, while others grant the courts personal jurisdiction only over defendants who reside, are in, or have an agent in the district. Rule 4 recognizes the personal jurisdiction that these statutes extend. Where no federal statute grants the federal court personal jurisdiction over a defendant in the action, Rule 4 authorizes the district court to extend personal jurisdiction to the **same extent as the long-arm statute** of the forum state. Rule 4's **100-mile rule** also extends federal-court personal jurisdiction over a necessary defendant or third-party defendant served within the district and not more than 100 miles from the court issuing the summons.

A defendant may **challenge personal jurisdiction** directly **by special appearance** in the court in which the plaintiff has filed the case. The defendant challenges personal jurisdiction directly must not commit an act, such as answering and defending, that the court will construe as consent to personal jurisdiction. Rule 12 and similar state rules require defendants to challenge personal jurisdiction by motion before the first responsive pleading and to allege lack of personal jurisdiction in any subsequent responsive pleading.

A defendant may alternatively attack personal jurisdiction **collaterally**, after the plaintiff has taken a default judgment in the court that the defendant maintains has no personal jurisdiction. Collateral attack occurs in the court in which the plaintiff attempts to enforce the prior judgment, such as in the defendant's home state where the defendant has assets on which the plaintiff can execute or income to garnish. A defendant who makes a special appearance to challenge jurisdiction in the original action but loses that challenge may not later collaterally attack on the same jurisdictional grounds.

C. Service of process...

Service of process refers to the procedure by which the plaintiff attempts to get the summons and complaint or other pleadings initiating a lawsuit into the defendant's hands and documents for the court that the plaintiff has done so or attempted to do so. Rule 4 and similar state rules authorize any person **at least eighteen years of age** and who is **not a party** to serve process. Rule 4 requires that the plaintiff accomplish service **within 90 days** of filing the complaint, although the court may extend the period on motion before it expires. State rules provide for similar periods. Rule 4 authorizes service on an individual defendant according to the forum state's rules or by **personal delivery** to the defendant, leaving the summons and complaint with a **person of suitable age and discretion** residing at the defendant's usual place of abode, or delivering to an agent whom law authorizes to receive process. Service on a **corporation** is typically by personal delivery to an **officer or agent** on whom the law authorizes service.

While the rules label service *of process*, as the procedure for getting the summons and complaint into the defendant's hands, the rules also provide for **service** of pleadings and other court papers beyond the summons and complaint. Rule 5 and similar state rules require a party to serve other parties or their counsel with pleadings, notices, and other court papers after initial service of process whenever those other parties or their counsel have **entered an appearance** in the case. If neither the defendant nor the defendant's

Civil Procedure

lawyer has appeared in the action, then other parties need not serve the defendant with those subsequent papers after the plaintiff serves or attempts to serve the defendant with process.

...and notice

Service of process raises constitutional **due-process** issues, particularly when the defendant fails to answer the complaint timely, suffering default judgment affecting important rights. Service of process must be by means **reasonably calculated to effect notice**. Service according to the above rules would typically satisfy this constitutional standard. Yet service rules and statutes also exist for **alternate service**, such as when a defendant has moved away without forwarding address, and the plaintiff is unable to locate the defendant after reasonable investigation. Alternate-service rules and orders may provide for **mailing** to the last known address, **advertising** the cause of action in the local newspaper or legal news, **posting** the process at the defendant's residence or at the courthouse, or even **online posting** to the defendant's social-media account.

Whatever means the court approves and plaintiff follows, service of process must satisfy the Supreme Court's *reasonably calculated* standard. While this functional standard requires **case-by-case** review, the Supreme Court tends to reject service by only one alternate means that relies on only **constructive notice**. For example, advertising only, mailing only, or posting only may well be insufficient, particularly when the service is not likely to reach the defendant. Multiple means, the best means possible or reasonably practical, and showing that the defendant is deliberately avoiding service, increase the likelihood that service is constitutionally sufficient. The Constitution also requires that notice include the action's title, number, and court, how and when to appear and defend, and the grounds for the action. Rule 12 and similar state rules permit defendants to move to dismiss an action for insufficient service of process. A defendant having suffered default in a prior action without notice may challenge the judgment's constitutionality in the subsequent enforcement action.

D. Venue...

As the introduction above indicates, **venue** involves issues having to do with efficiency of the courts and fairness and convenience to parties and witnesses, including discouraging undue forum shopping. The plaintiff chooses venue initially by filing the complaint in a court of that venue, presumably within the scope of the applicable venue statutes. When served with process out of that court, the defendant may then challenge venue as improper or seek transfer of venue to a more-convenient forum. **State and federal venue statutes** control original venue in state and federal courts, respectively. A plaintiff must file the case in a court that has venue under the applicable statute. First consider whether venue is proper, followed by sections on forum convenience and transfer of venue.

State venue statutes identify the locations (often counties) in which a state court has original venue for the action. Many state venue statutes,

Civil Procedure

particularly those for tort actions, locate venue in the county **where the cause of action arose**. State statutes may also place venue in the county of the **litigation's subject**, such as the disputed real property's location, under what law calls the **local-action doctrine**. Other venue statutes, particularly those for breach-of-contract actions, may specify the county where the **defendant resides or does business**, or if the defendant is from out of state, then where the plaintiff resides or does business. Venue statutes for divorce or other family law actions may specify the county where the children and at least one parent reside.

Venue in **federal court** involves choosing both the forum state *and* the district within the state if the state has more than one federal district. Federal venue ordinarily depends first on any applicable **special venue statute** and then on the general federal venue statute. For example, special federal venue statutes exist for removed actions and copyright and patent actions. A plaintiff may follow the special or general venue statute only if the special venue statute so provides. Federal courts may also follow the **local-action doctrine** in disputes involving real property.

The **general federal venue statute** requires a connection between the forum state and federal district within the state, on one hand, and either the parties or the events or property that they dispute, on the other hand. A federal district court has original venue when all **defendants reside** in the state and at least one defendant resides in the district. Venue law construes an individual defendant's *residence* to mean the one permanent home to which the individual intends to return when absent. Federal venue statute defines a corporation's residence much more broadly to include any district that has personal jurisdiction over the corporation.

Federal district courts also have venue when **substantial events giving rise to the claim** occurred in the district or **the disputed property** is in the district. Substantial events may mean less than a majority of events. Two or more districts may each venue, as long as significant material events occurred in the district. If a plaintiff cannot satisfy any of these federal original-venue provisions, then the plaintiff may file in any district having personal jurisdiction. Alien individuals and corporations face unlimited federal venue.

Defendants **challenge venue** with a motion under Rule 12 or similar state rules, when the plaintiff files a case in an improper venue. Defendants must do so as their **initial response**, on penalty of having waived the venue challenge. If a party later joins a new party whose joinder makes venue improper, then the court must dismiss the joined party if the joined party makes that motion. Dismissal of a party or case for improper venue is *not* a decision on the merits barring refiling in a proper court.

...forum non conveniens...

The doctrine of **forum non conveniens** addresses cases the court should not hear because of party or witness inconvenience or judicial efficiency, even though venue is proper. A court may dismiss under the doctrine, otherwise properly filed actions. Indeed, federal district courts may dismiss based on forum non conveniens *before* deciding whether they have

Civil Procedure

either personal or subject-matter jurisdiction. Forum non conveniens dismissals, though, are *not* decisions on the merits. Parties remain free to refile in the more convenient jurisdiction. When determining whether to dismiss under forum non conveniens, federal district court do not consider the favorability of law in the forum unless the law in the other forum is so clearly inadequate as to be no remedy at all.

...and transfer...

Courts determining that another forum is more convenient and efficient than their own forum need not dismiss the action under forum non conveniens but may instead **transfer** the action to the more-convenient forum. For example, federal and state statutes authorize transfer on grounds of convenience to parties and witnesses including not only the burden of travel to distant forums but also whether the court can compel attendance. The federal courts also have statutory authority to transfer venue when the plaintiff chose an improper venue or when the court has no personal jurisdiction. The federal district courts have **discretion** whether to dismiss the case or to transfer the case to a proper or more-convenient venue.

Federal law also authorizes transfer of **multi-district litigation** into a single district court, when panel concludes that convenience and efficiency compel consolidation of cases in different districts for pretrial procedures. A court must not transfer a case to a forum that does not have personal jurisdiction over the defendant. Forum-selection clauses are a significant but not controlling factor in a court's decision whether to transfer. A federal district court receiving a diversity-jurisdiction case on transfer must apply the law that the federal district court granting transfer would have applied. State courts have similar state statutory or court-rule authority to transfer venue to courts of other counties within the same state or to dismiss in favor of the plaintiff refiling in another state.

II.   Law applied by federal courts

Federal courts do not always apply federal law. They sometimes instead apply *state* law. In brief outline, the federal courts apply federal statutes, federal common law, and federal rules in cases involving **federal questions**. Federal-question cases present no significant questions of which law to apply. By contrast, state-law claims filed in federal court under **diversity jurisdiction** require the federal courts to determine what law applies to which case procedures and substantive issues. In those diversity cases, when a federal rule or statute clearly prescribes a court **procedure**, then the court applies the federal provision. The court applies the state's **substantive** law to the substantive state claim. The next two sections address in greater detail when the federal courts apply *state* law and when they apply *federal* law.

A. State law in federal court

Civil Procedure

The *Erie* **doctrine** holds in simplest form that federal courts in diversity cases follow state substantive law but federal procedural law. For example, if a manufacturer from another state files in federal court a contract-breach action against a distributor from the federal court's forum state, then the federal court will apply the forum state's contract law to the claim while applying federal discovery rules and other federal rules of procedure. The *Erie* doctrine, though, can in any one application require more than distinguishing between substance and procedure.

The full test of the *Erie* doctrine involves **balancing interests**. When a state law is **bound up with** state-created rights, then the state law is more likely to apply. Yet when the federal rule is an **essential characteristic** of the federal system, then the federal rule applies. Federal procedural rules are not to interfere with substantive rights but are otherwise **superior** to conflicting procedural provisions. For example, while state tort law would determine a plaintiff's tort recovery in a federal diversity case, the federal court would apply the federal discovery rule for medical examinations even if that federal rule conflicted with state rules. Federal appellate procedural rules also supplant contrary state procedural rules, such as for penalty interest on a judgment. If a federal procedural rule clearly applies, then follow it, not the contrary state rule.

State law governs in federal diversity cases founded on **both law and equity**. The federal courts construe federal procedural provisions narrowly to avoid supplanting state substantive law in diversity cases. Some issues, particularly those that are case-dispositive, mix procedural and substantive issues. In those instances, the federal court in a diversity case determines the degree to which the state provision is an integral part of state-law rights, **balancing** that determination against countervailing federal interests in control over the federal courts. When a federal court faces the question of which state's law to apply, the court looks to the **choice-of-law doctrine of the forum state**. State choice-of-law rules tend either to be the substantive law of the place where the cause of action arose but the procedural law of the forum state, or to involve a balancing of each state's interests in having its own law apply. Federal courts may not always have state substantive law showing them what to do in any one case. Most states permit a federal district or appellate court to **certify** a state-law question of **first impression** to the state's highest court for answer, at the state court's discretion.

B. Federal common law

The *Erie* doctrine does *not* abolish all **federal common law**. Federal common law interprets **federal statutes**. For example, if Congress constitutionally enacts broad legislation on a matter of interstate commerce, the federal courts may develop common law carrying out the legislation's object. Federal common law also interprets **federal procedural rules**, such as when the federal courts develop by case law the scope of discovery that the federal rules only broadly outline. Federal common law also carries out powers that the Constitution grants directly to federal courts, in enclaves of **special federal interests**, such as in admiralty and maritime law, and disputes

Civil Procedure
over federal contracts. Federal common law can also create a **federal defense** to a state claim, such as by federal preemption.

On a related subject, some federal statutes permit enforcement actions in **either state or federal court**. In such cases involving federal statutory actions, federal law governs just as much in state court as federal court. State courts commonly apply federal law to matters involving federal rights and interests, consistent with the Constitution's **supremacy clause**. For example, federal law governing interstate waterways applies in a state-court case, even if the federal law is case-based federal common law rather than drawn from a federal statute. When a state-court case implicates both federal and state interests, the courts apply the law of the entity, federal or state, that has the predominant interest.

III. Pretrial procedures

The Multistate Bar Examination's topics list emphasizes pretrial procedures as an exam topic. Pretrial-procedure topics include pleading and pleading amendment, Rule 11 certification of court papers and associated sanctions, joinder rules including class actions, discovery procedures, and other pretrial practice. Give these topics their due.

A. Preliminary injunctions...

Trial courts follow special procedures for orders and judgments involving **injunctions**. An injunction is an order or judgment requiring that a party do or refrain from doing something. Injunction actions typically involve early contested hearing on the plaintiff's **motion for preliminary injunction**. For the court to issue the requested preliminary injunction, Rule 65 and similar state rules require the plaintiff to show **likelihood of success** on the claim's merits, **irreparable harm** if the court grants no injunction, **inadequacy of damages**, and a **balance** of greater harm if the court grants no injunction than the harm if the court does grant injunction. If the court grants a preliminary injunction, then in theory the case proceeds through discovery to trial months later on the issue of whether the injunction should become permanent. In practice, many injunction actions resolve at the preliminary-injunction stage, whether preliminary injunction issues or not.

...and temporary restraining orders

Injunction actions often begin with a motion for **temporary restraining order**, made when the plaintiff files the initial complaint and before hearing on the motion for preliminary injunction. A motion for temporary restraining order seeks to **preserve the status quo** while the court adjudicates the rights and remedies that the complaint asserts. If giving the opposing party notice of the motion may trigger the adverse action that the motion seeks to prevent then the moving party may forgo notice. The court may then enter the requested restraining order on the condition that notice and contested hearing on preliminary injunction follow promptly.

Civil Procedure

B. Pleadings...

Pleadings are court papers, typically filed at a case's outset, that frame the legal and factual issues in a case. A plaintiff begins an action by filing a **complaint** with the court. Consistent with notice pleading practices, Rule 8 and similar state rules require a statement of jurisdiction, **short and plain** statement of the claim, and demand for relief, in clear, concise, and direct rather than technical form. A defendant may **counterclaim** against the plaintiff or file a **third-party complaint** adding third-party defendants. Parties may also **cross-claim** against one another at any of these levels.

Complaints, counterclaims, third-party complaints, and cross-claims ordinarily require the defending party to **answer**. Rule 8 and similar state rules provide that an answer may admit, deny, or otherwise address the opposing pleading's allegations. An answer's admissions are **judicial admissions** rather than evidentiary admissions, meaning that they resolve the issue in the other party's favor, precluding the admitting party from introducing contrary evidence. Parties may also answer **no contest** to an allegation, meaning that they admit the allegation only for the pending proceeding and not for other proceedings. A party who denies an allegation must do so responding to the allegation's substance, admitting true parts while denying the rest. Yet Rule 8 and similar state rules authorize a defendant in good faith to plead **lack of knowledge or information** sufficient to answer, which the court construes as denial. A failure to answer an allegation is an admission.

Rule 8 and similar state rules require a party answering a pleading to also plead any **affirmative defenses** that the party intends to reserve or pursue. Affirmative defenses can include such grounds as accord and satisfaction, assumption of the risk, comparative or contributory negligence, and failure of consideration. A defendant who does not plead affirmative defenses when answering loses them, although some courts require the plaintiff to show prejudice from their omission. Prejudice can include frustrating trial preparation or having to devote more to the case than if the defendant had pled the defense initially.

...and amended...

Rule 15 and similar state rules authorize parties to file **amended pleadings** under certain circumstances at various points during the litigation right through trial. A party may amend once **as a matter of course** before the opposing party responds or, if the rules require no response, then within a short period that the federal rules set at 20 days after serving the pleading. The automatic-amendment right enables counsel to correct or augment a pleading in which the answer or other review indicates a deficiency. In all other instances, the party desiring amendment must either obtain opposing counsel's consent or the court's leave by motion. Rule 15 and similar state rules require that the court **freely grant leave** when justice requires. Courts do not grant leave when amendment would be **futile** or would **prejudice** the defendant.

Civil Procedure

The date of the amendment's effectiveness can be critical, particularly when the original complaint failed to plead a claim that a limitations period would bar by the time of the amendment. In some instances, though, the law construes the amendment's date as if the pleader had pled the amendment in the original complaint. The **relation-back doctrine** applies when the limitations statute expressly states so. The doctrine also applies when the amendment asserts a matter that arose out of the same transaction or occurrence (common core of operative facts) as the original complaint. The doctrine also applies when the original complaint misnamed a party who knew of the action within the time for its service and knew that the complaint should have named it but for the mistake.

...and supplemental pleadings

While amended pleadings seek to correct deficiencies in the prior pleadings, **supplemental pleadings** instead update the pleadings with events that occurred after the pleading that the party seeks to supplement. For example, if an employee sued an employer for unlawful race discrimination in passing over the employee for promotion, and the employer fired the employee in retaliation for the lawsuit, the employee may seek to supplement the pleading to allege the fact of the firing and the additional legal claim of retaliation. Rule 15 and similar state rules authorize a party to **move to supplement** a proceeding and the court to grant the motion **on just terms**. Give the trial judge's discretion whether to grant the motion, the party seeking to supplement a pleading should act promptly when the need arises, demonstrate the need including the prejudice if the court refuses supplementation, and meet terms like scheduling extensions and payment of costs. Supplemental pleadings may in appropriate instances relate back to the date of the original filing.

C. Rule 11

Rule 11 and similar state rules are the means by which the courts ensure that lawyers who present papers to the court have solid grounds for doing so. The rules require that a party's **attorney of record**, and if the party is unrepresented then the party personally, **sign** every **court paper presented to the court**. The rules then construe the signature as the attorney's **certification** that the attorney has not presented the paper for any **improper purpose** and that the paper has **legal and factual support**. The rules permit lawyers to make **nonfrivolous arguments** to extend, modify, or reverse law, or to make new law. The rules also permit lawyers to make factual contentions that will likely have evidentiary support after reasonable investigation or discovery.

Violations of the rule for signature certification can result in **sanctions** against the lawyer, law firm, or party. A party may **move** for sanctions, or the court may impose sanctions **on its own after** an order to show cause and a **hearing**. Sanctions may include directives and monetary payments into court or to the moving party for costs and attorney's fees due

Civil Procedure

to the violation. Rule 11 does not apply to discovery requests, responses, objections, and motions.

D. Joinder of parties...

To bring a claim, a plaintiff must have **standing**. To have standing is to be an **interested party** or real party in interest, meaning to hold a sufficient stake in the case to advocate it vigorously and genuinely. For example, a landowner would have standing to sue over another's harmful invasion of the owner's land. Yet a nonprofit organization interested in conservation may or may not have sufficient stake to sue, depending on a variety of factors such as the organization's mission and membership. For another example, the trustee would typically have standing to litigate for the trust, while one of several trust beneficiaries may not have standing to act for the trust but would have standing to litigate the beneficiary's own interest.

A plaintiff must also have the **capacity** to sue, just as defendants must have the capacity to be sued. Capacity generally involves not the significance of the party's interest or stake but instead the party's capability, maturity, and mental competence. The federal rules refer to the state law of the party's domicile to determine the party's capacity. For example, in a certain state, a party may have to be at least age eighteen to have capacity, requiring appointment of a conservator to act on behalf of parties younger than eighteen.

Litigation, fundamentally adversarial in nature, ordinarily begins with at least one **plaintiff** suing at least one **defendant**. Joinder rules determine whether other party arrangements are also appropriate. Under Rule 20, a plaintiff may join **multiple plaintiffs or defendants** only when their interests arise out of the **same transaction or occurrence, or series** of transactions or occurrences, raising a **common law or fact question**. The limitation's purpose is to keep litigation to a manageable scope. Indeed, even when the rules permit a plaintiff to join multiple parties, the court may order **separate trials** to avoid prejudice and **drop or add parties** on just terms. Rule 42 permits the court to **consolidate** into a single claim separate actions that have a common law or fact question, to manage the court's docket most efficiently.

Whether to join multiple parties is in other ways not always the plaintiff's choice. The rules require a plaintiff to join **necessary parties**. Under Rule 19, the court will permit willing necessary parties to join, or compel unwilling necessary parties to join, or will dismiss the case if joinder is not feasible and the non-party is **indispensable**. Under Rule 19, a federal court need not join a necessary party whose joinder would destroy diversity jurisdiction. Under Rule 19, a non-party is necessary and joinder compulsory when the court **can only accord incomplete relief** without the party, relief would **impair the non-party's rights**, or nonjoinder could subject a party to **inconsistent obligations**. Under Rule 19, a non-joinable non-party is indispensable and the court must dismiss the case if judgment without the non-party would be **prejudicial**, **protective provisions cannot lessen the prejudice**, judgment is **inadequate** without the non-party, and the plaintiff has **other available remedies**.

Civil Procedure

While joinder of multiple plaintiffs and defendants is relatively broad, focusing on the same transaction or occurrence or series of transactions or occurrences, and common law or fact questions, the rules narrow when a defendant wants to bring in a **third party**. Under Rule 14, a defendant may within 14 days of answering **implead** only a third-party defendant who **is or may be liable to the defendant** for all or part of the claim. **Indemnity** and **contribution** are common grounds on which defendants implead third-party defendants. Under 28 USC §1367, federal courts have **supplemental jurisdiction** over third-party claims. Once a defendant impleads a third party, under Rule 14 a plaintiff may claim against the third party if the plaintiff's third-party claim relates to the original claim. The plaintiff may not claim against a third party if doing so would destroy diversity jurisdiction. Statute does not provide supplemental jurisdiction for a plaintiff's third-party claim.

Other joinder rules govern **intervention**, when a non-party wishes to join an action but no party is willing to join the non-party. Under Rule 24, non-parties may on timely motion intervene **as of right** to **prevent impairment of their rights**. For example, if parties to a foreclosure proceeding omit a non-party lienholder, that lienholder may intervene of right to ensure proper protection of the lien. By contrast, non-parties have only **permissive intervention** for **common law or fact questions**. For example, if parties litigate a driver's negligence in a motor-vehicle accident, a non-party who suffered injury in the same accident may request intervention to take advantage of the resolution of that same negligence question. Non-parties seeking to intervene as of right must show a **significantly protectable interest** that may be impaired without intervention.

Interpleader involves other party-joinder rules. Under Rule 22, a plaintiff may interplead two or more defendants when the plaintiff holds an asset over which those defendants make competing claims. For example, a liability insurer that due to its insured's negligence must pay its full liability limits to two or more competing claimants, may interplead all claimants before paying any of them, so as not to face claims beyond its limits. Congress has expanded federal-court jurisdiction for interpleader actions, reducing the diversity jurisdiction's $75,000 minimum to just $500 while requiring only minimal diversity rather than complete diversity. Venue and personal jurisdiction are also broader in federal interpleader actions than in other federal cases and injunctions easier to obtain.

...and claims...

The subject of **joinder of claims** begins with the claims that a plaintiff may join in the complaint. Rule 18 permits plaintiffs to join **as many or few unrelated claims** as the plaintiff determines. The plaintiff chooses the initial scope of litigation. In federal court, though, joined state-law claims that have no other federal jurisdictional basis must meet 28 USC §1367's **same-case-or-controversy requirement**. Joinder does not create federal jurisdiction over the joined claims. Each claim must stand on its own. While plaintiffs *may* join unrelated claims, plaintiffs generally *should* join claims that arise out of the **same transaction or occurrence**. The reason to join related claims in the first proceeding is that **claim preclusion**, addressed at the end of this

Civil Procedure

subject's outline, generally bars related claims that a plaintiff fails to join but attempts to litigate after a final judgment on the merits in a prior case. Plead related claims now, or risk seeing them barred later.

Claim joinder has similar rules when a defendant wishes to plead a **counterclaim** against a plaintiff. Joinder rules divide counterclaims into **permissive** counterclaims and **compulsory** counterclaims. Under Rule 13, a party *may* join permissive counterclaims, which are those that do *not* arise out of the same transaction or occurrence as the plaintiff's claim. Yet, a defendant *must* join compulsory counterclaims, which are those that *do* arise out of the **same transaction or occurrence** as the plaintiff's claim. Claim preclusion will likely bar a related counterclaim that the defendant fails to join. Federal courts apply a broad **logical-relationship test**, rather than a narrow immediate-connection test, to define compulsory counterclaims. Federal courts have supplemental jurisdiction over compulsory but not permissive counterclaims.

Cases involving multiple parties similarly aligned, such as multiple defendants or third-party defendants, create the prospect for **cross-claims** between those parties. Under Rule 13, a party may cross-claim against a party who is similarly aligned. However, cross-claims must relate to a transaction or occurrence already pled in a claim or counterclaim. To permit unrelated cross-claims would unduly complicate the litigation.

...(including class actions)

Class actions involve **class representatives** pursuing an action on behalf of numerous class members whom the class identifies not by name but by common characteristics. Under Rule 23, **judgment** in a class action, conducted in the name of one or more representatives who adequately represent the class, **binds class members**. Congress grants broad federal jurisdiction for class actions. Under 28 USC §1332, federal courts have **subject-matter jurisdiction** over class actions if all class claims aggregate to **$5 million** and at least one plaintiff and defendant are diverse, meaning **minimal diversity** rather than complete diversity. One defendant may remove a class action to federal court without the consent of other defendants. Federal law preempts state securities-law claims in **securities class actions**. **Choice of law**, often an issue in nationwide class actions, depends on showing constitutionally adequate significant contacts to apply a specific state's law.

For a class action to proceed under Rule 23, the court must **certify** the class at an early practicable time. Class certification first requires that the class representative show that the action meets **numerosity**, **commonality**, **typicality**, and **adequacy-of-representation** requirements. Numerosity requires impracticable joinder of all class members. Commonality requires law or fact questions common to all parties. Typicality requires a representative whose claims typify class members' claims. Adequate representation requires that the representative and class counsel have the commitment, skill, and resources to represent and protect the class.

In addition to satisfying these four conditions, class certification under Rule 23 also requires that the action be one of four types. For

Civil Procedure

certification, a class action must either prevent **incompatible standards, depletion of an insufficient common fund**, or **frustration of an individual injunction**, or enable resolution of **small individual damages claims**. For the latter damages-type class action aggregating individual small claims, the common law or fact questions must **predominate** over individual questions and a class action must be **superior** to individual resolution.

Class actions must satisfy constitutional due process including that class members have **notice** of the certification order with an opportunity to **opt out** of the action. Rule 23 requires that representatives give members notice of a class-action **settlement**, which the court must **approve or disapprove after hearing** class-member objections. The court may permit objecting class members to opt out of the settlement. Class counsel must obtain court approval of fees. **Settlement-only class actions**, in which the parties reach agreement before filing suit, must still satisfy certification requirements.

E. Discovery...

Discovery of evidence, playing an outsize role in civil litigation, begins with the filing of a case. The rules do not authorize pre-suit discovery, although Rule 27 and similar state rules permit depositions to **perpetuate testimony**, such as where a witness is terminally ill. Once a party files suit, Rule 26 limits the scope of discovery to **nonprivileged relevant matter proportional to case needs**. Discovery requests must first of all be likely to lead to admissible evidence relevant to pled claims or defenses. As to the proportionality requirement, courts balance benefit from the discovery against the discovery's cost and burden, party resources, amount in controversy, interests at stake, and other factors.

Federal and state discovery rules authorize certain discovery methods only between parties. **Interrogatories** between parties involve written questions that the responding party must answer in writing under oath. Rule 33 limits to twenty-five the number of interrogatories including subparts, although state rules for interrogatories may not have such a limit. While parties typically use interrogatories to discover facts, interrogatories may also ask for opinions, contentions, and application of law to fact. Rule 33 permits a responding party to refer the requester to business records when both sides would have the same burden of deriving answers. Parties routinely serve interrogatories on opposing parties.

Rule 36 and similar state rules also authorize parties to serve other parties with **admission requests**. An admission request is a written statement as to a matter of law or fact relating to the case, or as to the authenticity of documents, that the other party must admit or deny (under the federal rule, within 30 days) with particularity, giving reasons for denials. An admission establishes the matter beyond dispute, in the nature of a pleading or judicial admission rather than an evidentiary admission. Admission requests can help narrow the claims and defenses or save time proving the authenticity of documents.

Mental or physical examination is another discovery device limited to the parties. Indeed, under Rule 35, mental or physical examinations are

Civil Procedure

available only when a party has placed the party's **mental or physical condition in issue**. For example, a plaintiff in a personal-injury case necessarily places the plaintiff's mental or physical condition in issue, meaning that the defendant may demand a qualified medical-care provider's examination of the plaintiff. On the other hand, parties disputing contract breaches or fraud do not place their mental or physical condition in issue, meaning that examination is not available. When a party obtains examination of an opposing party, the party must produce the examiner's report.

Parties also routinely serve **production requests** on opposing parties or, with a subpoena, on non-parties. Rule 34 authorizes production requests for documents and things, including also inspection of property. When a non-party holds a party's records, such as in the case of employers, schools, or medical-care providers, a party may comply with a production request by authorizing the non-party's release of those records to the requesting party.

Rule 30 and similar state rules authorize parties to take **depositions** of both party and non-party, and both lay and expert, witnesses. A deposition is an out-of-court recorded and transcribed record of oral questioning, conducted in question-and-answer format as if in a court proceeding. A party taking a deposition must notify other parties whose counsel may attend to cross-examine the witness. Counsel note objections on the record for later ruling if necessary but may instruct their own clients not to answer questions requiring disclosure of privileged information. Parties may take depositions for discovery, to preserve testimony for trial, and for impeachment purposes.

...(including e-discovery)...

Given the large quantity today of electronically stored information, such as email and electronic files, Rule 34 and similar state rules specifically authorize parties to request production of electronically stored information. Indeed, while persons who have no reason to anticipate litigation take **safe harbor in good-faith routines** for the destruction of electronic information, on the contrary, persons who should **reasonably anticipate litigation** have a duty to preserve electronically stored information that may become evidence. Lawyers properly notify clients to institute a **litigation hold** as soon as reasonably anticipating litigation.

Parties may refuse discovery of electronically stored information that is **not reasonably accessible** because of undue burden or cost. Because of the high cost of producing some electronically stored information or of searching it for privileged material before production, parties may agree to (or the court may order) sampling, cost-shifting, quick-peek, and claw-back provisions. Rule 34 requires a responding party to produce electronically stored information in **native or reasonably useable format** without scrubbing metadata. Parties requesting electronically stored information may instead designate preferred format, to which responding parties may object on cost, security, or other basis. Whenever a party withholds privileged information from production, including scrubbing privileged metadata, the party should keep and produce a privilege log listing redactions.

...disclosure...

Civil Procedure

Rule 26 requires parties in federal court to make **early voluntary disclosures** without waiting on discovery requests. Parties must disclose testifying **experts' names, qualifications, and opinions**. Parties must also disclose **lay witnesses**, supporting **exhibits, damages computations**, and available **liability insurance**. Parties must make these disclosures twenty-one days before the Rule 16 conference.

Privileges, though, limit a party's duty to disclose. In federal court, the common law determines privileges. Civil litigation commonly involves two main privileges. The **attorney-client privilege** protects confidential communications between attorney and client including communications among corporate employees for the corporation's lawyer. **Inadvertent disclosure** does not waive the privilege if the discloser took reasonable steps to prevent disclosure.

The **attorney-work-product privilege** protects from discovery things that the attorneys in the proceeding prepare anticipating or during litigation. Unlike the attorney-client privilege, the opposing party may obtain discovery of attorney work product if showing substantial need, such as when a witness whom an attorney has interviewed has disappeared. The substantial-need exception to the attorney-work-product privilege, though, does not reach work product reflecting an attorney's mental impressions in the case, which remain protected. Parties must disclose to the other side when they withhold information as to which the party claims a privilege to enable the other side to evaluate and challenge the claim.

...and sanctions

Those who should reasonably anticipate litigation have a duty to take reasonable steps to **preserve evidence**. Failing to preserve evidence when that duty exists, or outright destruction of evidence, also known as **spoliation**, can lead to **sanctions** up to default or dismissal. When parties disagree over discovery, the requesting party may move under Rule 37 to **compel discovery**. In doing so, the moving party must certify to efforts to confer and resolve the disagreement with the other side. The party resisting discovery may move for **protective order** against unreasonably cumulative, duplicative, late, annoying, embarrassing, oppressing, burdensome, or expensive requests. Also, when parties fail or refuse to provide requested discovery in federal court, and the court orders discovery, the court must order the cost incurred in moving to compel unless the court finds the failure or refusal justified. If a party disobeys a discovery order, then the court may enforce the order up to default or dismissal and contempt sanctions.

F. Adjudication without a trial

Local federal rules adopted to comply with federal statutes, and similar state-court rules, authorize the court to support **alternative dispute resolution**, to resolve cases without extensive litigation and short of trial. These methods vary in their voluntary and coercive efforts toward resolution. **Early neutral evaluation** involves independent evaluators stating the case's

Civil Procedure

monetary value that the parties reject at the peril of paying the other side's costs if they fail to improve their position. **Offer of judgment** involves a party formally notifying of a settlement offer that the opposing party rejects at the peril of paying the offering party's costs if failing to obtain a more-favorable result. **Mediation** involves the parties hiring a trained professional to help the parties recognize interests, generate settlement options, and fashion voluntary relief.

When parties do settle voluntarily through alternative dispute resolution, they often do so by private agreement providing for dismissing the pending lawsuit with prejudice. Where enforcing a settlement agreement is a concern, the parties may incorporate the agreement by reference into the dismissal order so that the court can later reopen the case for enforcement if necessary. Where statute provides for prevailing-party attorney's fees, defendants may settle to avoid incurring those fees, which courts award only when entering judgment. Avoiding judgment may avoid payment of the other side's fees.

Arbitration is another form of alternative dispute resolution that both federal and state law and rules support, but one that involves a significantly greater degree of compulsion than the above methods. Arbitration involves a **neutral professional** or **balanced panel** deciding a case through streamlined private procedures. The prevailing party may enter the arbitration award as a court judgment for the court's enforcement. Courts generally review arbitration awards only for **evident bias** or **exceeded powers**. Parties may agree to arbitrate after filing a court case, or the parties may have contracted for arbitration in advance of any dispute, with either party compelling arbitration through contract enforcement. While arbitration clauses are generally enforceable as a favored means of private resolution, the courts will not enforce **unconscionable** arbitration clauses that fail to provide for fair resolution.

G. Pretrial conference and order

Trial courts typically hold an early scheduling conference, in federal court known as a **Rule 16 conference**, to address orderly resolution of the case. The court then issues a **scheduling order** including due dates for amending pleadings, concluding discovery, filing final witness and exhibit lists, and moving for summary judgment, and scheduling a final pretrial conference near the scheduled trial date. Failure to comply with the scheduling order may result in loss of procedural rights such as to call unlisted witnesses or introduce unlisted exhibits, or in other sanctions. At a Rule 16 pretrial conference, the court may also **dismiss insupportable claims and defenses**, typically those for which a party acknowledges having no support. The court may also use the pretrial conference to refer matters to a magistrate or master. Pretrial conferences under Rule 16 and similar state-court rules also encourage or require efforts at voluntary settlement, addressed above.

IV. Jury trials

Civil Procedure

Whether a judge or jury decides a case at trial depends on both whether the parties have a right to jury trial *and* whether at least one of the parties exercises that right. Rule 38 and similar state rules require at least one party to **demand** a jury trial when pleading. If no party demands a jury trial, then the judge will decide a jury-triable issue. Lawyer-conduct rules give *parties*, not their lawyers, the choice whether to try their claims before a judge or jury. Lawyers thus take care to ensure that they demand a jury trial when their clients wish one, or the client may lose that right, and the lawyer may have committed misconduct.

A. Right to jury trial

The **Seventh Amendment** guarantees federal civil litigants a right to jury trial only in certain cases. The Seventh Amendment defines federal civil jury rights by the **historical practice** for suits at common law when the states adopted the Amendment. The practice then and today grants jury-trial rights for tort and contract claims, and other **suits at law**, referring generally to damages cases. Parties do *not* have jury-trial rights in **equitable cases** seeking injunctive relief including, for example, divorce and other family-law cases and declaratory actions construing other rights of the parties.

Some cases involve both legal claims as to which the parties have jury-trial rights and equitable claims as to which they do not have those rights. In those cases, Rule 57 provides that a jury decides the legal claims and the judge the equitable claim. When history and practice provide no precedent for whether jury-trial rights exist, the courts look to **analogous claims**. For example, while federal statutory civil-rights damages claims did not exist at the Seventh Amendment's adoption, those claims are sufficiently like tort claims for the courts to grant jury trial. The courts look next to the **form of remedy**. If the claim is for damages, then a jury decides, while if the claim is for an injunction, then the judge decides. If the form of relief is mixed, then the courts look next to the **practical ability** of jury or judge to decide. State constitutions and law define state civil-jury-trial rights.

B. Selection...

When a party has a jury-trial right and demands jury trial, questions remain as to how many jurors to draw, how to draw them, and how they decide. Rule 48 and many state rules provide for a **minimum of six jurors**, although other states provide for a minimum of twelve jurors. The practice is to also seat **two alternate jurors** for the trial if one or two jurors must retire for illness or other cause, and then to draw off the two alternates if all other jurors remain to deliberate. Rule 48 requires juror **unanimity** to reach a verdict, unless the parties stipulate and the court accepts otherwise. Individual states may permit one or more dissenting jurors.

To ensure that jurors are qualified, they answer questionnaires that the court makes available to counsel for review. To ensure that jurors are not biased, the judge and counsel **voir dire** prospective jurors before seating them for trial. Counsel may **challenge for cause** any juror who demonstrates inability or unwillingness to follow the law in unbiased manner. After the

Civil Procedure

judge removes any biased jurors, each side may then strike up to three jurors in a **peremptory challenge** for which counsel need give no cause. Parties must exercise their peremptory challenges in racially and sexually non-discriminatory manner. Parties who strike jurors along racial or sexual lines must give non-discriminatory reasons for doing so when challenged. The other side may challenge those reasons as pretext.

...and composition of juries

Federal courts draw jurors from among **registered voters**. States may instead draw jurors using driver's licenses, state identification, or other candidate pools, creating a broader jury pool. Under federal law, jurors must be **U.S. citizens at least age eighteen** who reside in the district, know English well enough to complete the juror qualification form, have **no felony convictions** or pending felony charges, and have no mental or physical condition that would prevent them from serving. Federal law excuses active-duty military members, full-time firefighters and police officers, and full-time federal, state, and local government officials. Judges may excuse jurors for undue hardship or extreme inconvenience and under local rules often excusing those over age seventy, those who have served within the past two years, and volunteer emergency personnel.

C. Requests for and objections to jury instructions

Judges decide and instruct as to the law, while juries decide disputed fact issues, preserving Seventh Amendment jury-trial rights and similar jury rights under state provisions. Judges typically require that counsel submit **proposed jury instructions** in advance of trial. After jury draw, trials begin with **preliminary jury instructions**. Counsel then typically make opening statements before each party presents its case in chief and any rebuttal case. Judges instruct jurors as to any law issues that arise during those cases. **Final jury instructions** typically follow closing arguments, after which jurors deliberate. Judges may give further instructions during deliberation if any issues arise.

Counsel for the parties draw and propose jury instructions from **standard jury instructions**, also called *pattern* or *model* instructions. Counsel often also draft and propose **special jury instructions** to address new issues peculiar to the case that standard instructions do not address. Once the trial judge decides what instructions to give or reject, counsel for each party must **object on the record** to erroneous instruction or erroneous refusal to instruct, *before* the court reads instructions to the jury. If counsel fails to object on the record before instruction, then the party can lose appeal rights as to erroneous instructions, unless the instructions constitute **plain error** affecting the party's substantial rights.

V.   Motions

A motion is a procedural device that a party employs to bring an issue to the trial judge's attention for decision. A party files a motion with an

Civil Procedure

accompanying brief, reciting the facts and circumstances, and legal authority, supporting the requested relief. The opposing party files a response and opposing brief. The judge will then typically hear the motion in open court, often ruling from the bench, following which counsel for the prevailing party will present an order for the judge's signature. The judge may alternatively take the motion under advisement, writing an opinion and order later.

A. Pretrial motions...

Pretrial motions often take on outsized significance in civil litigation, to the point that some lawyers refer to their litigation work as *motion practice*. Motions often address pleading amendment or discovery issues, as explained above. Trial courts also hear and decide motions that dispose of claims, defenses, and entire cases, as the following sections show. Yet parties may find cause for other motions. For example, a party may move to **recuse** (remove) a judge when the judge exhibits bias or prejudice on which the party can reasonably question the judge's impartiality. The Supreme Court's due-process standard for judicial recusal requires that the moving party show **serious risk of actual bias**.

...including motions addressed to face of pleadings...

Rule 12 and similar state rules authorize a defendant to move for dismissal of a vague or ambiguous complaint or for an order that the plaintiff file a complaint with **more definite statement**. The defendant's motion must point out the complaint's defects. Courts facing a vague or ambiguous complaint are much more likely to require more definite statement than to dismiss without having given the plaintiff that chance. A plaintiff has corollary opportunity to move to strike an **insufficient defense** that the law does not support within the face of the complaint. Parties may also **move to strike** pleadings that, although legally sufficient, nonetheless contain **redundant, immaterial, impertinent,** or **scandalous** matters that distract or even damage the parties while lowering the dignity of the proceeding and court.

...motions to dismiss...

Courts may under certain circumstances grant either **voluntary dismissal** of a case at plaintiff's request or **involuntary dismissal** of a case at defendant's request. Rule 41 and similar state rules generally permit a plaintiff to voluntarily dismiss a case at plaintiff's election and without court order but only up until the defendant appears and defends. A plaintiff's first voluntary dismissal before the defendant has appeared is ordinarily **without prejudice**, meaning that the plaintiff may refile the case again later. Rule 41 construes voluntary dismissal of a second identical case as **with prejudice**, barring a later refiling. When, though, the defendant expends the effort of appearing in defense, Rule 41 and similar state rules generally require a court order for voluntary dismissal, giving the court the opportunity to impose fair terms including that dismissal with prejudice and payment of defendant's

Civil Procedure

costs or even fees if statute makes fees recoverable. A following section treats involuntary dismissals for failure to prosecute.

Rule 12(b)(6) and similar state rules authorize defendants to move to dismiss based on plaintiff's **failure to state a claim** on which to grant relief. Motions to dismiss for failure to state a claim test the complaint's **facial sufficiency**. The trial court deciding the motion must **accept as true all allegations** that the challenged complaint makes. When the plaintiff's complaint appears to inadvertently omit allegations necessary to state a legal claim, courts ordinarily grant leave to amend. If on the other hand, the plaintiff alleges clearly what the plaintiff intends but what does not make a legal claim, such that amendment appears **futile**, then the court may dismiss without leave to amend.

A defendant must ordinarily make a motion under Rule 12 or similar state rules **before answering** the defective complaint. Rule 12 delays the defendant's need to answer until 14 days after notice that the trial court denied the motion or postponed ruling until after trial. Yet after the pleadings close, a defendant may make a Rule 12 motion for **judgment on the pleadings** if developments in the case show that the parties no longer dispute material fact issues. In federal cases, the court may also dismiss a complaint that does not plead a **plausible** claim even if the claim is legally sufficient. For example, a pleading that alleges that the defendant negligently invited a harmful Martian landing might state a technical negligence claim but be well beyond plausibility.

...and summary judgment motions

Summary judgment allows trial courts to ensure that only meritorious claims and defenses reach trial. Under Rule 56, a party may move for summary judgment when there is **no genuine issue of material fact** and the party is entitled to judgment as a matter of law. The moving party, often but not always the defendant, need not produce any evidence supporting the motion. The moving party must instead show the court by motion and brief (often with accompanying exhibits) that the party opposing the motion, who has the burden of producing evidence, cannot do so on one or more claims, elements, or defenses. The party opposing a Rule 56 summary-judgment motion must respond with specific facts showing a genuine issue of material fact for trial. The party opposing the motion **may not rely on pleadings or allegations** but must instead support a response **by affidavit**, deposition testimony, or otherwise. Summary judgment does not always dispose of the entire case. Rule 56 authorize the court to grant **partial summary judgment**, preserving only those claims or defenses as to which the parties present a genuine issue of material fact for trial.

In evaluating a summary-judgment motion, the court must view the evidence in the **light most favorable to the party opposing summary judgment**. Doing so preserves the party's jury-trial right whenever a case presents disputed material fact issues. A summary-judgment motion's timing is important. The court may deny a motion or delay decision on the motion if the responding party has reason for not yet presenting facts justifying its opposition, such as that the motion came before the parties concluded

Civil Procedure

discovery. Supreme Court decisions may make summary judgment under Rule 56 more common than some state rules. For example, if the proof burden is higher (clear and convincing evidence rather than a preponderance), then the federal court must consider that higher burden when deciding a summary-judgment motion. Also, although a federal court must **draw inferences in the non-movant's favor**, if the only inferences are **implausible**, then the non-movant must come forward with more persuasive evidence.

B. Motions for judgments as a matter of law (directed verdicts...

Rule 50 authorizes a party to move for **judgment as a matter of law** (formerly called **directed verdict**) at the close of the opposing party's proofs at trial, where the evidence the opposing party presented did not satisfy that party's burden of proof on a claim or defense. The judge may grant judgment as a matter of law (direct a verdict), removing the claim or defense from jury consideration, where the evidence does not support the claim or defense. In civil-rights cases, federal courts follow a **burden-shifting framework**. After the plaintiff makes a prima-facie case, the defendant must show legitimate non-discriminatory reason, and then the plaintiff must show that the defendant's asserted reason is pretext for unlawful discrimination. The trial judge may grant judgment as a matter of law (directed verdict) at any stage at which a party did not come forward with the necessary evidence.

...and judgments notwithstanding the verdict)

A party who moves for judgment as a matter of law (directed verdict) before jury deliberation may **renew the motion** for judgment as a matter of law (formerly known as moving for **judgment notwithstanding the verdict**) after trial. The party who moves during trial and renews the motion after trial may then challenge on appeal the trial judge's adverse rulings on the motion and renewed motion. A party who does not move for judgment as a matter of law before jury deliberation may not do so after trial or challenge the sufficiency of evidence on appeal.

C. Post-trial motions, including motions for relief from judgment

Rule 60 authorizes a party suffering an adverse verdict and judgment to move for **relief from judgment**. Grounds include newly discovered evidence, fraud, clerical mistakes in the judgment, a void or discharged judgment, excusable neglect, and anything else justifying relief. A party moving for relief must do so within a reasonable time and no later than one year if for newly discovered evidence, fraud, or excusable neglect. Courts generally deny a motion when the moving party's carelessness or lack of diligence forms the motion's grounds.

...and for new trial

Civil Procedure

Rule 59 authorizes a party to move for new trial within 28 days after entry of judgment. Parties suffering adverse verdict and judgment may move for new trial when grounds for the motion affected their substantial rights and were not merely harmless error. Grounds for new trial include, among other things, **misconduct** by a party, counsel, witness, or juror, **errors** in the trial court's rulings, and **defects** in the jury's verdict or a **verdict against the great weight of the evidence**, treated further in a section below. Judges grant new trial when misconduct or other **irregularity** in the proceeding affected the substantial rights of the moving party, generally meaning to have affected the trial's outcome.

VI.   Verdicts and judgments

A **verdict** is the jury's announcement of its decision in open court after the jury concludes its deliberation. A verdict is not self-executing. Instead, the prevailing party typically prepares a proposed **judgment** for opposing counsel to review and approve, and for the trial judge to sign and court to enter. The judgment incorporates the jury's verdict. The judgment also adjusts the outcome according to rules and statutes for judgment interest, inflation, present value, taxable costs, prior settlements, and other matters. An opposing party may object to the proposed judgment, requiring the judgment's proponent to **move for judgment entry**. The trial judge then signs (and the court clerk enters) the contested judgment, typically after motion hearing.

A. Defaults...

A **default** is a court paper signed by the court clerk noting a party's failure to appear and defend as the rules require. Default begins with the clerk's **entry of default** and ends with the court's **default judgment**. A plaintiff obtains entry of default after the time expires for defendant to appear and defend, without the defendant having done so. If the defendant files an answer or a motion of certain type before the plaintiff requests default, then the plaintiff no longer has the right to default. When a defendant in a federal case files a Rule 12 motion before answering, the motion suspends the time to answer until after the court rules on the motion. Summonses state the time within which the defendant must appear and defend. Rule 12 generally requires that the defendant in a federal case respond within 21 days after service, although the rule extends the time to 60 days if the defendant waives service and grants the federal government 60 days in any case. State rules provide for similar periods.

Default does not usually enter automatically. Instead, plaintiff's counsel must ordinarily **request entry of default** after determining that default is appropriate. Plaintiff's counsel may, for instance, have granted defense counsel an extension of time within which to answer. The request for default entry typically requires an **affidavit** attesting to proper service, that the time to appear and defend has expired, and that defendant is not a minor, incompetent, on active-duty military service, or otherwise protected

Civil Procedure

against default. If the defendant appeared in the action but did not answer or otherwise defend, then the plaintiff must serve the default request on the defendant, giving the defendant an opportunity to contest its entry or to contest later entry of default judgment.

After the clerk enters default, the plaintiff may seek a **default judgment**. In cases involving uncertain damages, default judgment requires a **hearing on damages**. The defaulted defendant would have no right to contest liability but full opportunity to challenge damages. Pleadings in some cases, though, are able to allege damages in an amount certain. In those cases, the court may at the plaintiff's request enter judgment for the amount pled without first requiring hearing. Rule 54 and similar state rules prohibit default judgment from differing in kind or exceeding the amount that the prayer for relief demanded. Default procedures apply not just to plaintiffs suing defendants but also to counterclaims, crossclaims, and third-party practice. Any party who serves a pleading requiring response may request default entry, and any party who must respond but fails to do so may suffer default.

Rule 55 and similar state rules permit the court to **set aside default** on the defaulted party's good-cause showing. The law favors disposition of claims on their merits rather than on technical or procedural grounds. Thus, for example, a defendant whose lawyer misses a filing deadline by computational mistake or simple oversight may have good cause to set aside a default, particularly in a case involving substantial rights. Good cause may also depend on the culpability of the defaulted party's inaction and whether the defaulted party has a good defense to the action. The court must set aside a technically improper default and one that does not provide constitutionally adequate due process.

...and involuntary dismissals

Rule 41 and similar state rules authorize a defendant to move for **involuntary dismissal** where the plaintiff **fails to prosecute** the action. Involuntary dismissals involve the plaintiff's delay or inattention rather than misconduct or lack of merit in the claims. Unlike the common without-prejudice treatment of voluntary dismissals, involuntary dismissals are ordinarily **with prejudice**. Courts will ordinarily treat involuntary dismissals as adjudications on the merits, barring re-litigation unless the court specifically orders otherwise.

B. Jury verdicts—types

Counsel for each party may submit a proposed jury-verdict form. Model or pattern forms may exist depending on the type of case and the jurisdiction. Verdict forms are of two main types. A **general verdict** is a simple form asking not much more than which party prevails, and if the plaintiff, then for how much. A **special verdict** is a more-detailed form requiring jurors to answer a series of questions necessary for the court to enter judgment. A special verdict form's questions may be as to each element of a claim, forms of economic and non-economic damage, specific defenses, or other issues that the claims, defenses, and evidence raised. Special verdicts

Civil Procedure

enable parties not only to advocate for entry of judgment in the trial court but also to preserve issues for appeal. Once the judge approves, selects, or drafts the appropriate verdict form on which jurors will deliberate, the jury foreperson must complete and sign the form, reading it in open court to return the jury's verdict.

...and challenges

Counsel for each party may object to the verdict form that the trial judge adopts, when the verdict form does not accurately reflect the claims, defenses, or issues under the applicable law. Counsel must place objections on the record to preserve appeal rights. Parties may also challenge the jury's verdict by filing a motion for new trial. Grounds include **defects** in the jury's verdict such as failing to have completed the verdict form correctly or having reached an internally inconsistent verdict. For example, if the verdict form's instructions required the jury to assign fault among multiple parties totaling one-hundred percent, but the fault that the jury actually assigned totaled some percentage other than one hundred, then the verdict would reflect a defect likely warranting new trial.

Grounds for new trial also include a verdict **against the great weight of the evidence**. This challenge to the jury's verdict does not authorize the trial judge to substitute the judge's evaluation for that of the jury. Rather, the rare verdict, although supported by some evidence, may clearly appear to the trial judge to not have had the support of credible evidence and instead to have relied on false evidence, improper juror sympathy, or other juror bias or improper motive, resulting in miscarried justice and warranting new trial. Post-trial juror interviews may alternatively reveal jury tampering, juror research, or other juror influence by matters not admitted into evidence, as grounds for new trial. Jurors, though, may not **impeach their own verdict** as a ground for new trial, such as by admitting that they misunderstood the law or misapplied the law to the facts. Those verdicts would stand.

C. Judicial findings and conclusions

Judges decide cases when parties have no jury-trial right or choose not to demand a jury trial. Rule 52 and similar state rules require the judge presiding in a **bench trial** to make **findings of fact and conclusions of law**. Judges often request counsel for each party to propose those findings and conclusions for the judge to consider and adopt. Findings of fact and conclusions of law enable an appellate court to review the trial judge's decision on appeal. Rule 52 permits appellate courts to set aside only **clearly erroneous** findings and only after giving due regard to the trial judge's determination of **witness credibility**.

D. Effect

Courts have power to **enforce judgments**. Parties who suffer an adverse judgment often voluntarily comply without further court action. Otherwise, Rule 69 provides that prevailing parties in federal court may

Civil Procedure

enforce judgments using state enforcement procedures. Those procedures typically offer **garnishment** orders securing obligations (accounts, wages, and loans, for instance) owed to the judgment debtor. **Attachment** and **execution** on the judgment debtor's real or personal property are also available. Judgment creditors may also **discover debtor assets**. State laws offer judgment debtors limited housing, vehicle, tools, and other **exemptions** from enforcement. Rule 62 and similar state rules also offer parties short post-judgment **stays** to prepare motions and appeals. Parties may also post **bond** as a condition for stay pending appeal results. Courts also enforce judgments for specific acts using **contempt powers**.

Judgments, while enforceable as to their stated relief, also have the effect of **precluding further litigation**. Litigation's finality is an important civil-justice-system goal. Judgments can preclude continued litigation of both **claims** and **issues**, under related but different rules that the following two sections cover.

claim...

Claim preclusion, also known as **res judicata**, bars a party from re-litigating claims that the party litigated or could have litigated in a prior action that reached final judgment on the merits against the same party. For example, if parties litigate a breach-of-contract claim in a case that reaches a final judgment in favor of one and against the other party, but the losing party then files a new action involving the same breach-of-contract claim, the court would dismiss the new action as precluded. The parties in the prior and present actions must be the same or have been **in privity** or similar relationship such that the prior judgment should bind them. For example, a trustee who sues for the trust and loses would ordinarily have bound the trust and trust beneficiaries to the loss, barring their subsequent litigation even if they were not named parties.

For claim preclusion to apply, the prior case must also have raised the same claims as the party pursues in the subsequent case or the party must have been **able** to raise those same claims in the prior case. A party could have raised a claim in the prior case when the claim arises out of the **same transaction or occurrence**, or series of transactions or occurrences, sharing the same **fact nucleus** as the prior case. This claim-preclusion rule relates to the *use-it-or-lose-it* rule for **pleading joinder**, to plead all related claims. A prior judgment does not bar a subsequent claim if a party could *not* have raised the claim in the prior action, such as for lack of jurisdiction.

For claim preclusion to apply, the court in the prior action must also have reached **final judgment on the merits** for the judgment to preclude subsequent litigation. Still-pending actions in the trial court and judgments that remain on appeal are not yet final. In federal court, a prior judgment reaches the merits when dismissing the case for a Rule 12 failure to state a claim. Some states disagree, taking a dismissal on the pleadings as having not reached the merits. A judgment stating that it is on the merits does not mean that it is so. Substance, not form, controls, except that consent judgments bind the parties because contractual in nature.

Civil Procedure

As to choice of claim-preclusion law, federal courts apply the claim-preclusion rules of their **forum state** to determine the preclusive effect of prior state-court judgments. Constitutional **full faith and credit** requires that federal courts recognize state judgments in that respect. Federal common law governs the preclusive effect of a federal court federal-question decision in a prior case. The courts must also interpret claim-preclusion rules consistent with constitutional due process for notice and opportunity for hearing. A non-party to the prior case has had due process as to a claim that the non-party wishes to raise in a subsequent case but cannot do so because of claim preclusion, when the non-party succeeds to the same interest as a party in the prior case, controlled the prior adjudication, or had adequate representation in the prior case.

...and issue preclusion

Issue preclusion, also known as **collateral estoppel**, bars a party from re-litigating an identical issue that the prior litigation actually and necessarily decided against that same party. Issue preclusion differs from claim preclusion in that issue preclusion bars re-litigation of issues like agency, notice, duty, or control, rather than claims like breach of contract, fraud, or negligence. The prior case may not have decided the same *claim* but may have decided the same subsidiary *issue*.

Issue preclusion also differs from claim preclusion in that only the party whom issue preclusion binds in the subsequent case must have been a party to the prior case that decided the issue, rather than both parties having been parties to the prior case, as required for claim preclusion. A non-party to the prior case may thus apply issue preclusion in the subsequent case in **non-mutual** fashion, precluding only the party to the prior action without precluding the non-party. By contrast, claim preclusion must be mutual. A party who asserts issue preclusion in the subsequent action may also do so both **offensively** to establish the other party's liability and **defensively** to defeat the other party's claim.

Issue preclusion also differs from claim preclusion in that the prior case must have **actually decided** the issue, *not* just that the prior case *could have* done so, as for claim preclusion. Consent and default judgments do not generally actually litigate issues. General verdicts may actually decide issues or may not, depending on the number and types of claims that the general verdict decides. Because of their specificity, summary judgment and special verdicts generally do actually decide issues. An issue decided in the alternative to another decision is not necessarily decided and so is not issue preclusive.

Issue preclusion also works within a single case. The **law-of-the-case** doctrine bars a party from re-litigating an issue that the court already actually and necessarily decided **in the same case**. Issue preclusion, though, is a flexible doctrine. Courts may permit re-litigation of issues where a party had no opportunity to appeal the prior decision, the law changed, issue preclusion would interfere with a remedy scheme, or procedures are better in the second case.

Civil Procedure

VII.   Appealability and review

Federal and state civil-justice systems provide for appeal rights through rule and statute. Those provisions typically provide for one **appeal of right** following the trial court's final action. A prevailing party may **cross-appeal** if receiving less than full relief. A party's appeal of right is often to a mid-level appellate court, such as in the federal system to the U.S. Court of Appeals for the federal circuit of the district court's region. After a first appeal of right, the federal system and many state systems provide for discretionary **appeal by leave** to a second and higher appellate court. In the federal system, the U.S. Supreme Court conducts that discretionary review by writ of certiorari, although parties in certain cases may take direct appeal to the Supreme Court. Appellate courts may sanction parties for frivolous appeals.

A. Availability of interlocutory review

While most appeals occur after the trial court concludes the case, the federal system and many state systems permit some appellate review during trial court proceedings. For example, the federal courts make **interlocutory review** available when the trial court decides a **substantial dispute over controlling law**, appellate review of which may materially advance the litigation. The trial court thus invites the appellate court to hear the interlocutory appeal. The federal courts also make appellate review available in cases involving **multiple parties or claims**, when the court decides a claim or all claims as to a party, and the court certifies **no just reason for delay** in an appeal.

Federal law also authorizes interlocutory appeal of decisions in cases involving **injunctions, receiverships,** and **admiralty**. Federal law also authorizes appeal of **collateral orders** affecting important rights, when a challenge would not reach the appellate court if the party had to await final judgment. For example, when a court orders disclosure of privileged material and disclosure complying with the order would make pointless a later appeal after final judgment, then the party may have a right to immediate review. When a trial judge **usurps power**, such as issuing groundless contempt orders, appellate courts may also exercise supervisory authority under a **writ of mandamus**.

B. Final judgment rule

The **final-judgment rule** holds that a final judgment triggers a party's one appeal of right. Rule 54 provides that a judgment is a court paper, whether titled *judgment* or not, that **disposes of all remaining claims** in a pending case. Other than for the interlocutory review described just above, federal appellate courts generally have **jurisdiction** only over final judgments disposing of all claims. Federal Rule of Appellate Procedure 3 provides that a party initiates an appeal by **filing a notice with the district court**. Federal Rule of Appellate Procedure 4 requires that a party file an appeal as of right **within 30 days** from the date of the appealed judgment or order (60 days for

Civil Procedure

U.S.-government appellants). State rules may have shorter appeal periods. Federal and some state rules permit the trial court to **extend the appeal period** for excusable neglect or good cause.

C. Scope of review...

The scope of appellate review and applicable review standards influence appeal outcomes. As to scope of appellate review, the **harmless-error rule** prevents appellate courts from reversing for errors that did not affect the parties' substantial rights. Appellants must generally demonstrate that trial error likely affected the trial's outcome. For example, if a jury deciding a negligence claim in a personal-injury case returns a verdict in the plaintiff's favor on liability but awards only a small fraction of the plaintiff's claimed damages, then the plaintiff could challenge erroneous rulings or instructions as to damages but not erroneous rulings or instructions as to liability. The plaintiff won on liability, meaning that any liability errors did not harm the plaintiff.

...for judge...

Appellate **review standards** differ depending on who made the decision below, whether judge or jury, and if the judge, then what the judge decided. Appellate courts review a trial judge's *law* decisions **de novo**, meaning afresh without deference to the trial judge's decision. By contrast, appellate courts review a trial judge's *fact* decisions in a bench trial for **clear error**. The clearly erroneous standard respects the trial judge's credibility evaluations, permitting reversal only when the appellate court reaches a **definite and firm conviction** that the trial judge made a **mistake**. Appellate courts review docket-management issues, such as the time for discovery and whether to permit trial adjournments, for **abuse of discretion**.

...and jury

Appellate courts give greater deference to a jury's fact determinations. Appellate courts uphold jury factual determinations when supported by **substantial evidence**. Substantial evidence is more than a mere scintilla, enough that a reasonable mind could accept it to support a conclusion. Appellate courts do not reverse a jury verdict unless jurors had no **reasonable evidentiary basis** for the verdict, generally meaning the absence of testimony or exhibit rather than any weight of the evidence. Appellate courts will not reverse based on conflicting evidence when reasonable jurors could rationally resolve the conflict in the prevailing party's favor. Appellate courts instead defer to such jury findings as to witness credibility or the weight given testimony or exhibits, even when the appellate judges would have decided differently if acting as a trial decision maker.

Civil Procedure

Constitutional Law

B.   Constitutional Law

NOTE: The terms "Constitution," "constitutional," and "un-constitutional" refer to the federal Constitution unless indicated otherwise. Approximately half of the Constitutional Law questions on the MBE will be based on category IV, and approximately half will be based on the remaining categories—I, II, and III.

The Multistate Bar Examination focuses fully one half of its constitutional-law questions on just one of its four main subjects, **individual rights**. The other three main constitutional-law subjects, **judicial review**, **separation of powers**, and **federal/state relations** together comprise just one half (the other half) of the exam's constitutional-law questions. So, focus the bulk of your constitutional-law studies on the individual-rights subject, while not ignoring the other three areas. Begin with judicial review.

I.   The nature of judicial review

Judicial review refers to the power of the courts to determine whether actions of the *executive* and *legislative* branches of government violate the Constitution. For example, if the president were without legislative authority to order that coal no longer ship in interstate commerce, then a federal court might strike the president's order as beyond the president's exercise of an enumerated constitutional power. Similarly, if Congress were to enact legislation requiring churches to obtain a public certificate to operate, then a federal court might strike the law as violating the First Amendment's free-exercise-of-religion clause. Because the courts have no military, police, budget, or other powers to ensure that the other branches respect their determinations and follow their orders, the courts depend on public and official *respect* for the Constitution and trust in the *legitimacy* of the courts' exercise of their constitutional powers.

The Supreme Court has the power of **judicial review** not only over actions of the executive and legislative branches of the federal government but also as to the constitutionality of any *state* action, whether executive, legislative, or judicial. For a judicial-branch example, the Supreme Court has held that state courts must as a matter of constitutional due process provide free counsel for indigent defendants facing felony charges likely to result in incarceration. For a legislative-branch example, the Supreme Court has struck under the Constitution's equal-protection clause a state statute prohibiting interracial marriage. For an executive-branch example, the Supreme Court has struck under the equal-protection clause certain race-based preferences in state university admissions.

A. Organization and relationship of state and federal courts in a federal system

Constitutional Law

State constitutions and legislation differ from state to state as to the organization of state courts, although all states have both **trial courts** and **appellate courts**. Some trial courts may be courts of *general jurisdiction*, hearing all matters, while other trial courts may be courts of *limited jurisdiction*, hearing only family-law, criminal, business, or other special dockets, or matters having a value below a certain ceiling, such as in small-claims courts. Trial courts generally decide cases, with or without a jury depending on state constitution and statutory rights, after *trial* or *hearing* at which parties present evidence, resulting in findings and a judgment resolving the parties' claims and rights. Yet some trial courts also decide appeals taken from administrative agencies or from other trial courts of limited jurisdiction. For example, a nursing-home aide whose certification an administrative agency revoked for alleged patient abuse may appeal the revocation to a trial court acting like an appellate court or offering the appellant a fresh trial.

Parties who lose in the state trial court may appeal to the state appellate court. States typically provide one **appeal of right**. A panel of appellate judges, rather than a single trial judge, decides the appeal by majority, usually writing an opinion that informs the parties and public of the rationale. While some states have only one level of appellate court, many states have both a **mid-level** appellate court *and* a **state high court**. Appeals to the mid-level appellate court are then typically *of right*, while the state high court generally grants a second appeal only by the court's *discretion*, reserving that discretion for cases of obvious error or significant impact. Appellate courts may conclude the case by *affirming*, *reversing*, or *modifying* the lower court's judgment, or they may **remand** for further proceedings with the appellate court's direction.

The **federal judicial system** has similar organization to state judicial systems. Congress created federal district courts to serve as the primary trial courts in the federal system. The nation currently has nearly one-hundred federal districts including at least one in each state. Individual district court judges, who are lifetime presidential appointees with Senate advice and consent, decide cases after hearing or trial, with the help of magistrate judges whom the district-court bench employ on eight-year terms. Federal bankruptcy courts are a division of the district courts. Congress also created a Court of Federal Claims to hear monetary claims against the United States and a Court of International Trade.

Congress has also created United States Circuit Courts of Appeal as **mid-level federal appellate courts**, providing for eleven numbered circuits plus the District of Columbia and Federal Circuits. The Federal Circuit hears appeals from the Court of Claims and Court of International Trade. The other federal circuit courts of appeal including the District of Columbia Circuit hear appeals from the federal district courts within their geographic circuit. The federal appellate courts decide cases on the record below by majority opinion of a three-judge panel, giving deference to fact findings but not to law constructions. Parties who fail to prevail before the three-judge appellate bench may request *en banc* hearing before all judges of the circuit, the number varying from circuit to circuit. As indicated in greater detail below, the

Constitutional Law

Supreme Court has both **original jurisdiction** to hear some new cases in the manner of a trial court and **appellate jurisdiction** to hear cases that the federal circuit courts of appeal have already decided plus, as described below, some state decisions. The Supreme Court exercises its discretionary jurisdiction when the party losing the appeal below petitions the Supreme Court for a *writ of certiorari* that would order the appellate court below to convey the file to the Supreme Court for hearing.

The federal judicial system is, though, distinctly different from the state courts in that the federal courts are *all* courts of **limited jurisdiction**. A following section describes federal jurisdiction in brief, while the above civil-procedure subject outline describes federal jurisdiction in depth. In brief, Congress has provided for two primary forms of limited subject-matter jurisdiction for the federal district courts. **Federal-question** jurisdiction involves cases arising out of the Constitution or federal statutes, while **diversity** jurisdiction involves cases between parties from different states controverting matters of $75,000 in value. Federal district courts also hear cases involving the federal government as a party. In federal-question cases, they also have **supplemental jurisdiction** over state claims arising out of the same case or controversy.

As to the *relationship* of state to federal courts, the Supreme Court has the power of **judicial review** not only over actions of the executive and legislative branches of the federal government but also of *state court cases* arising under federal law or the Constitution. Thus, for example, if a state high court decided that a citizen had no Fourth Amendment right against a certain warrantless search, the Supreme Court could review and affirm or reverse that decision, or remand the case to the state courts for further hearing under the Supreme Court's direction as to the federal issue. The state courts also have the power to strike down their own state's laws based on the state or federal constitutions. The state courts do *not* have any role in reviewing federal-court cases.

B. Jurisdiction

Jurisdiction involves the power of a court to decide certain matters. A court must have jurisdiction over the parties and matter if its judgment is to have enforceable effect. The Constitution provides that the Supreme Court has **original jurisdiction** only over cases involving *ambassadors*, *foreign ministers*, or *consuls*, and when a state is a party including disputes between two states. For example, if one state sues another claiming interference with interstate commerce, the Supreme Court would have original jurisdiction to hear the case.

1. Congressional power to define and limit

In addition to its *original jurisdiction* under the Constitution, the Supreme Court has **appellate jurisdiction** as Congress provides. The Constitution expressly gives to Congress the power to define the Supreme

Constitutional Law

Court's appellate jurisdiction. Thus, Congress has provided for the Supreme Court's **discretionary** appellate jurisdiction under **writ of certiorari** to review decisions of the federal courts of appeals and state high courts arising under federal law or the Constitution. For example, if a prisoner claiming violation of Eighth Amendment rights against cruel-and-unusual punishment lost that claim in either a federal appellate court or state high court, then the prisoner could petition for a writ of certiorari from the Supreme Court, which could grant or deny the petition, to hear or refuse to hear the prisoner's further appeal of the case. Because the Constitution itself gives the Supreme Court **original jurisdiction** over cases involving *ambassadors*, *foreign ministers*, or *consuls*, and cases involving a *state as party*, Congress *cannot* limit that original jurisdiction. For example, if Congress enacted legislation purporting to deprive the Supreme Court of the ability to hear cases brought against states, then the Supreme Court would properly ignore the legislation to exercise its constitutional authority in those cases.

2. The Eleventh Amendment and state sovereign immunity

The **Eleventh Amendment**, adopted to overturn an early Supreme Court decision, limits private actions *against states* in the federal courts, stating that federal judicial power *does not extend* to such suits. Under the Eleventh Amendment, states typically get to decide when others may subject them to suits in federal court. States *may consent* to suit in federal court either by law or appearance in the case. Also, federal legislation may create private rights that individuals may enforce against state officials in federal court under certain limited circumstances, where the Constitution authorizes such suits. Thus, if an individual sues a state in federal court without the state's consent and without any authorizing federal legislation, the federal court *must* dismiss the action under the Eleventh Amendment. Yet if the suit alleges a violation of federal civil rights in a private right of action that Congress has authorized against state officials under constitutional authority, or if the state's lawyer appears with the state's consent to defend the federal action, then the federal court will not dismiss but will instead hear the case under certain circumstances.

Specific circumstances where the Supreme Court has held that the Constitution authorizes federal-court actions involving state interests include actions for *injunctions* and *declaratory relief* against state officials, enforcing federal civil rights authorized under the Constitution. Such actions do not violate the Eleventh Amendment or fall within qualified state sovereign immunity. An aggrieved individual must sue a state official in the official's *individual* rather than *official* capacity if the action is for money damages in federal court *and* must establish that the official violated a *clearly established* federal right, if the individual is to overcome the official's **qualified immunity**. In other cases, states *consent* to federal suits under state legislation acknowledging such consent. A state also consents to federal jurisdiction when the state removes litigation from state to federal court. States also consent to federal control when states accept federal funds

Constitutional Law

contingent on waiver of immunity. State sovereign immunity also extends to suits in state court. If a state has not consented to suit in state court, then the court must dismiss the state as a party.

C. Judicial review in operation

While the federal courts have the power of judicial review of federal executive and legislative actions, and state actions involving federal constitutional and statutory issues, judicial review entails *specific limitations* having constitutional dimension. Courts self-impose each of these limitations as a prudential matter to ensure the integrity, respect, and enforcement of their decisions through voluntary compliance or actions of the executive branch. As the following sections explain, these prudential limitations include that the federal courts must only decide an actual *case or controversy*. Federal courts must not determine the scope and application of a constitutional rule when the court could decide the matter on an *adequate and independent state ground*.

1. The "case or controversy" requirement...

The Constitution limits federal judicial power to **cases and controversies**. If a case does not satisfy the *case-or-controversy* requirement, then the court must dismiss the case. The following sections show that to present a case or controversy, a matter must require the federal court to do more than offer a merely *advisory opinion*. Parties appearing in cases before the federal courts must also have *standing*. Cases must be *ripe* for adjudication to present a case or controversy, and the matters that cases present must not be *moot*.

...including the prohibition on advisory opinions...

The constitutional prohibition against federal courts giving merely **advisory opinions** goes to the heart of the *case-or-controversy* requirement. To constitute a case or controversy, the matter before the court must be actual, real, and consequential, not theoretical. If courts gave merely advisory opinions, then interested persons would be free to disregard them, causing judgments to lose their *finality* and parties to lose the opportunity for judgment's *execution*. For example, if the president requests a recommendation from a federal aeronautics board as to the appropriate executive action to take to carry out certain legislation, the federal courts must refuse to review the board's recommendation, because to do otherwise would be to advise the president rather than review actual actions for their constitutionality. Although the federal courts must not give advisory opinions, Congress has properly authorized the federal courts to decide *declaratory-judgment* actions in which parties with a genuine dispute of consequence may obtain the court's declaration of party rights before either party has violated the right of the other.

...standing...

To satisfy the *case-or-controversy* requirement, a plaintiff initiating suit in federal court must also show that the party has **standing**, defined as a *concrete and particularized injury in fact*, either *actual or imminent*. The plaintiff must also trace the past or imminent injury to the defendant rather than a non-party. Finally, the plaintiff must show that the court's decision, if favorable to the plaintiff, is *likely to redress* the injury. Litigants ordinarily must raise their own rights rather than another's rights, to give the case *concrete adverseness*. For example, a landlord whose tenant is unable to pay rent would not from that circumstance have standing to sue in federal court the employer who fired the tenant in violation of federal civil-rights statutes. Only the tenant would have that standing. The plaintiff must, in effect, be the *interested party*. The federal courts will, though, look to state laws on guardianship, conservatorship, trusts, estates, and the like, to recognize the standing of representatives for minors, incapacitated persons, beneficiaries, and others having disabilities or special statuses warranting representation. The court or a party may raise standing issues at any time.

...ripeness...

While standing determines *who* may sue, the **ripeness** doctrine determines *when* a party may sue. The issue of ripeness arises in cases in which the plaintiff's harm has not yet occurred. You have just seen that a party may have standing not only when the party has already suffered injury but also when the party's injury is merely imminent. Determining ripeness requires a similar analysis of whether the party's injury is *likely, concrete*, and *imminent*. If instead, the injury remains too far off to be reasonably confident that it will in fact occur and be of consequence without court action, then the court must refuse to entertain the action as not yet ripe. For example, if a federal agency proposes a pipeline regulation that would, if taking effect, harm a pipeline venture, then the venture's prospective harm would not yet be ripe for federal-court adjudication because the agency had only proposed, rather than promulgated and begun to enforce, the regulation. Ripeness issues typically arise at the litigation's outset rather than later in time.

...and mootness

The parties must also show that their matter is not **moot**, if they are going to satisfy the federal court's case-or-controversy requirement. While ripeness determines whether a plaintiff brought a case *too soon*, mootness determines whether parties brought or continued to maintain a case *too late*. A case is moot when circumstances or events eliminate the controversy, leaving the court with nothing to decide that will change the parties' outcome in the dispute. For example, if a party with standing sues to enjoin a hospital from continuing violations of a federal anti-patient-dumping law, but the

Constitutional Law

hospital promptly ceases the violations, adopting a policy complying with the federal law, then the court may rule the case moot and dismiss. On the other hand, federal courts may continue to hear certain cases that would otherwise be moot when the issue is *capable of repetition yet evading review*, looking to the likelihood of recurrence *as to that plaintiff* although sometimes as to other similarly situated plaintiffs.

For examples of cases where courts may hear an otherwise moot claim, when a defendant voluntarily ceases action solely to *evade court action*, then the court may review, especially if the defendant remains in a position to repeat the alleged misconduct. Likewise, short time frames for things like school enrollment or graduation, or medical treatment, may repeatedly moot a matter, repeatedly frustrating its determination, such that the court may still review. Class actions present a special case where a representative's claim may become moot but without resolving class claims, in which case the court may hear the action. Courts generally look to the *reasonable expectation of recurrence* to determine whether to hear an otherwise moot claim but may also look to the *public significance* of the claim, such as for elections or trial access. Plaintiff's counsel owes a duty to bring a case's mootness to the court's attention when it occurs. The court and parties may raise mootness at any time.

2. The "adequate and independent state ground"

After the case-or-controversy requirement, a second prudential limitation on federal judicial review involves the **adequate-and-independent-state-ground** doctrine. The doctrine holds that when the Supreme Court reviews a petition for a writ of certiorari from a state high court that decided the case on both a federal ground subject to Supreme Court review *and* a state ground that would adequately and independently support the state high court's judgment, then the Supreme Court has no jurisdiction. The state ground must be enough to support the judgment without relying on the federal ground, and the state ground must also be independent of the federal ground rather than intertwined. For example, if a theater challenges a distributor's contract restrictions on showing films, as both unconscionable under state law and void under federal anti-trust law, and the state's trial and appellate courts find for the theater on both grounds, the Supreme Court will not review the federal-antitrust ground because the state ground was adequate and independent.

The adequate-and-independent-state-ground doctrine is a form of **abstention**. Abstention doctrine, applying to cases where the federal courts *have* jurisdiction but *refuse to exercise it*, is a complex area of law involving several different abstention forms applicable to different types of cases under different tests. The overriding construct, though, is that if a federal court can responsibly *defer to state law* applied in a parallel state-court proceeding to resolve a dispute before the federal court, then the federal court should do so. Abstention doctrine's goal is to reduce the tension between the federal and state judicial systems through the federal court's deference to state law, not

Constitutional Law

that state law is in any sense supreme, the opposite being true that federal law is supreme.

3. Political questions and justiciability

The **political-question** doctrine, another prudential limit on federal jurisdiction, addresses whether a federal court should decline to hear a case over which it would otherwise have jurisdiction, because the political branches, meaning the executive and legislature, should instead decide the issue as a political question. The federal executive and legislative branches may disagree on the political resolution of issues. When their disagreement is indeed *political* rather than a *constitutional* issue such as one involving separation of powers, then the federal courts must permit the political branches to determine that issue. The two principal factors in determining whether a question is political are whether the Constitution makes a *textually demonstrable commitment* of the question to a political branch or, on the other hand, whether the federal courts have *judicially discoverable and manageable standards* for resolving the case. For example, disputes between the president and Congress over foreign policy, such as the recognition of foreign states and forming or rescinding treaties, are often political questions, given the Constitution's textual commitment of those foreign-policy powers to the political branches.

II.   The separation of powers

In addition to creating and enumerating the powers of the **judicial branch**, addressed above, the Constitution separately creates and enumerates the powers of both a **legislative branch** and **executive branch**. In creating and defining the powers of three separate branches of government, the Constitution intended to check the power of each branch and balance the powers of the three branches. Thus, the following sections address first the powers of the legislative branch, then the powers of the executive branch, and then how the Constitution provides for certain *interbranch* relationships that require the branches to respect and cooperate with one another.

The bicameral **Congress**, constituted to enact legislation carrying out specific limited powers, includes the **Senate** and **House of Representatives**. One hundred senators, two elected to six-year terms from each state, comprise the Senate. Four-hundred-thirty-five representatives, elected to two-year terms and representing districts proportional to population within all fifty states, comprise the House. Representatives must be at least age twenty-five and have been a U.S. citizen for seven years, while senators must be at least thirty and been a U.S. citizen for nine years.

The **president**, elected to no more than two four-year terms, heads the unitary executive branch, constituted to carry out faithfully the laws that Congress enacts. The president must be a natural-born U.S. citizen, be at least thirty-five years old, and have resided in the U.S. for at least fourteen years. The president selects a vice-president running mate, the two standing for

Constitutional Law

election through state contests that elect to the Electoral College the number of delegates that is proportional to the senators and representatives from the state.

A. The powers of Congress

The Constitution expressly enumerates the powers of Congress, as the following sections address. Congress cannot exercise power without identifying its source in one of the Constitution's enumerated powers. Congress's principal powers include to **regulate interstate commerce**, to **tax** and **spend** for the general welfare, and to **declare war**, provide for the nation's **defense**, and guide **foreign affairs** in concert with the president. Congress also has powers under the **13th**, **14th**, and **15th Amendments**, together with other enumerated powers that Congress exercises less often.

1. Commerce...

The Constitution grants Congress the *exclusive* power to regulate commerce with **foreign nations** and **among the several states**. States must not enact laws that interfere with commerce between a state and foreign nation or **interstate commerce**. For example, companies located in a state must comply with that state's laws regulating domestic corporations, but if a domestic company contracts with a customer located in a foreign nation, only *federal* law, not *state* law, may regulate the domestic company's transaction with the foreign customer. Likewise, while a domestic company must comply with its own state's laws and the laws of any other state in which it does business, such as to register with the state for service of process, if the company contracts with a customer in another state, then the company would look only to federal law, not state law, for regulations affecting that interstate commerce.

One big question is what constitutes *interstate commerce*. Regulation affects *interstate commerce* in several ways. Congress may regulate *channels* of interstate commerce, meaning roads, waterways, and air travel, even when a stretch of transport, such as a segment of river or an airport location, lies entirely within a state. Congress may also regulate *instrumentalities* of interstate commerce including vehicles, equipment, and the activities of persons engaged in interstate commerce. For example, Congress may legislate vehicle safety, even as to within a state, given the use of vehicles in interstate commerce. Congress may also regulate items *crossing state lines*, such as agricultural produce, manufactured goods, and even electronic information relating to online interstate commerce.

Finally, in the commerce clause's greatest reach, Congress may regulate activities having a *substantial effect* on interstate commerce. For example, Congress may prohibit carriers from charging higher rates for goods shipped interstate than for goods shipped within the state or authorize a federal agency to intervene to prevent a labor strike at a single location of an employer that ships its product interstate. Congress may even authorize a federal agency to regulate how much wheat a farmer can grow for local consumption if the activity of growing wheat has a *substantial cumulative effect* on interstate commerce. Here, though, the Constitution limits Congress's commerce-clause reach to substantial *economic* effects. For example, Congress may not prohibit persons from carrying guns in a school zone or provide a civil remedy for victims of gender-motivated crimes because the restrictions affect personal safety rather than economic activity. The commerce clause also has negative implications preventing states from regulating interstate commerce, addressed in a later section.

...taxing and spending powers...

The Constitution's **general-welfare** clause grants Congress the power to both **tax** and **spend** for the general welfare. The general-welfare clause does *not* authorize Congress to enact laws for the general welfare but instead only to *tax* or *spend*. Congress may also *place conditions* on federal funding to influence states to adopt laws that regulate general welfare. For example, while Congress could not ban the sale of alcohol because of its harmful effects on health and safety, Congress could tax alcohol sales to fund programs of public education on those harmful effects. In the same example, Congress could require states to adopt a legal drinking age of twenty-one to receive federal highway funding, given the hazardous effects of drunk driving. Similarly, Congress may, in funding the arts, attach a condition that the grants that the federal agency awards be for works reflecting general standards of decency and respect. This example further reflects that Congress may delegate its spending powers to the executive branch if providing intelligible principles to guide agency discretion.

2. War...

The Constitution grants Congress express power to **declare war**. Congress also has the power of the purse to fund or not to fund military actions through legislation. Yet because the president holds the *commander-in-chief* power to direct the armed forces in pursuit of war's ends while also holding veto power over military-funding legislation, Congress and the president effectively *share* power to pursue those military ends. While the Supreme Court has given little guidance on the scope of Congress's war powers, it has held that Congress has the authority during wartime to prohibit the sale and distribution of distilled spirits as appropriate to focusing the nation's war effort, suggesting relatively broad war powers. On the other hand, the Supreme Court recently held that Congress does *not* have war-power authority to keep an alien held on territory that the nation controls from seeking a writ of habeas corpus to review the constitutionality of detention.

Congress has invoked its war power attempting to limit how and when presidents may conduct military actions, except after declaration of war, by statutory authorization, or in national emergency. Congress's resolution purports to require presidents to consult Congress, notify it of

Constitutional Law

military actions within forty-eight hours after initiating them, and limit to sixty days the duration of military actions without Congress's authorization of the use of force. Presidents have largely complied with those restrictions without acknowledging that Congress has the power to enact those restrictions.

...defense...

In addition to the power to declare war, Congress also has express power to create and maintain an army and navy, and to create and maintain a civilian militia, known as the *national guard*, while providing the terms on which the national government may call the militia into government service. These express powers give Congress broad authority to provide for **national defense** whether in war or peace. Specifically, Congress may provide for a military draft and selective-service system, enact wage and price controls over the entire economy during wartime, and restrict certain citizens during wartime. Congress may also establish military tribunals under a military-justice code that need not comply with the procedures required of Article III civilian courts, such as jury trial. In other respects, Congress shares with the president power over the nation's defense. For example, while the president nominates the secretary of defense, national security advisor, and other cabinet-level positions, the Senate must give advice and consent for the nominees to receive their appointments. Congress also sets the defense budget, subject to presidential veto.

...and foreign affairs powers

Like the powers of war and defense, Congress also shares with the president power over **foreign affairs**. While the president negotiates treaties and appoints ambassadors to foreign nations, the Senate decides whether to approve treaties under two-thirds super-majority vote. The Senate also confirms a president's nominees for ambassadorships and cabinet positions charged with carrying out foreign affairs, particularly secretary of state. Congress once again also holds the power of the purse to fund or not to fund the president's foreign-policy initiatives, such as foreign aid and funding for troops whom the president deploys in international crises. Congressional foreign-affairs committees can also investigate how the president conducts foreign affairs and the operation of federal agencies involved in those foreign affairs.

3. Power to enforce the 13th, 14th, and 15th Amendments

Congress has express power to enforce the **13th Amendment** abolishing slavery, the amendment so declaring that Congress may do so *by appropriate legislation*. Congress exercised its 13th Amendment power by granting all citizens the same right to contract as the right held by white citizens. The Supreme Court upheld that legislation insofar as denying non-

Constitutional Law

white citizens the same right to contract could be a *badge of slavery* that the 13th Amendment empowered Congress to prohibit.

Congress also has express power to enforce the **14th Amendment** including both its *equal-protection* and *due-process* clauses. Congress exercised that power in prohibiting discrimination based on race, sex, age, disability, and other protected characteristics, in housing, education, employment, and public accommodation, among other things. For example, the Supreme Court held that Congress properly relied on the amendment's authorization to enact legislation allowing citizens to sue states to redress disability discrimination. On the other hand, the Supreme Court held that Congress lacked the power to force the states to allow persons over age eighteen but under age twenty-one to vote because the 14th Amendment's equal-protection clause did not reach that far. The Supreme Court has also held that the 14th Amendment's express grant to Congress of the power to carry out the amendment through appropriate legislation did *not* empower Congress to grant individuals greater rights than the Supreme Court itself determined that the 14th Amendment granted.

Congress also has express power to enforce the **15th Amendment** guaranteeing that the federal and state governments would not deny any citizen the right to vote based on race, color, or prior servitude. As with the 13th and 14th Amendments, the 15th Amendment declares that Congress may do so *by appropriate legislation*. Congress exercised that power adopting a voting-rights act that both prohibits literacy tests to exercise the right to vote and requires states to submit changes to their voting laws to the U.S. attorney general for *preclearance*. The Supreme Court upheld both restrictions as appropriate legislation under Congress's 15th Amendment power, just as the Supreme Court upheld preclearance denial for a proposed voting change that, though neutral in language and intent, had an adverse racially discriminatory effect.

4. Other powers

Congress holds other express powers such as to **borrow money**, **coin money**, determine **bankruptcy** rules, determine the rules of the **naturalization** of foreign citizens, create the **post office**, provide for **copyrights**, and exercise authority over the **District of Columbia**. The Constitution includes among Congress's additional powers the **necessary-and-proper** clause to enact such legislation as is necessary and proper to carry into effect the above enumerated powers. The necessary-and-proper clause is *not* a new grant of general powers. The clause is instead an express grant of power to enact such legislation as *reasonably related* or *incidental* to carrying the other express grants into effect. The necessary-and-proper clause thus allows Congress to imply authority for legislation from the express grant of other powers. For example, while the Constitution does not authorize Congress to create a national bank, Congress's power to tax and spend for the general welfare impliedly authorize Congress to create a national bank as reasonably related to taxing and spending. Similarly, the necessary-and-

Constitutional Law

proper clause does not authorize Congress to impose an individual mandate to buy health insurance. The mandate so characterized does not reasonably relate to any enumerated power. Yet Congress may tax those who refuse to buy health insurance.

B. The powers of the president

The Constitution also expressly enumerates the powers of the president. Just as Congress must have constitutional authority to act, the president must find authority to act either in the Constitution or in statutes that Congress constitutionally enacts. The following sections address the president's principal constitutionally enumerated powers beginning with the power as **chief executive** to take care to execute faithfully the nation's laws. The Constitution also makes the president the **commander in chief** over the nation's military and gives the president the power to negotiate, but not to approve, **treaties** that the Senate must instead approve to put them into formal effect. The president has other **foreign-affairs** powers including to *appoint ambassadors* and a cabinet-member *secretary of state*, and to *recognize foreign states*. The president also has **appointment powers** over other cabinet officials, with the Senate's advice and consent.

1. As chief executive, including the "take care" clause

The Constitution expressly vests the **executive power** in the president, making the president the nation's **chief executive** to carry federal laws and national interests into effect. Although the Constitution says little more about the president's chief-executive role than that the president is to *take care that the laws be faithfully executed,* the chief-executive role means that the president oversees the vast federal bureaucracy. Key to that administrative role is the president's express power to appoint cabinet-level and senior officials of each executive-branch department and agency subject to the Senate's advice and consent, as more fully described below. The president works through those officials to implement Congress's legislative programs and policies. The administrative agencies that those officials direct *promulgate regulations* consistent with their authorizing legislation. As chief executive, the president also influences legislation through the Constitution's express responsibility to *address Congress* annually, statutory responsibility to submit annual budgets, and the Constitution's authority to veto legislation, requiring a two-thirds congressional override, as explained more fully below.

The *take-care* clause, though, does not require the president to carry out every law to its fullest effect. Indeed, the president's **pardon power** is an example of the president's discretion not only to determine the extent of enforcement but even to relieve individuals from federal law enforcement. That the Constitution vests the executive power in the president provides the president with authority to determine how to expend appropriations, when Congress grants that discretion. Yet the president must not cancel or impound appropriations that Congress grants and directs the president to expend.

Constitutional Law

Congress has carefully limited the president's statutory power to impound funds so as not to diminish Congress's appropriation power. The president must also not prevent an executive-branch official from carrying out a duty that Congress imposes.

2. As commander in chief

As noted above, the Constitution effectively divides war powers between Congress and the president by giving Congress the power to declare war and control war and other military funding, while designating the president as **commander in chief** over the nation's armed forces. The president's commander-in-chief power, though, is broad, plainly including the power to conduct war and the nation's defense. The president's commander-in-chief power may expand with congressional authorization, such as to blockade a port to defeat an insurrection, even without a declaration of war, try in military tribunals enemy combatants captured in the United States during a declared war, or declare as enemy combatants and detain without trial non-citizens captured during an authorized use of force. Yet without congressional authorization, the president must not exercise national-defense powers that the Constitution reserves to Congress, such as to authorize military trials of citizens in time of civil war or of non-citizen detainees without a declaration of war. And the president must not hold enemy combatants in territory that the United States controls without declaration of the detention grounds and due-process right to challenge the grounds before a neutral decisionmaker.

3. Treaty and foreign affairs powers

The president has express power to **make treaties** with foreign powers, subject to Senate concurrence by two-thirds majority. In modern practice, the Senate is not directly involved in negotiating treaties, which the president instead negotiates and signs, leaving their effect until after Senate approval. The Constitution identifies treaties as part of the *supreme law of the land* along with federal statutes. The president also has power implied from another article of the Constitution to make executive agreements with foreign powers, without Senate approval. Presidents have drawn authority for executive agreements, such as on trade matters, from other express executive powers such as to recognize foreign powers, or from adopted treaties or legislation. The Supreme Court has held that the president's power to make treaties authorizes the federal government to regulate state hunting methods, seasons, and limits under a migratory-bird treaty, although the president must not use treaty power to regulate activities reserved for state control. Although the Constitution does not directly address treaty termination, presidents have terminated treaties on their own, with the Supreme Court accepting that act over Senate objection.

Presidents draw foreign-affairs powers from constitutional grants of authority beyond the power to make treaties. The Constitution also expressly

Constitutional Law

extends to the president the powers to **appoint** and **receive ambassadors**. The president's power to appoint ambassadors affects and carries out the president's foreign policy. The president's power to receive ambassadors from other nations enables the president to recognize or reject the *legitimacy* of foreign governments. These two powers, together with the treaty power and (to a degree) the power as commander in chief, make the president the nation's *chief diplomat*. The president speaks to the nation's foreign affairs as head of government, acting through the appointed secretary of state overseeing the Department of State, and thus to the world as *head of state*. While these powers and positions give the president leading voice in foreign affairs, the Constitution checks the president's foreign-affairs powers not only through the Senate's role in approving treaties but also through Congress's power to appropriate or refuse to appropriate funds for foreign initiatives.

4. Appointment and removal of officials

The Constitution expressly authorizes the president to appoint certain public officials with Senate advice and consent. The **appointments clause** applies to *principal* officers rather than *inferior* officials. Cabinet-level officials are principal officers. The Constitution also expressly grants the president power to nominate Supreme Court justices, again subject to Senate advice and consent, and ambassadors as addressed above. Congress cannot remove from the president the president's constitutional power to nominate principal officers of the president's qualifications and choice. Congress can only legislate the qualifications of inferior officers, whose offices Congress creates. For example, although the president nominates justices of the president's own qualifications and choice to the constitutionally created Supreme Court, among other principal officers, Congress created the other federal courts and so can and does provide for the qualifications of other federal judges.

The Constitution expressly authorizes the president to fill vacancies when the Senate is *in recess*. A **recess appointment**, taking place *without* Senate advice and consent, lasts only until the next congressional session expires. A qualifying recess occurs only *between* congressional sessions *at the end of the year* or for other breaks longer than nine days, not shorter intra-session breaks, which the Senate typically keeps to under nine days using pro-forma proceedings if desiring to prevent presidential recess appointments. Gridlock over appointments is *not* grounds for the president expanding the recess-appointment power.

Although the Constitution does not address the power to remove federal officials, the Supreme Court has limited the president's removal power to only those principal officers who immediately serve the president. For example, the president cannot summarily remove over policy differences a trade commissioner whom federal legislation granted a seven-year term revocable only for malfeasance. Similarly, the president cannot remove a war-claims commissioner to install the president's own candidate, even when

Constitutional Law

the federal legislation creating the commission provided no such restrictive terms. The president also cannot remove special prosecutors whom the attorney general appoints under legislation that keeps the prosecutor in place until the investigative work is complete. On the other hand, Congress must not create an agency that performs executive functions, the officials of which only Congress can remove. Congress generally sets removal terms for inferior officers in offices that Congress creates, while the president removes political appointees from principal offices such as cabinet positions and ambassadors but of course not including members of the Supreme Court.

C. Federal inter-branch relationships

The above sections show several ways in which the Constitution checks and balances powers among the federal government's three coordinate branches. The following sections summarize these and other **inter-branch relationships** beginning with *congressional limits on the executive*. The executive, though, has its own constitutional checks on Congress, including that Congress must *present* legislation to the president and that the president has power to *veto* legislation or withhold action on legislation. The Constitution also limits the extent to which the coordinate branches can *delegate* their sole power to other branches. Finally, each branch has certain *immunities* from interference by other branches.

1. Congressional limits on the executive

The Constitution gives Congress several powers that act as checks on the president's power. As indicated in greater detail above, although the president serves as *commander in chief* over the nation's armed forces, only Congress can **declare war**. This check on presidential power creates a purposeful tension in roles that the executive and legislative branches have, in the absence of a formal war declaration since World War II but a nearly continuous series of military actions, worked out through war-powers resolutions requiring consultation, notice, and limits on the duration of military actions. In foreign affairs, although the president makes treaties, the Senate must **concur in treaties** by two-thirds super-majority vote for the treaties to take effect. The president must also have the Senate's advice and consent on the president's **appointment** of cabinet-level officials, ambassadors, and Supreme Court and other federal judges, again as addressed above in greater detail. Congress also approved, and the states adopted, a constitutional amendment limiting presidents to **two terms**.

Congress also holds **impeachment power** over the president and other executive officers. The House votes to impeach on a simple majority, after which the Senate tries the impeached officer to determine on a *two-thirds super-majority* vote whether to remove. Impeachment is not broadly discretionary and loosely political. Rather, the Constitution limits impeachment grounds to *treason*, *bribery*, and other *high crimes and misdemeanors*. The Senate must conclude that the impeached officer committed one or more of these specific acts to vote to remove. The Constitution defines treason as levying war against the United States, adhering to the nation's enemies, or giving enemies aid and comfort, and requires at least two witnesses to testify to treason. The Constitution does not define bribery or high crimes and misdemeanors. The latter phrase's historical meaning includes *corruption* of various kinds and *violations of public trust*. Two presidents have been impeached in House votes, one for firing a cabinet secretary in violation of legislation the constitutionality of which the president disputed and the other for perjury and obstruction of justice relating to personal conduct with a White House intern. The Senate acquitted both presidents of the charges.

Other congressional limits on presidential power include that although Congress must present legislation to the president who can *veto* that legislation, Congress can **override** the president's veto by two-thirds vote. Similarly, while the president must prepare an annual budget to present to Congress, Congress shapes and adopts the **budget**, which the president must carry out with only such limited discretionary power to withhold funds as Congress itself may grant. Congress can therefore fund initiatives that the president must implement against the president's judgment or *refuse* to fund initiatives that the president desires to pursue. Congress, in other words, holds the power of the purse over the president's policy initiatives. As addressed in greater detail above, the Constitution further requires the president to *take care* to *faithfully execute* the laws that Congress enacts, giving Congress the power to legislate to contravene or limit a president's policy initiatives.

2. The presentment requirement...

The Constitution expressly requires that Congress present to the president every bill that passes out of the House and Senate *before the bill becomes law*. The **presentment requirement** does not mean that the president can block all legislation. The requirement is merely to *present* proposed legislation, not to obtain the president's approval on it. The next section addresses the president's power to approve or disapprove of legislation, or withhold action. The presentment requirement's main function is to *preserve* the president's *veto power*. Yet the presentment requirement can at times be an effective check on Congress even when Congress is likely to adopt legislation in the face of a president's resistance. The requirement slows Congress's haste in adopting legislation, while the president considers whether to approve, veto, or take no action. The present requirement also prevents Congress and the president from altering the Constitution's three-step process for approving legislation involving passage in one legislative body, passage in the other body, and presentment to the president, as further addressed in a following section on *non-delegation doctrine*. To keep Congress from skirting the presentment requirement, the requirement expressly applies not only to substantive legislation but also to any *order*, *resolution*, or *vote* to which the concurrence of House and Senate are necessary.

...and the president's power to veto or to withhold action

The Constitution grants the president authority to **veto** legislation or resolutions that Congress passes out of the House and Senate and presents to the president. The president has *ten days* (not counting Sundays) to sign presented legislation or to reject and return it to the body from which it originated, typically although not necessarily with the veto's rationale. Congress may reconsider a vetoed bill immediately, setting aside other business to consider a veto override. Congress overrides a president's veto and adopts legislation only with a **two-thirds vote** of those present in both House and Senate. The president has no power to *alter* the presented legislation or resolution, only to sign it, reject and return it, or refuse to act. If the president refuses to act on legislation rather than signing or vetoing the legislation, then the legislation becomes law. However, if Congress presents the legislation to the president but adjourns before the president's ten-day period for considering the proposed legislation expires, and the president does not act while Congress remains in session, then the president's inaction becomes a **pocket veto** when Congress adjourns, and the proposed legislation does *not* become law.

3. Non-delegation doctrine

As briefly mentioned above, the *presentment requirement* reinforces that to enact laws, Congress and the president must follow the process of approval by one legislative body, approval by the other body, and presentment to the president. Congress and the president thus cannot legislate that one body of Congress or the president alone take legislative actions. To do so would be to improperly **delegate** to a single body or the president a legislative power that the Constitution's presentment requirement granted only to the bicameral bodies and coordinate branches. For example, Congress may grant the president administrative discretion in promulgating regulations to implement broad legislation. Yet Congress cannot through properly approved legislation grant overly broad administrative authority to the president, more akin to legislative authority, while reserving to one body or committee of Congress a power of *legislative veto* of administrative actions. Single-body legislative vetoes violate the Constitution's bicameralism and presentment requirement. Congress must also not grant the president authority to *cancel* legislation, such as in a line-item veto of broad budget authority. To do so violates the presentment requirement, in effect giving the president power to repeal part of a law.

Non-delegation doctrine applies in other areas, too. For example, Congress has the authority to empower executive officers like the comptroller general with executive discretion in implementing an approved budget. Yet Congress cannot reserve to itself the exclusive right to discharge the

Constitutional Law

comptroller general once appointed because to do so would be for Congress to reserve to itself an executive function. The president executes the laws, not Congress. If Congress were to have the power to both approve *and* *remove* executive officers to whom Congress granted discretionary authority, then Congress would in effect be exercising the president's executive function. Congress holds impeachment powers over the president and other executive officers, but Congress does not hold broader powers of removal.

4. Executive, legislative, and judicial immunities

The president has **absolute immunity** for executive acts while in office, without respect to the president's alleged good or bad faith in carrying out those official duties. By contrast, the president has *no* immunity for *personal* acts while in office and no right to delay proceedings seeking to hold the president responsible for personal acts before taking office. The president also has a qualified executive privilege to keep presidential papers and discussions confidential while in office, although the judicial branch, not the president, has the power to determine and limit the privilege's scope, such as to develop the facts in a criminal trial. The president also has the power of **reprieves and pardons** from federal crimes, although not from impeachment proceedings, civil proceedings, or state offenses. The president may exercise the pardon power to protect former executive officials from federal prosecution, affording a kind of immunity.

The Constitution's **speech-and-debate clause** grants members of Congress privilege from arrest while in congressional session and on the way to and from congressional sessions. Thus, the president, other executive officers, or anyone invoking the powers of the courts cannot interfere with the ability of members of Congress to attend sessions to speak, debate, and cast votes. However, the clause does *not* protect members of Congress from criminal conviction for conduct outside the sphere of *legislative activity*, such as taking bribes, even when conviction would interfere with a member completing a legislative term. The speech-and-debate clause also extends the **legislative privilege** to protect members of Congress from *questioning* in any place for any congressional speech or debate. Thus, a member of Congress may in session read and enter into the congressional record confidential national-security papers without later questioning over the papers' source. The Supreme Court has also held that the speech-and-debate clause protects congressional aides from questioning to the same extent as the member of Congress for whom the aide works. The speech-and-debate clause does *not*, however, protect members of Congress from questioning or responsibility over private publications in no way essential to their session speech and debate. The courts may enjoin publication dissemination of defamatory materials included in congressional reports.

III. The relation of nation and states in a federal system

Constitutional Law

The Constitution's federal system implicates relations of the federal government to the states. **Intergovernmental immunities** is one such federal/state subject, involving both federal immunity from state law and state immunity from federal law, the latter including the reach of the 10th Amendment. Limits on state authority also arise from other **federalism limits** including the Constitution's *supremacy clause* making federal law supreme and the negative implication of the commerce clause known as the *dormant commerce clause*. Another federalism question arises around Congress's ability to authorize otherwise invalid state action. Consider the following sections addressing these questions of the relations of the federal government to the states.

A. Intergovernmental immunities

Intergovernmental immunity between the federal government and state governments is an aspect of *sovereignty* that keeps federal and state agencies from intruding on one another's spheres. For example, a state may not exempt its own chartered banks from restrictions while imposing those restrictions on federally chartered banks because to do so elevates state interests and sovereignty over federal interests and sovereignty. Similarly, states may not exempt state and local-government pensions from state income tax while taxing federal-government pensions because to do so disrespects federal sovereignty. The Supreme Court construes intergovernmental immunity from the Constitution's structure of government while in the case of state immunity from federal law also relying on the express 10th Amendment immunity.

1. Federal immunity from state law

The sovereign **immunity** of the **federal** government from state law often applies to prevent states from *taxing* federal programs, properties, or personnel, as in the case of federal pensions referred to in the prior section, because to tax is to burden and discourage. The federal immunity from state taxation applies not only to *programs* such as federal pensions but also to federal *property*. States and locales may not tax federal lands and facilities in the manner that they tax privately owned lands and improvements to private lands. Federal immunity from state laws extends beyond taxation to prohibit states from imposing requirements for fees, licenses, and other restrictions. States, for example, do not register and license federally owned and operated vehicles. Federal immunity can also extend to quasi-governmental agencies like federally financed museums. Yet the federal government may *voluntarily* subject its personnel to state and local regulation, such as to require federal officials to obey local traffic and parking regulations to relieve urban congestion exacerbated by non-compliant operation of federal vehicles.

Constitutional Law

2. State immunity from federal law, including the 10th Amendment

The above section on the Eleventh Amendment and **state sovereign immunity** summarizes several specific circumstances where states and their agencies either have or do not have immunity from federal control. For example, the Constitution and its amendments authorize federal-court injunctive and declaratory actions against state officials, enforcing federal civil rights, as outside state sovereign immunity. As noted above, though, to overcome the **qualified immunity** of state officials, aggrieved individuals must sue state officials in the official's *individual* rather than *official* capacity if the action is for money damages *and* must establish that the official violated a *clearly established* federal right. States may also *consent* to federal suits under state legislation or when the state removes litigation from state to federal court. States also consent to federal control when states accept federal funds contingent on waiver of immunity.

Yet the sovereign immunity of state government from federal law draws its source not only from the Constitution's structure of federal and state sovereigns but also from the **10th Amendment**. The 10th Amendment *reserves to the states* or to the people any powers that the Constitution does not grant to the federal government or forbid the states. The 10th Amendment does *not* limit powers that the Constitution expressly grants to the federal government, such as to regulate interstate commerce or to tax and spend for the general welfare, even when those powers affect a state. For example, the federal government may apply Social Security provisions, employment laws, and wage-and-hours provisions to state personnel in the same manner that it does private employees. The federal government may also tax state sales of property in the same manner that it taxes private property sales. The federal government must *not*, though, **commandeer** state personnel and resources in ways that require states to enact or administer federal regulatory programs, such as to require states to take title to nuclear waste generated within the state.

B. Federalism-based limits on state authority

As the above introduction to this part indicates, in addition to federal sovereign immunity from state interference, other **federalism** constructs explicit or implicit in the Constitution necessarily limit state authority in other ways. The Supreme Court has over time developed a workable framework for determining the scope and impact of the *dormant commerce clause*, meaning the prohibition on certain state actions that interfere with interstate commerce, prohibitions that the Court construes from Congress's commerce-clause power. Another section below addresses the Constitution's explicit *supremacy clause*, holding treaties and federal law supreme over state enactments. Another section below addresses federalism questions arising around Congress's efforts to authorize otherwise invalid state action. Consider the following sections addressing these federalism questions.

Constitutional Law

1. Negative implications of the commerce clause

Congress has *commerce-clause* authority to regulate interstate commerce, as an above section addresses. Yet the commerce clause has a strong negative implication, referred to as the **dormant commerce clause**, preventing *states* from regulating interstate commerce. While states may impose burdens protecting local health and safety, states must not regulate in ways that reduce or curtail the flow of goods in and out of the state. Laws that **openly discriminate** against interstate commerce, given *strict scrutiny*, are presumptively invalid unless the state can show that the law is the only way to achieve a *compelling interest*. Laws that do not openly discriminate but instead **substantially burden** interstate commerce must be necessary to *directly advance* an important state interest and be the least restrictive means of doing so. Laws that place only **incidental burdens** on interstate commerce are presumptively valid when rationally related to a legitimate state interest unless the burden *substantially outweighs* the local benefit. States may, on the other hand, participate in the market without dormant-commerce-clause concern, such as buying products from only within the state or at higher prices from within the state. Under the dormant commerce clause, Congress may *expressly preempt* states from regulating economic activity, while federal legislation may also *impliedly preempt* state regulation.

2. Supremacy clause and preemption

The Constitution's **supremacy clause** expressly makes the Constitution, treaties adopted under the Constitution's terms and effective as domestic law, and federal laws duly enacted, to be the *supreme law* of the land. The supremacy clause thus ensures that federal law controls when in *conflict* with state law, again if the federal laws are otherwise constitutional. On the other hand, the supremacy clause alone does *not* prohibit states from enacting general health-and-safety or police-power legislation that pursues similar ends as federal laws enacted under Congress's commerce-clause power, authority to tax and spend for the general welfare, or other express constitutional powers. Thus, both federal and state laws may criminalize, prohibit, or otherwise regulate the same conduct, as long as the state laws are not obstacles to Congress's accomplishment of its objectives, such as to prohibit or require private conduct that would violate a federal enactment. The supremacy clause does *not* authorize Congress to veto state legislation but rather to legislate on its own in ways that take precedence over contrary state laws.

The supremacy clause does, on the other hand, enable Congress to explicitly or implicitly **preempt** state law from regulating in any area that Congress determines that it alone should control. For example, Congress may determine that only federal law and regulation should govern a national vaccine program, thus prohibiting states not only from further administrative regulations but also products liability for vaccines. Congress preempts state law *explicitly* by so stating in its federal legislative schemes. Congress preempts state law *implicitly* when it so comprehensively *occupies the field* as to indicate its intent to displace all state regulation. For example, Congress has at times and in ways so comprehensively regulated nuclear power, vehicle safety, tobacco-product advertising, medical devices, pharmaceuticals, and fuels, as to occupy those fields, displacing and preempting state law. However, for Congress to occupy a field and preempt state law, the federal enactment must be *necessary and proper* to implement an enumerated congressional power. In other words, the supremacy clause is not an authorization of federal power but instead a conflict-of-law rule making federal law supreme.

3. Authorization of otherwise invalid state action

Congress has the power to authorize state action that would **otherwise be invalid** as state regulation of interstate commerce. For example, while discriminatory state taxation of insurance transactions across state lines violates the *dormant commerce clause*, Congress may authorize states to impose those discriminatory taxes, in essence extending Congress's commerce-clause power to the states. Congress's intent, though, must be *unmistakably clear*. For example, just because Congress restricts interstate commerce in timber cut from federal lands does not authorize a state to do likewise as to state lands, absent clear congressional intent to extend that authority. The Supreme Court also holds that Congress may at times determine whether the states may regulate federal instrumentalities, where those federal instrumentalities would otherwise be immune from state regulation in the absence of Congress's authorization. For example, while federally chartered banks would ordinarily have sovereign immunity from state taxation, Congress may authorize state taxation of federal banks if Congress so wishes. On the other hand, while Congress can at times enlarge *state* power, states must *not* consent to enlarge *Congress's* power beyond what the Constitution authorizes, such as to unconstitutionally permit Congress to enact a local program that the state then administers and implements.

IV. Individual rights

The Constitution grants certain enumerated **individual rights** against federal and state government action. Individual rights are rights against *government* action, not generally *private* action, as the first section below addresses. Other sections below address **due process** as a principal individual right, including both *substantive* due process and *procedural* due process, and **equal protection** as a right against certain government classifications. The Constitution also grants individual rights against government **takings** of private property interests. Other constitutional protections treated below include rights under the *privileges-and-immunities* clause and *contracts* clause, and prohibitions against *unconstitutional*

Constitutional Law

conditions, *bills of attainder*, and *ex post facto laws*. The **First Amendment** guarantees other primary rights of *freedom of religion* and *freedom of expression*. Consider each of these rights in the following sections.

A. State action

State-action doctrine involves the principle that the Constitution provides a check on *government* rather than private action. Individual rights under the Constitution are thus rights against the federal and state governments taking certain actions. For example, the 1st Amendment right of free speech expressly guarantees that *Congress* not interfere with an individual's free-speech rights. Congress must not, for instance, enact legislation prohibiting individuals or corporations from advocating for tax reform. Those 1st Amendment protections would also extend to actions by federal agencies. Thus, the Internal Revenue Service must not adopt policies and practices that discriminate against individuals or organizations that advocate for tax reform. By contrast, the 1st Amendment does *not* prohibit private employers from interfering with employee speech, although other state and federal laws may offer that protection. Thus, a tax-preparer employer could prohibit its employees from advocating for tax reform in ways that interfere with the employer's business.

State action clearly includes the exercise of legislative, executive, or judicial authority. For example, a legislature's enactment of a law restricting employment or authorizing confiscation of controlled substances is state action, as are executive and regulatory efforts to implement those laws, and judicial proceedings to enforce those efforts. Yet state action can also arise when a government-regulated entity, particularly one that the state authorizes to act as a *monopoly* or in other *coercive* way for the state, acts in the challenged way out of its close state nexus. Thus, when a nonprofit association that the state authorizes to license professionals in its field denies an applicant a license, such that the applicant cannot practice the profession in that state, the association's actions are state actions subject to constitutional protections. Similarly, when a private contractor undertakes to enforce government parking regulations under a government contract requiring it to act precisely as government parking enforcement would act, the contractor's actions are state action subject to constitutional protections.

The *state-action doctrine* takes on special significance with respect to state-government action rather than federal action. The Constitution's Bill of Rights directs its protections toward *federal*-government action, not *state*-government action. The 1st Amendment prohibits *Congress* from restricting free speech, not the states from restricting free speech. The 14th Amendment's due-process clause, guaranteeing individuals due-process rights against *state*-government action, though, has enabled the Supreme Court to selectively **incorporate** certain Bill of Rights' individual rights into constitutional protections against the state. So, for example, while the 1st Amendment does *not* guarantee free speech against state-government action, the 14th Amendment *does* by incorporation of 1st Amendment rights guarantee

Constitutional Law

free speech against state action. Thus, the individual rights addressed below are rights against both federal action and state action unless otherwise indicated.

B. Due process

The 5th Amendment provides for **due process** of law in any *federal* proceeding to deprive any person of life, liberty, or property. Similarly, the 14th Amendment provides for due process in any *state* proceeding to deprive any person of life, liberty, or property. Due process involves two distinct forms of guaranteed right, *procedural due process* and *substantive due process*, each addressed immediately below. Before one determines what due process requires, one must determine whether government action threatens to deprive a person of *life, liberty,* or *property*. Thus, government actions threatening to deprive a person of *liberty* can include not only prosecution of crime on the penalty of incarceration but also enactment of laws prohibiting or restricting actions, such as when, where, or with what methods or equipment to work or recreate. Government actions threatening to deprive a person of *property* can include not only condemnation of buildings and lands, and seizure and forfeiture of personal property, but also fines, fees, and taxes. Not every burden on liberty and property rights rises to the level of constitutional protection. For example, while keeping a government job for which one has a contract providing job security is a protectible property right, a government job held at the government employer's will, terminable without cause, ordinarily would not be a protectible right because the government could terminate the employment at any time for any lawful reason or no reason at all.

1. Substantive due process

Substantive due process, in contrast to *procedural due process* addressed below, protects persons against laws that unduly burden *fundamental rights* or, if they do not burden fundamental rights, then are nonetheless arbitrary and irrational, even if the process of their enforcement is reasonable and fair. *Substantive* due process involves the impact of the law itself, not the procedure for enforcing it. For example, if police seized, forfeited, and sold a person's home and vehicle with full notice to the person who had full opportunity to dispute the police actions in a trial-like proceeding before an impartial judge, then those police actions would comply with *procedural* due process. Yet if the actions took place not, say, for the person's illegal manufacture and sale of controlled substances using home and vehicle, but instead because the person's street address came up in a government lottery that law had established to raise local law-enforcement funds, then the law on which the police acted would *not* satisfy substantive due process. The law would instead be random in its implementation and capricious in its destructive effect against innocent persons. See in the following two sections how the law distinguishes fundamental rights from

Constitutional Law

lesser rights and further articulates the two tests for substantive due process that the distinction entails.

a. Fundamental rights

The Supreme Court defines **fundamental rights** as involving certain specific autonomy and privacy interests, within a larger sphere of liberty interests. The rights to *marry*, *procreate*, and raise and maintain custody of *children*, form one set of fundamental rights. The rights to purchase and use *birth control*, and refuse *medical treatment*, form another set of fundamental rights. The rights to freedom of *religion*, freedom of *speech* and *association*, interstate *travel*, and *vote* form another set of fundamental rights. Government restrictions on these rights face **strict scrutiny**. Strict scrutiny requires the government to show that the restriction is the *most narrowly drawn* means of achieving a *compelling state end*. Example of statutes failing strict scrutiny for unduly restricting a fundamental right include a ban on the sale of contraceptives and a statute requiring non-custodial unmarried parents to receive counseling before marriage. The right to an abortion, while at one time clearly a fundamental right, has a current constitutional status that prevents states from imposing *undue burdens* on the woman's right, placing the right between fundamental rights and lesser rights addressed below. Because the government bears the burden of satisfying strict scrutiny, and because strict scrutiny's standard is so high, most enactments facing strict scrutiny fail to pass constitutional muster.

b. Other rights and interests

By contrast to due-process's *strict scrutiny* protections for fundamental rights, substantive due process offers only minimal protection for other life, liberty, and property rights and interests. The **rational-basis** test requires only that government show that its enactment bears a *rational relationship* to a *legitimate government purpose*. Also, unlike challenges to interference with fundamental rights in which the government bears the burden of showing that the measure passes strict scrutiny, the person challenging government interference with a non-fundamental right bears the burden of showing that the enactment is **arbitrary** and **irrational**. With a low threshold and the burden on the challenger, most enactments facing rational-basis review pass constitutional muster. For example, federal legislation requiring coal operators to compensate miners for injury on the job, even if the injury occurred before the legislation and the miner no longer works for the operator, relates rationally to the legitimate government purpose of income security for injured and disabled workers. The law need *not* be rational in every respect if its core addresses a legitimate object. For example, a law prohibiting opticians from fitting lenses in frames without an optometrist or ophthalmologist prescription reasonably relates to the quality of eye care even if it unreasonably prevents opticians from fitting old lenses in new frames. Laws easily satisfy rational-basis review.

Constitutional Law

2. Procedural due process

Procedural due process protects persons in their life, liberty, and property by ensuring that government processes are fair and impartial, particularly as to *notice* and *opportunity for meaningful hearing* before an impartial decisionmaker. For example, police seizure, forfeiture, and sale of a person's home and vehicle used in illegally manufacturing and selling controlled substances, without any notice to the person or opportunity to contest the action, would violate procedural due process, even though the statute's object to discourage and prevent illegal distribution of dangerous drugs was legitimate. Procedural due process does *not* concern itself with the nature of the right, whether fundamental or not, if the person challenging the process has a constitutionally adequate life, liberty, or property interest. For example, whenever the state institutionalizes a person, the process that the state uses must satisfy *procedural due process* because institutionalization involves deprivation of a significant liberty interest. Similarly, if the state were to terminate a supplier's one-year contract in mid year, the state must provide the supplier with procedural due process because terminating a one-year contract in mid year interferes with a significant property interest.

While *notice* and *opportunity for hearing* are due-process hallmarks, procedural due process is *flexible*, depending on the *personal interest*, risk of *process errors*, *state interest*, and state *burden of additional procedures*. Due-process questions can include, among other things, the specificity of the notice and charges, how long before government action the government must serve the notice, and whether hearing must take place before government action and whether counsel may be present, evidence rules apply, and witnesses must testify under oath and cross-examination. For example, terminating disability benefits on internal review and beneficiary notice may be constitutionally adequate, if the beneficiary has an opportunity to challenge the termination after it occurs, submit additional evidence of disability, and demand hearing if the challenge does not result in benefit resumption. On the other hand, termination of *welfare* benefits necessary for food and housing, or dismissal of a student from public grade school on allegations of truancy or other misconduct, would likely not satisfy due process without notice and opportunity for prior hearing, given the significance of the lost benefits and rights, and the probability of errors on allegations without hearing.

C. Equal protection

The 14th Amendment expressly guarantees **equal protection** of the laws as to state enactments. The 5th Amendment, while not including an equivalent *equal-protection clause*, incorporates through its due-process clause the 14th Amendment's equal-protection guarantees against federal enactments. Thus, both *federal* and *state* enactments must meet constitutional tests for equal protection. Equal-protection challenges require determining

Constitutional Law

whether the classification involves a *fundamental right*, *suspect classifications*, or *non-suspect classification*. As the following sections address, each classification involves applying a different test that the federal or state enactment must satisfy. Enactments affecting fundamental rights face *strict scrutiny*, while enactments affecting suspect classifications face *heightened scrutiny* and non-suspect classifications only *rational-basis review*.

1. Fundamental rights

Equal-protection analysis requires that classifications involving **fundamental rights** and **suspect classifications** face **strict scrutiny**. Equal-protection analysis defines fundamental rights as above for due-process analysis, including rights to *marry*, *procreate*, raise and maintain custody of *children*, use *birth control*, and refuse *medical treatment*, plus freedom of *religion*, *speech*, and *association*, interstate *travel*, and *vote*. The law continues to define suspect classifications as clearly including only classifications based on *race* and *national origin*. Thus, for example, a state law forbidding interracial marriage would constitute classifications based on both the fundamental right of marriage and the suspect classification of race. The classification, though, must be *purposefully* and *invidiously* discriminatory, looking to the legislative motive and intent. Neutral classifications adopted in good faith but that adversely impact fundamental rights or suspect classes do not require strict scrutiny, unless the challenge establishes that the asserted good faith was pretext for invidious discrimination.

Strict scrutiny of enactments affecting fundamental rights and suspect classifications requires that the government show that the law is *necessary*, also stated as *narrowly tailored*, to achieve a *compelling state interest*. Suspect classifications rarely survive strict scrutiny, a last clear example (other than affirmative action) involving World War II detention based on national origin for national-security purposes. Significantly, the law applies strict scrutiny not only to enactments that disadvantage minority groups by race or national origin but also to *affirmative-action* measures seeking to aid those groups. Affirmative-action programs must show their necessity to achieve a compelling government interest, such as remedying past racial discrimination or providing educational benefit from a diverse student body.

As to fundamental rights, strict scrutiny applies to enactments classifying voters, such as redistricting that dilutes *one person/one vote*, because voting is a fundamental right. Yet strict scrutiny does not apply to international travel, only interstate travel, because under the privileges-and-immunities clause, only interstate travel involves a fundamental right. Also, as noted above in the due-process section on fundamental rights, abortion is not a fundamental right, and so classifications based on abortion do not receive strict scrutiny, only the intermediate scrutiny involving the question of *undue burden*. Education is not a fundamental right.

Constitutional Law

2. Classifications subject to heightened scrutiny

Heightened or **intermediate scrutiny** applies to *quasi-suspect classifications* that, while not fully suspect warranting strict scrutiny, nonetheless bear some of the same indicia of concern. Intermediate scrutiny applies to classifications based on *sex* and classifications based on *illegitimacy*. Thus, for example, a public university that admits only members of one sex implicates the quasi-suspect classification of sex, while a statute that bars paternity actions five years after the child's birth involves the quasi-suspect classification of illegitimacy. Intermediate scrutiny for quasi-suspect classifications requires that the law *substantially relate* to an *important government objective*. Intermediate scrutiny thus elevates over rational-basis review both the necessary relationship, *substantial* rather than merely rational, and the significance of the end, *important* rather than merely legitimate. Under that standard, both above example enactments would likely fail, lacking the substantial relationship to the important end. Barring paternity actions after five years would reduce fraudulent and stale claims, but that end is not sufficiently important to distinguish between children under and over the five-year age. Similarly, single-sex education, while helpful to the important education end, bears an insufficiently substantial relationship to that important end to justify distinguishing between men and women, when co-ed education could achieve the same end.

3. Rational basis review

Non-suspect classifications face only **rational-basis review**. Non-suspect classifications can include any distinction not identified as a fundamental right or suspect classification. For example, a city that prohibits vehicle owners from advertising anything on their vehicles other than their own business or interest distinguishes between non-suspect classes of advertisers advertising on their own vehicles or on other vehicles. *Rational-basis review* requires only that the enactment *relate rationally* to a *legitimate government end*. Thus, the above enactment prohibiting non-owner advertising on vehicles would pass rational-basis review because the measure may reduce driving distractions and accident injuries. Importantly, enactments addressing non-suspect classifications enjoy a *presumption of constitutionality*, meaning that the challenger must show that the enactment is purely arbitrary and irrational in every respect, leaving the enactment without rational support for any legitimate end. Thus again, the above enactment banning non-owner vehicle advertising would not eliminate all vehicle advertising because owners could still advertise their own business, arguably leaving the law incompletely rational, but the limited rationality of a partial advertising ban satisfies the test.

Although a federal or state law need only relate rationally to a discernible end, the end itself must be *legitimate*. The courts defer generously to legislatures on *social welfare* and *economic* legislation as to the legitimacy of legislative ends. For example, social-welfare and economic classifications

Constitutional Law

based on age do not receive elevated scrutiny, need pass only rational-basis review, and routinely pass constitutional muster. Similarly, a state may prohibit public-university professors from negotiating over teaching loads in collective bargaining because the economic classification pursues the state's tuition-control end. Yet if instead the end that the law pursues violates another constitutional prohibition, then the law does not satisfy the rational-basis test. For example, if a state enacts a law that taxes out-of-state insurers at higher rates than in-state insurers, pursuing the rational end to reward in-state insurers for the employment and business that they bring to the state, the law nonetheless fails the rational-basis test because the end violates the dormant commerce clause for discriminating against interstate commerce. The law would be rational but its end illegitimate. Rational-basis review requires both rationality *and* legitimate end.

D. Takings

The federal government has the power of **eminent domain** to take private property anywhere in the nation for public use. Each state has equivalent power within the state. The federal and state governments exercise eminent domain to take private lands to build public roads, buildings, airports, ports, and other facilities. In those instances, the fact of a *taking* is obvious from the condemnation procedures that government follows to obtain *legal title* to the private land. Yet governments also take private property through *permanent physical occupation*, such as by building utility towers and running utility lines across private land. Governments also regulate private property through zoning and other land-use laws. When regulation eliminates *all economically viable use* of land, such as by prohibiting any building on seashore lots owned and valued exclusively for that purpose, the owner has a claim of *inverse condemnation*, just as if the government had completed a traditional taking. On the other hand, when government only temporarily interferes with private land without taking legal title, physically occupying the land, or regulating away all economically viable use, such as by conducting noisy and dangerous operations around, over, and across private lands, the government has not taken the land but may be liable for trespass or nuisance, unless the activities are so sustained as to be permanent.

The 5th Amendment restricts the federal government's eminent-domain power, while the 14th Amendment incorporates that restriction into a protection against state exercise of those same powers. The restrictions include that the power's exercise must be for **public use** and only with **just compensation**. The Supreme Court construes the *public use* condition broadly to include not only taking private land for public roads and facilities but also to convey to other private owners for *public purposes*. Thus, for example, a city may condemn blighted urban lands not just to build a public courthouse or jail but also to convey to private developers for private housing, offices, and commercial centers, for the public purpose of relieving blight and stimulating economic development. States vary in their constitutional, statutory, and common law interpretation of the tension between public *use*

Constitutional Law

and public *purpose*, some states limiting condemnation only to public use while others interpreting the right broadly to permit transfer to private ownership for development of private stadiums, arenas, performance halls, and other private development benefitting employment, the arts, and other public purposes.

Just compensation requires the government to pay **fair market value** to the private owner whose property the government condemns. Fair market value is *not* the value to the owner but instead what others would pay for the land on the open market in an arm's length exchange. Fair market value can thus *exceed* the value of the land to the private owner, where others would pay more for the land than the owner's use justifies, such as where the owner maintains a junkyard on the land but the land would support an office or apartment tower. Conversely, fair market value can also be *less* than the owner's value, where others would not pay the value in which the owner holds the land, such as where the owner's family has lived on the land for generations.

E. Other protections, including the privileges and immunities clauses...

The Constitution's **privileges-and-immunities** clause ensures that states grant out-of-state citizens the same privileges and immunities as citizens of the state. For example, although a state may require lawyers practicing in the state to obtain a license, the state must not refuse a license to any lawyer other than lawyers who reside in the state. The privileges-and-immunities clause applies to *fundamental rights* of individuals, granting no protection to corporations. A fundamental right is one that relates to an important economic or civil liberty. So, for an example of important *economic* liberty, a state may charge a higher fee for an out-of-stater to hunt or fish recreationally but not to obtain a commercial license to hunt or fish for a living, earning a living involving an important economic activity. For an example of an important *civil* liberty, a state may restrict all persons from a wilderness area but must not permit in-state residents access while refusing out-of-state residents access because *travel* is an important civil liberty. States must not discriminate against citizens of other states with respect to an individual's fundamental right unless the restriction closely relates to advancing a *substantial state interest*.

...the contracts clause...

The Constitution's **contracts clause**, embedded among several other Article I restrictions on state power, prohibits the states from impairing the right of individuals to contract. The prohibition prevents states from enacting laws that undermine contracts between private individuals. For example, a state could not pass a law that relieves a debtor from repaying a creditor an obligation owed under an *existing* contract. On the other hand, a state may pass laws governing *future* contracts, such as laws protecting tenants from

Constitutional Law

landlord overreaching, if those laws governing prospective contracts create greater security and stability in contracting. A state could not, though, pass a law stating simply that landlords cannot enforce rental contracts. To survive a contracts-clause challenge, a state law affecting contracts must not *substantially impair* existing contracts, must have *legitimate* broad, general, social or economic purpose, and must be *reasonable* for achieving that purpose. The contracts clause also prevents states from enacting laws that undermine the state's own obligations to private individuals. The prohibition seeks to ensure economic liberty and the integrity of obligations against state interference. Congress cannot use its own express powers to authorize the states to impair contracts.

...unconstitutional conditions...

The doctrine of **unconstitutional conditions** prohibits government from *conditioning* a person's receipt of a government benefit on the person's *waiver* of constitutionally protected rights. Because the government must not violate individual rights directly, the government must also not condition receipt of government benefits on giving up the right. The doctrine keeps government from forcing individuals to choose between a government benefit and a constitutionally protected right. For example, the federal government may not offer federal funding to treat a sexually transmitted disease conditioned on grant recipients adopting a policy opposing prostitution and sex trafficking because the policy would require *forced speech* violating 1st Amendment rights. Government grants may define their criteria and limits but must not leverage grant programs to regulate speech beyond the scope of the grant. Similarly, government may not condition employment as a teacher on the teacher giving up free-speech rights or deny unemployment benefits unless a religious adherent gives up religious rights not to work on a holy day.

Unconstitutional-conditions doctrine, though, is *not absolute*. Government may impose a condition *essential* to the government interest that the benefit promotes if the condition is *proportional* to the harm the benefit redresses. For example, a state may require a mall owner to permit non-disruptive petitioners to engage in free speech rights on the property, despite the owner's right to control the owner's own property without government taking, because unfettered freedom to exclude certain persons is not necessary to economically valuable use of the land, and the small impact of the government condition was proportional to the harm to public free speech that the government edict addressed. Yet a state cannot require a beachfront-property owner to donate without just compensation a public-access easement as a condition for a permit to build. In each case, one must identify the individual's constitutional right and the government's conditional burden on it, to measure proportionality.

...bills of attainder...

Constitutional Law

The Constitution prohibits both the federal and state governments from enacting **bills of attainder**. A bill of attainder purports to deprive a specific person of life, liberty, or property without due process of law. Thus, a bill of attainder must satisfy three conditions that it specify the affected *persons*, include *punishment*, and forgo *hearing*. For example, a federal or state statute must not prohibit specific classes of persons from obtaining employment. To do so would identify the persons, punish by depriving of employment rights, and prevent a hearing to preserve the right. Case law narrowly construes punishment and seldom upholds a bill-of-attainder challenge. Thus, for example, regulations denying specific persons government financial aid and statutes requisitioning the recordings and papers of a resigned president and his aides are not bills of attainder because they merely restrict noncontractual government benefits or affect personal-property rights.

...and ex post facto laws

The Constitution prohibits both the federal and state governments from enacting laws **ex post facto**. An ex-post-facto law *criminalizes previously lawful conduct* after the person has completed the conduct. Legislation that applies only prospectively rather than retrospectively does not violate the clause. The principle justifying the constitutional prohibition on ex-post-facto laws is that retrospective criminal laws are fundamentally unjust in denying persons the right and opportunity to conform their conduct to avoid punishment. The clause protects only against later-adopted *criminal* statutes, not enactments creating or affecting *civil* liability, although in distinguishing the two, the courts measure enactments by their effect rather than their form. A statute that punishes conduct will fall within the prohibition even if disguised as a civil rather than criminal sanction. Thus, for example, a retroactively imposed forfeiture for a crime could constitute an ex-post-facto criminal sanction. So, too, retroactive statutes that eliminate a defense to crime, increase punishment, or increase likelihood of conviction can also constitute impermissible ex-post-facto laws. Yet retroactive legislation requiring sex offenders to register constitutes only a civil regulatory scheme rather than criminal punishment and so does not violate the ex-post-facto-law prohibition. Nor does imposing civil commitment on a sexual predator after sentence.

F. First Amendment freedoms

First Amendment freedoms protect a wide range of fundamental religious and expressive freedoms through parallel rights against government interference. While the 1st Amendment restricts federal interference, the 14th Amendment incorporates 1st Amendment rights into protections against state interference as to the same 1st Amendment rights. Keep in mind the state-action requirement that the 1st and 14th Amendments apply to *government* interference with freedoms, not *private* interference. As to the specific

Constitutional Law

freedoms protected, the 1ˢᵗ Amendment begins with the *religious-freedom* clause including both its free-exercise and disestablishment provisions. The 1ˢᵗ Amendment also addresses several rights of *free expression* including freedom of speech, press, and association. In government regulation of expression, the law concerns itself first with whether government regulates the *content* of speech, regulates speech only in *content-neutral* fashion, or regulates *unprotected* or *commercial* speech, the classification determining the constitutional test for the regulation. Regulation of the expression or association of public-school students and of public employees, and of public benefits based on expression or association, raise other constitutional issues addressed below. The sections below also address regulation of expressive conduct and doctrines of prior restraints, vagueness, and overbreadth.

1. Freedom of religion and separation of church and state

The 1ˢᵗ Amendment's religious-freedom clause, again applying not only to federal laws but also, through the 14ᵗʰ Amendment, to state and local law, recognizes **freedom of religion** on one hand but also that government must not **establish** religion on the other hand. Government regulations that prohibit, burden, or interfere with the free exercise of religion, whether intentionally or in incidental effect, face rigorous constitutional review. On the other hand, government actions that recognize and accommodate religion must not endorse, support, and establish religion, for which law provides a rigorous three-part test, as the following sections address.

a. Free exercise

The 1ˢᵗ Amendment's **free-exercise clause** guarantees the right of individuals to adopt religious beliefs and practices of their choosing, unencumbered by government interference. The Supreme Court has in the past applied **strict scrutiny** to certain laws interfering with the free exercise of religion, requiring government to show that it *narrowly tailored* the law to directly advance a *compelling government interest*. Thus, for example, a law that denies unemployment benefits to individuals who are unable to work weekends because of Sabbath observance would violate the free-exercise rights of individuals whose religious beliefs compel Sabbath observance. The state must also not compel parents to educate their children beyond the eighth grade when their religious practice prohibits doing so. Similarly, a civil-service rule prohibiting public employees from displaying a religious symbol while at work on a public site would violate the free-exercise rights of individuals who adhere to religious beliefs requiring such display.

The free-exercise clause and establishment clause appear most in conflict when a neutral law interferes with a religious practice, causing the religious adherent to request an exemption that, while allowing free exercise, can simultaneously appear to endorse the practice. Thus, the Supreme Court has held both long ago and more recently that a *neutral law of general applicability* generally does *not* implicate the free-exercise clause. For

Constitutional Law

example, states may outlaw bigamy or smoking peyote even though doing so may interfere with some sects' religious practices. Similarly, government would have to show that it narrowly tailored a rule prohibiting safety officers from wearing any headgear, to advance a compelling state interest, for the rule to survive a free-exercise challenge by an officer whose religious practices required wearing headgear on occasion. Congress responded by enacting federal law requiring *strict scrutiny* of neutral measures interfering with religious practices, under which the Supreme Court struck the federal seizure of a ceremonial tea containing a controlled substance, in effect requiring government to exempt importation and use of the tea for religious observance. The Supreme Court struck the federal law to the extent that it would apply to state actions, although some states have adopted similar protective statutes.

b. Establishment

The 1st Amendment's **establishment clause** prohibits government endorsement or support of either a particular religion or of religion over non-religion. Thus, for example, laws must not establish a state religion, tax and spend to support religious activities, aid one religion or all religions generally, force anyone to attend religious observances or prevent them from doing so, or punish anyone for religious beliefs or the absence of religious beliefs. Government officials must also not in their official capacity participate in religious services or permit religious officials to participate in their religious capacity in government activities. The 1st Amendment **test** for an establishment-clause challenge first identifies the law's *secular* or *sectarian* purpose, striking laws that have sectarian rather than secular purpose. The test then asks whether the law's *primary effect* advances or inhibits religion, striking laws that do so. The test then asks whether the law fosters *excessive government entanglement with religion*, striking laws that do so. A law satisfies this test only when passing all three restrictions as to purpose, effect, and entanglement.

Thus, for example, a public university that permits private groups to use university buildings when not in the university's use would satisfy the above test if including a non-discrimination clause that allowed religious use. The general-use policy would have a secular purpose, neither primarily advance nor inhibit religion, and not excessively entangle the university in religion. Similarly, if a state authorizes local school districts to reimburse parents for transporting students to school, districts would satisfy the above test if including a non-discrimination clause that allowed reimbursement for transportation to religious schools. Non-discriminatory reimbursement would advance education's secular purpose, not primarily advance or inhibit religion, and entail no entanglement. Yet a law requiring every public-school classroom to post the Ten Commandments would have the unconstitutional primary effect of advancing religion even if including a statement as to the Commandments' secular role. So, too, would a rabbi's prayer at a high-school graduation ceremony. Similarly, a law identifying specific sects the

Constitutional Law

adherents to which qualify for Sabbath work relief would excessively entangle government in religion.

2. Freedom of expression

The 1st Amendment protects freedom of **speech** including **expressive conduct**. A section below specifically addresses regulation of expressive conduct, while each of the sections below address regulation of speech including its expressive-conduct form. The constitutional standards for whether government may regulate speech including expressive conduct depend first on whether the regulation identifies specific speech *content* or, conversely, is *neutral* as to content while simply regulating speech generally. Content-based regulations must satisfy a significantly higher constitutional standard than content-neutral regulations. The constitutional standard for regulating speech then excludes certain forms of speech from any protection, identifying *unprotected speech*. The constitutional standard also differs for *commercial speech*. Special issues also arise around *public-school* regulation of student speech, *public-employer* regulation of employee speech, and individual access to other public licenses and benefits subject limited by speech restrictions. The sections below also address the doctrines of *prior restraint*, *overbreadth*, and *vagueness*.

a. Content-based regulation of protected expression

Content-based regulations are those that identify and regulate specific subjects of speech, such as criticism of public policy, or forms of speech, such as profanity. For example, an ordinance that prohibits the display within one-hundred feet of the entrance of an abortion clinic any signs for or against abortion is a content-based regulation. For another example, if the state charges an individual with an offensive-conduct crime for wearing clothing in a court proceeding that displays a profanity in express protest of the military draft, the state will have pursued a content-based regulation, particularly if wearing clothing in court with other non-profane, non-critical messages would not have resulted in a charge. Ordinarily, content-based regulations receive **strict scrutiny**, requiring the government to justify the regulation by showing that it was *necessary*, meaning **narrowly tailored**, to achieve a **compelling state interest**. Strict scrutiny routinely means that the regulation will fail. For example, a regulation that prohibits public display within five-hundred feet of an embassy, of signs critical of foreign governments, fails under strict scrutiny as a content-based regulation. The government cannot articulate a compelling interest that such a ban would be necessary to advance. Importantly, a regulation need *not* restrict a certain *viewpoint*, such as pro or con, to constitute a content-based regulation. Thus, the above regulation would remain a content-based regulation subject to strict scrutiny even if it banned the display of *any* signs, whether critical or supportive of foreign governments.

Constitutional Law

On the other hand, regulation of **unprotected speech**, addressed in a section below, does *not* receive strict scrutiny even though it involves content-based regulation. The law excepts unprotected speech from strict scrutiny for content-based regulation. **Commercial speech** also receives its own form of constitutional review, even though commercial speech also involves content-based regulation. Thus, be sure after classifying the regulation as content based to confirm whether the regulation involves unprotected or commercial speech. Apply strict scrutiny only to other content-based regulations, not to unprotected or commercial speech.

b. Content-neutral regulation of protected expression

Content-neutral regulations, also known as *time, place, and manner* restrictions, are those that the government enacts and justifies *without reference* to the speech's *message* and instead based on the location or other circumstances of the speech. For example, a city ordinance that prohibits any private signs within ten feet of the curb of a city street, justified by the intent to remove distractions and obstructions to driver vision, is a content-neutral regulation. The message on any signs, whether political, commercial, or otherwise, would be of no consequence to the regulation's form, purpose, or enforcement. The law allows content-neutral speech regulation under **intermediate scrutiny**, when *justified without reference* to *content*, serving a *significant government interest*, and leaving open *ample alternative communication channels*. Thus, in the above example, the street-side sign ban justifies itself as to any sign without respect to message, serves a significant interest in avoiding vehicle accidents from distraction and obstruction, and leaves open ample alternative communication through signs further back on properties and on buildings. Intermediate scrutiny does *not* require that the regulation use narrowly tailored, least-restrictive means.

Content-neutral regulation may be constitutional **on its face** but unconstitutional **as applied**. A content-neutral regulation is constitutional on its face when it meets the above intermediate scrutiny. Yet if the government applies a facially constitutional, content-neutral regulation in a manner that tends to regulate only certain content, then the regulation will fail under the above intermediate scrutiny as applied. For example, if city officials applied the constitutional city street-side-sign ban in the above example only against campaign signs but not against commercial or other signs, and especially only against campaign signs that oppose city millage requests, then the court may treat the content-neutral ordinance as a content-based regulation *as applied* and strike the regulation as applied, under strict scrutiny rather than intermediate scrutiny.

The *locations* to which content-neutral regulations apply, whether to *public forums, limited public forums*, or *non-public forums*, matters in applying review standards. A **public forum** is a public place, such as a city park or sidewalk, where persons may freely congregate for free expression and speech. Content-based regulation of public forums receives *strict scrutiny*, unless restricting only unprotected speech such as obscenity or

Constitutional Law

incitement to violence, while content-neutral regulation of public forums receives the lower *intermediate scrutiny*. Thus in a content-neutral regulation, a city may prohibit all public events in a city park during late-night hours both to ensure public security and reduce noise in adjacent neighborhoods, each significant government interests, if the city permits use of the park at other times as an ample alternative communication channel. Government may also require organizations to obtain a permit for forum use to achieve the significant government interest in event coordination, safety, and security, and may deny a permit to an organization that does not comply with reasonable restrictions.

Some locations that are *not* freely open to the public can become *limited public forums* if certain members of the public have frequent access there for public uses. Regulation of limited public forums must satisfy intermediate scrutiny. For example, if a public school allows outside groups to use its gymnasium for events on weekends and evenings when not in school use, then the school's regulation of that forum must be content neutral and satisfy intermediate scrutiny. The school could not, for example, forbid use by an advocacy organization or political group while allowing use by literary or artistic organizations. Yet the limited public forum of a fairground may limit distribution of religious or other materials to designated locations to ensure efficient fairground operations.

Government may revoke all use of a *designated limited public forum*, such as the school gymnasium in the above example. On the other hand, government must not do so for a *traditional public forum*, such as the city park in the above example. Traditional public forums must remain open for free speech and expression, although reasonable content-neutral time, place, and manner restrictions serving significant government interests would be permissible. The government need not allow any free speech in a **non-public forum** such as a jail, airport, or military base. Thus, for example, government may convict students for trespassing on jail property even if doing so for peaceful demonstration. Government may also enact content-neutral regulations in those non-public spaces, such as for city-bus advertising. Similarly, a law may not prohibit all solicitation of private property owners because of the public-forum nature of a street but may restrict specific activities such as picketing of individual residences because of the captive nature of the residential audience.

c. Regulation of unprotected expression

Some speech receives no constitutional protection. Speech inciting **illegal activity** such as to suborn perjury or promote an illegal conspiracy, speech threatening **public safety** such as to yell *fire* in a crowded theater, **fraudulent misrepresentation**, and speech constituting **fighting words** all have no 1st Amendment protection. **Defamation** against private figures on private issues receives no 1st Amendment protection, although defamation involving *public officials* and *public figures* requires those persons to prove the speaker's *actual malice*, and defamation on *public issues* requires proof

Constitutional Law

of fault for liability and *actual malice* for presumed or punitive damages. **Obscenity**, defined as appealing to the prurient interest, patently offensive, and having no serious political, artistic, literary, or scientific value, also receives no 1st Amendment protection. **Child pornography**, whether obscene or not, also receives no 1st Amendment protection.

d. Regulation of commercial speech

Commercial speech typically proposes a commercial transaction, such as *advertising* the sale of a product or service. More broadly, commercial speech involves communication toward a consumer audience promoting the economic interest of the individual or corporation making or authorizing the communication. The law's treatment of commercial speech first requires that one distinguish *truthful* commercial expression, which the 1st Amendment protects, from *false* or *deceptive* commercial speech, which the law does not protect. Regulations may prohibit false and deceptive advertising, while also prohibiting advertising for illegal transactions. For example, regulations may prohibit misrepresenting an energy drink as having vitamins or other therapeutic properties that the drink does not in fact have. Yet just because a lawful product, such as alcohol, caffeine, or sugar, may be harmful to certain persons in certain situations does not justify greater regulation of commercial speech. If an energy-drink company wishes to advertise truthfully that its drink gives users a rush of energy, then it may do so despite other potential adverse effects.

Regulation of commercial speech receives **intermediate scrutiny**. Government must show that it has *narrowly tailored* the law restricting commercial speech so that the law *directly advances* an *important government interest*. First Amendment review of commercial speech thus receives less rigorous review than the strict scrutiny given to the content-based regulation of non-commercial speech and instead more like the intermediate scrutiny given to content-neutral regulation. Thus, although regulation of commercial speech is content-*based* regulation in that it restricts commercial content, the law treats commercial speech more like the law treats content-*neutral* regulations.

Because commercial speech receives less protection than non-commercial speech, the 1st Amendment permits greater government regulation of commercial speech. For example, lawyer-conduct rules may not only prohibit false or misleading lawyer advertising but may also prohibit in-person solicitation of potential clients for fees, whether by the lawyer or through another. Conduct rules may also prohibit lawyers from claiming *specialist* status or *certifications* other than as the rules permit, to avoid confusing the public as to the true nature and extent of professional expertise. Yet laws may not prohibit advertising the price of prescription drugs or alcohol because the value of price information for consumers outweighs the insubstantial state interest. The law does *not* consider the value of the product or service when applying the test. The law must treat alcohol as it does

Constitutional Law

healing drugs. Laws also should not *compel* commercial speech, such as requiring mushroom growers to pay for generic mushroom advertising.

e. Regulation of, or impositions upon, public school students...

Public-school students retain certain 1st Amendment rights against interference by school officials, whose public role satisfies the *state-action* requirement. Thus, for example, a public school may not ban students from wearing arm bands in symbolic protest of war, when the arm bands do not interfere with operation of the school. Public-school facilities can also constitute *limited public forums* regulation of which must satisfy intermediate scrutiny. For example, if a public school allows student groups to use school facilities after school and on weekends, then the school's regulation of that limited public forum must be content neutral and satisfy intermediate scrutiny. The school could not, for example, forbid use by certain student groups while allowing use by other student groups based on the messages each group promoted. However, orderly operation of the school's educational program may grant school officials greater ability to restrict free-speech rights. For example, a school principal may remove from a school newspaper information that could identify and embarrass individual students on issues of divorce and teen pregnancy.

...public employment...

Public employees also retain 1st Amendment rights against interference by their public-employee supervisors, whose public role satisfies the *state-action* requirement. Thus, a public school cannot fire a teacher who publishes a letter critical of the school board, unless the letter contains knowing or reckless falsehoods or substantially interferes with the teacher's ability to do the job. Similarly, a public school could not fire a teacher solely because the teacher called a radio show to complain about a new school dress code. A public school must also not condition employment as a teacher on the teacher giving up free-speech rights or require teachers to list organizations of which they have been a member, burdening associational rights. Nor may an elected supervisor fire, transfer, or deny promotion to subordinate public employees who support an opposition candidate. For protection, though, speech must generally address a matter of *public concern*. Thus, speech critical of a president's policies, made to a co-worker in a constable's office and not reducing public confidence in the office, would receive protection. Conversely, speech on the internal operation of a prosecutor's office, or carrying out official duties, would receive no protection because not addressing matters of public concern. Similarly, circulating writings critical of office management could so damage working relationships as to receive no 1st Amendment protection.

Constitutional Law

...licenses, or benefits based upon exercise of expressive or associational rights

The 1st Amendment also protects those who receive government licenses or benefits. As indicated in a section above, the doctrine of **unconstitutional conditions** prohibits government from *conditioning* a person's receipt of a government benefit on the person's *waiver* of constitutionally protected rights, including 1st Amendment rights. For example, as indicated above, the federal government may not offer federal grant funding conditioned on the grant recipient adopting a policy beyond the scope's grant and that constituted *forced speech* violating 1st Amendment rights. Similarly, government may not deny unemployment benefits unless a religious adherent gives up religious rights not to work on a holy day. Government may, on the other hand, impose a condition *essential* to the government interest that the benefit promotes if the condition is *proportional* to the harm the benefit redresses. For example, a state may require a mall owner to permit non-disruptive petitioners to engage in free speech rights on the property because unfettered freedom to exclude certain persons is not necessary to economically valuable use of the land. On the other hand, a state cannot require a beachfront-property owner to donate without just compensation a public-access easement as a condition for a permit to build. One identifies the individual's constitutional right and government burden to measure proportionality.

f. Regulation of expressive conduct

The 1st Amendment also protects **expressive conduct** also referred to as *symbolic speech*. Expressive conduct involves behavior that communicates a message that the law would protect if the behavior were instead speech. The law applies *strict scrutiny* to the content-based regulation of expressive conduct just as it would to content-based restrictions on speech. Thus, for example, a public school may not ban students from wearing arm bands in symbolic protest of war, when the arm bands do not interfere with operation of the school, as indicated above. Similarly, neither the federal government nor state law may ban desecration of the nation's flag in symbolic protest of national policy. Laws prohibiting non-obscene public nudity as expressive conduct also typically fail, although the Supreme Court has upheld a ban on totally nude public dancing as part of a general ban on public nudity and upheld a city ordinance prohibiting nude-dancing clubs for their negative secondary effects on the community. A compelling government interest can justify other narrowly tailored restrictions on expressive conduct. For example, burning a draft card in protest of war is certainly expressive conduct, yet the government has independent and important reason in the smooth operation of conscription to require individuals to maintain, and thus not to burn, their draft card.

g. Prior restraint...

Constitutional Law

A **prior restraint** is a law or order that prohibits speech or expression *before it occurs*, in the nature of *censorship*. The 1st Amendment prohibits most prior restraints. Thus, a state law may not authorize state officials to obtain an injunction against publication of scandalous materials, through which officials suppress a newspaper that scurrilously maligns local police. A prior restraint could conceivably pass *strict scrutiny* when narrowly tailored to achieve a compelling government interest such as national security in a time of war, but even there, efforts to restrain publication of confidential government historical war analyses or even publication of bomb construction have failed. Similarly, courts may have limited authority to restrict pretrial publicity to ensure a fair trial, but broad gag orders have failed. On the other hand, a school principal may remove from a school newspaper information that could identify and embarrass individual students on issues of divorce and teen pregnancy, as indicated above.

…vagueness, and overbreadth

In addition to the above restrictions and tests, laws regulating speech must not be **overbroad** or **vague**. The doctrines of overbreadth and vagueness address concerns over discouraging or *chilling* speech. Laws that are either overbroad or vague are unconstitutional whether the speech is otherwise protected or not. A law is overbroad when it regulates *substantially more* speech or expressive conduct than the 1st Amendment permits. For example, a law intended to outlaw unprotected obscenity would be overbroad for prohibiting photographs of unclothed persons because many such photographs would not be obscene. A law is vague when a reasonable person must *guess* what speech or expressive conduct the law permits. For example, a law intended to outlaw unprotected speech inciting imminent violence would be vague for prohibiting anything that might lead to a fight because one would have to guess at whether certain words or actions might lead to a fight.

3. Freedom of the press

The 1st Amendment explicitly protects **freedom of the press** against federal laws, just as the 1st Amendment protects freedom of speech. The 14th Amendment's due-process clause incorporates free-press protection against state laws. The law does not limit press freedoms to writings only or to professional journalists only but instead extends those freedoms to speech and to anyone, professional journalist or not. The law also does not limit press freedoms to news or politics but extends those freedoms to arts, entertainment, culture, and any other subject. The law makes no distinctions among protections for various subject. The law also does not consider the press viewpoint, whether positive or negative, constructive or destructive, hateful or helpful, or good or evil.

Constitutional Law

The above rules for *strict scrutiny* of content-based regulation and prior restraints, and *intermediate scrutiny* of content-neutral regulation and commercial speech, apply generally not only to protect speech but also to press freedoms. *Prior-restraint* protections, prohibiting suppression of speech before it occurs, are of particular concern for the press because of the interest of public officials in controlling media to promote government ends. Thus as indicated above, a state law may not authorize state officials to enjoin a newspaper's anticipated publication of materials critical of local police. Government efforts to restrain publications on national-security grounds have also failed. The law also permits only limited restraints on pretrial or trial publicity, prohibiting broad gag orders. On the other hand, as also indicated above, a school principal may remove from a school newspaper information that could identify and embarrass individual students on issues of divorce and teen pregnancy.

State **defamation** laws affecting the press and others must also comply with 1ˢᵗ Amendment restrictions. A defamation plaintiff who is a *public official*, defined as one who controls a government function, or *public figure*, defined as one universally well-known or who voluntarily participates in a public issue giving the person media access, must prove the defendant speaker's *actual malice*. Actual malice means that the speaker *knew or recklessly disregarded* the speech's falsehood. A plaintiff who is instead a private figure but defamed on a *public issue* need only prove the defendant speaker's *fault* for liability, although *actual malice* for presumed or punitive damages. If the press's publication was on a public issue, which it routinely is, then the defamation plaintiff must also retain the burden of proving the speech to be false.

4. Freedom of association

The 1ˢᵗ Amendment also protects the **freedom of association** against federal interference, drawn from the Amendment's rights of free speech and to *assemble* and *petition* the government. The 14ᵗʰ Amendment's due-process clause extends that protection to state laws that interfere with associational freedoms. The law applies *strict scrutiny* to government actions that require or forbid individuals to associate with one another or with viewpoints to which they object, or otherwise burden associational interests. For example, a law or order may not bar an advocacy organization from 1ˢᵗ Amendment activity in the state or prohibit the organization from urging individuals to enforce their rights. Likewise, a court may not hold the same organization in contempt for refusing to produce a membership list absent compelling interest to do so, when production of the list would threaten private associational rights. For a recent example, a state law may not require *quasi*-public employees to pay an agency fee to a union representing the workforce when those employees object to joining or supporting the union. State law may, on the other hand, require *full* public employees to do so.

Associational rights, though, depend on activities that organize or associate *to engage in speech*. By contrast, activity that involves mere

Constitutional Law

incidental social contact does not implicate association rights. Thus, for example, a state may restrict to certain ages public admission to licensed dance halls because social dance-hall contacts are not associations to engage in speech. Even when associational rights do apply, they are not absolute. Thus, states may burden associational rights with non-discrimination provisions, such as requiring large business or civic organizations to admit women, when the organizations exercising those rights have nearly indiscriminate membership requirements instead of *intimate* or *private* relation criteria. Yet government may not apply non-discrimination provisions to interfere with an organization's ability to present its message, such as by requiring a national-heritage organization to include in a parade individuals who would present a contrary social message.

Associational rights also apply to protect against overreaching *political-patronage* systems. Thus, while a government official may choose confidential policymaking subordinates based on political participation and views, government officials may not use political-party and patronage tests for employing lower-level, non-confidential, non-policymaking subordinates. To do so would interfere with associational rights. *Independent contractors* enjoy the same associational protection when forming government contracts. Government officials must not discriminate among contractors based on political party or patronage, or other associational rights. When government requires individuals to join public-employee unions or obtain professional licenses, government cannot compel those individuals to pay dues funding political or other advocacy to which the individual objects, other than to advance the specific employee or professional interests.

Contract Law

C.   Contract Law

NOTE: Examinees are to assume that Article 2 and Revised Article 1 of the Uniform Commercial Code have been adopted and are applicable when appropriate. Approximately half of the Contracts questions on the MBE will be based on categories I and IV, and approximately half will be based on the remaining categories—II, III, V, and VI. Approximately one-fourth of the Contracts questions on the MBE will be based on provisions of the Uniform Commercial Code, Article 2 and Revised Article 1.

The Multistate Bar Examination emphasizes certain contracts topics over other topics. The two general topics of (1) contract formation and (2) performance, breach, and discharge make up **one half** of the exam's contracts questions, while the four remaining general topics of (1) contracts defenses, (2) parol evidence and interpretation, (3) remedies, and (4) third-party rights make up only the remaining one of the exam's contracts questions. The examiners further indicate that **one quarter** of the exam's contract questions address the Uniform Commercial Code's Articles 1 General Provisions and 2 Sales, thus emphasizing the **sale of goods** over other contracts for the sale of services and land. Study contract-law topics comprehensively, but be sure to understand and recall rules on the formation, performance, breach, and discharge of contracts for the sale of goods.

I.   Formation of contracts

A **contract** is an agreement the promises within which the law will enforce. A **bilateral contract** is one in which the parties exchange promise for promise, such as when the seller of a home promises to convey title to the home while the buyer promises to pay for the home at a closing to take place in sixty days. A **unilateral contract** is one in which one party performs while the other party promises to perform, such as when a restaurant serves a meal for which the diner promises to pay when the meal is over. Formation of a legally binding contract requires both **mutual assent**, addressed in the next section, and **consideration**, addressed in a following section.

A. Mutual assent

A contract ordinarily requires **mutual assent**, usually satisfied by the parties expressing their agreement orally or in writing. The courts determine **express** assent *objectively*, using the meaning that a reasonable person would give to the communication, even if one of the parties intended some other meaning *subjectively*. For example, if parties negotiate and sign an agreement for the sale of a business, the seller believing the agreement to be real but the buyer intending the agreement to be a joke, then the seller may enforce the

Contract Law

agreement if the agreement and circumstances would lead the reasonable person to believe the agreement to be real.

While contracts ordinarily require *express* mutual assent, the law will also **infer** mutual assent from words that indicate assent only indirectly or from conduct indicating assent, to find an **implied-in-fact contract**. For example, if an owner asks a youth to detail the owner's car for $100, and the youth does so without having expressed assent, then the law will infer mutual assent from the owner's request and the youth's performance. The law will also find an **implied-in-law contract** without express or inferred mutual assent, where one party must compensate the other party for a benefit to avoid **unjust enrichment**. For example, if a mechanic boards a disabled boat at the owner's invitation to fix its broken engine so that the owner can motor back to dock, the law will enforce an implied contract in the mechanic's favor to prevent the owner from unjust enrichment. Implied-in-fact contracts are actual contracts, while implied-in-law contracts are legal fictions.

1. Offer...

Most contracts arise when one party makes an offer, and the other party accepts the offer. An **offer** expresses a party's willingness to form a contract, in terms sufficiently definite and complete (questions address in a later section) that an acceptance of the offer would form an enforceable contract. To constitute an offer, the party must first express the intent to form a contract. An offer creates a power of acceptance in the offeree. For example, a web designer may offer to create a website for an online retailer for $1,500, giving the retailer the power to accept the offer by reply email. If the retailer does so, then the offer and acceptance bind the parties to performing.

By contrast, an **invitation to deal** expresses a party's willingness to make or entertain an offer. Accepting an invitation to deal does not form a contract but instead opens negotiations over offers and acceptance. For example, if the above web designer instead asked whether the retailer would be *interested in* or *consider* a website for $1,500, the designer has not yet indicated the intent to form a contract but only an invitation to deal. An offer would require the designer to express that the designer *would* create the website for the quoted price. For another example, the law generally construes **advertisements** to the public to be invitations to deal rather than offers because advertisements are typically indefinite as to quantity, credit, and other material terms. Yet an advertisement that invites specific action while clearly indicating the offeror's willingness to be bound by that action can constitute an offer, particularly where quantity is not an issue. Thus, an advertisement that states that the first customer to arrive at the used-vehicle dealer's location dressed in a tiger suit gets half off of any vehicle under $5,000 is an offer to the first customer who accepts by that performance.

Similarly, an **auction** is an invitation to deal in the auctioned item, not an offer of the item. Auction bids are offers, each bid replacing the prior bid as an offer. The auctioneer accepts a bid only when the hammer falls.

Contract Law

Until the hammer falls, the owner of the auctioned item can remove the item from the auction, while before the hammer falls, the bidder may rescind the offer. Also, when a public or private entity puts a **contract out for bid**, the entity's request for contract bids is only an invitation to deal. The contract bids are offers. The entity may accept any bid but may also refuse all bids, rescinding the invitation to deal.

Offerees form a contract by accepting the offer. However, an offeree must accept before the offer **terminates** through revocation or lapse. Offers lapse when the time for acceptance that an offer state **expires**, if the offer states an expiration time, otherwise within a reasonable time. A face-to-face offer usually expires when the face-to-face ends unless the offeror suggests thinking over the offer, indicating intent that the offer remains open for a reasonable time. Importantly, even if an offer states that it will remain open for a specific period, an offeror may ordinarily revoke the offer earlier, unless the offer takes the form of an option contract or **firm offer** discussed below. An offeree's power to accept an offer also terminates when the offeree **rejects** the offer, even if the offer has not yet expired. Invitations to deal over an offer, such as asking if the offer is firm, or inquiries to clarify the offer, such asking if the offer includes or excludes certain performance, do *not* constitute a rejection.

An offeree's power to accept an offer also terminates when the offeree makes a counteroffer. A **counteroffer** is a new offer by the party receiving the other party's offer that varies the original offer's terms. A counteroffer **rejects** the offer while creating a right in the offeror to accept the counteroffer. For example, if a painter offers a homeowner to repaint all the home's interior walls for $2,000, and the homeowner counters with an offer to pay $1,500, the homeowner rejects the painter's offer but creates in the painter a right to accept the homeowner's counteroffer.

A **qualified**, **conditional**, or **partial acceptance** is a response to an offer that varies the offer's original terms and thus qualifies as a counteroffer, terminating the offer. On the other hand, a simple inquiry whether the offeror would consider different terms is *not* a counteroffer. Thus, if in the above example, rather than countering at $1,500 the painter's $2,000 offer to paint all interior walls, the homeowner agreed to pay the $2,000 but only if the painter also painted an exterior deck, the homeowner has made a qualified, conditional, or partial acceptance altering the offer's terms, and thus has rejected the painter's offer and made a counteroffer that the painter may accept. To obtain mutual assent and form a contract, an acceptance must ordinarily be a **mirror image** of the offer. An unconditional acceptance with an invitation to deal, though, operates as an acceptance rather than a rejection or counteroffer. Thus, if the homeowner in the above example agreed to pay the painter $2,000 for the work that the painter proposed but told the painter that the homeowner hoped that the painter would give the homeowner a price break if the painter finished the work more easily than expected, then the homeowner has accepted, and the painter may enforce the agreement without giving the suggested price break.

Contract Law

As noted above, an offeror may ordinarily terminate the offeree's power of acceptance by revoking an offer, even one open for a specific period, with exceptions described below. A revocation is effective when the offeree **receives** the revocation. The **mailbox rule**, on the other hand, holds *acceptance* effective when *placed in the mail*. Thus, if the offeror mails a revocation that does not reach the offeree until after the offeree has placed an acceptance in the mail, the offeree has accomplished the acceptance, and the parties have a valid contract, even if the offeror mailed the revocation before the offeree mailed the acceptance. An offeror may also accomplish revocation indirectly, when the offeree receives information from a reliable source other than the offeror that the offeror has taken definite action inconsistent with an intent to continue the offer. The offeror's **death** or **incapacity**, or a change in circumstance frustrating the offer's object, also terminates the offeree's power of acceptance.

An **option contract** is a contract promise, ordinarily supported by consideration, to keep an offer open for a specific period. An offeror **cannot revoke the offer** during the option period. Also, a rejection of or counteroffer to an offer held open by an option contract does not terminate the offeree's power of acceptance, unless the offeror relied to the offeror's detriment on the rejection or counteroffer. The party making the counteroffer may still accept the offer, forming a contract on the offer's terms. For example, if a pilot pays an airport operator $500 for an option to buy an airplane for $20,000 within the next ten days, then the operator may not revoke the offer within those ten days, and the pilot's offer within those ten days to pay $15,000 also does not terminate the operator's power of acceptance. The pilot may still pay the operator $20,000 within ten days in exchange for the airplane. **Death** of the offeror does *not* terminate an offeree's power of acceptance of an offer held open by an option contract if the performance is not personal to the offeror, such as in the above example of the airplane sale.

Nominal consideration is normally sufficient to support an option contract open for a specific period. Thus, if the pilot in the above example only gave $10 to hold open the option, then the offer remains open for the option period. Nominal consideration is *not* sufficient, though, to support a donative promise to make a gift. An option contract can also arise if the offeree has reasonably and foreseeably **relied** on the offer before accepting it. For example, if the operator in the above example offered to sell the airplane for $20,000 at any time in the next ten days while inviting the pilot to hire a mechanic to do a complete inspection, and the pilot promptly does so at a cost of $1,000, then the firm offer is likely irrevocable for those ten days because the pilot has incurred significant expense preparing to accept or reject the firm offer within its period. The law may even have **implied** that the offer would be irrevocable for a reasonable period while the pilot completed the inspection.

The Uniform Commercial Code also makes certain offers for the **sale of goods** irrevocable *without consideration*, and if the offer states no period, then for a reasonable time, a circumstance that the Code calls a **firm offer**. The Code, though, limits *firm offers* to no longer than **three months** whether

106

Contract Law

the firm offer specifies its open time or does not specify a time and is thus open only for a reasonable time. To be a firm offer under the Code, the offeror must be a *merchant* in the goods, as the Code defines, who makes the offer in a signed writing stating that the offer is open.

While traditionally, an offeror could revoke an offer for a unilateral contract, meaning one accepted only by performing, right up until the offeree had *completed* performance, the modern rule avoids unfairness by holding that once the offeree *begins* performance, that action creates an option contract to allow the offeree to complete performance within a reasonable time. For example, if an apartment manager offers to pay a snowplow service $500 if the service removes piles of snow from the parking area, the modern rule would hold the offer open as an option contract once the service began removing snow if the service completed the removal in a reasonable time. Merely *preparing* to perform, such as the service moving a truck to the parking area, would *not* be enough to create an option contract.

...and acceptance

An offeree must accept the offeror's offer while the offer remains open for the parties to form a contract. An **acceptance** ordinarily involves the offeree's timely communication to the offeror that the offeree agrees to the terms of the offer and will perform the offeree's side of the bargain. An untimely acceptance after an offer has expired is a *counteroffer*, not an acceptance. Ordinarily, **silence is not acceptance** unless the offeree *expressly indicates so*. For example, if an artist sends a customer a painting that the artist has for sale, the customer's nonresponse alone is not acceptance. Yet if the customer had told the artist to send the customer anything that the artist wishes to sell and that if the customer doesn't return it promptly, then the artist should consider it sold, then the customer had adequately indicated that the customer's silence *is* acceptance. Also, an offeree who **exercises dominion** over goods offered for sale accepts those goods at the stated offer price. So, in the above example, if the artist had sent the customer a painting, and without expressly indicating acceptance the customer had framed the painting and hung it on the customer's wall, then the customer would owe the artist for the painting at the stated price.

An offeree accepts an offer to a **bilateral contract**, meaning one that exchanges promise for promise, by *making the return promise* that the offer requires. The offeree simply performing, starting to do what the return promise would have required, instead of promising in return, does *not* form a contract. The offeree could not in that instance recover for the begun performance if the offeror revoked the offer. For example, if a homeowner asks a pool-cleaning company if it would agree to open and clean the homeowner's pool for $500, and instead of accepting the offer the company begins to clean the pool, the homeowner's revocation of the offer once the company began would leave the company without contract remedy. However, if the offeree *completes* the performance, then the offeree will ordinarily be able to compel the offeror's return performance, in this instance to pay for the pool cleaning.

Acceptance is usually by words but can be by **communicative actions** such as a nod of the head. **Circumstances** combined with actions may also communicate acceptance when equivalent to the offeree's communication of affirmative non-verbal acceptance. So, in the above example, if in response to the homeowner's offer the pool-cleaning company began immediately to clean the pool in front of the homeowner, then the company's action would communicate acceptance. An offeree, though, must usually **communicate acceptance** to the offeror, unless the offeror expressly **waives** acceptance. For example, if an insurer offered to insure a nonprofit organization and, in the offer, indicated that the nonprofit's board approval would constitute acceptance, then when the board approved, the nonprofit would have accepted the offer, and the insurer could not subsequently revoke even if not yet having heard of the approval and acceptance.

While offers to a bilateral contract typically require the offeree's return promise for acceptance, offers to **unilateral contracts** typically require the offeree's **performance** rather than promise. The offeree's promise to perform does not accept an offer of a unilateral contract. Only performance suffices to accept. Thus, if in the above example the insurer's offer instead indicated that the nonprofit's acceptance could only be by the nonprofit paying for the insurance electronically or in person, then the nonprofit's promise to pay would not accept the offer and would not form a contract. An offeree, who accepts a unilateral contract by performing, must within a reasonable time **notify** the offeror that the offeree has completed performance, if the offeree has reason to know that the offeror would not otherwise be aware of the offeree's performance, unless the offeror waives notice, knows that the offeror has completed, or should know within a reasonable time. If, for example, a business offered a snowplowing service $100 for each plowing of the business's parking lot, but the service waited six months to notify the business that the service had plowed the lot four times, then the business would no longer owe the contract obligation of payment unless the business actually knew or should have known. A reasonable effort to notify timely is sufficient if timely notice fails.

Sometimes, performance occurs by one having **no knowledge** of the offer for a unilateral contract. In such cases, *no contract forms* except in cases of a governmental entity's offer to pay a reward. Otherwise, the one completing performance must know of the offer. Thus, in the above example, if the snowplowing service gratuitously plowed the business's parking lot without knowing of the business's offer of a unilateral contract, then the business would have no obligation to pay if the service later learned of the offer and demanded payment. An offeree who responds to an offer that is **unclear** whether it requires a return promise (to form a bilateral contract) or instead a performance (to form a unilateral contract) may accept *either by promise or performance*. Likewise, the Uniform Commercial Code provides for contracts for the sale of goods that a party may accept an offer either by promise or performance *unless the offer unambiguously states otherwise*, if promise or performance is reasonable under the offer's circumstances. For example, if a manufacturer offers to buy supplies on prompt shipment, then the supplier may either promise to ship or actually ship the supplies, either promise or performance constituting acceptance. If the supplier ships **nonconforming goods** as its performance, then the supplier has accepted, formed a contract, and breached the contract. If, though, the supplier identifies the nonconforming goods as an **accommodation**, then the supplier has not formed or breached a contract but instead has counteroffered.

As indicated above, under the **mailbox rule**, an acceptance is effective on its dispatch, when placed in the mailbox, before the offeror receives the acceptance. **Option contracts** are an exception, where acceptance of the offer is effective only on the offeror's *receipt* of the offeree's acceptance. To be effective on dispatch under the mailbox rule, the acceptance must be timely, in *reasonable manner*, and *consistent with the offer* if the offer restricts the manner of acceptance. An acceptance is reasonable if by the same means, such as mail, email, fax, or delivery, as the offer, if the offer does not restrict the acceptance to other means. Thus, an offeree must accept only by mail an offer that specifies only mail acceptance, even if the offer was by email or fax. If the means of acceptance is unreasonable, then the mailbox rule does not apply, and an intervening revocation of the offer is effective, terminating the offer notwithstanding the unreasonable means of accepting. Yet if the unreasonable means of accepting nonetheless reaches the offeror before the offer expires or the offeror revokes it, then the acceptance is effective.

Because *rejection* or *counteroffer* is effective only on *receipt*, if the offeree dispatches a reasonable acceptance, the contract forms, and the offeree's subsequent rejection or counteroffer is ineffective even if the offeror receives the rejection or counteroffer before the acceptance, unless the offeror has **relied** to the offeror's detriment on the rejection or counteroffer. For example, if a purchaser offers to buy supplies from a supplier, and the supplier mails an acceptance of the offer but then emails a rejection, and the purchaser buys the supplies elsewhere relying on the emailed rejection, the mailed acceptance is ineffective to form a contract even though it would have formed a contract under the mailbox rule. On the other hand, if an offeree first mails a rejection or counteroffer but then, before the offeror has received the rejection or counteroffer, mails an acceptance, the mailbox rule does *not* apply, and whichever response the offeror receives first is effective.

2. Indefiniteness or absence of terms

Beyond bargained mutual assent through offer and acceptance with consideration, to be enforceable a contract must also be sufficiently **definite** and **complete**. An agreement the terms of which are so indefinite, or an agreement missing such material terms, as to leave the parties and court without reliable guide for measuring performance, is unenforceable. Similarly, an agreement that allows one party to **determine a material term** at a later date is ordinarily incomplete and unenforceable, as a mere

Contract Law

agreement to agree. Yet if the contract requires the parties to determine the term according to an objective measure, then the court may find the contract complete.

Thus, while **price** is usually a material term, the court may under the Uniform Commercial Code and common-law rule supply the price *if* the parties clearly intended a contract *and* supplied an objective measure for determining price. For example, a toy retailer and distributor who leave to the distributor the right to determine the price of a seasonal toy *according to the market price at season open* likely have a sufficiently complete contract, particularly if the market provides sufficiently objective and definite measures of price at season open. By contrast, **time of performance** is *not* usually a material term unless the parties or circumstances otherwise indicate because the court can typically construe a *reasonable time*, as the Uniform Commercial Code also provides. Other minor terms, such as the grade or color of a good, are also often non-material terms or terms that the court can construe from other communications or from the circumstances. Also, **partial performance** of an incomplete agreement can also supply missing terms, particularly if the parties do not dispute the partial performance that supplies the intended but missing terms.

The question of an agreement's definiteness and completeness also applies to offers. To be sufficiently definite and complete to constitute an offer, the party's expression must generally include at least the **subject matter**, **quantity**, and **price** terms. For example, if a local marina operator says that he will sell to a boater a *suitable* boat for a *fair price*, the operator has not sufficiently described the subject matter or price. By contrast, if the operator says that he will sell the boater a twelve-foot skiff for $2,500, then the operator has sufficiently described the subject matter and price to have made an offer. With the intent to contract and presence of fundamental terms, an expression is sufficient to constitute an offer even if missing other terms. For example, if the above offer permitted the boater to buy on regular payments but did not specify the payments, a court could supply those missing terms to find a sufficiently definite offer.

A **requirements contract**, under which a party promises to buy from a specific seller all of a good or service that the party's business or activity requires, is ordinarily enforceable without the quantity term. Likewise, an **output contract**, under which a party promises to sell to a specific buyer all of a good or service that the party's business produces, is ordinarily enforceable without the quantity term. In each instance, the buyer or seller has limited their options to buy from or sell to only a specific party, supplying the necessary consideration. The Uniform Commercial Code requires that the promisor in a requirements or output contract act in good faith according to commercial standards in that business, including that the requirement or output not be disproportionate to any estimates or to previous requirement or output. Going out of business to avoid the obligation is a breach in such contracts, while going out of business for other reasons is not a breach.

3. Implied-in-fact contract

Contract Law

In some instances, the law will find an **implied-in-fact contract** when the parties' agreement does not supply sufficiently definite terms. The agreement and its circumstances must, though, provide sufficient factual context for the court to infer the missing terms. A court must not supply its own terms. For example, a decorator may contract to decorate a new hotel's lobby for $25,000. While the contract may not supply any other detail, a court would likely construe that the decorator must use **best efforts** to do so, consistent with the decorator's profession and the hotel's trade. Yet if the parties left out the price term, and the factual context suggested no basis for a price, then the court would not supply the price, and the contract would remain fatally incomplete.

4. "Pre-contract" obligations based on reliance

Parties to a contract negotiation sometimes **rely** on the negotiations to *change their position*, anticipating that the parties will form a contract. For example, a tradesperson may turn down other jobs or may order tools or equipment for a job for which the tradesperson is negotiating with a builder. Parties ordinarily *bear their own costs or losses* from changes in anticipation of a contract, when contract negotiations break down and no contract results. Yet the law recognizes some grounds for **pre-contractual obligations**. A party may be liable for the other party's reliance costs if the party induced reliance through **misrepresentation** or made **specific promises** inviting reliance during negotiations. For example, if the builder in the above example specifically told the tradesperson that the builder would pay for tools and equipment that the tradesperson purchased anticipating the job, the builder would owe the tradesperson **pre-contract reliance damages** if the tradesperson did so but the parties didn't ultimately form a contract for the job. A party is also liable for pre-contract reliance damages if the party **benefited** from the other party's reliance, while knowing of and accepting the benefit. Thus, in the above example, if the tradesperson prepared the job site for the work, but the builder hired a different tradesperson at a lower cost relying on the first tradesperson's preparations, then the first tradesperson could recover those reliance losses. The law recognizes these **promissory estoppel** and **detrimental reliance** theories when the reliance is *reasonable, foreseeable*, and *detrimental*, and enforcement is necessary to *avoid injustice*. The law limits recovery to restoring the relying party to the pre-reliance position.

B. Consideration

Consideration is the bargained-for exchange of promises or performances having value the law recognizes. An exchange is bargained-for if each party's promise or performance induces the other's promise or performance. Accordingly, one's promise or performance of something having only nominal value, such as promising to pay ten dollars for a forty-

Contract Law

thousand-dollar vehicle, will ordinarily not be a bargained-for exchange. Nominal consideration is sufficient only to support an **option contract** to hold an offer open for a specific time or a **guarantee** to pay the debt of another. A promise or performance usually has value the law recognizes because the law does not normally concern itself with the adequacy or fairness of consensual exchange. However, *fungible exchanges* in which the parties exchange exactly the same thing are *not* consideration because lacking in value to induce exchange. Promises of love and affection also lack the requisite value.

Most contracts require both an *agreement* between the parties, meaning *mutual assent* to the same terms, and also *consideration*. If one party to an agreement fails to exchange consideration for the other party's promise, the party failing to exchange consideration cannot enforce the promise against the party making the promise. For example, when a handyman promises to power wash a house in exchange for the owner's promise to pay him $200, the parties have each given consideration in the form of exchanged promises, and either party may enforce the other's contractual promise. Exchanging a promise for an act also constitutes consideration. For example, in the above example, if the owner offers to pay the handyman $200 *if* the handyman power washes the house, and then the handyman does so, then the exchange of the owner's promise for the handyman's act constitutes consideration for an enforceable contract.

Certain types of bargained-for exchanges deserve specific mention. For example, **conditional promises** are those in which a party promises to perform an act only if the condition occurs. For example, if an entrepreneur promises a friend that the entrepreneur will invest in the friend's franchise if a certain national franchisor offers the friend a franchise, then the friend may enforce the entrepreneur's promise when the condition occurs, even though the condition may never have occurred. Conditional promises are almost always enforceable even when one party controls the condition, such as the friend deciding to buy a franchise in the above example. Similarly, **alternative promises**, in which the promisor gets to choose which consideration to perform, are valid as long as all choices have value that the law recognizes. Thus, a contractor who promises to either build a coach's deck or paint the coach's garage in exchange for the coach teaching the contractor's child to play baseball, has formed a contract that the coach may enforce. Multiple promises provide consideration if at least one of the promised performances has value the law recognizes.

As indicated above, the Uniform Commercial Code requires **no consideration** to hold open a **firm offer** to buy or sell goods for the offer's specific time. Courts will also find consideration improper when the promise is to forbear or relinquish an **unjust legal claim** such as not to file a frivolous lawsuit. The claim's validity must be reasonable, or the promisor must believe in good faith that the claim is reasonable. The next section addresses other consideration promises around **illusory promises**.

1. Bargain and exchange...

Contract Law

As discussed above, the concept of **bargain** forms the basis for requiring an exchange of **consideration**. To *bargain* is to negotiate the terms of an exchange to the point of agreement. Bargain constituting consideration for an enforceable contract may include not only *promises* of affirmative acts or *performing* the acts themselves, as above, but also promises to **refrain** from acting or actual **forbearance** from acting, in ways that the law entitles the promisor to act. For example, a landowner ordinarily has the legal right to exclude others from the land, even to sue entrants in trespass. Yet a landowner may promise a neighbor to forgo that right and agree to permit the neighbor to enter the land to park a trailer on it, in exchange for the neighbor's agreement to pay the landowner $500. The parties' bargain, relying on the landowner's forbearance and the neighbor's promise, constitutes an enforceable contract, if the parties have satisfied any other requirements such as the statute of frauds.

Some bargains do not constitute consideration for an enforceable contract because the bargain is only **illusory**. An illusory bargain is one in which the agreement **binds only one party** and not the other. Illusory bargains include agreements in which one party promises to perform but the other party promises to perform **only if the party wants to do so**. For example, if a furniture maker promises to buy all of the steel that it needs from a certain supplier, and the supplier promises to sell all of the steel *the supplier wants to sell* to the furniture maker, the bargain is illusory because it binds only the furniture maker and not the supplier to perform. Illusory bargains also include agreements in which one party promises to perform but the other party may terminate performance at will without notice. For example, if the supplier in the above example instead promised to sell all the steel that the furniture maker required but reserved to the supplier the right to cancel the contract at any time without notice, then the bargain would still be illusory because the supplier had not **limited its future options**. The Uniform Commercial Code requires reasonable notice before at-will termination and holds invalid, contracts without notice where enforcement would be unconscionable. A following section describes another kind of unenforceable agreement lacking the bargain aspect because of **preexisting duties**.

...and substitutes for bargain: "moral obligation"...

Bargain and consideration are key concepts for identifying enforceable contracts. Generally, **donative promises** in the nature of a gift are unenforceable for lack of consideration. For example, if a rich aunt promises to buy her nephew a sports car but later refuses, the nephew has no contract to enforce, not having given the aunt consideration in exchange for her promise. **Conditional donative promises** are also not enforceable, particularly when the condition is part of the gift. So, for example, if the rich aunt promised to give her nephew a sports car if he would go to the dealership to select it, and the nephew went to the dealership, the nephew would still have no enforceable contract because the nephew's performance was merely

Contract Law

an effort to carry out the gift. Yet if the parties to the agreement construe the condition as a bargain, then the agreement is no longer an unenforceable donative promise but instead an enforceable contract. So, for example, if the rich aunt promised her nephew a sports car if he kept out of trouble and neither smoked nor drank until he graduated from high school, and the nephew performed those bargained obligations, then the nephew would have an enforceable contract.

Other promises are enforceable even without bargained-for consideration, such as certain promises given in exchange for **moral consideration**, also called **past consideration** giving rise to moral obligation. For example, if a neighbor graciously mows a homeowner's expansive lawn all summer while the homeowner recuperates from a serious illness, and the homeowner subsequently promises to pay the neighbor for the labor and gas, the modern view makes the promise enforceable even though the neighbor's work was donative and the homeowner's promise motivated only by past benefit rather than bargain. The modern rule makes donative promises supported by moral consideration enforceable *if the benefit flowed to the promisor rather than to a third party.* So, for example, while the neighbor could enforce the above promise of the homeowner to pay for the lawn mowing the benefit from which flowed to the homeowner, if the neighbor also mowed another nearby neighbor's lawn for which the homeowner also promised to pay, the mowing neighbor could not enforce that other promise the benefit from which flowed not to the promising homeowner but to the nearby neighbor.

Traditionally, donative promises were enforceable only when made to pay a **past debt** barred by the **limitations period** or **bankruptcy**, or to perform a voidable obligation such as one made when still a minor (the latter rule treated in a following section). For example, if a consumer failed to pay credit card debt in the amount of $5,000, but the limitations period had run on the debt barring its enforcement, the credit-card company could nonetheless enforce the $5,000 obligation if the consumer renewed the promise, saying that the consumer would in fact pay it. Similarly, if the consumer had discharged the credit-card debt in bankruptcy, the credit-card company could nonetheless enforce the consumer's subsequent promise to pay the discharged debt. The statute of frauds in most jurisdictions requires a signed writing to renew a past debt, although not an obligation discharged in bankruptcy.

...reliance, and statutory substitutes

Another form of donative promise that a party may enforce even without bargained-for consideration involves a promisee's **reliance** on the promisor's promise. For example, a mentor may tell a protégé to go buy a new suit for which the mentor will pay. Even though the protégé has not bargained for a new suit, if the protégé relies on the mentor's promise to pay for a new suit and does so, then the protégé may enforce the mentor's promise. Other promises that can be enforceable even without bargained-for

Contract Law

consideration include **waiver of non-material conditions** of a bargain and promises made under special **statutory substitutes** such as promises **under seal**.

2. Modification of contracts: preexisting duties

Another form of unenforceable agreement missing the bargain aspect is an agreement in which one party promises only to do that which the *law already obligates the party to do*. The **preexisting-duty rule** holds three kinds of promises are not consideration to make the other party's promise enforceable. When a public official promises to do that which **public duty** already obligates the official to do, the parties have not bargained for the promise, which thus does not serve as consideration for the other party's promise. For example, if a firefighter, whose public duty already includes serving a district that covers a factory, promises the factory owner to watch the factory in exchange for $1,000, then the firefighter did not bargain for the $1,000 because of the public duty already owed. On the other hand, if the firefighter was off duty and agreed to inspect a factory for fire hazards, particularly a factory outside of the firefighter's district, then the firefighter would have bargained for the $1,000, and the firefighter could enforce the factory owner's promise.

Another kind of promise that does not amount to consideration is a party's promise to perform something that **law already requires** the person to perform. For example, if a passenger in a driver's car promises to pay the driver $50 in exchange for the driver's promise to drive with reasonable care, the driver cannot enforce the passenger's promise because the driver exchanged no consideration. The driver had a preexisting duty to drive with reasonable care. A third kind of agreement that the preexisting-duty rule holds to lack consideration is a promise to perform a **preexisting contractual duty**. For example, if a civil engineer agrees with a landowner to build a bridge over a creek on the land in exchange for $10,000, but then the engineer makes a subsequent agreement that the landowner will pay $15,000 for the same work, the bargain is illusory and unenforceable because the first agreement had already obligated the engineer to perform the same work. However, if the **obligation changes**, even in relatively small degrees, then the change serves as the new bargain for an enforceable new contract. So, for example, if the landowner requests a higher or longer bridge and agrees to pay the higher sum for it, the engineer's agreement to the change constitutes bargained performance. The preexisting-duty rule, though, does not apply if the obligor owes the original promise to *someone other than the new promisor*. Thus, if a performer contracts with a homeowner to perform a backyard concert, and then the neighbor promises to pay the performer an extra $500 if the performer goes through with the concert, the performer can enforce the neighbor's agreement.

Bargain also arises when the obligor had a **defense** to the original contract that the obligor waives or loses in the new agreement. For example, if parties contract orally for the sale of an interest in land, where the statute

Contract Law

of frauds would hold the agreement unenforceable, and then subsequently agree in writing to a higher price for the same interest, then the new bargain overcoming the statute-of-frauds defense satisfies the bargain requirement for an enforceable contract. A new agreement accommodating an **unanticipated change in circumstances** can also satisfy the new-bargain requirement. For example, if a farmer agrees to seed a landowner's field in the fall for $5,000, but torrential fall rains make the seeding impossible, the parties may reach a new and enforceable bargain for spring seeding at an adjusted price of $7,500. The Uniform Commercial Code also makes good-faith modifications of contracts for the **sale of goods** enforceable *without consideration*. Do not apply the legal-duty rule to the sale of goods. In the sale of goods, watch only for bad-faith, unfair, and inequitable modifications.

3. Compromise and settlement of claims

The compromise and settlement of claims involve other contract rules. An **accord** is an agreement to replace an old, disputed contract obligation with a new contract obligation. For example, if homebuyers had a contract for a builder to construct a home on a certain lot that the builder was refusing to perform, the homebuyers and builder could substitute a new agreement for the builder to build the home on a different lot where the builder was willing to perform. Either side could then perform or enforce the new accord. An accord is **executory** until performed. An **executory accord** that a promisor fails to perform enables the non-breaching party to enforce either the accord *or* the original obligation unless the parties' executory accord indicated the intent to replace the original obligation, in which case the non-breaching party could only enforce the substitute obligation. On the other hand, performance of an accord constitutes **satisfaction** of the entire obligation. In other words, **accord and satisfaction** is a defense to an action on the original obligation.

II.   Defenses to enforceability

Defenses to enforcement presume that the parties have formed a contract. A party seeking to enforce a contract must plead the contract, produce evidence of the contract, and at trial prove its existence and terms by a preponderance of the evidence. On the other hand, a party raising defenses to a contract has the same burdens of pleading those defenses, producing evidence of them, and proving them at trial by a preponderance of the evidence. Consider each of the following defenses.

A. Incapacity to contract

A party must have the **capacity** to contract. Capacity includes being of the **age of majority**, typically eighteen years of age. When a minor contracts, the other party cannot enforce the minor's promise because the minor lacked capacity. By contrast, the minor holds a **voidable** contract that

Contract Law

the minor *may* enforce if the minor wishes to do so. A voidable contract thus forms an exception to the usual mutuality requirement. For example, if a sixteen year old promised to pay $2,500 for a used car, the seller could not enforce the voidable obligation against the minor, even though the minor could enforce the obligation against the seller. Yet once the minor turned the age of majority, the promise would bind the now-adult buyer if the buyer affirmed the formerly voidable promise, although if the affirmance was for a lower price, such as $2,000, then the seller could only enforce that lower obligation.

B. Duress

A party whom the other party *threatened into a contract* may void the contract for **duress**. The clearest form of duress involves threats to do violence to the party or the party's acquaintance if the party does not accept and perform the contract. Threats to physically damage the party's property also constitute duress, as can threats to harm the party's economic wellbeing by unlawful or improper means, particularly if the party cannot avoid the harm by any means other than entering into the contract. While threats of criminal or other unlawful action can constitute duress, so can threats to do acts outside of the moral or other customary bounds of a business or profession, such as to defame, humiliate, or embarrass.

C. Undue influence

A party to a contract who shows that the other party induced the contract through **undue influence** may void the contract. Undue influence, often confused with *duress*, involves one party deliberately exercising such control over another whom the party knows to be subject to control, as to deprive that other of **free will** in forming the contract. A party claiming undue influence must prove the weakness or **susceptibility**, the other party's opportunity, and the other party's deliberate actions unfairly playing on that susceptibility, resulting in the contract. Undue influence typically occurs in *special relationships*. For example, if a caretaker for an elderly, socially isolated, and mentally weak property owner falsely tells the owner that the owner's adult children do not care for the owner, to induce the owner into selling the caretaker property for a fraction of the property's fair-market value, then the caretaker has unduly influenced the sale contracts, which the owner could then void.

D. Mistake, misunderstanding

The effect of **mistake** or **misunderstanding** on contract formation and enforcement depends on *classifying* the event. A **mutual mistake** is one in which both parties misperceive *in the same way* the actual terms and surrounding circumstances of the contract. In mutual mistake, the party who suffers the harm from mistake may **void** the contract, unless the contract did assigned risk of mistake to that party. For example, if parties contract for the sale of livestock of rare value, not knowing that the livestock had already died, then the parties' mutual mistake will enable the buyer, who would have paid for a dead animal, to void the contract. By contrast, if the parties knew that the animal was sick, and the buyer accepted that risk in forming the contract anyway, and the animal then died, the buyer could *not* void the contract. Contracts under mutual mistake are **voidable**, not void. The party suffering the loss from the mistake may enforce the agreement if that party so chooses. If on the other hand parties merely record their sound oral agreement in a **mistaken writing**, then the harmed party's remedy is to reform the writing rather than void the contract.

A **unilateral mistake** involves a contract in which only *one* party misperceives the actual terms or surrounding circumstances of the contract. In unilateral mistake, the contract ordinarily *remains enforceable*, meaning that the party who made the mistake bears the loss flowing from the mistake. For example, if a contractor submits a bid to an owner on a project that the contractor mistakenly believes to be just like the prior job that the contractor performed, on which the contractor profited, and the owner accepts the bid, the owner may enforce the contract even if the contractor's mistake means that the contractor incurs such additional costs as to lose on the contract. On the other hand, if a party *knows* or *should have known* that the other party has made a mistake, then the mistaken party may void the contract. Thus, in the above example, if the contractor's bid was a quarter of the other bids on the job, from which the owner knew or should have known of the contractor's mistake, then the contractor could void the contract. Some jurisdictions allow the mistaken party to void the contract even when the other party did not know nor should have known, if the other party had not yet relied on the contract.

Misunderstanding differs from *mistake* in that while mistake involves misperceptions of actual circumstances, misunderstanding involves disagreement over what the parties intended from terms susceptible of different, *equally reasonable meanings*. In cases of misunderstanding, the parties cannot enforce the agreement as a contract because they have not mutually assented to the terms. For example, a land-sale contract may call for the sale of land in a city of a certain name, with the seller reasonably intending a city of that name in one state while the buyer equally reasonably intends a city of that name in another state. Neither party can enforce the agreement. On the other hand, if one party's interpretation is more reasonable than the other party's interpretation, then the more reasonable interpretation prevails, and the parties have formed an enforceable contract. Thus, in the above example, if the buyer and seller both resided in the same state near the land that the seller intended, and the buyer's intended land was in a distant state to which seller and buyer had no plain connection, then the contract would be enforceable as to the seller's far-more-reasonable intention.

E. Fraud, misrepresentation, and nondisclosure

Contract Law

Fraud, also known as **misrepresentation**, in a contract's inducement makes the contract *voidable* at the election of the party so wrongly induced. Fraud involves a contracting party knowingly making a false representation of material fact to induce the other party's justifiable reliance to the other party's detriment in entering into the contract. For example, the seller of a used boat in dry dock who misrepresents the boat as seaworthy, knowing instead that the boat has severe leaks that substantially diminish the boat's value, has fraudulently induced the buyer into contracting, so that the buyer may void the contract on discovery of the fraud. While fraud's essence is the scheme, scam, or swindle, simple deliberate exaggerations or other misrepresentations of material terms can constitute fraud if the misstatements are of **objective, verifiable, measurable fact** rather than merely *opinion*, *predictions*, or *puffing*. Thus, if the seller in the above example merely asserted that the boat was a *good old boat*, the assertions would likely *not* be verifiably false and the contract not voidable.

The law may permit a party to rescind a contract when the other party **negligently** or even **innocently** misrepresents a material fact about which the representing party did *not* know. Those cases tend, though, to require that the parties have some *special relationship* requiring the representing party to investigate and disclose, such as when a statute requires that the party do so. Otherwise, the general **buyer beware** rule is that each party to a contract must do its own *due diligence*. For example, a home seller could enforce the home-sale contract even if carelessly misrepresenting the home as having no roof leaks, if the buyer had equal opportunity to inspect for and discover leaks. Yet if a statute required the seller to reasonably investigate and accurately disclose, and the buyer justifiably relied on the seller's careless misrepresentation, then the buyer could void the contract. Simple **omissions to disclose** are usually not actionable. Fraud typically requires an *affirmative misrepresentation.* Yet if a party has a statutory or fiduciary relationship requiring disclosure, or the party **actively conceals** conditions so that the other party cannot discover them, then the wronged party may void the contract.

F. Illegality, unconscionability, and public policy

An **illegal** contract is one the *object* of which is illegal, such as an agreement to rob a bank or counterfeit goods where the performance itself breaks the law, or one the *consideration* for which is illegal, such as a contract to provide illegal drugs to a tradesperson in exchange for the tradesperson's home-renovation work. Distinguish *illegal* contracts from contracts involving the *incapacity* to contract, such as with minors. While contracts involving incapacity to contract are merely *voidable* by the incapacitated party, and thus also *enforceable* by the incapacitated party at that party's election, illegal contracts are *void*, meaning that *neither* party may enforce the obligation.

An **unconscionable** contract is one so outrageous or immoral that it shocks the conscience. Courts measure unconscionability by factors

Contract Law

including the **equity** or **fairness** of the exchange, the relative **ability** of either party **to accept or reject** the exchange, relative **resources, information,** and **sophistication** of the parties. For example, if a parent desperately needs to buy medicine for a very sick child, and a wealthy neighbor offers to provide the funds in exchange for labor worth five times the funds, then a court may determine that the bargain is so nearly extortionate as to be immoral and unconscionable.

A contract against **public policy** is one that, while advantageous to one of the parties, the law refuses to enforce to protect the other party or because against the public interest. For instance, the law refuses to enforce contracts that promote conduct already against state or federal law, such as to sell contraband prescription drugs, and contracts that offend public morals, such as to pay for sexual acts. Employment agreements that prohibit employees from organizing into a labor union, or that waive worker's compensation rights or forbid medical leave, are other examples of contracts against public policy.

G. Statute of frauds

Parties may in general enforce promises in **oral agreements**. Yet the **statute of frauds** requires that for a party to enforce certain promises, the other party must have **signed a writing** memorializing the disputed promises. Contracts within the statute of frauds include contracts for the sale of an **interest in land** or for **goods for $500** or more, contracts in consideration of **marriage**, contracts to **guarantee** another's debt, also known as *suretyships*, and contracts that one **cannot perform within one year. Part performance** of a contract relating to an interest in land takes the contract out of the statute. Thus, if the seller conveys title to the buyer, performing the seller's side of the contract, the seller may compel the buyer to pay. Likewise, if the buyer takes possession and improves the land, the buyer may compel the seller to convey title. Part performance of a contract for the sale of goods takes the contract out of the statute but only *to the extent of the part performance*. Thus, the seller may compel the buyer to pay for goods already delivered and accepted, whereas the buyer may compel shipment of goods for which the buyer made and seller accepted payment. Also, in contracts for the sale of goods for $500 or more, the Uniform Commercial Code provides exceptions to the statute of frauds when the non-breaching party sends a signed written confirmation of an oral agreement, and the breaching party receives it but does not object to it within ten days.

Contracts in consideration of marriage are not contracts *to* marry, which are void as against public policy, but contracts to do certain things *when* the parties marry, such as to convey certain property or grant certain rights. As to contracts that the parties cannot perform within one year, the contract falls outside the statute if the parties have *any possibility* of completing the performance within one year. Thus, if a party promises to care for another's pet parrot for the rest of its life in exchange for $1,000, the parties may enforce the contract because the parrot could die within one year.

Contract Law

Also, if the parties fully perform a contract over its necessary span of more than one year, full performance removes the contract from the statute and enables enforcement. While suretyship contracts between the guarantor and creditor must be in a signed writing, a guarantor who promises the debtor to back up the debtor's debt need not have signed a writing for the *debtor* to enforce the promise. Similarly, if the guarantor's **main purpose** in guaranteeing a debt is for the guarantor's *own benefit*, then the creditor may enforce the oral promise.

Some oral agreements are not enforceable even when they fall outside the statute of frauds. Parties sometimes agree orally intending that they write and sign a contract memorializing their oral terms. Setting aside the question of the statute of frauds, an oral agreement that the parties *intend to reduce to writing* is nonetheless enforceable, *if* the parties intended their oral agreement to form a contract. By contrast, if the parties agreed orally that their agreement would be a contract *only if* written and signed, then the oral agreement is *not* a contract. In disputed cases, the courts look to whether parties typically write down that kind of contract, whether the parties' oral agreement was general or detailed, and the value of the contract, to help determine whether the parties intended an oral contract or a contract only once written and signed.

III. Parol evidence and interpretation

The **parol evidence rule** prohibits a party to a contract dispute from using evidence from *outside of the written contract* to modify or contradict those written contract terms. Only if the written terms are *unclear* as to their meaning may a party introduce evidence extrinsic to the contract, such as testimony of oral statements made in the negotiation of the contract that clarify the unclear terms. A party may also use parol evidence, meaning evidence from outside the written contract, to supply missing terms that are not so material and substantial as to make the agreement fail as a contract for lack of mutual assent. In no case, though, is parol evidence admissible to vary the plain language of the written terms.

When the terms of an offer or acceptance are so ambiguous that the parties disagree whether they have formed a contract, the court gives an ambiguous term its **objective** interpretation. The court construes the term to mean what a reasonable person would understand it to mean if in the party's position. For example, if an offeree responds "that's fine" to an offer under circumstances where the reasonable person would construe the statement as acceptance, then a contract forms. No contract forms, however, if construing the statement to mean acceptance or *not* to mean acceptance are **equally reasonable** because of some reasonable confusion over terms. For example, if a seller offers shipment by first rail, reasonably believing that first rail would be the next day, but the buyer accepts equally reasonably believing that first rail is the same day, because of an anomaly in published rail schedules, then the parties have not mutually assented as to the shipment term and cannot enforce either term.

Contract Law

If, however, a party knows that the other party attaches a **specific meaning** to an expression, and the party attaching that specific meaning does not know that the meaning differs from the meaning that the first party would ordinarily give it, then the contract forms around that specific meaning. A party may introduce **extrinsic evidence**, meaning evidence outside of the face of the contract such as the parties' oral statements in negotiations or the circumstances of the negotiation, to prove that the parties understood a certain meaning to an ambiguous term.

IV. Performance, breach, and discharge

The Multistate Bar Examination devotes one half of the contracts questions to contract formation, addressed in the first section of this contracts outline, and also this section on performance, breach, and discharge. Devote your studies to this section, just as you have to the subject of contract formation. **Performance** issues arise around **conditions** that may relieve a party from performing, the **impracticability** of performing, **discharge** of contractual performance, **warranties** of performance, and finally partial and substantial **breach** including **anticipatory repudiation**. First consider conditions of performance.

A. Conditions

Contracts do not always require prompt performance. In some cases, a contract expressly excuses performance until events satisfy a **condition** that only then triggers the obligation to perform. For example, the purchaser of a home may contract with a builder to renovate the home if the home's purchase closes. If the purchase does not close, then the buyer would have no obligation to pay the builder for work that the builder could not perform. In other cases, the circumstances **imply** a condition to performance that the contract does not expressly state. For example, a business owner may form a contract with an equipment-leasing company for the company to repair the owner's imaging device on any malfunction within the next two years. The contract implies the condition that the owner notifies the company of any malfunction so that the company can make the repair. If the owner fails to notify the company, then the company has no obligation to perform repairs about which it has no knowledge of the need.

1. Express

The law recognizes two forms of **express condition**. The first form, a **condition precedent**, excuses a party from performing until the condition occurs. The above example of the home buyer contracting for the builder's renovation only if the home-sale closes is an example of a condition precedent. The second form, a **condition subsequent**, excuses a party from *continuing to perform* after having begun performance, once the condition occurs. For example, a minor-league baseball player may sign a one-year contract to perform for the minor-league team but with the express condition that a call-up to the major leagues relieves the player from continuing the minor-league performance. So, with conditions *precedent*, the party has no duty to begin performance until the condition occurs, whereas with conditions *subsequent*, the condition's occurrence relieves the party from continuing to perform once the condition occurs. A party enforcing a contract has the duty to prove any conditions precedent that would trigger performance, while a party resisting enforcement has the duty to prove any conditions subsequent that would relieve continued performance.

Some contracts include a party's **satisfaction** as a condition precedent to the party's performance. For example, if a caterer contracts to cater a dinner party for $1,000 payable only on the host's satisfaction, then the host's satisfaction is a condition precedent to the host's obligation to pay. If the dinner does not satisfy the host, then the host does not pay. Satisfaction contracts use **subjective** satisfaction of the specific party when, as in the example just given, the condition's subject involves personal judgment or taste. By contrast, satisfaction contracts use **objective** measures of the trade or profession when the condition's subject involves commercial matters having objective standards. Thus, if a subcontract calls for installation of a furnace to the general contractor's satisfaction, the commercial nature of the performance measures the satisfaction *objectively*. The contractor cannot withhold satisfaction (withhold payment as return performance) by claiming that the work did not satisfy the contractor. Satisfaction of *third party*, though, such as a construction project's architect or engineer, typically requires *subjective* rather than *objective* satisfaction.

2. Constructive

Contracts may also **imply** certain **constructive conditions**. *Notice* is one common implication, as in the example in the above introduction to conditions, where the business owner would have to notify the equipment-leasing company of the need to repair the imaging device before the company had that obligation. Contract *performance* is another common implication. For example, if a company hires a new chief executive officer on a three-year contract at $500,000 per year, then the contract implies as a condition to the company's payment that the officer will show up for work to begin performance. If instead the officer accepts a better offer from another company before beginning to perform, then the company with whom the officer first contracted has no obligation to pay any part of the $500,000. Contracts also imply *cooperation*. Thus, in the above example, if the chief executive officer showed up for the first day of work, and the company refused to provide the officer with an office, office equipment and furniture, and administrative or secretarial support, then the company would have breached an implied term for cooperation.

3. Obligations of good faith and fair dealing in performance and enforcement of contracts

The parties to a contract owe the obligation to perform the contract in **good faith**. Good faith generally means that strict performance of the agreement is *not enough*, if in doing so the performing party intentionally defeats or frustrates the other party's contract object. The parties must live up to not just the contract's letter but also its *spirit*. For example, a sales-representative company that promises to do the best that it can to market an inventor's newly patented invention but then promptly forms a contract to market for a large corporation the invention's already successful and well-established competing product, leaving the company's best available efforts to be nothing more than posting the invention to a website, has violated the contract's spirit if not its letter, leaving the inventor with a remedy for breach of the good-faith duty. The Uniform Commercial Code defines good faith in the case of **merchants**, meaning those who deal in the good that is the contract's subject, as **honesty in fact** while following **reasonable commercial standards of fair dealing** in the trade. Thus, if in the sale of goods, one party follows the contract's strict terms but in ways that do not follow reasonable commercial standards for those goods, then the party will have violated the duty, leaving the other party with a remedy. For example, the produce seller who in transport fails to heat the produce against winter freezing, destroying the delivered produce, may have met the strict terms of delivery but not according to commercial delivery standards, leaving the grocer buyer with a breach remedy.

4. Suspension or excuse of conditions by waiver, election, or estoppel

In some cases, circumstances will **excuse** or **suspend** the condition so that the party relying on it to *not* perform will nonetheless have to perform even though the condition has not occurred. When a party *wrongfully interferes* with the occurrence of the condition on which the party relies to not perform, then the party loses the right to rely on it and must perform even though the condition has not occurred. For example, a project owner, who contracts with a builder to pay a $100,000 bonus if the builder can get the owner a certificate of occupancy for a new office building within one year, may not refuse to sign the application for the certificate simply to prevent the builder from collecting the duly earned bonus. Similarly, a party deliberately shutting down its business to avoid a loss on a requirement or output contract wrongfully interferes with the requirements or output condition, suspending the condition and allowing the other party to pursue contract-breach remedies.

5. Prospective inability to perform: effect on other party

The law excuses a party's performance in certain circumstances when the party learns that the other party is *unable* to perform. A party's **prospective inability to perform** generally relieves the other party's performance in contracts where the relieved party must perform first but can

Contract Law

see that the other party will then be unable to perform. For example, a contract may require that a buyer pay for goods in advance by a certain date, following which the seller will deliver the goods. If before payment, fire destroys the seller's business, making the seller clearly unable to perform, then the buyer need not make the advance payment. The opposite may also be true that in a contract to supply goods first, followed by payment, a seller may learn that the buyer is unable to pay, thus relieving the seller from supplying the goods.

Insecurity alone, though, does not automatically and entirely relieve performance. When a party appears unable to pay for the performance that the party owing performance has not yet begun or completed, the insecure party may under the Uniform Commercial Code and common law **demand assurances**. If the party whose circumstances suggest inability to pay, such as having filed for *bankruptcy*, provides adequate assurances, then the other party must perform despite the bankruptcy. Yet the absence of those assurances, required under the Uniform Commercial Code within thirty days, relieves the insecure party from performing, the bankrupt or insolvent party having presumptively repudiated the contract.

Disputes between contracting parties, including the issues of *prospective inability to perform* and *insecurity*, often implicate what the contract may require as to the party's **order of performance**. While some contracts clearly require one party to perform before the other party performs, many contracts are silent as to the order of performance. The rule in such cases is generally that the performance that *takes longer* is the *first* performance. For example, if a landowner contracts to pay $5,000 to a well driller to drill a well for water, without specifying whether payment or drilling comes first, then the drilling would come first because it takes longer than payment. If, on the other hand, performance time is equal, *simultaneous*, and instantaneous, such as in the delivery of goods in exchange for payment, then performance by each is a **condition** to the other party's performance. Thus, if a party delivers the goods at the indicated time and place, but the other party is not present with the payment, the paying party's absence excuses the delivering party's performance.

B. Impracticability and frustration of purpose

The law excuses performance made **impractical** by occurrences that the contracting parties did not anticipate and that make performance extremely and unreasonably difficult. For example, the parties need not perform when unanticipated events *destroy* the contract's *subject matter*, such as when a fire destroys a home under a sale contract not yet closed. For another example, the parties need not perform when law reform makes the contract's subject *illegal*, such as when a new ordinance outlaws barroom bare-knuckles cage matches in a city where producers had contracted with a bar for such an event. For another example, the parties need not perform when supplies designated from a specific place are no longer available, such

Contract Law

as when a decorating contract calls for rugs imported from a location where war and embargoes suddenly prevent the supply.

Construction contracts differ depending on whether the contractor has *begun* the work and whether the work is for *new* construction or only for *renovation* or repair. If flooding or other disaster destroys a construction site before the contractor begins, then the **impracticability** of beginning relieves the contractor of performing. If, however, the contractor begins, and fire, earthquake, or other event damages the incomplete construction, then the contractor must continue to perform if still able, notwithstanding the additional difficulty and expense of the work. If the contract, though, is only for repair, then the destruction of the building or work relieves the contractor even if the contractor has begun, although the contractor could recover for the partial work performed. Contracts for the **sale of goods** under the Uniform Commercial Code depend on whether the contract identified *specific goods*, in which case their destruction relieves the parties from performing, whereas if the goods were *fungible commodities*, the parties must still perform.

In **personal-services** contracts, where performance depends on the special skill of the person promising performance, that person's death or *permanent incapacity* excuses performance. If, on the other hand, the party promising personal service only falls temporarily ill, making performance *impractical* rather than impossible, then the illness *suspends* rather than *relieves* performance, unless the contract provides otherwise. When the performer recovers, the obligation resumes unless changes in circumstance substantially increase either party's burden, in which case the changes relieve both parties from performing. For example, if a comedian contracts to perform on a specific date at a specific venue but suffers stroke permanently disabling the performer, then **impracticability** of continuing with the contract excuses the performer and venue from performing. Yet if the comedian only fell ill with hoarseness preventing performance on the specific date, then the comedian and venue could each insist on a rescheduled performance, unless some other reason made rescheduling unduly burdensome on either party.

C. Discharge of contractual duties

Substantial performance of contract obligations satisfying the implied condition to perform typically **discharges** a party from remaining contract obligations. Contracts other than for the sale of goods do not ordinarily require perfect performance but only *substantial* performance. **Substantial performance** is conduct that fulfills the contract's *essential purpose*. Factors include the percentage of total benefit that the performance provided, whether damages can make up for the performance shortfall, and the good or bad faith in which the performing party acted. For example, if a builder contracts to build a new home one feature of which is to be Italian-marble kitchen countertops, but the builder builds a home with marble countertops from another source because of an interruption in supply, then the performance would be substantial because a small percentage of the total contract, done in

Contract Law

good faith, and redressed by damages for any (presumably small) difference in marble-supply costs.

The Uniform Commercial Code, though, requires **perfect tender** in contracts for the sale of goods, in effect reversing the rule of substantial performance. The perfect-tender rule provides an exception when the seller's time to perform has not yet expired and, on notice of imperfect tender, the seller informs the buyer that the seller will **cure** the imperfect tender by delivering conforming goods. For example, if a contract calls for a parts supplier to deliver ten-thousand galvanized fasteners to a jobsite within one week, the parts supplier delivers ten-thousand fasteners that are *not* galvanized, but the parts supplier still has several days yet to perform before the week concludes, then the parts supplier may notify the buyer that conforming galvanized fasteners are on the way and may then enforce the contract when curing the nonconformity.

The Uniform Commercial Code also provides relief from the perfect-tender rule in the case of **installment contracts**. If a nonconforming delivery in an installment contract does not *substantially impair* the full contract, then the seller may assure the buyer of the seller's ability and willingness to perform, and may cure the nonconformity. Thus, in the above example, if the supplier made a first of several promised installment shipments, and the first shipment representing only a relatively insubstantial part of the overall contract was nonconforming, then the supplier could promptly assure the buyer that conforming installments were coming, and then accordingly perform in conformity, enforcing the contract. If, on the other hand, nonconforming tender causes the other party some damage, even if not substantially impairing the full contract, then the party may recover that damage to cure the nonconformity.

Parties may **discharge** one another from performing a contract in ways other than *substantial performance* or, in the case of the sale of goods, *perfect tender*. **Mutual rescission** is a first form of discharge in which both parties agree to relieve one another from performing the contract, before either party begins performance. If, on the other hand, one party has already performed and only the other party still owes performance, then the parties cannot rescind. Instead, the parties may agree to **release** the non-performing party from further obligation. However, release after one party performs requires **consideration** to support the new agreement. For example, if an employer adopts a new policy that denies paid personal-leave days to employees already working under contract providing for those paid leave days, and the employees are willing to release the employer from the paid-leave-days obligation, then the employer must provide some consideration such as a one-time bonus or a wage increase to ensure that the employer can enforce the release if necessary.

D. Express and implied warranties in sale-of-goods contracts

Contracts for the sale of goods under the Uniform Commercial Code give rise to both *express* and *implied warranties* as to the *quality* of the contract goods. **Express warranties** involve affirmative statements, descriptions, and other representations as to the quality of the goods, whether in the contract or in advertising, product packaging, product instructions, or other locations. A seller whose product does not meet those express warranties is subject to an action for **warranty breach**. For example, if the seller of a hair-coloring product represented that it would change the user's hair to approximately the color represented on the product package, but the product instead uniformly changed hair to a distinctly different and unnatural color, then the seller would have breached its warranty, giving purchasers remedies in breach.

The Uniform Commercial Code also provides for **implied warranties** breaches of which give rise to a cause of action. The first implied warranty is one of **merchantability**, defined as *fitness for* the product's *ordinary purpose*. For example, if a manufacturer sells a lawn mower, then the product should mow lawns as its ordinary purpose, failing which the purchaser has a cause of action for breach of the implied warranty of merchantability. The second implied warranty is of *fitness for particular purpose*. If the product's seller knows of the buyer's particular need and supplies the product in response to that need, then the seller has impliedly warranted the product for the buyer's particular purpose even if the seller did not design or market the product for that purpose. Thus, if a homeowner visits a hardware store asking for a product that mulches leaves, and the hardware store sells the homeowner a lawn mower to mulch accomplish that particular purpose, but the lawn mower fails to do so, then the homeowner has an action for breach of the warranty of fitness for particular purpose.

The law imposes implied warranties only on **merchants**, meaning those who regularly deal in the goods that are the contract's object. One-time sellers such as at garage sales do not impliedly warrant the used product's fitness. **Damages** can include not only loss of the product but also harm to other personal or real property, and personal injury or death. States adopt different Uniform Commercial Code options as to whom product warranties reach and protect, whether only family members and guests of immediate buyers or any foreseeable user. The Uniform Commercial Code also permits certain warranty **disclaimers**, although consumer-protection and other laws generally void disclaimers as to liability for personal injury or death, and disclaimers of the implied warranty of merchantability.

E. Substantial and partial breach...

A **breach** of the contract gives rise to a cause of action in the non-breaching party to recover damages due to the breach. Yet breach by one party does not always relieve the other party from performing. Whether the breach relieves the other party from performing depends on whether the breach is **substantial**. Factors include the *extent* of performance, whether the breach was *intentional* or *careless*, whether the breaching party will *continue* to perform, the extent of the *benefit* from the performance, whether *damages* will suffice, and the *effect* on the breaching party of relieving the non-breaching party from performing. For example, if an arborist contracts to remove six large and two small trees from the grounds of a corporate office, but the arborist removes only the large trees leaving the small trees, then the corporation would still have to pay for the substantial work that the arborist performed, because the arborist's breach was only **partial** rather than substantial. The corporation would still have a breach-of-contract remedy addressing the cost of removing the remaining two small trees.

On the other hand, a contract may expressly require a party to complete *all* performance before obligating the other party to perform. Thus, in the above example, if the contract expressly made the arborist removing *every* tree a condition to *any* payment from the corporation, perhaps because the corporation had a special need for grounds clear of all trees, then the contract would have relieved the corporation from any payment, notwithstanding the rule of substantial performance. In effect, the non-breaching party's options depend on characterizing the other party's breach. If the contract required complete performance as a condition for the non-breaching party to perform, or if the breaching party's breach was substantial, then the non-breaching party may either terminate the contract and sue for damages, or continue with the contract but also still sue for resulting loss. If, on the other hand, the contract does not require complete performance as a condition to the non-breaching party's performance, and the breach is only **partial** rather than substantial, then the non-breaching party must perform but may still sue for resulting loss.

...and anticipatory repudiation

The law also relieves a party from performing a contract when the other party **repudiates** the contract. **Anticipatory repudiation** occurs when, before the party's performance is due under the contract, the party informs the other party that the first party refuses to perform the contract. Anticipatory repudiation relieves the non-repudiating party from performance. For example, if a sculptor contracts to sell a sculpture to a patron but then emails the patron that the sculptor refuses to go through with the contract, then the sculptor has anticipatorily breached, relieving the patron from paying for the sculpture and giving the patron a contract-breach action, whether the contract called for payment before, at the time of, or after the sculpture's delivery.

Repudiation can occur either through words *or actions*. In the same example, if the sculptor contracts to sell the sculpture to one patron but before delivery conveys the sculpture to another patron, the sculptor's actions will have repudiated the contract as to the first patron, relieving that patron from performing and giving the patron a contract-breach action. Repudiation must, though, involve an **unconditional refusal** rather than mere expression of uncertainty or doubt. Recall, though, that such expressions may give grounds for the non-breaching party to claim insecurity in the other party's *prospective inability to perform*, suspending the non-breaching party's obligation to perform and giving the non-breaching party grounds to demand assurances.

Contract Law

A party who repudiates may **retract** the repudiation if doing so before performance is due *and* before the other party accepts or relies on the repudiation. In breach-of-contract actions based on repudiation, the non-breaching party had the duty to mitigate damages.

V.   Remedies

Contract-breach **remedies** begin with protecting the non-breaching party's **expectation interest** through damages measures based on that interest. Beyond the non-breaching party's expectation interest, the non-breaching party may also have incurred **consequential damages,** or the contract may have provided for **liquidated damages** that courts will recognize if not constituting a **penalty.** Non-breaching parties also have an obligation to minimize the **consequences** of breach and to **mitigate** damages. Contract remedies may also include **specific performance** of the contract as an alternative to damages remedies, or **injunctions** in **declaratory-judgment** actions. The law may alternatively provide **rescission** and **reliance** remedies, the latter even in the case when the parties formed no contract. Breaching parties may have their own limited remedies and rights, all treated in the following sections.

A. Measure of damages for breach; protecting the expectation interest

A primary measure of contract-breach damages involves meeting the non-breaching party's **expectation interest**. Expectation damages compensate the non-breaching party for the loss of the *benefit of the bargain*, meaning the value that the party reasonably expected from the other party's contract performance. Expectation damages involve a *make-whole* remedy, placing the non-breaching party in the financial position the party would have been *but for the breach*. That remedy requires paying whatever costs the non-breaching party incurred in performing plus any profit that party would have made, or less any loss the party would have suffered, if the other party had not breached. For example, if a cotton supplier contracts to sell one-thousand bushels of cotton to a mill at ten dollars per bushel, giving a total $10,000 contract price, and the mill pays $5,000 in advance, but the price of cotton doubles to twenty dollars per bushel before the delivery date and so the supplier breaches, the mill may recover the $5,000 that it paid *plus the difference* between the ten-dollar contract price and twenty-dollar market price, representing the profit that it would have made. The mill lost the expectation interest of getting cotton worth $20,000 for a price of $10,000. If, on the hand, the market price of cotton had declined to five dollars a bushel, the mill could recover its $5,000 advance but would have to deduct the $5,000 loss that it would have incurred from agreeing to pay $10,000 for cotton having a value of only $5,000 on the delivery date. The mill's damages for breach in that case would be zero, although as discussed below, it could still recover the $5,000 down payment under a *restitution* theory.

Contract Law

A party claiming expectation damages must prove those damages to a **reasonable certainty**, meaning in the above example that the mill must present proof of the lost cotton's market value at delivery. If the party cannot prove damages to a reasonable certainty, then the court may limit the recovery to **nominal** damages, meaning a token amount such as one dollar or ten dollars to confirm the conclusion that the party breached. Whether a party can prove reasonably certain expectation losses or not, the court may award **incidental damages**, meaning expenses reasonably incurred in such things as receipt, inspection, and storage of rejected goods, and other *commercially reasonable* charges, expenses or commissions in connection with buying replacement goods, and other reasonable expense incident to the breach.

B. Consequential damages: causation, certainty, and foreseeability

The law provides for **consequential damages** in addition to expectation damages. While expectation damages put the non-breaching party in the financial position that the party would have been if the breach had not occurred, consequential damages instead look to other, additional losses that the non-breaching party incurred because of the breach. Thus, if because of the breach the non-breaching party suffered bodily injury or property damage, or lost expenses or profits in transactions with third parties, then the non-breaching party may recover those consequential damages in addition to expectation damages.

For a court to award consequential damages, the parties must have *contemplated* consequential damages, meaning that the damages must have been **foreseeable** to the breaching party *when* the parties *made the contract*, for the other party to recover those damages. The question of foreseeability is whether the breaching party actual foresaw those potential losses *or should have foreseen* them. For example, if a medical laboratory contracts for an equipment supplier to deliver a dozen new blood-testing machines on a specific date because the laboratory has a big new hospital to serve, and the supplier knows or should know of the laboratory's special need to serve the new hospital, then the supplier's failure to deliver the machines timely, breaching the contract, exposes the supplier to the laboratory's consequence of losing the hospital's testing business and even breaching a contract with the hospital. Yet the laboratory recovers those consequential damages *only if* it contemplated or should have foreseen those losses.

Consequential damages must also be **reasonably certain**, including that the breach must be the **factual cause** of the losses, for a party to recover them. The uncertainty of damages often arises around claims for lost profits. If, for example, a food distributor fails to supply a hot-dog stand with hot-dog buns for a summer-holiday weekend, and the hot-dog stand shows that it accordingly lost substantial profitable hot-dog sales, then the stand may claim those lost profits as an expectation recovery. Established businesses have less difficulty showing the reasonable certainty of lost profits than do new businesses. Thus, if a sidewalk entrepreneur had decided to try for the first

Contract Law

time to sell hot dogs over the same weekend and had the same supplier breach, with no prior record of sales on which to rely, the entrepreneur may be unable to establish lost profits to a reasonable certainty.

When a party is unable to prove reasonably certain consequential damages, the court may award only **nominal damages**, which involve a *token award*, such as one dollar or ten dollars, to confirm the conclusion of breach in the absence of reliable proof of reasonably certain damages. For example, a new company that must promptly close without any sales because of a supplier's breach of contract may have no reliable evidence on which to prove reasonably certain consequential damages. The failed company could, after all, have lost money if it had been able to open, meaning that the supplier's breach could have *saved* the company's investors additional losses. If the company could not prove reasonably certain damages, then the company may recover only nominal damages. Whether a party can prove reasonably certain consequential damages or not, the party may recover **incidental damages** for commercially reasonable expenses incurred as a result of the breach, as described in the prior section.

C. Liquidated damages and penalties

A contract may provide for **liquidated damages**, which involve either a specific amount in damages or a specific manner of calculating damages, as the parties negotiated in advance and included in the contract in the event of breach. A court will ordinarily enforce liquidated damages only if the court would find damages *difficult to calculate* in the event of breach and the liquidated damages *reasonably forecast* what damages would be in the event of breach. For example, if a corporation creates a new division that contracts with a software engineer to develop a new online service, and the contract provides for $25,000 in liquidated damages if the engineer fails or refuses to perform, a court would likely enforce the clause because of the uncertainty of the new division's damages, if $25,000 approximated the size and value of potential losses. If the court instead construes the liquidated-damages clause as a **penalty** to punish breach, then the court must not enforce the clause. Liquidated damages must *compensate*, not punish.

Also, distinguish liquidated damages from **punitive damages** awarded to punish particularly reprehensible misconduct. Generally, parties *may not recover punitive damages* for contract breach. Punitive damages depend on statutory or other law applied to specific forms of serious misconduct in special situations. For example, a landlord who while evicting a tenant for nonpayment of rent sets the tenant's personal property out on the curb, leading to the property's loss or destruction, may owe the tenant double or triple damages under a special statute so providing to discourage landlords from self-help.

D. Avoidable consequences and mitigation of damages

Contract Law

In the event of breach, parties have the obligation to *avoid consequences* that would increase the loss. The doctrine of **avoidable consequences** bars remedies for those losses that the non-breaching party could have reasonably avoided. For example, if a fire-suppression company breaches its contract to install sprinklers in an owner's warehouse, and a fire starts in the warehouse about which the owner is aware with the reasonable means to prevent it, then the owner must employ those means rather than allow the fire to consume the warehouse and then sue the company for consequential damages.

Similarly, a non-breaching party has an obligation to **mitigate damages**. Mitigating damages requires the non-breaching party to seek reasonable *substitute performance* to keep damages to their minimum. For example, if a grower needs a butane delivery from its fuel supplier to operate its orchard heaters during a frost, but the supplier fails to deliver the fuel, the grower must obtain the fuel from another source if reasonably available rather than allow the orchard to freeze and then sue the supplier for those consequential damages.

Likewise, employees terminated in breach of employment contract must seek other employment rather than expect the breaching employer to pay indefinitely for the lost income. Employees need only seek and accept *comparable jobs*, not any job unfitted to their qualifications. In the same way, the Uniform Commercial Code requires buyers in the sale of goods to seek substitute goods, what the Code calls **cover**, if the seller breaches. The Code bars damages that the buyer could have avoided if the buyer had sought cover as the Code requires. Similarly, construction contractors must seek substitute performance to complete the construction contract, when a subcontract fails to perform. If the contractor does not attempt in good faith to mitigate damages, then the contractor cannot claim the consequential damages, such as the contractor's failure to complete the construction on time under the contractor's own contract. Non-breaching parties may, though, recover in contract-breach damages additional costs incurred in mitigating damages.

E. Rescission and reformation

In some cases, the courts will provide the equitable remedy of **rescission**, having the purpose and effect of *undoing* the contract to place the parties once again in as close a position as possible to where they were before forming the contract. Rescission requires that each party return any property, funds, or other benefit that they received, as far as able. Neither party receives damages. After rescission, neither party has any remaining right to enforce the contract. Rescission presumes that the parties formed a contract. If the parties did not form a contract but nonetheless bestowed some benefit on one another, then the proper remedy is a pre-contractual *reliance* recovery. The party seeking rescission must show equitable grounds such as fraud, duress, or undue influence, or the contract's unconscionability. For example, if a sly caretaker unduly influenced a vulnerable nursing-home resident into conveying valuable jewelry to the caretaker for a fraction of its value, then

Contract Law

the court would likely rescind the contract, requiring the caretaker to restore the jewelry to the resident.

By contrast, **reformation** does not undo the contract but instead remakes or reforms the contract to reflect the intentions of the parties who formed it. The party seeking reformation must show the grounds such as palpable error in the contract contradicting the parties' actual intentions or ambiguity in the contract that requires clarification to reflect the parties' true intentions. For example, a seller may contract with a buyer for the sale of a two-acre parcel of land but mistakenly describe a five-acre parcel in the metes-and-bounds description. While the description might typically control, if the seller shows that the parties clearly intended only the sale of the two acres and that the description constituted a plain error in the agreement, then the court will reform the contract to reflect the sale of the two-acre parcel. Similarly, if the parties intend a two-acre sale but leave the description ambiguous as to the size and contours of the parcel, then the court may accept proofs resolving the ambiguity, from which the court may order the contract's reformation to eliminate the ambiguity.

F. Specific performance...

In some contract breaches, damages are an *inadequate remedy*. In those instances, particularly as the Uniform Commercial Code provides, in contracts having *unique goods* as their subject, the court may award **specific performance** instead of contract damages. Specific performance, an equitable rather than legal remedy, involves a court order that the breaching party must perform its contract obligation. For example, if the owner of a rare antique automobile contracts to sell the vehicle to a collector but then refuses, the collector may enforce the contract by specific performance, obtaining the vehicle rather than damages. Similarly, a buyer of real property, routinely determined unique, would receive title to the property in specific performance.

...injunction against breach...

The courts will not enforce some unique contracts by specific performance but instead by **injunction**. An injunction is a court order prohibiting a person or corporation from doing a specific act. In the case of contract breach, if the court could not force the party to perform the contract, then the court could instead **enjoin** the party from performing the same act to fulfill some other contract. For example, courts will not enforce employment contracts by specific performance because to do so would force the employee to serve against the employee's will. The court may instead enjoin the employee from providing the same services to another employer, particularly a competing employer, for the contract period. Thus, if an entertainer contracts to perform at a casino in a large resort city for a period of one year for one million dollars but repudiates the contract in favor of performing for a competing casino for two million dollars, the first casino may obtain an

Contract Law

injunction enjoining the entertainer from performing for the one-year contract period. Generally, to obtain an injunction, a party must show the legal right to a remedy, *irreparable harm* that damages do not adequately compensate, that *not* granting an injunction would lead to greater harm than *granting* an injunction would cause, and that the balance of public and private interests falls in favor of an injunction. Courts also have power to grant *temporary restraining orders* and *preliminary injunctions* before permanent injunction.

...and declaratory judgment

In some instances, the parties to a contract dispute the contract's terms but at the same wish to avoid a breach. When the parties face a genuine dispute over contract terms, they may turn to the court in a **declaratory-judgment action** for a ruling from the court construing the parties' rights. Neither party may yet have breached the contract, but if the parties can show the court that they hold genuine and substantial interests in resolving an impending dispute, the court will hear evidence and issue a declaratory judgment construing the contract rights. The declaratory judgment may also include an injunction carrying out the court's declaratory ruling. For example, an insurer and insured may dispute whether the insurer owes coverage for a claim that a third party has made against the insurer. Rather than leave the insured without defense and indemnity, the insurer may retain counsel to defend the insured in the third party's liability action but simultaneously seek a declaratory judgment determining whether the insurance contract requires the insurer to defend and indemnify.

G. Restitutionary and reliance recoveries

As an above section explains, the law recognizes some grounds for **pre-contractual obligations** in the form of **reliance recoveries**. A party may be liable for the other party's reliance costs if the party induced reliance through **misrepresentation** or made **specific promises** inviting reliance during negotiations. A party is also liable for pre-contract reliance damages if the party **benefited** from the other party's reliance, while knowing of and accepting the benefit. The example given above is that of a tradesperson who prepared a job site for work that the tradesperson expected to perform under a contract that the tradesperson was negotiating with a builder. When the builder hired a different tradesperson at a lower cost relying on the first tradesperson's preparations, then the first tradesperson could recover those reliance losses. The law recognizes these **promissory estoppel** and **detrimental reliance** theories when the reliance is *reasonable, foreseeable,* and *detrimental,* and enforcement is necessary to *avoid injustice.* The law limits recovery to restoring the relying party to the pre-reliance position.

Restitution is a related recovery involving one party providing a benefit to another a contract that turns out to be unenforceable. Restitution is available in a contract that *would have resulted in loss* to the non-breaching party, when the non-breaching party has already performed at least in part

Contract Law

before the other party breaches the contract. Recall that in measuring *expectation* damages, the non-breaching party must deduct any losses that the non-breaching party saved because of the breach to arrive at those damages. Yet in *restitution*, the non-breaching party may recover any benefit that the non-breaching party provided to the breaching party before the breach. Restitution prevents the breaching party from unjust enrichment at the non-breaching party's expense, undoing each party's actions to restore to each the interest that they held before any contract performance began. When literal restoration is impossible, such as where a party performed a service rather than transferred an interest or asset, restitution may instead require that the party receiving the service pay the value of its benefit. For example, if a marina hires a painter to paint its docks, but halfway through the job the waters rise so high to make the remaining contract performance impracticable, then the court may award the painter the value of the painting to that point, even though the contract is no longer enforceable.

H. Remedial rights of breaching parties

A party's contract breach does **not** eliminate the party's own contract rights unless the breach is material and substantial, going to the root of the parties' contract. Indeed, when the time to perform has not yet expired, and the performing party receives notice that the performance does not meet the contract terms, the party may **cure** the incomplete or inadequate performance, for instance in a contract for the sale of goods by tendering conforming goods to replace the nonconforming goods.

VI.   Third-party rights

Law ordinarily limits the rights arising out of a contract to the parties to the contract. Yet parties form some contracts intending to benefit a non-party to the contract whom the law identifies as a **third-party beneficiary**. In other instances, a party may **assign** the party's contract rights to a non-party whom the law identifies as an **assignee,** or conversely, a party may **delegate** its obligation to perform the contract to a non-party. The sections below address these rights and interests of non-parties to the original contract.

A. Third-party beneficiaries

A **third-party beneficiary** is a non-party to the contract whom the parties to the contract favored in some respect when forming the contract. The sections below address **intended beneficiaries,** meaning those whom the parties desired to benefit when forming the contract, and **incidental beneficiaries,** meaning those whom the parties did not intend to benefit but nonetheless did benefit in some unplanned manner. Third-party beneficiaries may in certain circumstances seek to enforce their rights or, conversely, may in certain circumstances lose their ability to enforce their rights in the contract to which they were not a party.

Contract Law

1. Intended beneficiaries

Some contracts clearly express the parties' intent to benefit a non-party to the contract, thus making that non-party a **third-party beneficiary**. Other contracts only imply from circumstance that the parties intend to benefit a non-party to the contract, such as when a party intends to favor a non-party relative or friend with a *gift* arising out of the contract's performance or a party intends to *extinguish* a non-party *debt* through the contract's performance. For example, a contract for a vehicle's purchase may direct that the seller deliver the vehicle to the buyer's beloved nephew, implying a third-party beneficiary gift. For another example, a contract for constructing a deck may direct the payor to pay a supplier whom the tradesperson constructing the deck owes a supply debt. In either case, the third-party beneficiary could show the intent to benefit.

2. Incidental beneficiaries

The law identifies as an **incidental beneficiary** a third-party to the contract whom the parties did *not* intend to benefit and whose benefit arose without the parties have planned it. If, for example, a homeowner contracts with a builder for an addition to the home, and the builder plans to hire several subcontractors, neither party would have intended the contract to benefit those subcontractors. Their benefit would instead have been *incidental* to the contract. They would have no right to enforce the contract, no event triggering any vesting. The contract may even list the subcontractors whom the contractor planned to use, but their interests would remain incidental to the contract, the full benefit of which would remain between the homeowner and contractor.

3. Impairment or extinguishment of third-party rights

Parties to the contract may **impair** or **extinguish** a third-party beneficiary's rights at any time before the beneficiary's rights **vest**. Parties may do so by changing or terminating the contract. A third-party beneficiary's rights *vest* when the third-party beneficiary *changes position relying* on the contract, such as when selling a vehicle anticipating the contract's vehicle gift. Third-party-beneficiary rights also vest if the parties request that the beneficiary *assent* to the contract or if the contract states a *condition when rights vest* and the condition then occurs. For example, if a rich aunt contracted with a vehicle dealer to convey a new vehicle to her niece when the niece graduated from high school, indicating in the contract the intent that the niece's right to select the vehicle would vest on graduation, then the niece's right would vest at graduation, after which the parties could no longer impair or extinguish the niece's right. Before the niece graduated and her right vested, the rich aunt could change the gift from her niece to her nephew or terminate the contract entirely if the dealer agreed. Parties may impair or extinguish the rights of *incidental* beneficiaries at any time.

4. Enforcement by the promisee

Third-party beneficiaries, those whom the parties intend to benefit, have the advantage of being able to *enforce* the contract against either party to the contract once the third-party beneficiary's rights **vest**. So, in the above example, when the rich aunt contracted with the vehicle dealer to convey a new vehicle to her niece when the niece graduated from high school, indicating in the contract the intent that the niece's right to select the vehicle would vest on graduation, and the niece did in fact graduate before the parties changed that contract, then the niece could enforce that right once the graduation occurred, although not before. Only *intended beneficiaries* may enforce the contract, and they may only enforce once their rights vest. *Incidental* beneficiaries may *not* enforce the contract.

B. Assignment of rights and delegation of duties

Parties do not always perform their own contracts, and parties do not always receive the benefit of their own contracts. Parties may in certain instances **assign** their contract rights and **delegate** their contract duties to a non-party to the contract. *Assignment* is the act of transferring the contract benefit to a non-party to the contract, while *delegation* is the act of transferring to a non-party the obligation to perform the contract. Assignment and delegation may go together or be apart. In shorthand, to *assign* a contract can also mean to transfer both the benefit and the obligation. Generally, though, a party assigning to another the contract's benefit need not have the benefitted person's consent, while on the other hand, a party delegating contract duties to another must have that person's consent to perform in the delegating party's place.

Assignees gain the **right to sue** the party who owes the assigning party the obligation to perform the transferred right. For example, if an investor assigns to his adult daughter the right to receive royalties from an oil-well investment, then the daughter may sue the party who owes the royalties if the party does not pay the royalties per the contract. The assignee suing on the contract need only show that they received the assignment. An assignment must adequately indicate the assignor's intent to benefit the assignee with the contract performance *and* to relieve the party owing performance from performing any longer for the assignor. In other words, the party owing performance cannot owe *two* performances. If the party owing performance performs for the contracting party before receiving notice of the contracting party's assignment, such as in the above example paying the royalty to the investor rather than the adult daughter, then the payment satisfies the obligation.

Non-parties accepting a **delegation of duties**, while owing the contract performance, have the same defenses as the contracting party who

Contract Law

transferred the obligation. Thus, for example, if the contracting party who delegated the duty also assigned the right to advance payment as a condition to performance, then the non-party taking the delegation of duty and right to payment could await the payment condition in the same manner that the delegating party could have awaited payment if the party had not made the delegation. Importantly, the party owed performance may enforce performance against the party who made the delegation. In other words, delegation alone does not relieve the delegating party from contract liability. Indeed, the non-party accepting delegation is *not* directly liable to the party expecting performance unless *consideration* supported the delegation, in which case the non-party accepting delegation is liable to either the delegating party or the party owed the performance.

Criminal Law and Procedure

D.   Criminal Law and Procedure

NOTE: Approximately half of the Criminal Law and Procedure questions on the MBE will be based on category V, and approximately half will be based on the remaining categories—I, II, III, and IV.

The Multistate Bar Examination emphasizes certain criminal law and procedure topics. The exam devotes one half of the criminal law and procedure questions to the Part V subject of **constitutional protections** of the accused, what the above title refers to as *criminal procedure*. Focus your studies on criminal procedure, while giving due attention to the other four *criminal law* subjects. Those other four subjects include **homicide, other crimes, inchoate crimes** referring to *attempts*, *conspiracy*, and *solicitation* but dealing also with other parties to crime, and finally **general principles** of criminal law. Begin your review of criminal law and procedure with the topic of homicide.

I.   Homicide

Homicide involves the unlawful killing of one by another. Not all killings carry criminal sanction. For example, killing in self-defense, defense of others such as in reasonable use of deadly force by law enforcement, or war, or to carry out lawful capital punishment, would not carry criminal sanction. Significantly, the subject of homicide involves both *intended* and *unintended* killings. The law of homicide assigns different crimes, and may assign different degrees of those crimes, depending on how its definitions treat the actor's state of mind, the circumstances, and the conduct that led to or accompanied the killing. Homicide crimes include *murder* in various degrees, *manslaughter*, and *reckless* or *negligent homicide*. Murder is the most-serious form of homicide. Manslaughter involves an intentional unlawful killing that does not reach the level of murder because of the mitigating circumstance of provocation. Reckless and negligent homicide involve less-culpable states of mind. Consider murder's primary definition next and then manslaughter and reckless or negligent homicide in later sections.

The common law defines **murder** as the *unlawful killing* of another with *malice aforethought*. Malice aforethought is a term of art that encompasses certain *intentional* killings but also other *unintended* killings. For example, malice aforethought includes not only intent to kill but also intent to cause serious bodily injury when the actions results in death. Malice aforethought also includes the intent to commit certain felonies when the intent results in death. Intentional acts done with depraved indifference to life, when the acts result in death, also satisfy malice aforethought. Sections below first address intended killings and then address unintended killings, following the common-law definitions for murder.

Modern statutes in many states modify the common-law rules into **first-degree** murder, **second-degree** murder, and **capital** murder, meaning

Criminal Law and Procedure

murder for which death is a possible penalty. *First-degree murder* includes premeditated killings involving reasoning or deliberation (not an impulse killing) and felony murder (addressed below). First-degree murder can also include murder by explosives or torture and of an on-duty police officer, while some jurisdictions also continue to include as first-degree murder traditional categories of murder by poison or lying in wait. *Second-degree murder*, which is a lesser-included offense (a topic addressed well below) of first-degree murder, involves the other forms of killing with malice aforethought, such as death after intended serious injury or depraved indifference, plus killing during or in flight from a non-dangerous felony (those felonies that do not qualify for felony murder). *Capital murder*, defined differently from state to state and not recognized in all states, involves first-degree murder with an aggravating circumstance such as killing of a judge, witness, or on-duty police officer, multiple killings, or killing for hire.

A. Intended killings

Malice aforethought includes the **intent to kill**, generally meaning acts done with the objective of bringing about the death of another. The intent-to-kill form of malice aforethought relates to *premeditation* and *deliberation*, treated in the following section. Not all intentional killings, though, even those beyond the categories of justified killings described above, are murder. A following section defines *provocation* and addresses its effect on an intentional killing.

1. Premeditation, deliberation

Malice aforethought carries involves **premeditation** and **deliberation**, indeed in modern statutes as distinct elements. *Premeditation* plainly includes planning to kill. Thus, an actor who considers and procures a death weapon, plans to meet the homicide victim at the killing's location, and then carries out the act as planned, will have premeditated the killing. *Deliberation* involves **reflection**, suggesting the opportunity to give one's thoughts a second look, toward the killing act. For example, thought and choice as to the means of killing, and the location, purpose, and consequence of killing, may all indicate deliberation, even though none of those factors are necessary to deliberation. *Motive*, for another example, is not a necessary element of premeditation and deliberation. An actor need not have a motive to satisfy premeditation and deliberation. Indeed, premeditation and deliberation need not extend significantly beyond the moment of the killing act. An actor who decides on the spot to kill another person and does so right then may still have premeditated and deliberated the act, satisfying malice aforethought.

2. Provocation

Criminal Law and Procedure

Voluntary manslaughter is an intentional killing that does not rise to murder's level because of the mitigating circumstance of **provocation**. Provocation's definition has both *objective* and *subjective* conditions. To reduce a conviction from murder to manslaughter, the provocation must be such as would cause a reasonable person to lose control *and* must also have caused the defendant to have lost control. In other words, if a reasonable person *would have* lost control but the defendant did *not* lose control and instead acted without provocation's effect, then the crime remains murder, not manslaughter. In the same way, if the defendant lost control but the reasonable person would *not* have done so, then the crime remains murder, not manslaughter.

Provocation can take many forms but often involves the victim's offense to or with the defendant's intimate family member, such as being caught in *adultery* with the defendant's spouse. Some cases even hold that hearing of adultery, not merely catching the victim in the act, can be provocation. Similarly, a *serious assault* such as firing a gun or swinging a knife or sword at the defendant, or *serious battery*, can constitute provocation, if the defendant reacts impulsively in response, setting aside for a later section whether the assault or battery warranted the defendant to kill in self-defense. Thus, fights in which one of the participants dies support a manslaughter conviction of the surviving participant, unless the surviving participant acted unfairly in the fight such as by pulling out and using a gun, in which case the action may support a murder conviction. *Words alone*, though, do *not* constitute provocation no matter how offensive.

Provocation depends on a second condition in addition to its adequacy to provoke. The defendant must not have *calmed down* from the provocation's effect. The defendant must also show that the reasonable person would not have calmed down from the effect. Thus, this second condition having to do with a cooling-off period has the same objective-and-subjective quality as the adequacy of the provocation to provoke both the defendant and the reasonable person. So, for example, if the defendant discovered the victim in a sexual act with the defendant's spouse but left the scene long enough for the provocation's impulsive effect to dissipate, then a subsequent intentional killing would be murder, not manslaughter. Similarly, if the defendant did not calm down but the reasonable person would have given a similar interlude, then the killing would be murder, not manslaughter.

B. Unintended killings

While *malice aforethought* clearly includes intent to kill, constituting the core premeditated and deliberated form of murder, *malice aforethought* sufficient to support a murder charge also includes certain **unintended killings**. The intent to cause *serious injury* that then results in death is one such form of unintended killing satisfying malice aforethought, as the next section addresses. The intent to commit certain felonies when death results in their course, known as *felony murder*, is another unintended killing that satisfies malice aforethought, as a following section addresses. Also,

Criminal Law and Procedure

intentional acts done with *depraved indifference* to life, when the acts result in death, also satisfy malice aforethought, as another following section describes. Another section below addresses *misdemeanor manslaughter*.

1. Intent to injure

The **intent to seriously injure** another also satisfies the *malice aforethought* element of common-law murder, when the victim dies from the serious injuries. The actor need not intend that the victim die and may even intend that the victim *not* die, if the actor intended serious injury and death resulted. The intent must be to injure *seriously*, not simply to cause minor or moderate injury. For example, to intentionally slap or punch someone may not qualify as the intent to cause serious injury, depending on factors such as the relative strength or weakness of actor and victim, force and location of the slap or punch, and awareness of the victim. Yet to intend to shoot a gun, cut with a knife, or strike with a heavy metal object may constitute intent to injure seriously, again, depending on several factors.

2. Reckless and negligent killings

Actions taken with **depraved indifference** to human life also satisfy the *malice aforethought* element of common-law murder, when those actions result in death. The law also calls this form *depraved-heart murder*. Depraved indifference involves the actor's *subjective state of mind*, where the actor knows that the acts carry **unusually high risk** of death or serious injury to another but undertakes them anyway, with resulting death. If, on the other hand, the actor does *not* know of the unusually high risk, even though the reasonable person would know, then the actor has *not* exhibited depraved indifference to satisfy the malice-aforethought element of common-law murder, and acquittal on that charge must follow.

Involuntary manslaughter is another crime of unintended killing. Involuntary manslaughter ordinarily involves *criminal negligence. Criminal negligence* need not involve a crime but must involve *unreasonably high* risk of death, which is more than ordinary civil negligence requires. In contrast to the subjective state of mind necessary for depraved indifference, the lesser crime of involuntary manslaughter does *not* involve the actor's *subjective* state of mind but instead involves an *objective* standard of conduct. Involuntary manslaughter does not consider what the actor knew or did not know. Moreover, the conduct necessary for involuntary manslaughter involves a lower degree of risk than the conduct necessary to convict of murder based on depraved indifference. The *criminal negligence* necessary to satisfy involuntary manslaughter involves *unreasonably high* risk of death that the jury would accept as criminal. Involuntary manslaughter thus differs from murder based on depraved indifference in both the state of mind and reprehensibility of the conduct.

Some states further divide the involuntary-manslaughter forms of unintended killings into *involuntary manslaughter* and *negligent homicide*.

In those states, involuntary manslaughter requires action involving a higher *reckless* degree of risk of death, while negligent homicide instead accepts merely *unreasonably high* risk to satisfy the crime. Because these are objective rather than subject standards, an actor can be guilty of the reckless form of involuntary manslaughter without appreciating the reckless degree of risk or guilty of negligent homicide without knowing of the unreasonably high risk. These objective judgments reflect a community sense of propriety rather than an investigation into the wrongdoer's own state of mind. Together, the three charges of murder based on depraved indifference, involuntary manslaughter of the reckless kind, and criminal negligence account for a range of behavior.

Thus, for example, a motor-vehicle driver who in road rage rams another vehicle off an interstate highway while traveling at high speed probably exhibits depraved indifference sufficient to convict of murder if the road-rage victim dies. By contrast, one who drives well over 100 miles per hour on a public highway with a 60 mile-per-hour speed limit, but without intending to strike other vehicles, probably exhibits recklessness because of the reckless risk of death. Drunk driving also typically involves a reckless degree of risk although in severe cases can constitute depraved indifference. In further contrast, one who drives 75 or 80 miles per hour in a 60 mile-per-hour zone may be exhibiting a merely unreasonably high risk of death warranting a negligent homicide charge if death ensues. Many modern statutes classify these unintended vehicle-death crimes as **vehicular manslaughter**.

3. Felony murder

Another mental state that *malice aforethought* includes is the intent to commit certain felonies, during which, or in fleeing from which, a death results. For example, if a person robs a bank but then in a getaway vehicle accidentally drives over and kills someone in flight, then the person will have committed felony murder, even though the death was accidental. The robbery felony would have satisfied the malice-aforethought element of murder. The **felony-murder** form of malice aforethought depends, though, on the commission of a *dangerous* felony traditionally including only *burglary, robbery, arson, kidnapping, escape,* and *sex crimes*. At common law, felony murder involved death occurring during the commission or attempted commission of *any* felony, but under modern developments, death resulting during non-dangerous felonies such as criminal fraud does *not* support a felony-murder charge.

Some states limit felony-murder charges to only foreseeable deaths, although broadly construing foreseeability to include such things as a security guard's accidental death in pursuit of the one committing the qualifying crime. Most states also require that the predicate felony, such as robbery or rape, be independent of the killing. If, for instance, a person commits a battery from which the victim subsequently dies, then the felony-murder form of malice aforethought usually does *not* apply because the battery was the

Criminal Law and Procedure

direct cause of the killing rather than an independent predicate crime. In that circumstance, the law would convict of murder, if at all, only under the intent-to-seriously-injure form of malice aforethought. A few states require the prosecution to prove not only the underlying felony and resulting death but also *malice*, proven by the intent to kill or cause grievous bodily harm, or extreme and reckless indifference to the value of human life.

Some jurisdictions also apply an *agency* rule to felony murder, requiring that the death result from the defendant's own acts or the acts of the defendant's co-felon agent. If instead a security guard accidentally shot and killed someone while trying to prevent the felony, then those jurisdictions would not find felony murder, although other jurisdictions still would. Other jurisdictions refuse to find felony murder if the death was of one of the co-felons rather than someone not involved in the crime. Felony murder does extend, though, to deaths occurring after the crime while the defendant is still in flight from the crime, up until the defendant reaches a place of *temporary safety*. Thus, if the defendant escapes to a hideout for an hour but then accidentally kills someone after resuming flight, the circumstances no longer support a felony-murder charge.

4. Misdemeanor manslaughter

Misdemeanor manslaughter, another form of *involuntary manslaughter*, is a final crime of unintended killing. Recall that only certain dangerous felonies, including burglary, robbery, arson, kidnapping, escape, and sex crimes, can support a felony-murder charge. Felonies like criminal fraud and misdemeanors punishable by imprisonment for less than one year do *not* support a felony-murder charge. These lesser crimes, though, *do* support a misdemeanor-manslaughter charge. Thus, causing death during commission of or flight from a crime *not counting for felony* murder supports a misdemeanor-manslaughter charge. If death results from one of these lesser crimes such as criminal fraud or a misdemeanor crime punishable by imprisonment of less than one year, then the crime supports a misdemeanor-manslaughter charge.

II. Other crimes

The common law defines several other personal and property crimes not involving killing. Property crimes include **theft** or *larceny* and the related crime of **receiving stolen goods**, crimes of **possession**, and the more-serious property crimes of **robbery**, **burglary**, and **arson**. Personal crimes include **assault**, **battery**, the sex crimes of **rape** and **statutory rape**, and **kidnapping**. Consider the definition and application of each in the following sections.

A. Theft...

Criminal Law and Procedure

The common law defines **larceny** as both a *trespassory taking and a carrying away* of the personal property of another with the intent to *permanently deprive* the owner or other rightful possessor of the property. The trespassory-taking element means to *intentionally dispossess without consent.* The personal property can be anything tangible that the wrongdoer can take and carry away, from money or jewelry to household or commercial goods and even vehicles, equipment, and livestock of value, although not household pets. Under the common law, larceny does *not* apply to intangibles like stocks, bonds, and vehicle titles, even when represented by a record or certificate that the wrongdoer can carry away. **Modern statutes**, though, alter the common law to include intangible property within the scope of larceny, so that the thief who steals stock certificates from an office, or a vehicle title from a car even without stealing the car, commits larceny.

Any minor intentional movement of the property will satisfy larceny's *carrying-away* element. The wrongdoer need not escape to relative safety with the property if the wrongdoer *possesses* and *intentionally moves* the property. Thus, the thief who takes a co-worker's wallet off the co-worker's desk and puts it in the thief's pocket intending to steal it has taken the property and, with any movement, carried it away, even if promptly caught. A wrongdoer who causes an innocent agent to accomplish the taking and carrying away also commits larceny, such as if the thief asked a friend to go get the thief's wallet, directing the friend to the co-worker's wallet instead, and the friend brought it to the thief. The taking, though, must be intentional and wrongful. Retrieving and moving one's own bag into which someone else has placed their property would not constitute larceny if the bag's owner did not know of the other's property or intended to return it to the owner rather than deprive the owner of it. Indeed, the law recognizes a person's **claim of right** to the property as a crime-specific defense. Taking property in the good-faith belief that one owns or has a legal right to it is not larceny.

Larceny by trick is a related crime but one in which the wrongdoer first gains the property not by secret action but instead by *misrepresenting* facts to its owner. For example, if a wrongdoer intentionally misrepresented to the owner of a laptop computer that the computer was the wrongdoer's computer, so that the wrongdoer could take it and carry it away intending permanent deprivation, then the wrongdoer would have committed larceny by trick. Traditional law does not regard a false promise of future performance to be a sufficient misrepresentation to support a larceny-by-trick charge. Thus, if the wrongdoer in the above example asked to borrow the owner's computer, ensuring that the wrongdoer would bring it back in an hour, then the false assurance would not support a larceny-by-trick charge even if the wrongdoer never intended to bring back the computer. The modern rule, though, reaches the opposite result, recognizing a false promise that the wrongdoer *never intended to keep* as sufficient to support a larceny-by-trick charge.

The **Model Penal Code** redefines common-law larceny and related crimes under the single crime of **theft**, involving the wrongdoer acting with the intent of depriving another person of personal property that the wrongdoer

Criminal Law and Procedure

has taken. The Code defines *depriving* to include permanent withholding of the property *or* withholding it long enough for it to have lost most of its value, withholding it for ransom, or disposing of it in a way that makes its recovery unlikely. Code defenses to theft include the suspect being unaware that the property belonged to another, the suspect taking it under honest claim of right, or taking the property intending to buy it immediately or reasonably believing that the owner would consent to its use.

Embezzlement is a similar crime to theft but one that begins with the property lawfully in the wrongdoer's hands. In embezzlement, one who lawfully holds the property of another with the other's consent converts, or misappropriates, the property with the intent to conceal the conversion from the property's owner. To convert another's property is to interfere with the owner's right, using the property in a way other than that which the owner authorized on relinquishing the property to the wrongdoer. For example, an advisor who secretly draws investments out of a customer's account for the advisor's own use has committed embezzlement. Similarly, a tradesman who borrows a homeowner's ladder for a job but then sells the ladder to another rather than return it to the owner has committed embezzlement. By contrast, one who takes the property unlawfully in the first instance, without the owner's initial consent, commits larceny, not embezzlement, such as if the tradesman simply stole the ladder rather than borrowing it in the first instance.

The related crime of **false pretenses** involves a wrongdoer tricking the owner of property into passing title to the wrongdoer. The false-pretenses crime differs from embezzlement in that with false pretenses, the wrongdoer obtains title, meaning authorized possession, although by misrepresentation, whereas with embezzlement, the wrongdoer never obtains title, only unauthorized possession. For example, a scheming builder who convinces a naïve homeowner that the homeowner must grant the builder a deed for the builder to do renovation work and then secretly conveys the deed to an investor, has committed false pretenses. If, on the other hand, the owner had offered the builder the deed in trust and the builder had subsequently absconded with it, then the act would be embezzlement rather than false pretenses.

...and receiving stolen goods

Receiving stolen goods relates closely to the crime of larceny. The crime of receiving stolen goods involves *knowingly* receiving stolen property while *intending to permanently deprive* the owner of those goods. Someone must have *stolen* the goods before passing them to the defendant. Receiving borrowed or lost goods with the intent of depriving the owner of them, for instance, will not support a receiving-stolen-goods charge. The person receiving the goods must also *know* that another stole them, although the person need not know how, when, or from whom another stole the goods, if circumstances nonetheless indicate theft. For example, taking high-value jewelry from a disreputable individual not in the jewelry business, when the individual has no credible explanation for coming into their possession, may

Criminal Law and Procedure

satisfy the knowledge requirement. The person must also intend the owner's *permanent deprivation*. A person who comes into possession of stolen goods only intending to return them has not committed the receiving-stolen-goods crime.

B. Robbery

The crime of **robbery** involves taking the personal property of another in the person's presence, by *force or violence*, or its threat, intending to permanently deprive the person of the property. Robbery is thus *larceny by force* in which the prosecution must prove larceny's elements plus the force-or-threat element. The property must be in the person's presence, meaning either on the person's presence, within the person's reach, or near enough that the person could prevent the theft by action but for the threat. The degree of force or threat doesn't matter, no matter how minor. Grabbing a purse out of another's hand is sufficient to constitute robbery, just as would be shooting a person or threatening to shoot. *Some* force must be used or threatened, though. Secretly slipping a wallet from another's pocket or bag would not support a robbery charge, only larceny. The intent, too, must be to *permanently deprive* another of the other's property. If the actor mistakenly thought that the property was the actor's own, or had no intent to permanently deprive the possessor of it, then the act is not robbery.

When the robber accomplishes the crime by **threat** rather than applied force, the prosecution must show that the robber's threat produced the victim's fear *and* that the victim's fear was *reasonable*. If either fear or reasonableness are absent, then robbery is not the crime. Moreover, the threat must be of *death or bodily injury*, not other extortion such as to embarrass or defame, although a threat to *destroy one's dwelling* also suffices. A threat of death or bodily injury made against the victim's relative or a person in the victim's presence will also suffice, such as if the robber were to demand the victim's property on threat of shooting a bystander. Any threat, though, must be for imminent harm rather than future action. Demanding property on threat of returning a day later in violence is not robbery.

While common-law robbery requires the use of force or threat to take the property, the **Model Penal Code** defines robbery more broadly to include any use of force during the theft, even if the force was only incidental rather than necessary to taking the property. The common law treats any robbery, whether of valuable goods or by use of weapon or not, as a felony. Modern statutes, while still treating all robbery as a felony, may include **aggravated robbery** for situations involving the wrongdoer's use of a weapon to accomplish the crime and increase the punishment accordingly.

C. Burglary

Common-law **burglary** involves *breaking and entering a dwelling* of another *at night* intending to *commit a felony inside*. The law construes the **breaking** element broadly to include not just breaking down a door or shattering a window but instead any even slight use of force to create or enlarge an opening to enter. Thus, opening an unlocked door or opening further an already-open window satisfies the element, although under the common law, if a door or other entry point is already open enough for entry and the actor does not open it further, then breaking has not occurred. Even *constructive* breaking will do, involving creating an entrance through threat, fraud, or a co-conspirator inside letting the burglar in. The breaking, though, must be into the dwelling *of another*. Breaking into one's own dwelling is not burglary, unless one has rented it to another, the rental excludes the owner's entry, and the owner nonetheless enters intending to steal or commit another felony inside.

The common law construes burglary's **entering** element broadly to include not only the slightest partial entry of the burglar's foot or hand but also constructive entries by others under the defendant's control. The entry of a tool used to create an opening, like a crowbar forced through under a window frame, does not constitute entry, but entry of a tool designed to steal, such a pole slid through a window to hook and remove an item, does constitute entry. The common law also requires that the entry be into an inhabited **dwelling**, defined as a place that persons regularly use for sleeping, even if the building also has other uses. A building under construction as a dwelling does not become a dwelling until occupied, but once occupied as a dwelling, the building remains a dwelling even while persons who regularly sleep there are away.

A person need not break into any specific part of the dwelling for the act to support a burglary conviction. Breaking and entering a vestibule will do even if the burglar intends the crime in an interior room. If the person enters the dwelling without having to break in but then breaks into an interior room, the interior breaking satisfies the breaking element of the burglary crime. Breaking and entering buildings that are near but apart from a dwelling does not support a burglary conviction unless those buildings are within the **curtilage**, defined as an area of land forming one enclosure with an inhabited dwelling. Thus, breaking and entering a shed or barn within an area that forms one enclosure with an inhabited dwelling would support a burglary conviction.

The person's entry must be with the intent to **commit a felony** inside. Felonies are generally crimes punishable by more than one year of imprisonment. The typical intended felony would be *larceny*, to steal something from inside the dwelling, but other felonies will also satisfy the element, including crimes of violence like assault, battery, and rape. The person need *not* actually commit the felony to suffer burglary conviction. The crime is complete once the person breaks and enters with felony intent, even if the person then decides not to go through with the felony. On the other hand, forming the intent to commit a felony *after* one has broken and entered does not constitute burglary, such as opening and entering a neighbor's door on a friendly errand but then deciding to steal something in sight. If an entrant completes the intended felony, such as larceny or rape, then the entrant can suffer both the burglary conviction and other felony conviction.

Criminal Law and Procedure

Modern statutes define burglary more broadly, such as to *knowingly enter* or *remain unlawfully in* a building intending to commit a crime inside. Modern statutes may not require a *breaking* element at all, so that walking in through an already-open door to commit a felony inside would still support a burglary conviction. Similarly, modern statutes may not require that the entry be *at night*, so that entries during the day would also support a burglary conviction. Modern statutes may also not require that the building be a *dwelling*, so that entering an office or commercial structure with the intent to commit a felony inside would support a burglary conviction. And modern statutes may find a burglary if the entrant initially had no intent to commit a felony when entering but forms that intent once inside. Modern statutes may also define degrees of burglary, reserving **first-degree burglary** for entrants of inhabited dwellings with a weapon used to commit an assault.

D. Assault...

Criminal **assault** in its common-law form involves *attempting to commit a battery*. The next section addresses the battery crime. Consistent with the law of attempts, addressed in a later section, the actor must not only subjectively intend to commit a battery but must also *take a step* toward accomplishing the battery. Assault in its modern conception includes not just an attempt at battery but also *intentionally placing the victim in fear of a battery*. This modern formulation of assault requires that the victim *apprehend* the imminent intentional harmful contact, usually by seeing it but possibly by hearing or otherwise sensing it. Assault also requires that the harm appear *imminent*. A threat to hurt someone tomorrow, even if real, is not assault. Also, words alone do not constitute assault. Assault requires some volitional act, such as seeming to reach for a gun or knife while making verbal threats or threatening actions.

To satisfy the modern formulation of assault, the victim's apprehension of the imminent intentional harmful contact must be both *reasonable* and *actual*. If, for instance, a person has an unusually heightened and distorted sense of fear, such as apprehending a battery from an innocent offer to shake hands, where the reasonable person would not have apprehended anything harmful, then the person offering the handshake has not committed an assault. If, on the other hand, a reasonable person *would* anticipate a battery from a certain action, such as another pointing a gun at the person along with words threatening an imminent shooting, but the person does *not* anticipate a battery, for instance knowing that the gun is unloaded or a toy gun, then no assault has occurred. Simple assault is a *misdemeanor*, while **aggravated assault**, involving either intent to kill or use of a deadly weapon, is a felony.

...and battery

Criminal **battery**, as distinguished from the civil tort of battery, involves intentional *unlawful use of force* against another. The person must

Criminal Law and Procedure

have either intended the act or acted negligently, where the person should have known that harmful or offensive touching would result. The person must also have caused *contact*, although the contact need not be person to person but can instead be such as bullet or rock to person. Thus, intentionally punching someone in the face is an obvious battery, as is shooting another intentionally, but so can be shoving a chair into the other or throwing a snowball striking the other, although some modern statutes require injury if the touching is not otherwise offensive. The touching necessary to sustain a battery charge can be either harmful *or* offensive. Thus, punching someone in the stomach obviously satisfies the harm-or-offense element, but so does intentionally touching another intimately without their permission when society would regard the touching as offensive.

The contact must, as just suggested, be harmful or offensive so *to the reasonable person*. For example, society might ordinarily tolerate and even encourage a polite tap or cheerful clap on the shoulder of another. Yet if the other has already indicated *refusal* to accept any contact, as for instance in a previously intimate relationship, then one who proceeds with initiating the harmful or offensive contact knowing the circumstances can have committed a battery. The victim's consent may, on the other hand, establish that the contact was *not* offensive, although the actor must not exceed the consent. If the actor exceeds the consent, causes injury, or intends to cause serious injury, then the action supports a battery conviction notwithstanding initial consent. While simply battery is generally a *misdemeanor*, jurisdictions often recognize felony **aggravated battery** committed with intent to kill or with a deadly weapon, or when resulting in serious injury.

E. Rape...

The common-law crime of **rape** involves a man *forcing sexual intercourse* on a woman not the man's wife, without the woman's consent. Under the common law, rape required at least some penetration, even minimal, of the female victim's genitalia, as the victim resisted. Modern statutes rename rape as **sexual assault** and redefine it to include *forcing another person to submit to sex acts* against will. Modern statutes thus broaden significantly the sex acts that qualify, beyond sexual intercourse involving penetration, to include other statutorily defined sex acts. Modern statutes also make the crime gender neutral so that either men or women may commit sexual assault. Modern statutes differ, though, on whether a husband can commit rape on the husband's wife, although the statutes leave open the possibility of assault and battery charges.

The common law and modern requirements of *force* and *lack of consent* together indicate that the perpetrator must have unlawfully overcome the victim's will, either by literal physical force *or* by threat of imminent harm. Force is not required if the perpetrator accomplishes the act using threat of imminent harm. Thus, while **consent** ordinarily defeats a rape charge, acquiescence under threat of imminent harm is *not* consent. A *mentally deficient*, heavily *intoxicated*, or *drugged* person may also not be capable of consent, so that the actor who commits the requisite sex act under those circumstances may be guilty of rape.

The effectiveness of consent through *fraud* depends on the circumstances. If the perpetrator's misrepresentation is as to the *intended conduct*, fraud in fact, then consent is ineffective, and the perpetrator is guilty of rape. Thus, if the actor proposes and victim consents to an examination but the actor commits sexual intercourse instead, then rape is the appropriate charge. If on the other hand the actor misrepresents the *context* for the acknowledged sex act, fraud *in the inducement*, such as if the actor falsely suggests medical or social value to intercourse to gain the victim's consent, and the victim consents, then rape is *not* an appropriate charge. Misrepresentation or trick as to identity, claiming to be someone other than who the actor is, does not affect consent, which remains valid. Jurisdictions disagree over whether a misrepresentation as to marital status, claiming marriage when knowing that marriage was not the fact, affects consent.

The actor must have the requisite guilty *state of mind*, knowing that the sex act is against the other's will. Mistaken belief that the other has consented to the act ordinarily defeats a rape charge, given the absence of the knowledge from which to construe the guilty mind. Some jurisdictions, though, require not only that the actor honestly and in good faith believe that the other had consented but also that the belief be *reasonable*. In those jurisdictions, if the reasonable person would *not* have construed consent from the other's words and actions, and the circumstances, then the sex act would remain rape. Some jurisdictions still retain a common-law age defense that a boy under age fourteen is incapable of the rape crime, although other jurisdictions alter the defense to a rebuttable presumption, while many others no longer recognize any such age defense.

...statutory rape

The crime of **statutory rape** involves sexual intercourse with a person, in some jurisdictions only a girl rather than a girl or boy, who is under the legal age of consent, without regard to consent. The state's statute establishes the legal age, often *under age sixteen*. Statutory rape occurs even if the underage person consents, the law conclusively presuming the invalidity of consent. Statutory rape is also a *strict liability* crime without a requisite state of mind. The actor is guilty not only if the underage person consent but also if the underage person claims to be, and looks to be, older than the age of consent. Some states relieve the actor of statutory rape if the actor's age is close to the victim's age, such as a sixteen-year-old boy having sexual intercourse with an underage fifteen-year-old girl.

F. Kidnapping

At common law, the crime of **kidnapping** involves the *secret confinement* or *movement* of a person by *force or threat*, intending to *hold* the victim *against the victim's will*. Kidnapping essentially involves *forcible*

Criminal Law and Procedure

moving of another. Courts disagree, though, on the extent to which the actor must move the person for the action to qualify as kidnapping. Some courts accept *any* movement as sufficient to satisfy that element of the crime, while other courts require *substantial* movement to ensure that the action qualifies as criminally reprehensible. Jurisdictions also differ on how the wrongdoer must accomplish the forceful movement. The core form of kidnapping involves the victim's **confinement** by force or threat to accomplish the movement, although other jurisdictions accept that movement accomplished by *fraud* also suffices. Thus, locking the victim in a vehicle's trunk to accomplish movement would clearly be kidnapping, but in some jurisdictions, so would be posing as a taxi driver while moving the victim not to the victim's requested destination but toward the kidnapper's intended destination.

Kidnapping is an intent crime. The actor must intend, while knowing that the actor lacks lawful authority, to move the victim by force or to confine the victim for movement, as the specific jurisdiction requires. If instead, the actor *accidentally* confines and moves a person, such as not realizing that they are in a vehicle or its trailer, or believes that the actor has lawful authority, such as to apprehend a suspected wrongdoer, then the actor has not committed kidnapping. Also, if the specific jurisdiction requires a *purpose* for the confinement and transport, as some jurisdictions require confinement and movement for *ransom*, then the actor must have that specific purpose as the actor's state of mind. If instead, the actor confined and moved the person out of a practical joke or for the victim's own safety or the safety of another, where the jurisdiction required confinement and movement for ransom, then the actor has not committed kidnapping. Many states, though, do not require proof of the movement's purpose. Kidnapping is a *felony* under both the common law and modern statutes, although many jurisdictions also recognize **aggravated kidnapping** when done for ransom or extortion. Other jurisdictions construe safe release as a mitigating circumstance.

G. Arson

The common-law crime of **arson** involves the *malicious burning* of the *inhabited dwelling of another*. The *malice* element of arson refers to the intent to commit a wrongful act without justification or excuse. The law defines arson's *inhabited-dwelling* element the same as the definition of a dwelling for burglary, meaning a building in which persons *regularly sleep*, whether including other non-residential functions or not. Arson requires that the fire that the suspect set accomplish at least *some* damage to the dwelling, such as charring some part of the structure, although the damage need not be extensive. Discoloration from heat or smoke does not constitute sufficient damage to support an arson charge.

Damage from an explosion is also not enough to support a common-law arson charge unless the explosion causes a fire that damages the dwelling. Because arson's mens rea is **malice**, defined as intent to commit a wrongful act, the actor need not necessarily intend to burn the dwelling. The actor's

Criminal Law and Procedure

knowing that the actions would burn the dwelling, or the actor's intentionally creating a high-risk fire hazard, such as the explosion example just given, suffices for arson's state-of-mind element. Careless actions leading to burning of the dwelling, though, are not sufficient. The burning must also be of the dwelling *of another* rather than the actor's own dwelling, although intentionally setting one's own dwelling afire, creating a high risk that a neighboring dwelling would also catch fire, satisfies arson's state-of-mind element if indeed the neighboring dwelling catches fire.

Modern statutes expand these common-law arson elements. Modern statutes eliminate the *dwelling* requirement, recognizing arson to include the intentional burning of any building. A few statutes even expand arson's reach to include burning the *personal property* of another, although imposing a lesser punishment. Modern statutes also eliminate the requirement that the building belong to another. Under modern statutes, intentionally burning *one's own* building constitutes arson, if the owner knew or should have known that the burning created risk to other people, or if the owner set the fire to defraud the owner's fire insurer. Modern statutes also loosen the *burning* requirement so that one who starts *any* fire intending to damage or destroy a building commits arson even if the fire does not reach and damage the building. Indeed, modern statutes accept damage done by intentional explosion even if no fire ensues. Arson is a felony under both the common law and modern statutes.

H. Possession offenses

Federal and state statutory **possession offenses** involve unlawful *knowing* and *intentional* possession of controlled or illegal substances, stolen goods, and other *contraband* like drug paraphernalia, without justification. For example, federal and state laws control certain prescription or other substances, such as opioids and amphetamines, and make illegal the manufacture, distribution, or possession of other substances, such as cocaine and heroin. Other laws regulate possession of materials or equipment for drug manufacturing, and possession of stolen items. When a person possesses a contraband item outside of the terms of the federal or state controls, or possesses an illegal substance, then the person commits the possession offense unless having a legal excuse. Possession offenses do *not* require intent to sell or distribute the items, which is a more-serious crime often proven in drug cases by the larger quantity and purer form of the controlled or illegal substance, or other direct or circumstantial evidence of intended sale. Possession laws may also ban possession of drug paraphernalia, like syringes or pipes if either already used with drugs (proven from residue) or purchased explicitly for drug use.

Possession typically entails personal, physical *control* over the substance or item, such as to intentionally have it on one's person or in one's vehicle or home where one can use, move, or dispose of it. Persons can share possession if they share control, such as by purposefully concealing it together in a shared vehicle or home, under either's physical control. As to

Criminal Law and Procedure

the required **state of mind**, the person need *not* know that a substance or item is illegal or controlled but *must* know what the substances or items are, such as that the drug is the methamphetamine, *and* must intend to possess them. Thus, a person who intentionally carries what the person knows to be methamphetamine, but who does not know that methamphetamine is a controlled substance or that possessing it is illegal, would still have committed the possession offense.

III.   Inchoate crimes; parties

The following sections first address the **inchoate crimes** of *attempt, conspiracy,* and *solicitation,* and then the potential **parties** to crimes, referring to the law of **accessories** to crime. These sections show that the law does not limit criminal responsibility to the persons who commit the personal harms or property theft or damage. Criminal responsibility extends to those who take substantial steps to commit crimes, agree and act in concert with others to commit crimes, encourage others to commit crimes, and interfere with law-enforcement apprehension of others who commit crimes. First consider the inchoate offenses and then the accomplice offenses.

A. Inchoate offenses

Inchoate crimes, also known as *incomplete crimes* although in law recognized as complete crimes in themselves, involve intentional criminal acts directed toward the promotion or completion of other crimes not necessarily executed. An inchoate crime is an offense in which the actor *intends a result* that the actor does not need to achieve to complete the inchoate crime. Inchoate crimes include crimes of **attempt** in which the actor takes a substantial step toward completing an underlying crime that the actor does not complete, crimes of **solicitation** in which the actor requests another to commit an underlying crime, and crimes of **conspiracy** in which two or more agree to commit an underlying crime while taking an overt act to further the agreement.

1. Attempts

A common-law **attempt** crime involves the *specific intent* to commit any felony or misdemeanor crime together with *taking a step* to accomplish the crime. By **specific intent**, the law means that the actor must intend an act necessary to commit the crime or an act that will result in the crime *and* intend the result of the crime, the latter requirement being the nature of specific-intent crimes. For example, someone who intends to break into an unoccupied house to stay warm and sleep one night, and attempts to do so but is caught trying to pick the door lock, has *not* committed attempted burglary because the actor, while trying to break and enter, had no intent to commit a felony inside, which is the result of the burglary crime. Thus, the only kind of *attempted murder* that a person can commit is the form of murder based on intent to kill. Any lesser intent, such as intent to seriously injure or depraved indifference, cannot satisfy an attempt crime's requirement that the person intend the crime's result, which in the case of murder is death.

When the law of attempt requires *taking a step* toward committing the underlying crime, the law requires more than mere **preparation**, defined as the act or process of devising means of committing a crime. A person may muse all that the person wishes about how the person would go about a crime, without having committed the crime's attempt. Yet when, under the Model Penal Code, the person takes a *substantial step* in the crime's commission, constituting *strong evidence* of the person's criminal purpose, the person has completed the attempt crime. Examples include lying in wait for the victim, luring the victim toward the planned crime scene, staking out the crime scene, entering the place of the crime, moving things necessary to commit the crime to the crime scene, or soliciting another to help with the crime. Casing several potential victims or crime sites is not enough.

Questions arise when the crime that the actor attempts is not possible. Attempt crimes treat **factual impossibility**, meaning things that the actor cannot physically accomplish, differently from **legal impossibility**, meaning things that the actor can accomplish but that are not a crime. An actor commits an attempt *even when the crime is factually impossible* but not when the crime is legally impossible, meaning not when the attempted action is not a crime. Another question arises when a person begins an attempt but then **withdraws** before completing the crime. The traditional rule held the actor responsible even if withdrawing. Yet the Model Penal code recognizes withdrawal as a defense if the actor abandoned *voluntarily* rather than because of the crime's difficulty or fear of discovery and arrest, and withdrew *completely*, cancelling all plans rather than merely delaying them for a later attempt.

Significantly, the law of attempts recognizes the **merger** of the attempt into the completed underlying crime. A prosecution cannot convict of both the attempt and the crime the attempt meant to commit. The attempt merges into the crime unless the actor does not complete the crime, in which case a prosecution may only convict for the attempt. Also, because an attempt is a **lesser-included** offense of the crime that the attempt intends to commit, meaning that the underlying crime includes all elements of the attempt, a prosecution cannot pursue an attempt charge after trial of the underlying crime results in an acquittal. To try the lesser-included attempt would violate the Constitution's double-jeopardy clause. The common law punishes attempts less than the crime, but the Model Penal Code permits the same punishments.

2. Conspiracy

The common-law crime of **conspiracy** involves an *agreement* between two or more to commit a criminal act together. The law of most jurisdictions adds an element that the common law did *not* require, which is that one of the conspirators commit an *overt act* furthering at least one of the

Criminal Law and Procedure

agreement's criminal objectives. To satisfy conspiracy's state-of-mind element, the conspirator must intend the agreement *and* intend the overt act furthering its criminal objective. Thus, a person who *says* that the person agrees to help commit a murder but who instead intends to turn in to authorities the other who sought the agreement has not formed the required *intent to agree*. Likewise, if the person says *and means* that the person agrees to commit a murder but then does not intend any act that furthers the agreement, even though the person's acts may unintentionally do so, has not formed the required *intent to act*. Prosecutors do, though, typically use circumstances to prove intent, conspirators not often admitting to elements of the crime. Courts disagree on whether the actor must know that the objective on which the actor agrees is in law a crime.

As to the **overt-act** element that most jurisdictions require to complete the conspiracy crime, beyond the common-law requirements, an overt act *by any of the conspirators* and *at any location and time* will satisfy the element. For example, if two agree to commit a murder a week hence, but just one procures the murder weapon the next day, then both will have committed the conspiracy crime, the act of one satisfying that element as to the conspiracy of both without respect to location or time. Yet under the common law, *at least two persons must intend their agreement* for either to have committed conspiracy. If one does not intend, for instance if an undercover officer, then the other who does intend still has not committed conspiracy. On the other hand, if two intend their agreement, then a third whose act furthers the agreement is a part of the conspiracy and may suffer conviction for the crime. Thus, if two agree to commit a murder, and a third procures and supplies the weapon for the crime, then all three have committed the conspiracy, the third's assistance *implying* agreement.

If conspirators form a *single agreement*, then they commit a single conspiracy crime no matter how many crimes they agree to commit within the single conspiracy. For example, if the agreement is to illegally purchase prescription drugs online to manufacture, distribute, and sell those drugs while laundering the profits through a sporting-goods store, then the parties to the agreement commit a single conspiracy even though multiple underlying crimes. The common law treats conspiracy as a *misdemeanor*, while modern statutes differ, and the Model Penal Code would punish conspiracy the same as the most-serious of the conspiracies target crimes. The Model Penal Code also broadens conspiracy's scope by eliminating the requirement that at least two must intend to agree. If one intends agreement but does so with an undercover officer who does not intend agreement, then the Model Penal Code would find a conspiracy crime. If the defendant agrees and intends agreement, then the defendant commits the crime, even if no one else intends the agreement that they reflect.

As with criminal attempts, if a conspiracy completes the target crime, then some jurisdictions have in the past held that the conspiracy charge **merges** into the completed target crime, and prosecutors cannot convict the conspirators of both the conspiracy and the completed target crime. Modern statutes, though, do *not* merge conspiracy into the completed target crime.

Criminal Law and Procedure

The Constitution's double-jeopardy clause does not require that they do so because conspiracy is *not* a lesser-included offense of the target crime, which would contain no *agreement* element. Yet if trials result in acquittals of all others whom prosecutors could charge with the conspiracy, then under the common law, the remaining alleged conspirator is also free of the charge, given that prosecutors must prove agreement. The Model Penal Code reaches the opposite result because it recognizes agreement of only one as sufficient.

As with attempts, *factual impossibility* is not a conspiracy defense. The common law refuses to recognize withdrawal as a conspiracy defense, but as with attempts, the Model Penal Code recognizes withdrawal as a conspiracy defense if voluntary and complete, although the withdrawing conspirator must also *prevent the target crime*. Under the ***Pinkerton* rule**, conspirators have criminal responsibility for reasonably foreseeable crimes that other conspirators commit furthering the conspiracy and that are the conspiracy's necessary or natural consequences. Thus, if two agree to a vehicle kidnapping and sexual assault but the victim and others foreseeably die in the conspiracy's course, both could suffer conviction for all crimes relating to the deaths, no matter which conspirator caused them. Withdrawal, though, would relieve a conspirator from responsibility for the conspiracy's other crimes after withdrawal, if the withdrawing conspirators timely communicates the withdrawal to the other conspirators. A conspirator is no longer responsible for other crimes once the conspiracy ends, which occurs when the conspiracy accomplishes its object. *Wharton's rule* prohibits a conspiracy conviction of two persons for an offense that requires two persons to commit.

3. Solicitation

The crime of **solicitation** involves *advising, encouraging, requesting,* or otherwise *inducing* another to *commit or join in committing a crime*. The person must have the *intent* to cause the other to commit the crime. Any of the above acts of soliciting complete the solicitation crime whether the person solicited commits the crime or not. Thus, soliciting an undercover agent or other person who never commits the crime, forms an intent to commit the crime, responds affirmatively or negatively to the request, or was in a position to be influenced by the request, still completes the solicitation crime.

If the solicited person commits the crime, then the person soliciting the crime is an **accessory before the fact**, as the next section addresses, whom prosecutors may convict both for solicitation *and* as an accessory. If, however, the person soliciting the crime also commits the crime, then the soliciting crime *merges* into the solicited crime, and the person both soliciting the crime and committing the crime suffers conviction only for the solicited crime. Because solicitation is a *lesser included offense* of the solicited crime, the Constitution's double-jeopardy clause bars a person's trial on solicitation after acquittal of the person on the solicited crime. The common law treats solicitation as a *misdemeanor* even if the requested crime is a felony, while

Criminal Law and Procedure

the Model Penal Code would punish solicitation to the same extent as the solicited crime.

B. Parties to crime

The common law of **accessories** or **accomplices** to crime deals with persons who *assist* or *encourage* others to commit a completed crime. The common law classifies accessory crimes by whether the actor *encourages or assists* in the crime's commission *before*, *during*, or *after* the crime, distinguishing using the terms *principals* or *accessories*. **Principals** are those who commit the crime or assist or encourage *at and during* its commission. By contrast, **accessories** are those who assist or encourage the crime *before* or *after* its commission but *not* at and during its commission. Either assistance, such as providing material or logistical support, *or* encouragement, such as simple urging without material or logistical support, suffices for accessory conviction. Assistance or urging need *not* be necessary to the crime's commission, although the principal must at least hear the encouragement. Significantly, for a person to be either a principal *or* an accessory, the crime must have occurred. A person cannot be an accessory to a crime that did not occur. Conviction as an accessory requires the *intent* to assist or encourage the crime that the principal completes *and* intent that the crime occur. *Unknowing* assistance does not make a person an accessory to crime. Nor does assisting or urging without intending the crime's commission. An accomplice must provide *actual* assistance, which can be physical or psychological, or by purposeful omission.

The common law further classifies principals and accessories. A principal **in the first degree** is the crime's perpetrator, including one who accomplishes the crime through an innocent other, such as getting an innocent friend to pass off what the perpetrator knows to be counterfeit money. A principal **in the second degree** is a person who is present at the crime's time and location to assist or encourage the first-degree principal in committing the crime, such as the driver who intentionally drivers the robber to the bank and then drives the robber away after the crime. Assisting from some distance, such as outside the crime scene in the getaway vehicle or conducting surveillance nearby, qualifies as presence during the crime. An **accessory before the fact** is a person who assists or encourages a principal *before* the principal commits the completed crime but who is not present at the crime's time and location. An **accessory after the fact** is a person who, knowing that another has committed a crime, assists the other to escape detection, capture, or punishment. The common law does not recognize after-the-fact accessories for mere misdemeanors.

Despite these distinctions, the common law treats both principals and accessories as having committed the crime itself, for instance treating an accessory to murder as a conviction for murder. Modern statutes tend to simply eliminate the distinction between *principals* and *accessories before the fact*, accomplishing the same end. In the modern view, accessories before the fact are simply principals to the crime. Modern statutes, though, retain the *accessory-after-the-fact* classification, imposing a less-severe punishment for assistance after the crime. A consequence of the modern statutes is that accessories before the fact can suffer conviction for the crime without the principal suffering conviction, given that the modern statutes treat accessories before the fact as principals in the crime.

IV.   General principles

General principles of criminal law apply to the above crimes. Those principles include the treatment of **acts and omissions**, involved persons' **state of mind** including treatment of mistakes, questions of **responsibility** of the mentally disordered or intoxicated, issues of **causation**, defenses of **justification** and **excuse**, and also the **jurisdiction** of courts to hear criminal cases. The following sections address these general principles.

A. Acts and omissions

Criminal law concerns itself with the **actus reus**, referring to the criminally wrongful act constituting that material, observable conduct that must occur for conviction of the crime. Acts involve observable human conduct, whether voluntary or involuntary. Crimes generally depend on acts, not merely status or thoughts. Thus, public drunkenness can be a crime, but being an alcoholic is not. Specific acts, such as to break and enter a dwelling of another at night to commit a felony inside, define certain crimes, such as burglary, in the absence of which a prosecutor cannot convict. General acts, such as to kill another, define other classes of crime, such as homicide. In either case, though, the prosecution must prove the requisite *affirmative*, *volitional*, and *conscious* act to obtain a conviction. Reflex actions like convulsions are not such acts. Sleepwalkers or narcoleptics (those who suddenly fall asleep without warning) cannot commit crimes, unless the crime involves carelessness for not avoiding the unconscious act.

Criminal law also concerns itself with **omissions**, referring to a person's criminal failure to perform something that the law considers a duty. Persons have *no general duty to act* including such as to come to another's aid or rescue. Thus, in cases based on omissions, prosecutors must first prove the *duty to act* and then the defendant's *knowledge* of the duty and *ability* to act. If a person does not know of the need to act or has no ability to act as the duty would require, then the person cannot have committed a crime based on the duty. On the other hand, a person ordinarily need not know that not acting *is a crime*, only that the person owes a duty. In other words, ignorance of the law is no excuse. Yet if the crime on which the prosecution would base the duty requires **willful** failure to act, then by the definition of willful, the defendant must know that not acting is a crime. As to the requirement that the defendant must be *able* to act, the law may require that the defendant call for help if the defendant cannot act alone but can call for assistance.

Criminal law recognizes a duty to act when the defendant has a **special relationship** with the victim. For example, a parent owes a duty not

Criminal Law and Procedure

to neglect the parent's child, as may a husband owe the same duty to a wife, or a guardian owe the same duty to a ward. Employers may owe duties to protect or rescue employees. **Statutes** can also create duties to act, including within special relationships, such as when a statute requires a ship's captain to search for an overboard passenger or a bus driver or airline pilot to seek emergency medical care for a passenger. **Contracts** can also create duties to act, for example around another's medical care in the case of an aide or physical security in the case of a bodyguard. **Volunteering** to act can also create a duty, such as when a person professes rescue on which the other relies but then abandons the rescue without notice, leaving the other worse off. Causing another's need for rescue can also create a duty to do so, as in knowingly causing the peril but then knowingly failing to assist. *Moral duties*, though, are not sufficient to give rise to criminal prosecution for failure to act.

B. State of mind

In addition to defining the criminal *acts* that define a crime, criminal law also concerns itself with the actor's **mens rea**, referring to the required *guilty state of mind* to convict of the crime. The following section describes several different states of mind that various crimes may require, including *general intent, specific intent, recklessness*, and *criminal negligence*. A following section describes *strict-liability crimes* requiring no specific state of mind, and then another following section describes the effect of *mistake* on the required state of mind. Several Multistate Bar Examination criminal-law questions, whether on homicide, burglary, kidnap, or other crimes, will require you to recognize and distinguish the required state of mind.

1. Required mental state

Criminal law recognizes **intent** as one state of mind necessary for certain crimes, referring to the actor's will and volitional toward a desired objective. Other crimes involve **recklessness**, referring to will and volitional *not* directed toward the criminal objective but that create a *substantial risk* of bringing it about. Other crimes involve criminal **negligence**, which refers to a careless state of mind sufficiently gross or extreme as to produce acts worthy of punishing as crime. Mens rea, the guilty state of mind for the crime, is *not* motive, which refers instead to the reason for the crime. Prosecutors use *motive* evidence simply to bolster that the defendant intended to commit and did commit the crime. Proving intent, though, is sufficient to convict without proving motive. Conversely, proving motive without proving intent does not convict.

Criminal law deploys two forms of intent, *general intent* and *specific intent*, to define two different classes of crimes. **General intent** involves the choice, decision, will, and volition to commit an *illegal act* that leads to the crime. For example, if a jurisdiction defines the crime of mayhem as intentional disfigurement of another, then mayhem is a general-intent crime

Criminal Law and Procedure

because a prosecutor need only prove the intent to act in a way that results in disfigurement, such as to cut another's face with a knife. The defendant need *not* have intended to disfigure, intended to break the law, or know that the act is illegal. Proof of the intent to cut another's face with a knife would be sufficient to convict along with proof of the act. Indeed, circumstantial evidence of the intent to act is generally all that would be necessary to prove general intent. If the crime does not define the necessary state of mind, then the crime is a *general-intent* crime.

By contrast, **specific-intent** crimes require a prosecutor to prove *both* the actor's general intent to do the illegal act *and* the *specific goal* toward which the actor directed the act. To commit a burglary, for example, involving breaking and entering a dwelling of another at night to commit a felony inside, the actor must intend not only intent to break and enter but also the *specific purpose* for breaking and entering, which is to commit a felony inside. Without proof of that specific intent to commit a felony inside, a jury could not convict the actor of burglary, which is a specific-intent crime. The jury would need the prosecutor's proof of the actor's specific intent. Circumstantial evidence from the intent to act is generally not sufficient to prove specific intent. The actor in the prior example might have been breaking and entering for innocent, even helpful reasons, when the burglary crime requires proof of a criminal purpose.

Crimes that require only **recklessness** or **negligence** do not distinguish between general intent and specific intent. Proof of these guilty states of mind instead depends on showing the required degree of *carelessness*, having to do with not avoiding high risk of causing the result that completes the crime. Recklessness, applicable to *involuntary manslaughter* and *reckless endangerment*, involves more risk than negligence, applicable for instance to *negligent homicide*. Thus, driving while extremely intoxicated would constitute recklessness, but driving well over the speed limit would at most constitute negligence, sufficient to support a conviction if the actor unintentionally struck and killed a pedestrian. Other crimes require the states of mind of either *malice* or *willfulness*, without a generally agreed definition of either term.

2. Strict liability

Criminal law also recognizes a class of **strict-liability** crimes including, for example, statutory rape and bigamy. Prosecutors need prove no intent to establish a strict-liability crime. If, for instance, spouses file for divorce, and the husband soon tells the wife that the divorce is complete when the divorce is not complete, the wife's remarriage while still married would constitute bigamy, even if the wife reasonably believed that she was divorced. A prosecutor would not need any proof of the wife's state of mind but could instead convict solely with proof of the latter marriage in the absence of a valid divorce from the prior marriage. On the other hand, merely because a statute defining a crime omits any mention of intent does *not* mean that the statute calls for a strict-liability crime. Courts will construe the legislative

Criminal Law and Procedure

intent from things such as the class of crimes, inserting the intent element where the legislature plainly so intended.

3. Mistake of fact or law

Mistake of fact can in certain cases relieve the actor from criminal responsibility. Mistake of fact involves an actor proceeding while honestly believing that the circumstances are different than they are. The effect of mistake depends on the crime's required state of mind. Mistake of fact most clearly relieves an actor of criminal responsibility as to *specific-intent* crimes, where the actor must intend to bring about a result, not simply intend to act in a manner that leads to the completed crime. For example, prosecutors cannot convict of burglary a person who mistakenly breaks and enters another's dwelling that the person mistakenly believes to be the person's own dwelling, given that burglary is a specific-intent crime. By contrast, mistake of fact generally does not relieve an actor of *strict-liability* crimes such as bigamy, where marrying a second wife while still married to a first wife would constitute the crime even if the bigamist reasonably believed that divorce had terminated the first marriage.

Although some refer to mistake of fact as a *defense*, to the contrary, the *prosecution* must prove the requisite intent, meaning that the prosecution must overcome with proof beyond a reasonable doubt any effect of the defendant's alleged mistake. Common-law jurisdictions tend to require that the mistake was *reasonable*, although some jurisdictions do not require reasonableness for the mistake to relieve the defendant of responsibility for a *specific-intent* crime. The Model Penal Code eliminates the reasonableness requirement, so that any mistake that obviates the required intent relieves the defendant of the crime. If, on the other hand, mistake does *not* affect the crime's required state of mind, then conviction remains possible notwithstanding the mistake. For example, if the crime of selling illegal narcotics does not require the seller to know the specific narcotics sold, then prosecutors could convict the seller who reasonably believed that the sale involved one illegal substance when the sale in fact involved a different illegal substance.

The law treats **mistake of law** differently than mistake of *fact*. A mistake of law involves an actor's misunderstanding as to what the law requires or prohibits in a certain situation, rather than, as in mistake of fact, what the factual circumstances of that situation are. Mistake of law will generally defeat a charge when the crime requires the actor to know that the actor is *committing a crime* but not when the crime merely requires the actor to know the *circumstances* of the crime. For example, the crime of *larceny* requires an actor to intend to permanently deprive another of the other's personal property. A mistaken belief that the law granted ownership to the one who finds another's property could defeat that specific intent to deprive another of *the other's* property. For another example, an actor who does not know that the law makes certain taxes due cannot commit the tax-evasion crime requiring knowledge of overdue taxes. Mistake of law can also be a valid defense when the actor relies on a statute or agency interpretation later held unconstitutional or court opinion later reversed, such as for law enforcement to enter for search and seizure.

Yet for other crimes that do *not* require knowledge that the conduct is wrongful, mistake of law will not relieve the actor of criminal responsibility. For example, if a state made it a felony to remove any personal property from another's dwelling, and an actor broke into and entered a neighbor's home to retrieve the actor's own personal property, mistakenly believing that the law permitted the actor to do so, then prosecutors could convict the actor of the removing-personal-property crime because it did not require proof of intent to commit a crime. These instances fall under the rubric that *ignorance of the law is no excuse*. Indeed, jurisdictions routinely hold that relying on a lawyer's mistaken advice as to the law does not relieve the client of the crime. Unless the crime requires the actor to know that the actor is committing a crime, mistake of law or reliance on lawyer opinions about law does not relieve the crime.

C. Responsibility

In assigning criminal **responsibility**, criminal law also concerns itself with the actor's *capability* of knowing the circumstances, consequences, and punishments of crime. The issue of responsibility arises around *mental disorders* that contribute to crime and both voluntary and involuntary *intoxication* contributing to crime, addressed in the next two sections.

1. Mental disorder

Mental disorder can affect whether an actor has committed a crime. Some jurisdictions hold that a defendant's *diminished capacity* can make the defendant unable to form the specific intent required for certain crimes. For example, a person of diminished capacity may not have appreciated, relative to a larceny charge, that the personal property the person took to make his own belonged to another, thus relieving the person of that charge. Diminished capacity does not, however, relieve of general-intent crimes. While specific-intent crimes like burglary and larceny require specific intent to commit a felony or intent to deprive another of property, relieved by incapacity to form the specific intent, one of diminished capacity could still be guilty of a general-intent crime like rape where the intent to act, without other intent, satisfies the required state of mind. Indeed, if diminished capacity relieves an actor of a specific-intent crime, the actor may still be guilty of a lesser-included general-intent crime, such as for a rape after a breaking and entering that but for diminished capacity would also have been a burglary crime.

Diminished capacity differs from the *insanity* defense. While diminished capacity can prove that the defendant *did not have the required intent*, the insanity defense seeks to prove that the defendant was *incapable of morally reprehensible behavior*. The insane do not know what they are doing or are unable to control what they do. Those who have diminished capacity know and control what they do but do not intend certain consequences. Most jurisdictions recognize only the insanity defense, not diminished capacity, focusing on a *mental disease or defect* that either affects the actor's ability to know right from wrong or to conform behavior to the law. Conversely, the Model Penal Code would allow diminished capacity in relief of both specific-intent and general-intent crimes. On the other hand, **incompetency** to stand trial is a procedural defense in criminal proceedings, when the trial judge determines after hearing that the defendant cannot understand the charge and proceedings, communicate with counsel, and make decisions about the case.

Criminal law also recognizes **infancy** to affect criminal responsibility when the actor is of such young age as not to have the mental capacity to form the guilty state of mind for crime. The common law presumes that children under age seven are *incapable* of crime. The common law grants children age seven to fourteen benefit only a *rebuttable presumption* of incapability that prosecutors may, for any crime other than rape, rebut with appropriate evidence that the child knew both the nature *and reprehensibility* of the criminal act. Some jurisdictions have increased the minimum age of responsibility, while others extend the rebuttable presumption to younger or older ages. In all instances, the age that matters is the age at the time of the crime, not age at trial, and the chronological age, not mental age. For these purposes, the law treats a sixteen-year-old young man as age sixteen even if the young man only has the maturity or mental powers of a six-year-old child, although such a young man may then prove diminished capacity.

2. Intoxication

Intoxication can also affect criminal responsibility, depending on whether the intoxication was voluntary or involuntary. Involuntary intoxication involves consuming a drink or substance that the actor did not know was intoxicating or consumed under duress. The Model Penal Code also recognized *pathological intoxication* as involuntary, when the actor unknowingly suffers a disproportionately severe effect from consuming a substance and amount that would not intoxicate the normal person. **Involuntary intoxication** becomes a complete defense when making the actor not know what the actor is doing or unable to control it, no matter the specific or general intent required for the crime. By contrast, **voluntary intoxication** is in most jurisdictions no defense unless the intoxication defeats the specific intent required for the crime. Thus, voluntary intoxication might defeat a charge for burglary, a specific-intent crime, if the intoxicated person thought that he was entering his own house, but would not relieve of rape, a general-intent crime.

A few jurisdictions reject voluntary intoxication as relief from any crime. A few other jurisdictions allow voluntary intoxication to relieve not only specific-intent but also general-intent crimes. The Model Penal Code would examine how voluntary intoxication affects proof of the requisite

Criminal Law and Procedure

knowledge element. If the crime requires purpose, knowledge, or willfulness, then proof of voluntary intoxication eliminating that knowledge would relieve the actor of the crime. By contrast, voluntary intoxication would *not* relieve a defendant of a crime that required only proof of recklessness or criminal negligence, as the Model Penal Code only requires for most crimes. Obviously, voluntary intoxication also does not affect conviction for crimes in which intoxication is itself an element, such as *public drunkenness* or *drunk driving*, although *involuntary* intoxication could be a defense to such crimes.

D. Causation

Causation issues arise in criminal law when the crime requires proof of a *result* instead of simply an act. For example, homicide charges generally require proof that the defendant's act caused the victim's death. While in many cases, such as many shootings, the proof will be easy, in other cases the act may be only one factor in bringing about the death or even a disputed factor, such as where the victim dies not of the shooting but of a heart attack. In such cases where the prosecution must prove a *result*, criminal law requires proof of both **factual cause** and **proximate cause**.

Factual cause typically involves proving that *but for* the criminal act, the required result would not have occurred, such as but for the shooting the victim would not have died. Factual cause does *not* require that the prosecution prove that the criminal act was the *only* cause. A criminal act may combine with other factual causes, such as the victim's weak constitution, the cold weather, or delays in an ambulance's arrival, to bring about the result that the crime requires. Criminal law treats a perpetrator's *speeding up* a criminal result, such as shooting to death a person whom someone else had already shot and who would soon have died from the prior shot, as a factual cause of the result.

Criminal law applies an alternative **substantial-factor rule** where but-for causation fails, when two act concurrently, and each action would have brought about the result. Thus, when two actors shoot the victim simultaneously, and the victim would have died from either actor's shot, *both* actors bear criminal responsibility, even though *neither* would have been the but-for cause of the victim's death. On the other hand, criminal law *relieves* an actor of criminal responsibility under but-for causation, when the criminal act *comes to rest* and later events cause the result. Thus, if an actor, intending to kill, heaves an axe at another as the other comes through a door, and the axe misses but sticks in the wall over the door, and hours later the axe falls from the wall onto the other's head killing him as he passes through the door once again, then the actor will not bear criminal responsibility as he would had the axe struck and killed initially.

Proximate cause involves a legal judgment of whether the act and result are sufficiently close. To satisfy proximate cause, the required result must be the criminal act's *natural and probable consequence*. Thus, when a shooting victim dies from bleeding to death, the death is clearly the natural and probable result of the shooting because one could foresee and predict

Criminal Law and Procedure

such a demise. Proximate cause does not generally consider pre-existing conditions, like a victim's weak heart, for the results of which the actor would remain criminal responsible. Instead, proximate-cause issues arise with unusual or unexpected results from *subsequent events*. Thus, proximate cause would be more difficult to prove, although still present, if a shooting victim died fleeing from the shooter, by running into the street and getting hit by a car. In such cases, the law looks to the foreseeability of subsequent events that intervene between the criminal act and its result, such as the car striking the victim in the prior example. A superseding event set in motion after the criminal act can interrupt causation, relieving the actor of criminal responsibility, if sufficiently extraordinary and unforeseeable. By contrast, foreseeable subsequent events, even including poor medical care, do *not* relieve the actor of criminal responsibility.

E. Justification and excuse

Criminal law recognizes various justifications and excuses for crime. The **necessity** defense justifies and excuses a criminal act in an emergency not of the actor's own making, when the criminal act is necessary to avoid greater imminent harm than the criminal act causes. The actor's *reasonable belief* of the necessity to act satisfies the justification, even if the actor turns out to be wrong and the criminal act is unnecessary. The actor must also be reasonable in believing that the criminal act is the *only way*, and thus necessary, to prevent greater harm, even if the actor turns out once again to be wrong. For example, a raging fire could justify an actor in setting fire to one structure to avoid the raging fire from consuming a whole row of structures, if the actor's belief in the necessity of acting and warrant of the action were both reasonable. If the actor were wrong in either belief, the actor would still have the necessity defense, unless either belief was unreasonable. Also, if the actor created the necessity, then the actor has no necessity defense. Economic necessity, such as needing to steal for food, does not justify the crime.

Criminal law also recognizes a defense of **duress** under certain conditions. Duress involves another person, not a natural force as in the necessity defense but instead a person, *threatening* and *forcing* the defendant to commit a criminal act. The defendant must prove the threat, not simply reasonable belief in a non-existent threat. The common law requires that the threat have been of *serious injury or death*, although modern laws often allow threats of lesser harm to support the defense. Threats against the defendant *or against others*, even strangers, support the duress defense. The threats, though, must be of *immediate* harm, not future harm, and the defendant's criminal act must be the *only way* to avoid the harm. Duress defends any crime other than crimes involving killing or attempted killing. Even in homicide crimes, though, duress may prove lack of the premeditation necessary to support a murder conviction, reducing the conviction to manslaughter.

Criminal Law and Procedure

Criminal law also recognizes **self-defense** as justifying and excuse what would otherwise be a crime. Self-defense involves a person's use of *reasonable force* to defend the person against another's imminent threat to use force against the person. Self-defense is commonly a defense to *assault* charges or *battery* charges. In those cases, the defendant must prove the defendant's *reasonable belief* that the force that the defendant used was necessary for lawful self-defense. Reasonable belief, rather than accurate belief, is enough. The reasonably mistaken defendant retains self-defense as a justification for the crime. The *unreasonably* mistaken defendant loses the self-defense right, although a mistaken belief in the right of self-defense may reduce a murder charge to manslaughter.

A defendant using **deadly force** in self defense must also show that the person threatened *serious injury or death*, not just any harm. Using deadly force in self-defense also implicates the question of **retreat**. The common law requires that the person using deadly force must first look for an opportunity to retreat and find none that would provide *complete safety*. Retreat is not necessary where the defendant reasonably believes that the defendant remains exposed to the threat. Retreat is also not required from one's own home. Many jurisdictions abandon the common-law duty to retreat. Some jurisdictions also recognize a *battered-woman-syndrome* defense extending justification to a woman who kills her abuser in response to an episode, when the justification lies not in the imminent threat but in continued abuse within a relationship that the abuser will not allow to end.

An aggressor who initiates a *fight* does *not* ordinarily have a right of self-defense as the fight escalates, unless the initial fight was without deadly force and the respondent escalates the fight to make a deadly threat. The aggressor may also act in self-defense when the aggressor *withdraws* from the fight but the respondent resumes the fight, becoming the aggressor. As indicated briefly above, a person may not use force in self-defense unless reasonably believing that doing so is *lawful*. Thus, to resist an officer's *arrest* without reasonable belief in the lawfulness of resistance does not justify a person's use of force. In other words, some jurisdictions allow a person to use reasonable force in self-defense to an unlawful arrest. Most jurisdictions, though, have abandoned a right of resistance to unlawful arrest and instead hold that a person must submit to *even unlawful arrest* if the person knows that an officer is making the arrest.

Criminal law also recognizes a justification to **defend others**. Generally, a person may use reasonable force in defense of others. Jurisdictions differ, though, on whether the person using force has a right to defend only those who have a relationship to the person. Some jurisdictions require a parent/child or husband/wife relationship to the one threatened, although most jurisdictions permit defense of any others. Jurisdictions also differ on whether the person using force may be *mistaken* in the other's need for defense. The traditional **alter-ego** rule grants the defense if the person defended would have had the right of self-defense. Most jurisdictions today follow the Model Penal Code, granting the defense of others whenever the actor reasonably believes in the need for that defense.

Criminal Law and Procedure

Criminal law also recognizes a limited right to **defend property**. A person may use reasonable, nondeadly force to protect property on the defendant's person or to prevent an intrusion into real property, if the person's use of force appears reasonably necessary for the property's imminent defense. Defense of property, though, is more limited than defense of persons. A person has no right to use *deadly force* in defense of property, although that right does arise when the threat extends to persons and is a deadly threat. Some jurisdictions allow deadly force to defend a dwelling even without risk of death to persons in the dwelling. In any case, though, the threat must be imminent. The law does not justify use of force to forestall later threat to property.

The law also does not allow the use of force to **recover** property other than on or about the premises from which, and at the time of which, the wrongdoer attempts to take it. In other words, the law limits use of force to recover property only to its *hot pursuit*. The law also discourages using *mechanical devices* that inflict force to defend property. The traditional rule allowed such devices only if the person deploying the device would have had the right to use the same amount of force as the device inflicted if the person had been present. The Model Penal Code, though, prohibits any use of mechanical force that could cause death or serious injury. The common law permitted an occupant's use of deadly force to prevent an intrusion into the occupant's dwelling if the owner first gave a warning not to enter. Modern statutes limit that right of deadly force to situations where the occupant reasonably believes that the intruder intends to commit a felony or hurt someone within the dwelling.

F. Jurisdiction

Criminal-case **jurisdiction** involves a court's power to enter judgment of conviction and punish the defendant. Without jurisdiction, a judgment is void. Generally, federal courts have jurisdiction over *federal offenses*, meaning those that Congress defines. Federal criminal jurisdiction typically involves crime on federal lands such as military bases and federal parks, and crimes that either involve interstate transport, such as kidnappings crossing state lines, or affect interstate commerce, such as drug distribution. State courts have jurisdiction over *state offenses* that the state's legislature defines, typically occurring within the state's borders. States may grant jurisdiction to different courts within the state, often depending on whether the crime is a misdemeanor or felony, or involves a youth or adult offender.

Federal and state courts may have **concurrent jurisdiction** where crimes occur in part on federal lands and in part on non-federal land within the state. In such instances, the federal courts hear the federal charges and the state courts the state charges. State courts of different states may also have concurrent jurisdiction where crimes occur in part in one state and in part in another state. In such instances, the state courts of one state will hear that state's charges, while the state courts of the other state will hear that state's charges. The courts of one jurisdiction do not hear the charges of

Criminal Law and Procedure

another jurisdiction. The first jurisdiction to charge often hears the charges first, although prosecutors from different jurisdictions typically attempt to agree on which jurisdiction should proceed first.

V.   Constitutional protection of accused persons

The Constitution protects the accused against federal action, and through the 14th Amendment's due-process clause against state action, in several ways. The 4th and 14th Amendments protect against unreasonable **arrest, search,** and **seizure.** Due-process rights restrict how and when investigators can obtain and prosecutors can use **confessions,** compel **self-incrimination,** and use **lineups** and other identification procedures. Due process also guarantees a **right to counsel.** The accused must also have a **fair trial. Guilty pleas** require other fair procedures. The Constitution also prohibits **double jeopardy** and **cruel-and-unusual punishment.** The Constitution also dictates that the prosecution carry certain **burdens of proof** and **persuasion.** An accused person also has certain rights regarding **appeals** and **error.** The following sections address each of these constitutional protections.

A. Arrest...

The 4th and 14th Amendments grant certain protections against **unlawful arrest.** An arrest involves a police officer taking a person into custody against the person's will for purposes of criminal prosecution. The common law permits warrantless arrest of a person committing either a *breach of the peace* or *felony.* The 4th Amendment, though, permits warrantless arrest in a public place on **probable cause** that the person arrested has committed a crime. Under the 4th Amendment standard, an officer may arrest a person on a minor traffic charge even when a citation would have been more reasonable, although statutes may limit the officer's broad constitutional scope for arrest. If, on the other hand, an officer must enter a home or other place where a person has a reasonable expectation of privacy to make an arrest, then the officer must have a warrant, unless exigent circumstances excuse a warrant or the person consents. Warrants must issue only on probable cause. *Probable cause* for an arrest requires that the arresting officer have *reasonable basis* for believing that the arrestee has committed a crime or is committing a crime, based on factual and practical considerations under the *totality of the circumstances.* An officer has no constitutional obligation to tell an arrestee the reason for an arrest.

The primary protection against unlawful arrests, such as arrests without a warrant when law requires a warrant *or* arrests on an invalid warrant issued without probable cause, is that the arrestee's confession made while illegally in custody is inadmissible at a later trial. The court must also suppress physical evidence including such as fingerprints, blood tests, and DNA obtained from an illegal arrest. When, however, the detention continues under other circumstances such that the connection between the illegal arrest

Criminal Law and Procedure

and confession becomes so *attenuated* as not to *taint* the confession, then the confession becomes admissible. The law excuses certain violations of these rights, admitting rather than excluding evidence recovered from the unlawful arrest. A good-faith exception to exclusion arises when an officer *reasonably believes*, due to the mistake of a court clerk or other court officer, that a judge or magistrate has issued a warrant. The good-faith exception does *not* extend to members of the law-enforcement team including prosecutors, investigators, and officers.

The protections against arrest without probable cause or warrant extend to *all* restraints of persons by authorities, not just to formal arrests. However, the Constitution does *not* require probable cause for certain police interactions with those suspected of involvement in crime. Police may **stop and frisk** on *reasonable articulable suspicion* that a crime has occurred, is in process, or is about to occur, referred to as *criminal activity afoot*. A stop is a *brief, non-intrusive* delay of a person so that the officer can confirm or dispel the officer's suspicion. For example, an officer may stop a person who stands on a street corner the officer knows to be a place where vehicles stop for the occupants to buy drugs, if the person makes furtive movements to hide something and move away from the officer as the officer approaches. A lawful stop may entail a *frisk* for weapons if the officer has a *reasonable and articulable suspicion* that the detainee is *armed and dangerous*, the frisk involving a *patdown* of the person's outer clothing. The officer must not manipulate anything that the officer feels in the patdown unless the *plain feel* without manipulation indicates contraband. Thus, the officer suspecting a drug sale in the above example could manipulate and remove an object that on patdown felt like the suspected drugs would feel.

...search...

The 4th and 14th Amendments guarantee a right against **unreasonable government searches**. The search must involve federal or state action. **State action**, though, can reach beyond searches by government officials to include searches by private persons working with or under the direction of law enforcement. Thus, state action includes a family member who retrieves a murder weapon from inside a home at an officer's request. A search, too, can involve minimal conduct such as moving aside an object to get a better view of potential evidence of crime. Thus, a warrantless search under *exigent circumstances* ordinarily permits recovery of evidence *in plain view*, but moving an object would be a search beyond what plain view permits.

To constitute a search, though, the investigation must be of a location as to which the defendant has a **reasonable expectation of privacy**. Authorities may under any conditions recover evidence in locations, such as a yard or street, where the defendant has no reasonable expectation of privacy. The **open-fields** doctrine holds that a defendant has no reasonable expectation of privacy in areas outside the *curtilage*, referring to the immediate surroundings and attached structures of a home, even when signs or fencing discourage entry. Thus, evidence recovered without a warrant from private fields does not implicate constitutionally protected privacy, although opening a box inside a garage attached to a home would implicate privacy, requiring a warrant or exception. Privacy also does not protect evidence within the **public purview**, referring to subject to public inspection, such as sounds, vehicle exteriors, odors, bank records, garbage out for collection, and things visible from the air or from public spaces. A search also occurs when the officer trespasses on a constitutionally protected area looking for evidence of a crime. Although police may approach the front door to perform a *knock and talk*, like the public under social license, they may not trespass to look for evidence of a crime.

Although generally, validly sought and executed warrants authorize searches, not every search requires a warrant. Many exceptions to the search warrant rule have been created. **Consent** of one whom authorities reasonably believe has access to the premises, even if not the defendant and even if the person giving consent does not in fact have the authority to do so, makes a search legal. Thus, one who answers an officer's knock on the door and invites the officer in for a search would have apparent authority to give consent, even if the person turns out to be a trespasser. A person must freely and voluntarily give consent, the totality of circumstances determine. A person may limit the scope of consent. For example, a person may consent to search of a motor-vehicle's passenger compartment but refuse to consent to search the vehicle's trunk. A person may revoke consent after giving it. When two share authority to consent to search, and both are present, the refusal of either one prevents the search. Authorities may seize evidence **in plain view** from any lawful location. Thus, if they lawfully enter a home in response to a report of domestic violence, then they may seize evidence of crimes other than domestic violence that they see in plain view within the home. The officer must, though, have lawfully entered, must have authority to seize the items, and the items must be readily apparent as contraband, without manipulation.

Authorities may also search **incident to lawful arrest**. Authorities may search the person whom they lawfully arrest and take into custody, and, for protection, search any area *within the arrestee's reach*. Thus, when arresting a drunk driver, police may search the glove compartment within the driver's reach but not the trunk. The reach or *wingspan* moves with the arrestee, giving officers greater scope to search as the arrestee moves. Search incident to arrest extends to recently occupied vehicles unless the officer places the recent occupant in the police cruiser, where the arrestee no longer poses a danger risk. The officer may still search the vehicle incident to arrest when the officer has reason to believe that evidence of the arrest crime is in the vehicle. As indicated above in the section on arrest, authorities may also search in limited fashion in a **stop and frisk**. Police may stop a suspect when they have *reasonable suspicion* of criminal behavior and frisk when reasonably believing that the person may be *armed and dangerous*. Acting on an unarticulated hunch is not reasonable suspicion, but acting on behavior that, though not providing probable cause of crime, nevertheless suggests the possibility of criminal behavior is reasonable suspicion. Again, as indicated

Criminal Law and Procedure

above, the frisk that reasonable suspicion permits, though, is only a *patdown* of the *outer clothing* for weapons. If in a lawful patdown an officer discovers an object that, *without manipulation*, readily feels like it may be a weapon or evidence of the suspected crime, then the officer may remove the object for inspection.

The law also does not require a warrant for a **vehicle search**, or search of other moveable transportation such as a boat, if authorities have probable cause to believe the vehicle contains evidence, instrumentalities, contraband, or fruits of crime. The search, though, can only be as invasive as necessary to discover what the authorities have probable cause to believe may have been evidence of the suspected crime. Thus, if the suspected crime is smuggling persons, then authorities could only search the vehicle or boat for persons, not opening small spaces to search for drugs or other contraband. And if the vehicle is no longer moveable, then the authorities would need a warrant. Like the vehicle exception, authorities may also search under exigent circumstances such as in **emergencies** and **hot pursuit**, when a suspect could easily move or destroy evidence. Thus, if a suspect enters private property, authorities may pursue the suspect there and seize evidence in plain view, even if the property does not belong to the suspect and the evidence involves a different person's crime.

If these circumstances do not permit or justify a search, then authorities must obtain a **warrant** to search, from a neutral and detached judge or magistrate. A judge or magistrate must find **probable cause** to issue a warrant. Probable cause depends on authorities showing that a reasonable person would believe that the location that authorities request to search has crime evidence such as a homicide weapon, instrumentalities such drug-manufacturing equipment, contraband such as the materials to manufacture drug, or fruits such as stolen goods. Authorities may demonstrate probable cause using sworn testimony, if recorded, or an affidavit, including an affidavit based on hearsay that a court could not admit against a defendant charged with crime. The affidavit or testimony must supply sufficient credible information for probable cause. The law presumes that police officers are reliable affiants due to their training and experience. Officers may include in their affidavit information from victims and other witnesses. The law usually requires that officers must knock and announce their authority to search before entering the search location. A knock-and-announce violation does *not* result in exclusion of the evidence. The law also permits certain administrative searches, not for law enforcement but for compliance with regulations, and special-needs searches, such as for drug screening of transportation employees.

The **exclusionary rule** requires a court in a criminal proceeding to exclude evidence that authorities obtained in violation of the defendant's 4th and 14th Amendment right against unreasonable search and seizure. The *fruit-of-the-poisonous-tree* doctrine further requires the court to exclude evidence that authorities discover later because of the discoveries made in the illegal search, unless authorities show an independent *lawful* source leading to the same evidence or can show that discovery was *inevitable*. For example, if

Criminal Law and Procedure

authorities search an office illegally, discovering illegal drugs, the exclusionary rule would exclude the drugs. If authorities also discover writings that lead authorities to more illegal drugs, then the fruit-of-the-poisonous-tree doctrine would exclude the other drugs, too, unless authorities could point to a lawful way in which they would have discovered the other drugs, such as an informant's information, or that they would inevitably have discovered the other drugs. Also, when authorities conduct a search in a *good-faith belief* that the search is legal, then the exclusionary rule does *not* exclude the evidence. An officer's belief that the law does not require a warrant can constitute good faith, as can conducting a search under an invalid warrant that the officer believes valid. On the other hand, an officer who knows or should know that a warrant is invalid has not conducted a search in good faith. The exclusionary rule does *not* bar use of the evidence for **impeachment** or, under the *attenuation* exception, when an independent source other than the unlawful search also led to the evidence's discovery.

...and seizure

The above discussion about *unlawful arrest* derives from the Constitution's 4th and 14th Amendment protections against **unreasonable government seizures**. The law defines a *seizure* as occurring when, under a totality of the circumstances, a reasonable person would not feel free to terminate an encounter with law enforcement or to refuse an officer's request. A seizure requires some application of force *or* submission to the officer's authority to use force.

B. Confessions and privilege against self-incrimination

The 5th and 14th Amendments guarantee a **privilege against self-incrimination** as to interrogation in custody by authorities. Under *Miranda v Arizona*, the privilege requires authorities to read an arrestee those rights so that the arrestee may then knowingly assert or waive those privileges. The rights are **to remain silent** and **have your attorney present during questioning**. Authorities, though, must read an arrestee the equivalent of *you have the right to remain silent, anything said can and will be used against you in court, you have the right to an attorney now and during questioning,* and *if you cannot afford one, the court will provide one.* Prosecutors cannot use at trial against a defendant a statement that the defendant made *while in custody* and *under interrogation,* unless authorities advised the defendant of those rights and defendant knowingly, intelligently, and voluntarily chose to waive them.

An arrestee must unequivocally assert the **right to remain silent** *before* giving the incriminating statement, not after. Incriminating statements made after waiving the right are admissible. An arrestee, though, may at any time *reassert* the right to remain silent as to any further statements. Authorities must stop questioning *on the offense for which authorities hold the arrestee* as soon as an arrestee asserts the right. After a break and

Criminal Law and Procedure

refreshed *Miranda* warnings, authorities may question about other offenses, although the arrestee may then reassert the right to remain silent. Authorities may question *without* warnings when *public safety* requires the arrestee's information. For example, if circumstances indicate other nearby suspects, a dangerous weapon, or an endangered victim, then an officer making an arrestee may question the arrestee without warnings. Statements that an arrestee makes under the public-safety exception are admissible at trial. Booking officers need not give the warnings simply to process for jail. Only persons, not corporations, may assert the right to remain silent. The privilege protects only the arrestee, not others. A court need not exclude statements that the arrestee makes that incriminate others. The privilege protects only statements, not against blood tests, DNA tests, handwriting samples, or recovery of other physical evidence.

Much as an arrestee must clearly and unequivocally assert the right to remain silent, as to the **right to an attorney**, an arrestee must affirmatively request the attorney, indicating that the arrestee will not answer questions without counsel present. Authorities must then stop all questioning, whether about the crime for which authorities arrested the suspect or about other crimes. Officers may re-approach the arrestee after *fourteen or more days* have elapsed. The right is to a *lawyer*, not anyone else such as a therapist, minister, friend, or relative. Authorities may continue questioning if the arrestee asks for anyone other than a lawyer. Also, the rights to remain silent and to an attorney protect against *interrogation*, meaning questioning, including any statements that a reasonable person would construe to be to elicit a response. A polite request to tell what happened is interrogation. On the other hand, greetings and amiable conversation on topics unrelated to the crime are not interrogation, although when a person in custody asserts the privilege, all talk must stop.

Authorities need give *Miranda* warnings before questioning only when the suspect is in **custody**. Custody first implies state action. The suspect need only be in a position where *a reasonable person would believe* that authorities have *restrained the suspect's movement against the suspect's will*. The circumstances do not implicate the privilege if a suspect starts voluntarily chatting at a bar with undercover officers whom the suspect does not know are authorities. While an arrest constitutes custody, custody does *not* require arrest or other physical restraint, such as handcuffs or jail. Custody does not even require that the suspect feel restrained, if a *reasonable person* would believe that the circumstances indicated that the person was not free to go. An order to stop or freeze constitutes restraint, although a request to stop, leaving open the freedom to ignore or decline the request, does not. Routine traffic stops do not constitute custody. Nor do probation or other interviews in an office or police station when the interviewee arrived freely and remains free to go, even if law required the interview. Once adversarial proceedings begin, the right to counsel applies to any interrogation.

As indicated above, a suspect in custody may **waive** the rights to remain silent and to have counsel present during questioning. In disputes, the prosecution must prove the waiver, which the court will *not* imply a waiver

Criminal Law and Procedure

from a defendant's silence. If the court implies waiver from other evidence, then the evidence must show that the waiver was *intelligent*, meaning that the defendant understood the rights, and *voluntary*, meaning without threat, trick, or cajolery. While signing a waiver form proves waiver, so will the defendant's telling the defendant's story after having heard the warnings. The court must not, though, imply waiver from the defendant speaking *before* the warning. Holding others, including the defendant's wife, until the defendant speaks makes a waiver involuntary.

C. Lineups and other forms of identification

The Constitution also shapes how authorities may conduct a **lineup** of the suspect with others for identification purposes. An accused's due-process rights mandate that authorities must conduct lineups in ways that are not *unduly suggestive*, conducive to *irreparable mistaken identity*. The effect of a violation of the defendant's constitutional rights relating to lineups is to exclude *in-court* identification based on the constitutionally defective *out-of-court* lineup, unless the witness has an independent source for identification. The constitutional concern is that once an unduly suggestive lineup causes a witness to identify the defendant, the witness will thereafter persist in identifying the defendant even when clearly mistaken due to the unduly suggestive initial identification. Thus, if officers conduct a **showup** involving only the defendant, where officers identify the defendant as the probable perpetrator, then the procedure is unduly suggestive. Likewise, if, in a lineup, the defendant is the only one of a certain sex, ethnicity, or distinct height or weight, and handcuffs, dress, demeanor, or other circumstances further suggest identification, then the lineup may be unduly suggestive. The protections against unduly suggestive lineups extend to the suspect's *photographic lineup* or *photo identification*. The suspect, though, bears the burden of proving the procedure unduly suggestive, creating a substantial likelihood of misidentification.

The Supreme Court has also held under the 6th and 14th Amendments that a post-arrest in-person lineup is a **critical stage** in a criminal proceeding at which the defendant has a *right to counsel*. Thus, a post-arrest in-person lineup must not be unduly suggestive *and* must occur only in the presence of the defendant's counsel who can monitor the procedure for constitutional or other defect. The right to counsel, though, does not attach until prosecution initiates a formal proceeding with a charge. The right to counsel also does *not* extend to photographic lineups or photo identification. Only the due-process clause reaches photographic procedures, which must not be unduly suggestive. These protections do not extend to processes involving the collection of physical evidence such as blood and DNA because those processes are not as susceptible to error or influence.

D. Right to counsel

Criminal Law and Procedure

The 5th and 14th Amendment **right to counsel** during custodial interrogation differs from the 6th and 14th Amendment right to have the **effective assistance of counsel** at trial. The 6th Amendment makes the right to counsel explicit for *all criminal prosecutions*, interpreted to mean felony proceedings, misdemeanor proceedings that *result in* imprisonment, and juvenile delinquency hearings. The right to effective assistance of counsel applies at all **critical stages** of these proceedings, defined to mean from custodial interrogations and post-arrest lineups, through arraignment, preliminary hearings, post-charge lineups, and trial, to guilty pleas, sentencing, and appeals. While under the 5th Amendment right to remain silent, authorities must stop *all* questioning if the defendant objects, the 6th Amendment right to effective assistance prohibits only offense-specific questioning.

For a convicted defendant to prove *ineffective* assistance to get a new trial, the court must find both deficient performance *and* that the deficiency *affected the outcome*, commonly known as the *prejudice prong*. Proving that the trial would have had a different result requires a substantial showing. Unsuccessful tactics, such as deciding not to object to certain improper questions because the questions and answers have no import, do not alone establish ineffective assistance. Nor does refusal to do as the defendant requested. Yet failing to object to a charge barred by the statute of limitations is ineffective assistance because it both constitutes deficient performance *and* plainly affected the outcome, which by law would have been dismissal of the charge.

E. Fair trial...

The 6th and 14th Amendments guarantee an accused in a criminal proceeding rights to a **fair trial** including that the trial be *speedy* and *public*, and, if the charges can result in imprisonment for more than six months, then also before an *impartial jury* from the district of the alleged crime. **Speedy trial** depends on balancing the length of delay with the reasons for delay, the defendant's assertion of the right, and the prejudice from delay. Violation of the speedy-trial right mandates the charge's dismissal. **Public trial** requires that the court permit the public to attend and observe the trial unless an overriding interest such as to prevent undue influence on jurors from trial publicity requires closure as a narrowly tailored remedy. Fair trial also ordinarily requires that the court permit the defendant to confront and cross-examine the prosecution's witnesses, which the Constitution's **confrontation clause** separately guarantees. Due process also requires the court to permit the defendant to present the defendant's own testimony and own witnesses, including if necessary to cross-examine and impeach those witnesses.

Jury trial, where mandated for charges entailing potential imprisonment of more than six months, in federal proceedings requires the *unanimous* vote of at least *six* jurors to reach conviction. The 14th Amendment, though, does *not* require that state juries reach unanimity on conviction unless the jury has only six members. State criminal proceedings

Criminal Law and Procedure

may convict on non-unanimous votes, if conviction entails agreement of at least six jurors. Courts address the 6th and 14th Amendments' requirement for **impartial jurors** through jury voir dire in which the court must permit the defendant's counsel to examine jurors for bias. The court must remove jurors who exhibit bias, although a defendant cannot challenge a conviction for juror bias if the court permitted the defendant to exercise *peremptory challenges*. The court must draw jurors from a representative cross-section of the community without excluding groups systematically in the process. The prosecution must not exclude jurors based on *race or sex* during jury voir dire. A defendant may require the prosecution to disclose the non-discriminatory reasons for striking jurors, and the court may examine the disclosure for pretext.

Due-process rights addresses other aspects of fairness and unfairness. For example, a judge may not receive compensation based on fine and costs imposed on a defendant whom the judge convicts. Due process would also grant a new trial if the judge or jurors exhibit bias or prejudice. For example, if trial publicity intimidates jurors into convicting, then the proceeding will have violated the convicted defendant's due-process rights. Courts must guard jurors against the influence of trial publicity. For another example, due process would prohibit trying a defendant in prison clothes, handcuffs, leg irons, or other indicia of imprisonment, as unduly suggestive of guilt. **Visible restraints** undermine the *presumption of innocence*.

...and guilty pleas

A defendant in a criminal proceeding has the right to plead *not guilty*, *guilty*, or nolo contendere, meaning *no contest*, having the effect in the criminal proceeding of a guilty plea. A federal court has the discretion to reject a no-contest plea after considering the interests of the defendant and of the public in efficient administration. A defendant's refusal or inability to plead requires the court to enter a not-guilty plea. The court must not accept a **guilty plea** or no-contest plea until the court ensures that the defendant *understands* the charges, proceeding, and plea, and has offered the plea *voluntarily* without threats or promises apart from the plea agreement. The trial judge must ordinarily do so in open court. When informing the defendant of the charge's nature, the judge must state both the *mandatory minimum* and the *maximum* penalties. The judge must state the defendant's right to a jury trial and to appointed counsel if indigent, and state that a guilty plea results in conviction without jury trial. The court must reject a guilty plea that the defendant has not made knowingly and voluntarily. Federal and state court rules also typically require that the court confirm a guilty plea's *factual basis*.

F. Double jeopardy

The 5th and 14th Amendments' **double-jeopardy clause** prohibits government from trying an accused on the same charges twice. The clause prohibits second prosecution for the same offense after either a conviction *or*

Criminal Law and Procedure

an acquittal. A trial begins for purposes of counting double jeopardy when the judge swears the first witness in a bench trial or swears the jury in a jury trial. See a following section on appeals for double-jeopardy rules after appeal. The clause also prohibits multiple punishments for the same offense, although the punishments must be *criminal*. Government may seek civil forfeiture or civil confinement after having pursued a criminal charge. The test for what constitutes the **same offense** focuses on the statutory elements. The clause generally bars re-prosecution for both greater and lesser-included offenses sharing same elements, although prosecution on the lesser offense, such as battery does, not preclude prosecution on a greater offense, such as murder, if the additional necessary element, such as death, accrues after the first trial. The clause applies to any prosecution, whether felony or misdemeanor, that may result in death, imprisonment, or fine. On the other hand, the double-jeopardy clause does *not* prohibit prosecution by *separate sovereigns* such as by both the federal government and a state government, even if the federal and state charges that each prosecution pursued were substantially the same. Local government may *not*, though, pursue state charges that the state has already tried because a state and its locales arise under the same sovereign.

G. Cruel and unusual punishment

The 8th Amendment prohibits **cruel-and-unusual punishment**. The definition of cruel and unusual depends on the case and changing societal norms, not any precise definition. The *crime* for which the court punishes, the *length* of the punishment, and the *nature* of the punishment can all help establish that it is cruel and unusual, and thus unconstitutional. Thus, a crime that punishes a person in any way for a mental disability or a disease is certainly cruel and unusual. Yet more commonly, punishment that is *grossly disproportionate* to the crime is cruel and unusual. Thus, a ten-year sentence at hard labor for a petty shoplifting conviction would be cruel and unusual. Punishment that is so severe relative to the crime that it unnecessarily degrades the defendant's dignity is more likely cruel and unusual.

H. Burdens of proof and persuasion

The 5th and 14th Amendments require that the prosecution prove every element of a crime **beyond a reasonable doubt**. If the prosecution proves several elements beyond a reasonable doubt but any single element to a lesser degree, then the jury must acquit the defendant. It also elevates the prosecution's proof burden well above, not just slightly above, the preponderance standard that most civil cases apply. The Supreme Court has not further defined the beyond-a-reasonable-doubt standard other than to say that the burden is *less* than substantial doubt or grave uncertainty, and that conviction does *not* require moral certainty. Thus, cases involving error in the standard's application often involve *jury instructions*. The Supreme Court has not mandated a specific instruction, but instructions must communicate

Criminal Law and Procedure

to the jury that the prosecution must establish guilt *beyond a reasonable doubt* as to each element. Courts should also instruct that the provision grants the defendant a *presumption of innocence.*

The beyond-a-reasonable-doubt standard does *not* apply to fact questions over whether the court should admit evidence over constitutional objection. The court may decide those objections based on a preponderance-of-the-evidence standard. For example, if a defendant objects to admission of evidence recovered in an allegedly unreasonable search, then the trial judge may resolve by a preponderance of evidence the dispute over the search's reasonableness, and admit the evidence even if the prosecution did not establish the search's reasonableness beyond a reasonable doubt. The court may also apply a lower evidentiary standard to disputes over consent to a search, the right to counsel, waiver of the right to remain silent, and the factual basis for ruling on other rights and objections.

I. Appeal and error

A defendant whom a trial court has convicted and sentenced may **appeal**, asking the appellate court to review the lower-court proceedings not for trivial or inconsequential errors but for **error** that may have *affected the outcome*. The appellate court may affirm or reverse the lower court's judgment. If the appellate court reverses, then it may remand for retrial of the case after the trial court corrects the error. If the reversal was for lack of evidence on one or more elements, then the appellate court may remand for entry of dismissal. Defendants who suffered conviction under *guilty plea* may in most jurisdictions appeal only if the appellate court grants permission because of a defect in the plea procedure. By contrast, defendants who suffered conviction after trial have an *appeal of right* including the *right to appellate counsel*. Defendants whom the trial court sentenced to death also have a right of appeal. Prosecutors may not appeal acquittals. When a defendant appeals a conviction, though, the prosecution may appeal pre-trial rulings admitting or excluding evidence.

Grounds for appeal include insufficient evidence on one or more of the elements of the crime, error of law by the court such as in evidentiary rulings or jury instructions, prosecutorial misconduct, witness misconduct, juror misconduct, and ineffective assistance of defense counsel, among other irregularities and defects in the proceeding that may have affected the outcome. Juror misconduct can include juror experiments, unauthorized juror scene views, juror research, juror outside influence including out-of-court communications with the attorneys, defendant, or witnesses, and juror drug or alcohol abuse, although not juror disagreements over evidentiary weight or interpretation of law instructions. As indicated above, unauthorized assistance of counsel must involve more than ineffective strategy but instead deficient performance affecting the outcome. An appellate court does not review **harmless errors**, meaning errors that affected no substantial right of the appealing party and that did not change the verdict.

Criminal Law and Procedure

When a defendant successfully appeals conviction, the prosecution may proceed with a retrial of the appealed charge and conviction without offending the Constitution's double-jeopardy clause. The prosecution may also retry a case when the defendant requests and the court grants a mistrial or when other *manifest necessity*, such as a deadlocked jury or defense counsel's misconduct, warrants retrial. However, the prosecution may *not* retry a case if the appellate court rules that first trial based conviction on inadequate evidence. Also, the prosecution may *not* try a defendant on a greater charger, such as murder, after the defendant successfully appeals a lesser charge, such as manslaughter.

Evidence

E.   Evidence

NOTE: All Evidence questions should be answered according to the Federal Rules of Evidence, as restyled in 2011. Approximately one-third of the Evidence questions on the MBE will be based on category I, one-third on category V, and one-third on the remaining categories—II, III, and IV.

The Multistate Bar Examination emphasizes certain evidence topics. One third of the evidence questions address **presentation of evidence**, of which introducing evidence and impeaching, contradicting, and rehabilitating witnesses form the biggest part. **Hearsay** takes up another one third of the evidence questions. Focus your studies on these two topics, particularly on hearsay. Only one third of civil-procedure questions address the remaining three categories of relevancy, privileges, and writings or recordings. Construe evidence rules to be **fair**, to **eliminate expense and delay**, and above all to **ascertain truth** while securing a just determination. All references to rules in this section are to the Federal Rules of Evidence.

I.   Presentation of evidence

In general, parties have the obligation to gather and present evidence, although a court may call a witness on its own, allowing each party to cross-examine. The court may also examine a party's witness. Evidence rules, though, require satisfaction of certain *conditions* to introduce and gain the admission of evidence, such as **personal knowledge** of a **competent witness**. The rules also dictate the court's control of the mode and order of **witness examination**. The rules also closely control **impeachment**, **contradiction**, and **rehabilitation** of witnesses. Consider these preliminary questions before moving on to relevancy, privileges, and other evidence subjects.

A. Introduction of evidence

The court decides preliminary questions about **witness qualifications** and **admissibility of evidence**. As indicated above, the court need not follow the evidence rules when making a preliminary fact determination as to the admissibility of evidence. For example, if a party questions whether an opposing party's witness has the necessary personal knowledge of the matter from which to testify, the court determines whether the witness has that necessary knowledge and may accept hearsay or other inadmissible evidence to make that determination.

1. Requirement of personal knowledge

One of the single most-significant evidence rules is that lay witnesses may testify only if having **personal knowledge** of the matter. For example, a witness may testify to observations that the witness made of a broken piece

Evidence

of furniture that caused the plaintiff's injury, but the court would not allow the witness to guess, conjecture, or speculate as to how the furniture broke, how long it had remained broken, or who was responsible for its inspection and repair, unless the party offering that testimony first demonstrated the witness's **factual basis**. The law calls that process **laying the foundation** for the witness's testimony. A party may lay the factual foundation for lay testimony using the witness's own testimony such as "I was present to see the disputed event happen," or using other evidence such as the testimony of another witness that the first witness was indeed present. Expert witnesses, treated below, do not need personal knowledge of the factual basis for their expert opinions when they reasonably and customarily rely on other sources.

2. Refreshing recollection

A witness may use a writing to **refresh memory** while testifying or before testifying. The adverse party may **inspect** the writing, **cross-examine** the witness on it, and **offer as evidence** any portion relating to the testimony, although the party producing the writing may ask the court to inspect in camera and delete unrelated portions. For example, a police officer testifying in a motor-vehicle-accident case may use the officer's accident report to refresh the officer's testimony, but the party calling the officer must supply the report to the adverse party who may cross-examine the officer on the report's contents and even offer the report as evidence. If the prosecution refuses to produce a writing used to refresh a witness's testimony, then the court must strike the witness's testimony or declare a mistrial.

3. Objections and offers of proof

Objections and **offers of proof** play an important role in preserving errors for appellate review. A party may **claim error** to **admit evidence** only if the error affects a party's **substantial right** and the party timely objects or moves to strike, stating the ground unless apparent. A party may claim error to exclude evidence only if the party makes an **offer of proof**, unless the context made the evidence's substance apparent. On the other hand, an appellate court may take notice of a **plain error** affecting a substantial right, even if the appealing party did not properly preserve the error that the party claims. Once the court rules, a party need not **renew** an objection or offer of proof to preserve a claim of error for appeal. In ruling, the court may make any statement about the character or form of the evidence or about the objection. Yet to the extent practicable, the court must not allow inadmissible evidence to reach the jury.

4. Lay opinions

A witness whom a party does not qualify as an expert may nonetheless give a **lay opinion** on certain conditions. The lay witness must base the opinion on the witness's **own perception**, unlike expert witnesses

Evidence

who may rely on other sources for their factual basis. The lay opinion must help the jury understand the witness's testimony or decide a material fact. The lay witness must also *not* base the opinion on the scientific, technical, or other specialized knowledge of an expert, unless the lay person can demonstrate that they have such peculiar knowledge and thus qualify as an expert in the matter on which they are about to opine. For example, an eyewitness to a motor-vehicle accident allegedly involving a vehicle's excessive speed may give a speed estimate based on the witness's own observation of the vehicle moving along the highway relative to the speed of other vehicles including the witness's own vehicle, particularly if the estimate would help the jury understand what the witness meant in testifying that the vehicle was going *fast*. Yet the witness must not base the estimate on skid marks or other reconstruction requiring expert knowledge.

5. Competency of witnesses

Every person is **competent** to testify in federal court unless a federal evidence rule provides otherwise. Yet state law governs witness competency as to a state-law claim or defense. To qualify as competent, a witness must give an **oath or affirmation** to testify truthfully. The oath or affirmation need not take any particular form. For example, a child witness's acknowledgment that the child knows what telling the truth means and that the child will do so, suffices to satisfy the oath-or-affirmation requirement. Interpreters must give an oath or affirmation for true translation. A presiding judge is not competent to testify, and no objection is necessary to preserve the error. Jurors may not testify before other jurors at trial. With certain exceptions, jurors may generally not testify during an inquiry into the validity of a verdict or indictment, about deliberations, anything affecting juror votes, or any juror mental processes concerning the verdict. A juror may, though, testify about whether extraneous prejudicial information reached a juror, outside influence reached a juror, or jurors made mistakes on the verdict form. Also, a threshold showing that a juror exhibited overt racial bias casting serious doubt on the fairness and impartiality of deliberations and resulting verdict, allows the court to determine whether racial animus significantly motivated the jury's vote to convict.

6. Judicial notice

A court may **judicially notice** an adjudicative fact that the parties do not reasonably dispute when the fact is **generally known** within the court's jurisdiction or the court can determine the fact accurately and readily from sources that a reasonable person cannot question. For example, the court may take notice from an official calculator that the sun rose at a specific time on a specific date, in a case involving whether the defendant should have had vehicle headlights on at the time of a motor-vehicle accident. At any stage of the case, the court may take judicial notice **on its own** but must take judicial notice when a party asks and supplies the necessary information. The court

Evidence

must hear a party objecting to judicial notice. The court must instruct the jury to accept the noticed fact as **conclusive in a civil case** but that **in a criminal case the jury decides** whether to accept the noticed fact.

7. Roles of judge and jury

The judge in a jury trial determines the **admissibility** of evidence, while the jury determines the **weight** to give the evidence. Judges determine admissibility after hearing **preliminary evidence** going to admissibility, such as facts affecting the existence or scope of a privilege or whether a witness has personal knowledge of the testimony's subject. Judges also hear the parties' objections to and arguments for admissibility. Judges may hear preliminary evidence, objections, and arguments with the jury present in the courtroom, giving appropriate instructions for jurors to disregard those matters, or may excuse jurors to take evidence and hear objections and arguments outside of the jury's presence.

8. Limited admissibility

If the court admits evidence for one purpose but not for another purpose, then the court on request must **restrict the evidence** to its proper scope and **instruct the jury** accordingly. For example, a court may admit evidence of a subsequent remedial repair for a personal-injury plaintiff to prove the contested issue of whether repair before the injury was feasible. On defendant's request, the court must instruct the jury *not* to use the same evidence to infer the defendant's admission that the defendant was negligent in not making the earlier repair.

B. Presumptions

A **presumption** establishes that the party with the burden of producing evidence on the issue to which the presumption applies has satisfied that burden. Presumptions involve policy judgments that the circumstance giving rise to the presumption should have the effect of satisfactory evidence. For example, a party who **destroys evidence** when the party should reasonably anticipate litigation involving that evidence may face a presumption that the evidence would have been adverse. Similarly, a party who **violates a safety statute** may face a presumption that the party was negligent as to the risk against which the statute protected. **State law governs** presumptions for civil claims and defenses for which state law supplies the rule of decision. Unless a statute or rule provides otherwise, the party against whom the law directs a presumption **must produce evidence** to rebut the presumption. A presumption **does not shift the burden of persuasion**, which remains on the party who had it originally.

C. Mode and order

Evidence

The **mode** of examining witnesses involves a party calling a witness on **direct examination**, asking questions of the witness that the witness must answer. The opposing party then **cross-examines** the witness, again asking questions that the witness must answer but within the scope of the direct examination. The party calling the witness may then **rebut** within the scope of the cross-examination and the opposing party rebut within the scope of the rebuttal. The order of calling witnesses traditionally involves the prosecutor or plaintiff calling witnesses in a **case in chief** followed by the defendant calling witnesses in the defendant's case in chief and then each party calling **rebuttal** witnesses.

1. Control by court

The court controls the **mode and order** of examining witnesses and presenting evidence. The court does so to **reveal truth**, **protect witnesses** from harassment and undue embarrassment, and **avoid wasting time**. For example, traditionally, in a civil case the plaintiff presents the plaintiff's case in chief first, followed by the defendant's case in chief, followed by any rebuttal cases. Yet if the defendant admits the complaint's allegations and pleads a contested counterclaim in setoff, then to save time and make for more-orderly presentations, the court could switch the order so that the defendant begins with the defendant's case in chief on the contested counterclaim, followed by the plaintiff's case in chief responding to that counterclaim, and any rebuttal cases.

2. Scope of examination

A party may address any relevant issue in the course of a witness's **direct examination**. The party must address all of the witness's relevant testimony in a single direct examination, having no right to call the party again later. By contrast, **cross-examination** must not go beyond the direct examination's scope, although a cross-examiner may inquire into the witness's credibility. The court may, however, allow broader cross-examination, such as to save time or for witness convenience. For example, if the plaintiff in a medical-malpractice case calls a treating physician to attest only to the malpractice and not to damages, but defense counsel has a single damages question for the treater, then the court may allow the question to relieve the treater from having to return to court in the defendant's case in chief to answer a single question.

3. Form of questions

A party is not to ask **leading questions** on direct examination. A leading question is one that suggests the desired answer, such as questions beginning, "Isn't it true that ...?" A party may lead on direct examination when necessary to develop the witness's testimony, such as to establish witness qualifications or foundation for the coming testimony. For example,

Evidence

the arguably leading question, "Where were you on the night of the shooting, August 10, 2016?" suggests a shooting, time, and date but nonetheless appropriately elicits the foundation for coming testimony. However, an obviously leading question, "Did you see the defendant pull out a Ruger handgun and fire three times at the decedent?" would be inappropriate as on critical questions of identity and action. The court should, however, ordinarily allow leading questions on **cross-examination** and when a party calls a **hostile witness** or **adverse party**.

4. Exclusion of witnesses

If a party asks, the court must order witnesses **sequestered** (excluded from the courtroom) so that they cannot hear other testimony. Parties and attorneys must not inform a sequestered witness about other testimony before the sequestered witness testifies. The court may also sequester witnesses on its own. Yet the court must not sequester an individual **party**, an officer or employee of a corporate party whom the party's attorney has designated the party's representative, or a person whose presence a party shows to be essential to presenting the party's claim or defense. For example, the court may exclude from the courtroom eyewitnesses whom a party plans to call in a negligence case to prove the circumstances of an industrial accident. The court would not, though, in the same case exclude an expert witness whom a party shows would rely on the in-court testimony to give an expert opinion.

D. Impeachment, contradiction, and rehabilitation

To **impeach** a witness is to attack the witness's credibility for telling the truth. To **contradict** a witness is to offer evidence tending to prove the opposite of a fact to which the witness testified. To **rehabilitate** a witness is to present evidence of the witness's credibility after the opposing party attacks the witness's credibility. The following sections show methods and examples for impeachment, contradiction, and rehabilitation.

1. Inconsistent statements and conduct

A party may examine a witness about a **prior inconsistent statement**. The party need not show the witness the statement but, if asked, must show the opposing party's attorney. For example, if an expert witness testifies for the plaintiff in a products-liability case as to the product's design defect, defense counsel may cross-examine the expert using statements inconsistent with the expert's testimony, drawn from the expert's report, correspondence, or deposition. While an opposing party's statement is admissible **as evidence**, a party may offer a non-party witness's prior inconsistent statement as evidence only if the witness has a chance to explain or deny the statement and the adverse party has a chance to examine the witness on it.

Evidence

2. Bias and interest

A party may at any time show the **bias** or **interest** of a witness to impeach the witness's credibility and veracity. Evidence of bias or interest does not contradict the witness's testimony on a material issue. Instead, evidence of bias or interest suggests to the jury that the jury *should not believe* the witness because of influence from the bias or interest. For instance, counsel on cross-examination may attempt to show that an adverse witness has a financial interest in the case's outcome or a family or friendship relationship with the opposing party that has influenced the witness to tell a mistruth. For another example, counsel for a defendant insurer may on cross-examination show that a witness does not like insurance companies because of prior disputes with them, influencing the witness's testimony. Any party, including the party who calls the witness, may impeach a witness's credibility.

3. Conviction of crime

A party may under certain circumstances offer a witness's **criminal conviction** to attack the witness's character for truthfulness. The criminal conviction must have been punishable by **imprisonment for more than one year** or involved **dishonest act or false statement**. If the witness under attack is the **defendant in a criminal case**, or the conviction and release from confinement are **more than ten years past**, then the court must admit the conviction only if its probative value outweighs its prejudicial effect. A conviction is admissible if still on appeal but is not admissible if the witness received a pardon or equivalent rehabilitation. Juvenile adjudications are admissible only in criminal cases to attack a witness other than the defendant, and if the adjudication would have been admissible if an adult offense and evidence is necessary to determine guilt or innocence.

4. Specific instances of conduct

A party may not use **extrinsic evidence** to prove **specific instances of conduct** to attack or support **witness character** for truthfulness. For example, a party may not ask a witness on direct examination about a time that they told the truth at personal expense. Yet the court may allow a party to **cross-examine** on specific instances probative of the character for truthfulness or untruthfulness of the witness. For example, a party may ask a witness on cross-examination about lies on the witness's resume and job application, to show that the witness had the character for untruthfulness. The court may also allow a party to cross-examine a witness on specific instances of another witness's conduct, about whose character the witness has testified. For example, if a witness testifies that another witness has the reputation for truthfulness, a party may cross-examine the witness about a time when the purportedly truthful witness had lied about the witness's age to go into a bar and drink.

Evidence

5. Character for truthfulness

A party may attack or support a witness's credibility using testimony about the witness's **reputation** for having a character for *untruthfulness* or in the form of an **opinion** about that character. For example, a witness may testify for one party that a witness for the opposing party had a wide reputation for telling lies and may also opine on the other witness's dissembling character. Yet reputation and opinion evidence of *truthful* character is admissible only after a party has attacked the witness's character for truthfulness. Thus, the opposing party in the prior example could call another witness to testify that the witness whom the other side called a liar instead had a good reputation for truthtelling. A party may not use a witness's religion to attack or support the witness's credibility.

6. Ability to observe, remember, or relate accurately

A party may at any time attack or support a witness's ability to **observe**, **remember**, or **relate** accurately, no matter which party has called the witness. Testimony, particularly eyewitness testimony, is both powerful and notoriously untrustworthy. To attack a witness's observation, memory, and communication is not to undermine the witness's credibility. To the contrary, the witness may reasonably and firmly believe that the witness is telling the truth. The problem with witness testimony may instead be that the witness was in a poor position to observe such as at a distance, has poor memory such as due to medication or lack of sleep, or has poor abilities to relate observations such as due to language obstacles or nervousness. Parties may confirm or refute a witness's ability to observe, remember, and relate, through the witness who testifies to the recollection or through other witnesses who have personal knowledge of the first witness's ability to observe, remember, and relate.

7. Impeachment of hearsay declarants

Hearsay statements, or hearsay-like out-of-court statements, are often admissible under a hearsay exclusion or exception. When the court admits an out-of-court statement either as outside the hearsay definition or within a hearsay exception, the party opposing the statement may **attack the absent declarant's credibility** as if the declarant were testifying. For example, the party opposing the declarant's statement may do so by offering the declarant's prior inconsistent statement, showing the declarant's bias or interest, or showing the declarant's inability to observe, remember, or relate. The party opposing the statement may also call the declarant as a witness and examine the declarant as if on cross-examination, if the declarant is available.

8. Rehabilitation of impeached witnesses

Evidence

To **rehabilitate** a witness is to present evidence bolstering the witness's credibility after an attack on the witness's credibility. The party initially calling the witness ordinarily rehabilitates the witness after the opposing party attacks the witness's credibility on cross-examination. For example, a party may call an employee witness to testify to the employer's full performance of a disputed contract. If on cross-examination opposing counsel elicits the witness's testimony that the witness has worked only for this employer for many years and needs the job, suggesting that financial interest has influenced the employee's testimony, then on redirect the employer's counsel may show that the witness's alleged financial interest in the outcome does not exist in that the employee would still have a job whether the employer lost or won the lawsuit.

9. Contradiction

To **contradict** a witness is to offer evidence tending to prove the opposite of a fact to which the witness testified. Parties may contradict witnesses with other evidence freely. Ordinarily, the party opposing the party who called the witness would be the party to contradict the witness. For example, if the plaintiff in a motor-vehicle-accident case calls an eyewitness to testify that the defendant motorist ran a red light, then defense counsel would be contradicting that testimony by calling another eyewitness who testified that the light was instead green. Yet a party may **contradict the party's own witness**. For example, if a witness mistakenly testifies to the wrong date of a transaction, counsel may on direct examination call the witness's attention to an exhibit to contradict and correct the date to which the witness had mistakenly testified.

E. Proceedings to which evidence rules apply

The **Federal Rules of Evidence** apply to proceedings before U.S. district courts, U.S. bankruptcy and magistrate judges, and U.S. courts of appeals. In those courts, the Federal Rules of Evidence apply to **civil** cases and proceedings including bankruptcy, admiralty, and maritime cases, **criminal** cases and proceedings, and **contempt** proceedings except when the court acts summarily. The Federal Rules of Evidence, though, do *not* apply to the court's preliminary determination of a fact question governing admissibility, grand-jury proceedings, or miscellaneous proceedings like extradition or rendition, issuing an arrest warrant, criminal summons, or search warrant, preliminary examination in a criminal case, sentencing, granting or revoking probation or supervised release, or considering whether to release on bail.

II. Relevancy and reasons for excluding relevant evidence

The **court** decides whether to admit or exclude evidence depending, among other things, on whether the evidence is **relevant**. When evidence's

Evidence

relevance depends on other facts, the evidence's proponent must introduce to the court proof of those other facts. For example, if a terminated employee offers evidence in a race-discrimination case that a manager was racially biased, the employee would first have to show that the manager made or influenced the employee's termination. A court may admit proposed evidence without that proof on condition that the evidence's proponent must introduce the proof later. The court must conduct a hearing on the evidence's admissibility **outside the jury's presence** if the evidence involves a confession or the testimony of a criminal-case defendant who requests a hearing, or if justice otherwise requires. A criminal-case defendant may testify on a preliminary question of admissibility without becoming subject to cross-examination on other issues.

A. Probative value

Outcomes of trials and evidentiary hearings often depend on the **probative value** of evidence. Parties on both sides often present at least *some* evidence on each dispositive issue, leaving the factfinder to determine which side has the *greater weight* of the evidence or, more significantly, whether the party with the **burden of proof** has met that proof burden. For example, the prosecution in a criminal case has the burden to prove issues **beyond a reasonable doubt**, meaning that the evidence must meet that constitutional standard. The plaintiff in most civil cases need only prove each element of the claim to be **more probable than not**, while the defendant has the same proof burden on defenses. Some civil claims, such as fraud and defamation, may carry a higher **clear-and-convincing evidence** proof burden. Thus, evidence's probative value is a significant issue.

1. Relevancy

Relevant evidence makes a material fact, meaning one of consequence to the action, **more probable or less probable** than it would be without the evidence. For example, if one eyewitness identifies the defendant as the robber in a criminal case making that robbery charge, but another eyewitness identifies a different suspect, the testimony of both eyewitnesses is relevant evidence, one to make identification more probable and the other to make it less so. Yet if a third eyewitness identifies a friend as the driver of a bus that passed by the scene an hour earlier, the evidence is irrelevant as of no consequence to the robbery charge. Relevant evidence is admissible unless the Constitution, a federal statute, the evidence rules, or other Supreme Court rules provide otherwise. Irrelevant evidence is not admissible.

2. Exclusion for unfair prejudice, confusion, or waste of time

A court may exclude relevant evidence if unfair prejudice, confusing the issues, misleading the jury, undue delay, wasting time, or needlessly cumulative evidence **substantially outweigh the evidence's probative**

Evidence

value. For example, while evidence that the plaintiff in a personal-injury case was a substance abuser before injury may tend to show that the plaintiff's injury caused somewhat less wage loss than predicted averages, the jury might give such unfair weight to that prejudicial evidence because of public attitudes against substance abusers that the court should not admit the evidence. The non-material issue of substance abuse might also confuse or mislead the jury from the material issues of fault and damages. Similarly, a court may refuse to admit the testimony of a fourth witness whom the proponent offers on the same issue to which three prior witnesses testified convincingly.

B. Authentication and identification

A party offering an item of evidence, such as a photograph or business record, must **authenticate** the evidence. To authenticate evidence is to show that the item **is what the proponent claims it to be**. A party may authenticate evidence by any reasonable means. A common means is the testimony of a witness through whom the party offers the item. For example, a police officer may testify that the photographs the personal-injury plaintiff calling the officer offers as an exhibit show the scene as it appeared without change immediately after the accident. The court should then admit the photographs as authenticated.

Authentication concerns can arise around both writings and recordings. A lay person who knows the **handwriting** of another may authenticate the writing as by that other, but handwriting experts may also do so by comparing the writing to an authenticated specimen. Persons familiar with another's **voice** may identify a recording as that of the alleged speaker. Persons familiar with calling a person or business on the **telephone** may authenticate that a certain call reached that person or business. Persons familiar with the recording or filing of **public records** may authenticate documents from those records, or the records may carry their own indicia of reliability. A witness can also authenticate **ancient documents** more than twenty years old when found in their likely place without suspicion over authenticity, or those circumstances can carry their own sufficient indicia of reliability. A party may also authenticate an item by describing the **process or system** that produced it, such as for temperature records.

Other items are **self-authenticating**, making them admissible without a witness attesting, or other circumstances showing, that the items are what they purport to be. **Domestic documents** bearing the **public seal** of any national, state, or local entity, and with an *executing signature*, are self-authenticating. Foreign public documents are self-authenticating only when accompanied by a diplomatic or consular official's final certification of authenticity. Copies of **public records** recorded or filed in a public office under law, when the custodian certifies the record, are self-authenticating. Books, pamphlets, or other publications issued by public authorities are self-authenticating, as are **newspapers** and **periodicals**. Tags or labels that businesses affix to goods can authenticate origin and ownership. **Notarized**

Evidence

acknowledgments self-authenticate the documents on which they appear, as do certifications of domestic records of regularly conducted activities and foreign records if false certification is subject to criminal penalty. Signed **commercial paper** is self-authenticating.

C. Character and related concepts

Character evidence is evidence that a party offers to show that the person whose character is in question *acted in a certain way* on a certain occasion, through the influence of a lasting attribute or disposition. The evidence rules *disfavor* and thus sharply restrict character evidence. The first following section gives the broad outline of how the rules treat character evidence. The next section shows the method for using character evidence in the limited instances when permitted, while the remaining sections of this part show other special instances for character evidence.

1. Admissibility of character

Evidence of a person's **character** is not ordinarily admissible to prove that the person acted in accordance with that character. For example, the plaintiff in a motor-vehicle-accident case could not use evidence that the defendant driver had a careless character to prove that the defendant drove carelessly causing the accident. Yet a **defendant in a criminal case** may offer evidence of the defendant's own character, which the prosecutor may then rebut. A defendant in a criminal case may also offer evidence of the alleged **victim's character**, which the prosecutor may rebut and then offer the defendant's character. A party may also offer evidence of a witness's character to **impeach credibility**, although as the next section indicates, the offer must be by certain method.

2. Methods of proving character

When character is admissible, a party must prove it by **reputation** or **opinion**. For example, when a defendant in a criminal case wants to prove the defendant's good character, the defendant's witnesses must testify only that the defendant's reputation is good or that they have a good opinion of the defendant, not that the defendant did specific good things. Only the character witness's **cross-examiner** may inquire into specific instances of the characterized person's conduct. Yet when a person's character is an **essential element** in the case, then parties may prove that character element using specific instances of the person's conduct. For example, if the state, to remove a neglected child, must prove the parent's unfitness, then the state may show specific instances of unfitness like leaving the child alone and hungry, or with guns and drug dealers.

3. Habit and routine practice

Evidence

A person's **habit** or an organization's **routine practice** is admissible to prove that the person or organization acted accordingly. For example, a vehicle owner suing the vehicle's insurer to recover for the vehicle's theft may testify that the plaintiff had the habit of locking the vehicle, if locking the vehicle is a material issue. Similarly, an office manager trying to explain why an electronic record was missing may testify that the office's routine practice is to delete such records at the close of every business day. The court may admit habit or routine evidence whether corroborated or not.

4. Other crimes, acts, transactions, and events

A party cannot use evidence of a crime, wrong, or other act to prove a person's character **to show that the person acted accordingly**. Yet a party may use evidence of a crime, wrong, or other act to prove **motive, opportunity, intent, preparation, plan, knowledge, identity, absence of mistake**, or **lack of accident**. For example, a prosecutor could not use a defendant's prior theft to prove that the defendant had the character to steal again later relating to the charge, but the prosecutor could use the defendant's prior theft of equipment used to accomplish the charged theft, to show the defendant's plan and preparation. A prosecutor must notify the defendant of any such evidence that the prosecutor intends to offer at trial if the defendant asks. The court must exclude the prosecutor's character evidence if the prosecutor fails to give pretrial notice when asked, unless the prosecutor can show good cause for the failure.

5. Prior sexual misconduct of a defendant

The prosecutor in a **sexual-assault case** may offer evidence that the defendant committed any other sexual assault, when that evidence is relevant to any material issue. For example, if the defendant dispute's the defendant's ability to accomplish the assault, then the prosecutor could offer evidence of other accomplished assaults to prove that the defendant was indeed capable. The prosecutor must disclose the witness statements or summary of expected testimony at least 15 days before trial or later if the court allows for good cause. The same rules apply to a criminal case accusing a defendant of **child molestation**. The plaintiff in a **civil case** alleging sexual assault or child molestation may, on the same conditions, offer evidence that the defendant committed other such acts.

D. Expert testimony

A party may call an **expert witness** to give opinion testimony on a material issue that is a proper subject for expert testimony. **Opinion testimony** addresses inferences and conclusions drawn from facts rather than offering facts. For example, lay witnesses would establish the facts and circumstances of an equipment injury, while human-factors expert would opine as to the equipment's safe or unsafe design, and mechanical engineers

Evidence

would opine as to alternative feasible safer designs. Experts may testify in the form of opinions or otherwise. For example, lay witnesses would establish the circumstances of a shooting death, while expert medical examiners would testify to both to the anatomical injuries, constituting factual testimony, and the medical cause of death, constituting opinion testimony.

A court may also **appoint on expert** on its own, although only voluntary rather than involuntary experts. A **court-appointed expert** must advise the parties of any findings. Parties may depose a court-appointed expert. The court or any party may call the expert to testify, and any party may cross-examine, including the party calling the expert. The court compensates a court-appointed expert in a criminal or condemnation case, from funds that law provides. In other cases, the parties compensate the court-appointed expert as the court directs, with compensation then charged like other costs. The court may authorize disclosure to the jury that the court appointed the expert.

1. Qualifications of witnesses

A party calling an expert witness to give opinion testimony must qualify the witness as an expert. A party may qualify an expert witness in preliminary questions put to the witness at trial, or the court may hold a pretrial hearing to qualify expert witnesses. Any combination of **knowledge**, **skill**, **experience**, **training**, or **education** may qualify an expert witness. Unless statute requires otherwise, an expert need not hold any specific education, licensure, certification, training, or experience. For example, an expert orthopedic surgeon in a medical-malpractice case may testify to the standard of care for a back surgery that the defendant neurosurgeon performed, if the orthopedic surgeon demonstrates knowledge of that standard from experience performing back surgeries. Yet if an applicable state statute requires that an expert have the same education and certification as the defendant medical-care provider, then the orthopedic surgeon would not qualify to testify against the neurosurgeon.

2. Bases of testimony

A party must show a reliable **basis** for an expert opinion. An expert must base an opinion on **sufficient facts or other data**. An expert may rely on facts or data that the expert has either **personally observed**, such as by examining a person or thing, or that a party **related to the expert**, such as by supply of records and depositions. The facts **need not be admissible** to admit the expert's opinion, if experts reasonably rely on such facts, like hospital consult records that contain expert hearsay. An expert may disclose inadmissible facts to the jury only if probative value substantially outweighs prejudicial effect in helping the jury evaluate the opinion. An expert may state an opinion without testifying to the underlying facts or data, unless the court otherwise directs, but the opposing party may require the expert to disclose the facts or data on cross-examination.

Evidence

3. Ultimate issue rule

An expert may generally testify to an **ultimate issue**, such as in a products-liability case whether the product was defective, medical-malpractice case the defendant breached the standard of care, or negligence case the defendant was negligent. In a **criminal case**, though, an expert witness must not state an opinion about whether the defendant had the mental state that an element of the crime or of a defense required. For example, the prosecutor in a murder case must not ask a psychological expert to opine on whether the defendant acted with a depraved heart, just as the defense counsel must not ask the same expert whether the defendant acted in the heat of passion. The trier of fact must alone decide ultimate issues in criminal cases.

4. Reliability and relevancy

An expert opinion must be **reliable** to be admissible, with the court acting as gatekeeper. The reliability of an expert opinion depends on the quality of the **scientific principles and methods** that the expert applies. The quality of the scientific principles and methods depends on factors such as **publication**, **peer review**, **testability**, **error rate**, and **general acceptance**. The expert must also have reliably applied the principles and methods to the case. For example, an automotive engineer who uses accepted physics principles of force, momentum, and center of gravity, to measure a vehicle's roll-over propensity, using photographs and measurements of yaw marks and vehicle damage from the actual scene, demonstrates a reliable basis. An expert who is unfamiliar with those principles or lacks the scene data to which to apply those principles fails to demonstrate a reliable basis.

An expert opinion must also be **relevant**, meaning having the tendency to make a material fact more likely or less likely than the fact would be without the opinion. For example, a psychological expert may opine from neuropsychological testing that the plaintiff employee in a discrimination case suffers severe depression, if mental and emotional distress including depression is a part of the plaintiff's damage claim. Yet the psychological expert must not opine as to the plaintiff's general good character, kindness, gentleness, and deservedness, when those qualities have nothing to do with the claim, particularly insofar as the irrelevant testimony would distract the jury from the material liability and damages issues.

5. Proper subject matter for expert testimony

An expert's opinion must be a **proper subject matter** for expert testimony for the opinion to be admissible. An expert opinion is a proper subject matter if the expert's **scientific**, **technical**, or **other specialized knowledge** helps the trier of fact **understand the evidence** or **determine a fact in issue**. For example, an expert mechanical engineer may explain to a jury in a product-failure case how certain machine functions work, so that the

Evidence

jury can understand other expert testimony that the product had design and materials defects. Yet experts could generally *not* opine as to the value of an injured plaintiff's non-economic loss such as pain and suffering, and mental and emotional distress, because that valuation does not involve scientific, technical, or other specialized knowledge.

E. Real, demonstrative, and experimental evidence

Real evidence involves physical items involved in the case that the jury can inspect first-hand, drawing their own sensual conclusions. For example, the gun allegedly involved in a disputed shooting or the allegedly defective product that injured the plaintiff would both be items of real evidence. The court admits real evidence when relevant to a material issue, not unduly prejudicial, and authenticated under those rules explained in a section below, establishing that the physical item is that which the party offering the item purports it to be. So, for example, a detective witness may authenticate that the gun the prosecutor offers into evidence is the gun recovered from the defendant's possession, ballistics testing of which confirms as the gun involved in the shooting.

By contrast to real evidence, **demonstrative evidence** involves models, illustrations, animations, and other depictions and devices that a party uses at trial or hearing to demonstrate or explain facts on which the party's case or theory of the case relies. While the court may closely guard the use in court of demonstrative evidence, particularly when the opposing party objects to its usefulness, confusion, waste, or prejudice, the court does not formally admit demonstrative evidence as an exhibit for the jury to consider in its deliberations. Demonstrative evidence's role is done when the demonstration in court concludes.

Experimental evidence is like demonstrative evidence in those respects, except that experimental evidence shows a jury a principle or process on which the party's case or theory relies rather than illustrating a fact in evidence. When a party offers experimental evidence solely to demonstrate a scientific principle, the conditions for the experiment need not approximate the conditions of the event that the litigation disputes. However, if a party purports to prove the occurrence of the disputed event with an in-court experiment, then the court will exclude the experimental evidence unless conditions are substantially similar to those of the actual event.

III.   Privileges and other policy exclusions

Courts exclude evidence as to which a party has a **privilege**, unless law provides an exception to the privilege. **Federal common law** governs privileges in federal court unless the Constitution, a federal statute, or Supreme Court rules provide otherwise, except that state law governs privilege as to a state-law claim or defense. Thus in a federal civil-rights action, federal common law would determine whether a party has an attorney-work product privilege as to witness statements that the party's attorney takes.

Yet if the plaintiff joins a supplemental state civil-rights claim, and state law offers a privilege as to communications within a state administrative proceeding, then the state-law privilege will apply as to the supplemental state claim.

A. Spousal immunity and marital communications

Two types of **marital privilege** arise when a party calls one spouse to testify against another spouse. The **testimonial privilege** permits a spouse to *refuse to testify* against the other spouse *in criminal cases only*. In the instance of the testimonial privilege, the *witness spouse* holds the privilege, deciding whether to exercise the privilege or not, although the privilege ends when the marriage ends. The law sometimes characterizes the testimonial privilege as a privilege of **spousal immunity** from testifying. The other marital privilege involves the **marital-communications privilege** that excludes evidence of private communications between spouses during the marriage *in both civil and criminal cases*. The marital-communications privilege applies to both words and communicative acts, and protects both the testifying and non-testifying spouse, either spouse having the right to assert the privilege. The marital-communications privilege does not apply to actions in which the spouses oppose one another as parties, such as in a divorce.

B. Attorney-client...

Clients have an **attorney-client privilege** to refuse to disclose, and to prevent others from disclosing, **confidential** communications between client and attorney, **made for obtaining legal advice**. The person asserting the privilege must be the attorney's client or have sought to become a client at disclosure. For example, a deponent may refuse to answer questions asking what the deponent's lawyer told the deponent to prepare for the deposition. The communication must be confidential between attorney and client, without the presence of **third persons**. Thus, if a lawyer and client discuss the client's legal matter at a dinner party attended by others, then the communication is not within the privilege. The communication also must not have been to commit or conceal a **crime or fraud** related to the lawyer's services. Thus, if a client tells the lawyer that the client is going to kill an adverse witness in a pending criminal matter, using the lawyer's subpoena to locate and lure the witness, then the communication is not within the privilege.

Parties may **waive** the attorney-client privilege. When a party discloses a privileged matter in a federal proceeding or to a federal office or agency, the waiver includes undisclosed information only if the party intended the waiver, the information is on the same subject, and the parties should consider the information together. If instead the party inadvertently disclosed the information, then the party does not waive the privilege if the party took reasonable steps to prevent disclosure and rectify the error. When

Evidence

the party discloses the information in a state proceeding, the disclosure does not operate as a waiver in a federal proceeding if the disclosure would not be a waiver if made in a federal proceeding or is not a waiver under the law of the state where the disclosure occurred. A federal court may nonetheless order that the party has not waived the privilege.

...and work product

Under the **attorney-work-product privilege**, an opposing party ordinarily may not compel disclosure of materials prepared by or for an attorney preparing for or in the course of litigation. For example, an opposing party may not demand production of witness statements that a lawyer obtained, memoranda and summaries that the lawyer's assistants prepared for the lawyer or timelines and descriptions that the lawyer's client prepared for the lawyer. An opposing party may compel disclosure of work product after showing **substantial need** for the material and **undue hardship** in obtaining it from another source. For example, if an opposing party is unable to obtain statements from witnesses who have died or moved away, then the party may be able to obtain statements that the opposing party or its counsel took from those witnesses before they were no longer available. Parties may **waive** the attorney-work-product privilege under the same rules for waiver of the attorney-client privilege.

C. Physician/psychotherapist-patient

While the Federal Rules of Evidence and federal common law do not generally recognize a **physician/patient privilege**, the rules defer to state-law privileges on state claims and defenses. State laws generally do recognize a physician/patient privilege. The patient holds the privilege, deciding whether to disclose the patient's medical information. However, to maintain an action that places the patient's physical, mental, or psychological condition in issue, the plaintiff must **waive** the privilege. So, for example, the plaintiff in a personal-injury case must make the plaintiff's medical records and treating care providers' testimony available to the defendant. Similarly, a civil-rights or employment-rights plaintiff who claims mental and emotional distress from the defendant's tortious actions must waive the privilege to allow the defendant to obtain and review the plaintiff's mental-health records.

D. Other privileges

As indicated above, the Federal Rules of Evidence and federal common law do not generally recognize other privileges beyond the attorney-client and attorney-work-product privileges. However, when a plaintiff brings a state-law supplemental claim or state-law diversity-of-citizenship case in federal court or the defendant asserts state-law defenses, then other state-law privileges in addition to the above marital and physician/patient privileges may arise. Other state-law privileges may include the

Evidence

accountant/client privilege and priest-penitent privileges. Note again, however, that a plaintiff who asserts a claim involving matters within evidentiary privileges must generally waive those privileges to maintain the claim.

E. Insurance coverage

A party may not offer evidence of **liability insurance** to prove whether the covered person or entity was negligent but may offer the evidence to prove witness bias or to prove **agency, ownership**, or **control**, or for other purposes. For example, a plaintiff in a products-liability case may not offer evidence of the manufacturer's liability insurance to prove that the manufacturer's products were defectively designed and made but may offer the insurance evidence if the manufacturer denies that it owned or controlled the insured product line. Similarly, the plaintiff in the same case could offer the evidence to impeach the insurance claim representative's testimony that the plaintiff had admitted the plaintiff's own fault, showing instead that the representative's testimony reflected bias for the insurer and insured, and financial interest in reducing the recovery.

F. Remedial measures

When a defendant in a civil case takes **subsequent remedial measures** that would have made the plaintiff's harm less likely, then the plaintiff may not use evidence of those measures to prove negligence, a product defect, need for warning, or other culpable conduct. The plaintiff may use subsequent measures for other purposes such as impeachment or, when the defendant opens the door, to prove disputed **ownership, control**, or **feasibility** of the measures. For example, the plaintiff in a trip-and-fall case could not use evidence of the defendant's repair of the sidewalk crack over which plaintiff tripped to show that the defendant was negligent for not repairing it earlier, but if the defendant at trial denied that the defendant controlled the sidewalk, then the plaintiff could use the repair to prove control.

G. Compromise, payment of medical expenses...

A party may not use **offers to compromise** a disputed claim, or related promises, actions, or statements, to prove the claim or to impeach by prior inconsistent statement. Similarly, a party may not use offers to pay medical or similar expenses from injury to prove liability for the injury. For example, the plaintiff patient in a medical-malpractice case may not offer evidence that the defendant physician made a substantial settlement offer or that the physician apologized during settlement negotiations, to prove that the physician committed malpractice. Yet actions and statements made during negotiations in a **criminal case** are admissible, as are actions and statements made during negotiations with a public office over regulatory, investigative,

Evidence

or enforcement matters. A party may also offer offers to compromise to prove witness bias, refute a claim of undue delay, or prove obstruction of a criminal investigation or prosecution.

...and plea negotiations

A prosecutor or plaintiff may not offer a **withdrawn guilty plea, no-contest plea**, or **statement** made during a plea proceeding or discussions. For example, the plaintiff in a civil case for battery may not use the defendant's no-contest plea in a criminal case making the same battery charge, to prove the defendant's liability. Yet a prosecutor or plaintiff may use other statements made during a plea proceeding or discussions that should be part of such statements already introduced. A prosecutor may also use statements made in plea proceedings or discussions in a criminal proceeding for perjury or false statement, if the defendant made the statement under oath, on the record, and with counsel present.

H. Past sexual conduct of a victim

A defendant in a civil or criminal case alleging the defendant's sexual misconduct may *not* offer evidence to prove that the victim engaged in **other sexual behavior** or to prove the victim's **sexual predisposition**. For example, an accused may not offer other witnesses with whom the victim had consensual sex, to prove promiscuous behavior leading to the accused act. In criminal cases, though, the defendant may offer specific instances of the victim's sexual behavior to prove that **someone else** was the source of semen, injury, or other physical evidence. An accused may also offer specific instances when the victim **consented** to sex **with the accused**, to prove consent to the charged act. Prosecutors may also offer specific instances when the victim consented to sex with the accused.

In a civil case alleging sexual misconduct, a defendant may offer evidence to prove the victim's sexual behavior or predisposition if the evidence's probative value substantially outweighs the danger of harm to any victim and of unfair prejudice to any party. Yet the court may admit evidence of the victim's reputation only if the victim placed it in controversy. When a defendant intends to offer evidence of a victim's sexual behavior, then the defendant must, at least 14 days before trial, **move for the evidence's admission** while describing the evidence and its purpose, serving all parties, and notifying the victim. The court must then conduct **in camera hearing** to hear the victim and parties, sealing the record.

IV. Writings, recordings, and photographs

Special rules apply to proving the contents of writings. One question that arises, addressed in the next section, is whether the writing's proponent must produce the **original writing** rather than a copy, under the **best-evidence rule**. A second question is whether a party may prove written content through testimony rather than the writing. The answer to that second question is that a party may only prove written content, other than through the writing itself, when using the testimony or written statement of the party against whom the party offers the content. Generally, **the court** determines whether a party may prove written content other than through the original writing, although the jury determines whether a disputed writing is the original, ever existed, or had the content that testimony asserts that it did.

A. Requirement of original

Under the **best-evidence rule**, a party introducing writings, recordings, or photographs to prove their contents must offer the original unless otherwise an exception allows a copy. However, the rules immediately provide that a **duplicate** is admissible *to the same extent as the original* unless an opposing party raises a *genuine question* about the original's authenticity or other circumstances make admitting the duplicate unfair. The rules further provide that the party need not offer the original and may use other evidence of content for **lost**, **destroyed**, or **unavailable** originals, or when the writing does not closely address a controlling issue. So, for example, parties in a personal-injury case may routinely offer copies of medical records rather than the original records, although if circumstances suggested an altered original, then the court may require the original record. A party may also use a copy to prove the content of a certified official record or official record that a witness testifies to be correct, and may prove the content by testimony when no copy is available.

B. Summaries

Litigation can involve **voluminous writings**, the complete contents and effect of which jurors could not conveniently examine, digest, and appreciate in court. For example, a business may claim substantial and enduring lost profits, based on voluminous financial records, due to a competitor's unfair competition. In those circumstances, the party advocating its position from voluminous writings may use a **summary**, **chart**, or **calculation** to prove contents that the factfinder cannot conveniently examine in court. The business in the above example may offer a summary or chart calculating the business loss from the voluminous records. The party must make the voluminous originals or duplicates available for the opposing party's examination and copying. The court may also order the party to produce the voluminous writings in court.

C. Completeness rule

When a party offers all or part of a single writing or recording, the adverse party may offer any other part or any other writing or recording that the jury should in fairness consider at the same time. For example, if the respondent employer in a worker's compensation case offers a medical

Evidence

examiner's report, the claimant employee may at the same time offer exhibits attached to the report.

V. Hearsay and circumstances of its admissibility

Questions on **hearsay** make up one third of the Multistate Bar Examination's evidence questions. You must know hearsay rules to do well on the evidence subjects. Hearsay is a complex subject because its proper treatment requires first recognizing what is and is not hearsay, and then, for hearsay statements, recalling and applying a large number of exceptions. Treat the hearsay subject as you would treat several separate subjects, including the hearsay definition, exclusions from hearsay, and hearsay exceptions. While the general rule is that hearsay is **inadmissible**, the rule defines hearsay *not to include* significant out-of-court statements. The hearsay rule also has so many exceptions that *hearsay is often admissible*. Note, too, that even if the hearsay rule excludes a statement, the court may still admit the statement if it has **equivalent circumstantial guarantees of trustworthiness**, is more probative on a material issue than any other reasonably available evidence, and if justice so requires, although the proponent must give pretrial notice of the intent to offer the otherwise-inadmissible hearsay statement.

A. Definition of hearsay

Hearsay has both a functional definition and categorical exclusions from that definition. You must know both the functional definition and categorical exclusions. The functional definition in the next section requires that you evaluate first whether evidence involves an out-of-court statement and, if so, then the *purpose* for which the party offers the statement relative to the case's issues. The categorical exclusions in the following two sections remove from the definition of hearsay two kinds of out-of-court statements that ordinarily would be hearsay but for their categorical exclusion. Do not think of the categorical exclusions as exceptions to the hearsay rule because the rules treat exclusions differently from exceptions.

1. What is hearsay

Hearsay means a statement that a declarant does not make while testifying at the current trial or hearing, that is, instead makes **outside of court**, that a party offers in court to **prove what the statement asserts**. For example, a prosecution witness who testifies in a criminal case that a neighbor told the witness that the defendant was the one who committed the crime is testifying to hearsay. The declarant neighbor identified in an out-of-court statement the defendant as the one who committed the crime, which was exactly what the prosecution meant to prove in offering the statement. By contrast, if the prosecution asked the witness who committed the crime, and the witness testified from first-hand observation that the defendant had done so, then the statement would not be hearsay because not out of court. Similarly, if the prosecution asked a witness whether the victim of a shooting was able to speak, and the witness answered saying that the victim had indeed said that the victim loved his wife, then the statement would not be hearsay because not used to prove that the victim loved his wife but to prove that the victim could speak.

Out-of-court statements include both **oral and written** assertions, meaning that the hearsay rule can apply to both testimony and offers of exhibits. Thus, in-court testimony about out-of-court conversations implicates hearsay, while in-court offers of out-of-court writings also implicate hearsay. Out-of-court statements can also include **nonverbal conduct**, such as nods of the head or pointing at someone in identification, when intended as an assertion. Thus, if a prosecution witness testifies that just before dying the victim pointed at the defendant when asked who shot the victim, then the victim's pointing involves hearsay. One would then search for an exception.

2. Prior statements by witness

The hearsay definition expressly excludes some **prior inconsistent statements** by witnesses. If the prior inconsistent statement's declarant is testifying under cross-examination about the prior statement, and the declarant gave the prior statement **under oath** in a proceeding including in a deposition, then the prior inconsistent statement is not hearsay. For example, when a party in a motor-vehicle-accident case cross-examines a police officer about a deposition that the officer gave in the case, to show that the officer testified on deposition to the opposite of the officer's testimony on direct examination, the officer's deposition testimony is not hearsay.

The same rule allows a party to rebut a charge of recent fabrication and rehabilitate an impeached witness using a **prior consistent statement**. A prior consistent out-of-court statement is not hearsay if the declarant is testifying under cross-examination about the prior statement, and the party uses the prior statement to rebut a charge that the declarant recently fabricated the statement from improper influence or motive, or to rehabilitate the declarant's credibility. For example, to rehabilitate the officer in the above example, the party calling the officer may on redirect, after cross-examination impeachment, refer the officer to the officer's accident report recording the officer's statement consistent with the officer's testimony. That report's statement would not be hearsay when used to rehabilitate the officer's credibility. A party may also use a prior consistent statement under cross-examination of the declarant when the statement identifies a person as someone the declarant perceived earlier.

3. Statements attributable to party-opponent

The hearsay definition also expressly excludes some **statements of the party opponent**. For a party to use a statement of a party opponent as

Evidence

outside of the hearsay definition, the party must offer the statement against the opposing party. For example, the wife in a divorce proceeding contesting a property division may testify that her husband had told her that he still owned a certain business interest that at trial the husband testified he had instead conveyed away. The husband's out-of-court statement would not be hearsay because used against him in the proceeding. The statement must also be one that the party either made, adopted as true, or authorized another to make, or if a corporate party, then the party's agent or employee made within the scope of that relationship, if other evidence establishes the employment or agency and scope. Coconspirator statements furthering the conspiracy also qualify as statements of a party opponent, if other evidence establishes the conspiracy.

4. Multiple hearsay

Parties may wish to offer out-of-court statements that include other out-of-court statements, implicating **multiple hearsay**. For example, a party may ask a witness to testify to what an out-of-court declarant said *that a third person said*. The out-of-court declarant's statement would be one level of hearsay and the third person's statement a second level of hearsay. For another example, a party may offer an exhibit that is hearsay at its own level but that also contains a person's statement at a second level of hearsay. The hearsay rule requires that you examine each level of hearsay to determine its admissibility. Hearsay within hearsay is admissible only if both levels of its hearsay are admissible. For example, if the exhibit just mentioned was a business record within that hearsay exception, and the person's statement within it a statement of physical condition within that hearsay exception, then the exhibit would be admissible.

B. Present sense impressions and excited utterances

The hearsay rule includes many exceptions. **Present sense impressions** are a first exception to the hearsay rule, admissible whether the declarant is available or not. A present sense impression is a statement describing or explaining an event or condition that the declarant is then perceiving. For example, a witness could testify to a declarant's statement, "Look at the man pointing a gun," because the declarant was describing a present perception. The **excited utterance** is a related hearsay exception in which the declarant describes a startling event under the described event's stress. So, for example, the above witness could add that the declarant also said, "That man just shot the woman!" because the statement would be under the described event's stress.

C. Statements of mental, emotional, or physical condition

Another hearsay exception exists, whether the declarant is available or not, for a witness's testimony as to a declarant's **then-existing state of**

Evidence

mind or emotional, sensory, or physical condition. For example, a witness could testify to a declarant's statement of motive, intent, or plan such as, "I'm so angry that I may just shoot him," or other bodily condition such as, "My stomach is so upset that I feel like throwing up." The then-existing-state-of-mind exception does *not* reach a statement of memory to prove the fact remembered, such as, "Oh, I just remembered that the tall man dressed in green was the shooter" to prove who shot, unless the statement relates to the validity or terms of the declarant's will, such as, "Oh, I just remembered that I did want my niece included in the bequest."

D. Statements for purposes of medical diagnosis and treatment

Another hearsay exception exists, whether the declarant is available or not, for statements made for **medical diagnosis or treatment**. For example, a medical record offered as an exhibit and recording, "Patient reports significant abdominal pain in the right lower quadrant," would fall within the statement-made-for-medical-diagnosis exception. The statement must be reasonably pertinent to the diagnosis and treatment, describing medical history, part or present symptoms, and their inception and causes. So, for example, an offered medical record could include, "Patient reports no prior symptoms until struck in the abdomen," within the hearsay exception but could not include, "Patient identifies man as wearing green jacket and red baseball cap," because the latter statement would not be reasonably pertinent to medical diagnosis.

E. Past recollection recorded

Another hearsay exception exists, whether the declarant is available or not, for **recorded recollections**, also known as *past recollection recorded*. The recorded recollection must be on a matter the witness once knew but now cannot recall and that the witness made when the matter was fresh in the witness's mind. The admitted record may be read into evidence but *not* received as an exhibit unless offered by the opposing party. For example, a police officer testifying as a witness may read from the officer's own accident report made at the accident scene as to the location of the vehicles and their relative damage, when the officer does not recall those details. The court would not admit the accident report as an exhibit unless the opposing party offered it. If the accident report recorded witness statements at the scene, those statements would be a second level of hearsay and need other hearsay exception.

F. Business records

Another hearsay exception exists, whether the declarant is available or not, for **records of a regularly conducted activity**. The records may include acts, events, conditions, opinions, or diagnoses. Someone must have made the record on their own **knowledge** or when receiving information from

Evidence

someone with knowledge. An organization must have created and kept the record in the course of regularly conducted activity. A custodian or other qualified witness must show these conditions unless a rule or statute certifies the record, and the record must not be otherwise untrustworthy. For example, the court in a breach-of-contract case may admit an account statement showing the defendant account debtor's charges and payments, on the plaintiff business's account manager's testimony that the manager kept the record in the regular course of the business. The exception also applies to the **absence** of a record. Thus, the admitted account statement in the above example could also establish the absence of the debtor's payment.

G. Public records and reports

Another hearsay exception exists, whether the declarant is available or not, for **public records**. The record must state the **activities of a government office** under a **legal duty to report**. For example, the court could admit a driver's license history offered under the testimony of a recordskeeper for a secretary-of-state office, in any proceeding in which the driver's license history is a material issue, such as a license-revocation proceeding or a civil case for negligent hiring. The exception also includes records of births, deaths, or marriages reported to a public office under a legal duty. The public-records exception does *not* include law-enforcement records offered in a criminal case or public-investigation records in a civil case or against the government in a criminal case. The records must appear otherwise trustworthy. The exception also applies to the **absence** of a public record after **diligent search**. Thus, the admitted driver's license history in the above example could also establish the absence of the license's prior revocation or reinstatement, or a county clerk's diligent search for a marriage record could establish that one did not exist.

H. Learned treatises

Another hearsay exception exists, whether the declarant is available or not, for statements in **learned treatises**, periodicals, or pamphlets. The statement's proponent must have expert testimony or judicial notice establish the statement as **reliable authority**. The proponent must also call the statement to an expert witness's attention on cross-examination or on direct examination show that the expert relied on the statement. For example, on defense counsel's cross-examination of the plaintiff's physician expert in a medical-malpractice case, defense counsel may show the physician a medical treatise, have the physician acknowledge that the treatise is authoritative in the physician's field, and then challenge the physician with a statement from the treatise that contradicts the physician's testimony on direct examination. A party may read the statement into evidence but not offer the statement as an exhibit.

I. Former testimony; depositions

Evidence

The next hearsay exceptions require that the **declarant is unavailable** as a witness. A declarant is *unavailable* when a **privilege** protects the declarant from disclosing or when the declarant **refused** to testify, does not **remember**, or cannot attend because of **death** or **illness**. A declarant is also unavailable when the party seeking the statement's admission has **not been able to procure** the declarant's attendance or testimony after reasonable effort. Yet if the proponent caused the declarant's unavailability, then the exception does not apply.

When the declarant is unavailable, a hearsay exception exists for **former testimony** that the declarant gave as a witness at a trial, hearing, or deposition in any proceeding. The former testimony's proponent must offer the former testimony against a party who had (or in a civil case a party whose predecessor in interest had) an opportunity and similar motive to examine the unavailable declarant. For example, the husband seeking child custody in a divorce action may offer the deposition testimony in the same case of a caseworker who after investigation testified on deposition to the relative fitness of each parent, if the caseworker subsequently suffered stroke and mental incapacity. The husband could not offer the deposition if the caseworker remained available.

J. Statements against interest

When the declarant is unavailable, another hearsay exception exists for **statements against interest**. A statement against interest is one that a reasonable person in the declarant's position would have made **only if believing its truth** because **so contrary to the declarant's interest**. For example, the plaintiff employee in a wrongful-termination case may testify that the employer's human-resources director who fired the plaintiff admitted to the employee in the firing that the employee had been a good employee. The director's admission would tend to work so strongly against the employer's litigation interest that the director must have believed the statement to be true. In criminal cases where the statement would expose the declarant to criminal liability, corroborating circumstances must clearly indicate the statement's trustworthiness.

K. Other exceptions to the hearsay rule

Multiple other small exceptions to the hearsay rule exist, whether the declarant is available or not. One such exception is for regularly kept **records of religious organizations** about personal or family history, such as statements of birth, legitimacy, ancestry, marriage, divorce, or death. Another such exception is for statements in **certificates of marriage, baptism, and similar ceremonies**, made by persons authorized to perform the certified act, attesting to the act, and issued near the time. Another exception is for statements in **family records** such as a Bible, genealogy, chart, ring engraving, portrait inscription, or burial or urn engraving. Another

Evidence

exception is for **recorded documents** affecting **property interests** if admitted to prove the original recorded document's contents.

Other hearsay exceptions exist, whether the declarant is available or not, for statements in **ancient documents** at least twenty years old and having established authenticity. **Market reports** and other commercial publications, including quotations, lists, directories, or other compilations on which the public or persons in particular occupations generally rely, are also excepted from hearsay, whether declarants are available or not. Reputation concerning **personal or family history** among a person's family or associates, or in the community, concerning the person's birth, adoption, legitimacy, ancestry, marriage, divorce, death, or adoption, are also excepted, declarant available or not.

A hearsay exception also exists for **reputation within a community**, arising before the controversy, concerning **boundaries of land** or customs that affect the land. For example, a witness could testify that certain city lands had long had the reputation and use as a public gathering space or park. The exception also applies to **general historical events** important to that community, state, or nation, such as witness testimony that a key protest against segregation had occurred long ago occurred in the public park. Reputation for a person's **character** among the person's associates or in the community is also admissible, such as testimony that the plaintiff employee in an employment-retaliation case had a reputation among co-workers as a hard worker.

Judgments of conviction are also admissible over a hearsay objection, unless taken under nolo-contendere plea. The conviction must have been for crime punishable by death or by imprisonment for more than a year, and offered to prove a fact essential to the judgment. For example, a plaintiff customer in a negligent-hiring claim against a broker, whose financial advisor embezzled the customer's funds, may offer the advisor's prior embezzlement conviction to show that the broker should have performed a background check and not have hired the advisor after discovering the conviction. Judgments admitted to prove a matter of personal, family, or general history, or boundaries, are also admissible even though hearsay.

Certain other hearsay statements are admissible only if the declarant is unavailable. For example, in a prosecution for homicide or in a civil case, a statement that the deceased declarant made about the cause of the declarant's **imminent death** is admissible. For example, the prosecution in a murder case could call a witness to testify that the dying declarant said that the defendant shot him. The hearsay rule also permits a witness to testify to a statement about the witness's own birth, adoption, legitimacy, ancestry, adoption, or similar personal or family history, or the same about the witness's family member, even though the witness had no way of acquiring personal knowledge about that fact. For example, a witness could testify that the witness was born or adopted on a certain date and had an older brother born on a certain date, even though that information would have been secondhand to the witness.

Evidence

Finally, the hearsay rule permits a witness to testify to a statement that a declarant made, when the party offers the statement against a party who **intentionally caused the declarant's unavailability**. Thus, the plaintiff estate in a wrongful-death case based on battery may offer a witness's testimony that the decedent said that the defendant had threatened to kill the decedent, the defendant having caused the decedent's unavailability.

L. Right to confront witnesses

The Sixth Amendment's **confrontation clause** provides that all **criminal prosecutions** must afford the accused the right to confront the witnesses against the accused. The court must ensure that witnesses in criminal cases testify **under oath**, understanding the trial's serious nature. The court must also ensure that the accused has the opportunity to **cross-examine** witnesses who testify against the accused. The court must also ensure that jurors can **assess the credibility** of prosecution witnesses by observing their behavior. The Sixth Amendment does *not* bar admission of an unavailable witness's prior testimony against the same defendant when the defendant had equivalent motive and full opportunity to cross-examine the witness. While face-to-face confrontation and cross-examination are ordinarily required, the court may protect abused children from further serious emotional distress by allowing cross-examination only by one-way closed-circuit television. The court may also limit cross-examination when the defendant has exhausted it and further cross-examination would be harassing.

Real Property Law

F.   Real Property Law

NOTE: Approximately one-fifth of the Real Property questions on the MBE will be based on each of the categories I through V.

The Multistate Bar Examination lists many real-property topics in five different areas, giving each area roughly equal weight in the number of questions asked. The areas include **ownership** of real property, special **rights in land**, **contracts** for the sale of land, **mortgages** and other security devices, and finally **title** to land. Study real-property law comprehensively rather than focusing on any one area. Do *not* let specific difficult subjects bog down your studies. The large number of topics and roughly equal treatment of subject areas warrant broad studies rather than deep studies on any one topic.

As you review this part on real-property law, keep in mind that the Multistate Bar Examination tests you on *real*-property law, not *personal*-property law. So while principles of gifts, bailments, or finders may appear on the state portion of the bar exam, you won't encounter them on the Multistate Bar Examination. Also, the Multistate Bar Examination's topic list is not always intuitive. For example, the topic list begins discussing present and future estates but doesn't mention the necessarily intertwined *rule against perpetuities* until a later section. Follow the cross references for related concepts.

I.   Ownership

The **ownership** of real property implicates five different issue areas under the Multistate Bar Examination topics list. The first ownership issue area involves the types of **present estates**. The second ownership issue area involves the types of **future interests** and special issues that future interests raise. The third ownership issue area involves the types of **co-tenancies** in land and issues having to do with their use, severance, and partition. The fourth ownership issue area involves the relationship of **landlords** to **tenants**. The exam's topics list for the ownership issue area ends with the treatment of **special problems** of ownership. Property ownership is a broad concept referring to the bundle of rights that owners of property acquire and responsibilities that they assume when they own land. The Multistate Bar Examination, though, focuses *estates* in land, describing the types of interests that one may hold in land. The law classifies types of estate in land generally by the *duration* of the interest, always accounting for the *entire* duration of interests in the land.

A. Present estates

Discussion of ownership sensibly begins with **present estates**. The following sections on **present estates** treat *fees simple, defeasible* fees simple, and *life estates*. **Present estates** arise when an owner has the ability to take possession of the property immediately. The four types of present estates categorize interests based on the duration of the expected possession. **Fee-simple** estates have an *infinite* duration, although they can terminate earlier on some event, as in **defeasible fees** discussed in a following section. **Fee-tail** estates last until the grantee's bloodline terminates. **Life estates** last only for the grantee's life of the grantee. A **term of years** lasts for a fixed period of any duration, not necessarily in years. The first three estates are **freehold estates** while the fourth estate, a term of years, is a **non-freehold estate** and the feudal predecessor of the landlord-tenant law of today. The landlord-tenant discussion in a following section thus also addresses non-freehold estates.

1. Fees simple

The term **fee simple** is shorthand for the **fee simple absolute**. When a person owns property in fee simple absolute, the person has the theoretical right to hold the property in perpetuity. Fee-simply estates are **alienable**, which means that the owner may sell or transfer the land to another, and **inheritable**, which means that the owner may devise the land by will to another, who would then own the property in perpetuity. The vast majority of land sales today transfer fee simple absolute.

The way that the parties write a land transaction determines the estate that they transfer. The language needed to create a fee simple absolute is *to A and A's heirs*, where *A* refers to the buyer's full legal name that would appear in the transfer documents. This language includes **words of purchase** and **words of limitation**. The words of purchase in this transaction are *to A*. The words of limitation in the transaction are *and A's heirs*. Traditionally, the law required the words *and A's heirs* to show that the seller intended to deliver fee-simple estate to the purchaser. Today, however, a transaction *to A* suffices to transfer fee simple. Modern law presumes fee-simple transactions unless the parties use other words of limitation.

2. Defeasible fees simple

Defeasible fee-simple estates are estates in fee simple that *end on a stated future event*. By *defeasible*, the law means terminable on the occurrence of the stated condition or event. By contrast, the owner of a fee simple *absolute*, rather than a *defeasible* fee, holds the property in perpetuity unaffected by future events. A grantor creates a defeasible fee estate when wanting to control the property's use and ownership. The law recognizes **three types of defeasible fee estates**, a fee simple *determinable*, a fee simple *subject to condition subsequent*, and a fee simple *subject to executory limitation*. The type of defeasible fee depends on the words of limitation used in the transfer that creates the interest.

A fee simple **determinable** is an estate that would be a fee simple absolute but for the language of the conveyance that attaches a condition to the property's ownership. The law calls the **condition subsequent** the event that would terminate the fee-simple interest. For example, a conveyance from

Real Property Law

grantor *to A so long as A never commits a felony on the property* includes the condition subsequent that A not commit a felony on the property. Thus, A owns the property in fee simple, but if A commits a felony on the property, A's fee simple terminates, and the property automatically reverts to the grantor who created A's interest. When a grantor creates a fee-simple determinable, the law calls the grantor's future interest a **possibility of reverter**. Reverter happens automatically by law when the condition subsequent occurs. To create a fee-simple determinable, the conveyance must include *durational* words of limitation indicating the intent that the possessory estate will end automatically on the happening of the stated condition. Typical words of limitation that suggest a fee-simple determinable include *so long as, during, while, unless,* and *until*. When one of these words addresses a condition subsequent, then the purchaser acquires a present possessory fee-simple determinable, while the grantor retains a possibility of reverter.

A fee simple **subject to condition subsequent** relates closely to the fee-simple determinable. Here, though, with a fee simple subject to condition subsequent, while the owner holds in fee simple, the grantor has attached a condition subsequent that will *not* automatically terminate the owner's fee-simple title. Instead, the grantor retains a future interest called a **right of entry** that gives the grantor the *option* to take the property back *or* let the owner keep the property. The conveyance's **words of limitation** determine whether the fee simple is determinable or, instead, subject to condition subsequent. Typical words of limitation for a fee simple subject to condition subsequent include *but if, provided that, on condition that, if, however,* and *provided, however.* For example, a fee simple subject to condition subsequent arises in a conveyance *from O to A, but if A commits a felony on the property, then O may reenter and retake the property.* These words of limitation are expressly conditional *and discretionary,* reflected here in the operative word *may,* rather than purely durational. The grantor may invoke *or ignore* the condition's occurrence.

The final form of fee simple, a fee simple **subject to executory limitation**, is easier to distinguish. Like a fee simple determinable and fee simple subject to condition subsequent, the owner possesses the property in fee simple but subject to a condition subsequent that may terminate the interest. Yet for a fee simple *subject to executory limitation,* the person who takes the property when the condition subsequent occurs is a third party rather than the original grantor or grantor's heirs or assigns. If the interest doesn't revert to the original grantor, then the purchaser has a fee simple subject to executory limitation. For example, a fee simple subject to executory limitation arises in a conveyance from grantor *to A, but if A ever commits a felony on the property, then to C.* The fact that a third party, C in this case, would get the property if A committed a felony on the property indicates the executory limitation. The law calls the third party's interest the **executory interest**, discussed in the future interest section below. If the condition subsequent occurs, then the property automatically goes to the third party.

Real Property Law

3. Life estates

A **life estate** is a third type of freehold estate. As the estate's name implies, the owner of a life estate owns the property for the *duration of the owner's lifetime*, whether that lifetime lasts one day or fifty years. Because of a life estate's limited and uncertain duration, a life estate is *not* inheritable or descendible. A life estate's owner has nothing left to give on demise. On the other hand, life estates are *alienable*, meaning that the owner can sell or transfer a life estate, although the law continues to measure the transferred life estate's term by the original life tenant's life, not the life of the person who received the life estate. The most common way that transfer documents create a life estate are with the language *to A for life* or *to A for A's natural life*. All life estates include a future interest because the property must go somewhere after the life tenant dies. The future interest can either be a reversion or remainder as following sections discuss in more detail.

B. Future interests

A second ownership area to address after present estates involves **future interests**. Future interests include *reversions*, both vested and contingent *remainders*, *executory interests*, and finally *possibilities of reverter* including powers of termination. A following section also addresses special rules affecting these interests. Generally, a **future interest** arises when a person must wait until some future time in order to take possession of the property. Estates involve the property's timeline of ownership. The present interest owner possesses the property for some duration, then the **future interest holder** may come into possession of the property after the present estate ends. Future interests belong to two categories, those retained by the original grantor and those held by a third party. Interests retained by the grantor include *reversions, possibilities of reverter*, and *rights of entry*. Interests granted a third party include *vested remainders, contingent remainders*, and *executory interests*, all addressed in the following sections.

1. Reversions

A **reversion** is a future interest that the grantor retains when transferring a present interest less than the grantor owns. For example, a conveyance from grantor *to A for life* creates a life estate in A with a *reversion in fee simple* in the grantor. When the grantor both doesn't convey the grantor's entire interest in the property and doesn't say to whom the property passes after the lesser estate ends, then the law construes a reversion in the original grantor or grantor's heirs or devisees if the grantor has already died when the present possessory estate ends. Thus, reversion is an interest that returns to the grantor. The law also recognizes a **possibility of reverter** and **right of entry**, each arising only in limited circumstances when the present possessory estate ends. As stated above as to defeasible fees, **possibilities of reverter** arise only when the present possessory estate is a fee simple determinable, that is, when the determinable fee ends automatically on the condition's occurrence. A **right of entry** arises only when the present possessory estate is a fee simple subject to condition subsequent, that is, when the grantor has the option of retaking the land after the condition occurs. A following section addresses these latter interests.

2. Remainders, vested and contingent

A **remainder** is a future interest granted to a third party after the present possessory estate ends naturally. Two conditions define remainders. First, the future interest must go to a third party, not revert to the grantor or the grantor's heirs or assigns. Second, the remainder holder must wait until the natural end of the prior possessory estate to take possession. This last point is critical to determining whether the future interest left over is an executory interest or some type of remainder, which the next section addresses.

Remainders can be either **vested remainders** or **contingent remainders**. A vested remainder is one that an *ascertained person* holds, meaning someone named, *and* that is not subject to a condition precedent. A condition precedent is an event that must occur before the person obtains the future interest. For example, the transaction from grantor *to A for life, then to B if B attains the age of 21*, includes a condition precedent to B obtaining the estate that B must attain the age of 21. Thus, B's interest is *not* a vested remainder but instead a **contingent remainder** because of the condition precedent. Similarly, a grant *to A for life, then to B's children*, when B has no children, would be a grant to unascertained persons and thus create only a contingent rather than vested remainder. Again, a contingent remainder involves either an unascertained owner or one who receives the interest subject to a condition precedent. A vested remainder cannot be contingent.

Contingent remainders can vest either when the condition precedent occurs or the unascertained person is ascertained. Thus, in the prior example, if the grantor had granted *to A for life, then to B's children*, and B then had a child, that child would take a *vested* rather than contingent remainder as an ascertained person within the grant. Because B could have other children, the child already born would have a vested remainder **subject to open** to account for the interests of any other children subsequently born to B. Thus, if when B died, B had three children, then those three children would have **indefeasibly vested remainders** because no further births could dilute their interests. Each child would have a one-third interest in the property as tenants in common.

Grantors can form **alternative contingent remainders** when the grantor creates two options for what will happen to the property. For example, the grantor creates alternative contingent remainders in the conveyance from grantor *to A for life, then to B if B reaches 21, but if B does not reach 21, then to C*. In this conveyance, B has a contingent remainder conditioned on B's reaching age 21. Here, though, the grant holds that if B doesn't reach age 21, then the property goes to C. The grantor retains no reversion here because of the stated alternatives.

3. Executory interests

Executory interests are a third type of future interest, one that the grantor creates *in a third party*. Executory interests relate closely to vested and contingent remainders. Yet an executory interest is a future interest in a third party that takes effect only *when a condition subsequent divests, or terminates, the interest that precedes the executory interest.* Executory interests vest when someone else loses a vested interest. For example, in the conveyance from grantor *to A for life, then to B, but if B does not reach the age of 21, then to C*, we have already seen that B has a vested remainder that B could lose if B dies before 21. The ability of B to lose the interest means that B's interest is *subject to divestment*. The possibility of divestment creates C's executory interest, which would vest only if B died before reaching age 21. An executory interest also arises in C in the conveyance from grantor *to A for life, then to B, but if B joins a biker gang, then to C*. Here, if B receives the property on A's death but then joins a biker gang, the condition subsequent occurring would divest B's defeasible fee simple, vesting C's executory interest.

4. Possibilities of reverter, powers of termination

As the defeasible-fee section addresses, a **possibility of reverter** is the future interest that remains after a fee-simple determinable. A **fee-simple determinable** is an estate that would be a fee-simple absolute but for the conveyance's language of the conveyance attaching a **condition subsequent** to ownership. For example, a conveyance from grantor *to A so long as A never commits a felony on the property* means that A takes the property in fee simple, but if the condition subsequent occurs, A committing a felony on the property, A loses the property, which automatically reverts to the grantor. A fee simple determinable arises whenever the grantor has a future interest, called a **possibility of reverter**. Reverter happens automatically by operation of law on the condition's occurrence.

Also as the defeasible-fee section states, a **right of entry**, also known as a **power of termination**, is the future interest that arises from a fee simple **subject to condition subsequent**. Recall that a fee simple subject to condition subsequent relates closely to the **fee simple determinable**. For any defeasible fee, the owner holds in fee simple, but the grantor attached a **condition subsequent** that could cause the person to lose their present possessory interest. Yet unlike the fee simple determinable, the owner does *not* lose the fee-simple interest automatically on the condition's occurrence. Rather, the grantor retains the **right of entry**, or **power of termination**, to take the property back *or not* at the grantor's option. The **words of limitation** in the conveyance determine the interest. A fee simple subject to condition subsequent arises under words of limitation like *but if, provided that, on* *condition that, if, however,* or *provided, however.* For example, a fee simple subject to condition subsequent arises in a conveyance *from O to A, but if A commits a felony on the property, then O may reenter and retake the property.*

5. Rules affecting these interests

The law recognizes several rules that limit *dead-hand control* over real property, meaning how long and how much a person can control what happens to the person's property after the person's death. The rules seek to ensure reasonable *alienability* and *marketability* of property. One of those rules, the **rule against perpetuities**, the Multistate Bar Examination's topics list treats under a following Special Problems section. Others of these rules no longer apply in most jurisdictions. For example, a few states still follow a rule for the **destructibility of contingent remainders**. In those few jurisdictions, the rule eliminates any contingent remainder that has not vested by the time that all preceding life estates have terminated. The rule for destructibility of contingent remainders ensures that the law can ascertain the person who would have the discretion to exercise a possibility of reverter.

The law continues to recognize a **merger rule** holding that when a person who owns a vested life estate acquires the vested future interest behind the life estate, the two vested estates merge into one fee-simple title. For example, in the conveyance *from O to A for life, remainder to B*, if B then sells B's future interest to the life-estate holder A, then A would own both the present vested life estate *and* B's vested remainder, the two interests of which would merge into fee-simple title in A.

The **rule in Shelley's Case**, in the few states that still recognize it, applies where a life tenant's heirs hold the remainder to the life tenant's present interest, to merge the interests into the life tenant in fee simple absolute. Thus, in a conveyance *from O to A for life, remainder to A's heirs*, the rule in Shelly's Case would give A the fee-simple title to the property. Having a grant of a life estate that also gives that person's heirs the remainder merge into fee-simple title in the life estate holder gives the grantee the ability to convey the property in fee-simple absolute, promoting the land's marketability. Buyers need not wait for the life-estate holder to die to ensure that they properly ascertain, and gain conveyance from, the persons who hold the remainder interests. Only one person, the grantee of the life estate, need sign the deed conveying fee-simple title.

The **doctrine of worthier title**, again in the few states that continue to recognize it, works like the rule in Shelley's Case to simplify future interests, except that the rule applies to future-interest conveyances back to the grantor's own heirs. Thus, the doctrine of worthier title would treat a conveyance *from O to A for life, remainder to O's heirs* as simply leaving the grantor a reversion, as if the conveyance were just *from O to A for life.* The doctrine of worthier title destroys remainders to the grantor's own heirs in favor of leaving the grantor a reversion. Again, the rule promotes the land's marketability because otherwise, buyers could not ascertain a grantor's heirs until the grantor died. The doctrine of worthier title allows the grantor and life tenant to convey the property while both are still alive.

C. Co-tenancy

Another area to address on ownership, after treating present estates and future interests above, involves **co-tenancies** between or among owners. Grantors may divide ownership interests among two or more persons, creating co-tenancies. Co-tenancies come in two different *types*, treated in the following sections. Co-tenancies also involve the *severance* of co-tenancies or their *partition*, each addressed in following sections. Another following section addresses the *relations* of co-tenants in their common use of the property. This part on co-tenancies then ends with rules on *alienability*, *descendibility*, and *devisability*.

1. Types

The following two sections address **tenancies in common** and **joint tenancies**, as the two types of co-tenancy. As the sections illustrate, one significant distinction between the two types of co-tenancy has to do with *rights of survivorship*, addressing the question of whether a co-tenant's heirs or devisees receive the co-tenant's interest on the co-tenant's death or, instead, the other co-tenant or co-tenants receive the interest. Tenancies in common differ from joint tenancies in other ways, too, such as the ability to form and hold unequal shares, and rights of use and conveyance. As to each type of co-tenancy, the *grantor's language* determines the type of co-tenancy formed. Ensure that you recognize the language that forms each type, while being able to distinguish the survivorship, use, and other rights afforded as to each type.

a. Tenancy in common

A **tenancy in common** is a type of co-tenancy that does *not* grant *survivorship rights* in the co-tenants. *Tenant*, in this context, does *not* mean one taking under a lease but instead means a co-owner in fee-simple title. Each of two or more tenants in common owns an alienable and inheritable share of the property. In contrast to a joint tenancy, tenants in common may own *unequal shares* that they can freely transfer to other owners either during life or at death by inheritance or will. Because death does not terminate the tenant in common's interest, the interest passes as the tenant directs in a will or law directs by intestacy. Whether tenants in common own equal or unequal shares, all tenants in common have the right to occupy and use all or any part of the property. A tenant in common's ownership interest is an **undivided** interest. Thus, if tenants in common own a home, then each may use any part of the home, even if one tenant owns a one-quarter share and the other tenant owns three quarters.

Real Property Law

Either tenant in common may sell their share so that the remaining co-tenant would share with a new tenant in common. Language *from grantor to A and B* creates a tenancy in common, as would more-specific language *to A and B as tenants in common.* Tenants in common may also receive their interests from separate conveyance documents. Thus, a grantor may convey fee-simple title to an owner who then conveys a tenancy in common to a co-tenant with the owner. Either co-tenant may then convey to other co-tenants whose interests arise out of those other conveyance documents. A tenancy in common differs from a joint tenancy in this additional respect, insofar as only a single conveyance document can create a joint tenancy.

b. Joint tenancy

A **joint tenancy** is a co-tenancy in which two or more co-tenants have equal undivided interests in the property with *rights of survivorship.* Thus, if a joint tenant dies, the other joint tenant or joint tenants receive the deceased joint tenant's interest automatically by operation of law. Joint tenants all have equal rights of the property's use. Unlike in a tenancy in common, joint tenants cannot own unequal shares. Language *from grantor to A and B as joint tenants* or *to A and B with full rights of survivorship* creates a joint tenancy, if the co-tenants have *unity of time, title, interest,* and *possession,* meaning that they take at precisely the same time, under the same document, with the same interest, and the same right of possession. The conveyance language must indicate the grantor's intent to create rights of survivorship either by saying so or by indicating that the grantees take as joint tenants. A conveyance that does not indicate the intent to create a joint tenancy or rights of survivorship instead creates a tenancy in common. As indicated in the prior section, only a single conveyance document can create a joint tenancy. A joint tenant may alienate, meaning transfer, the joint tenant's interest, but in doing so the joint tenant severs the joint tenancy and creates a tenancy in common.

A **tenancy by the entireties** is a joint tenancy between married individuals. Language *from grantor to A and B as tenants by the entireties,* or *to A and B as husband and wife,* creates a tenancy by the entireties, if A and B are in fact married. Most states also presume a tenancy by the entirety from a grant *to A and B as joint tenants* if A and B are then married. If grantees are not married but receive property in a grant indicating rights of survivorship, then they can be at most joint tenants. If they divorce, then they become tenants in common. An advantage of a tenancy by the entireties over a joint tenancy or tenancy in common is that a creditor of only one spouse cannot in execution reach the spouse's tenancy-by-the-entirety interest. Married couples hold entireties property free from the claims of creditors of either spouse, if the creditor has a claim only against one of the spouses. Creditors whose claims are against both spouses can reach entireties property. Unlike both tenancies in common and joint tenancies, tenants by the entireties cannot convey away their individual interests.

Real Property Law

2. Severance

Severance refers to the process, whether intentional or inadvertent, of converting a joint tenancy into a tenancy in common. Severance is significant because it *destroys the right of survivorship* that accompanies a joint tenancy. Joint tenants may agree to sever their joint tenancy, as for instance by agreeing to sell the land and divide the proceeds. Also, one joint tenant may convey away the interest, in doing so severing the joint tenancy and leaving the grantee in a tenancy in common with the other co-tenants who remain joint tenants as to one another. Lease of a joint tenancy does not, in most states, sever the joint tenancy in favor of a tenancy in common. Yet a joint tenant can by other action indicate the intent to sever and in doing so accomplish it, for instance by conveying to a trustee for the co-tenant's own benefit, or in some states, to the co-tenant's self, thus destroying the unity of time and title. Indeed, a conveyance to a trust, trustee, conservator, or other individual would inadvertently destroy the unity of time and title, and sever the joint tenancy, even if the co-tenant had not so intended.

3. Partition

Tenants in common and joint tenants may at any time seek **partition** of the land. Partition involves equitable division of the land to represent each co-tenant's individual interest. A court may at the request of any co-tenant impose and enforce partition, if the co-tenants cannot agree. Some real property co-tenants can easily divide, while other real property they cannot. Partition may thus be **in-kind**, accomplishing a physical division of the property, or partition may be **by sale** if the court cannot divide the property, division is impractical, or division is not in the co-tenants' best interests. Co-tenants must divide sale proceeds equitably to represent their individual interests.

4. Relations among cotenants

Co-tenants, whether tenants in common or joint tenants, share the rights of possession and rent, and share in responsibility. One co-tenant may not **oust** another co-tenant from possession. Most jurisdictions do *not* require one co-tenant to pay another co-tenant rent even if the co-tenant has the property's only use *unless* the co-tenant ousts the other co-tenant, in which case the tenant in possession may owe for the other's lost use. Co-tenants share in **rents** received from the premises. Thus, if one co-tenant collects rents but refuses to share, other co-tenants may enforce their right to a fair share. Co-tenants generally *share expenses*, each having a right to make the other contribute as necessary. Thus, if one co-tenant pays real-property taxes, mortgage payments, and reasonably necessary insurance, upkeep, or repair expenses to which other co-tenants refuse to contribute, then the paying co-tenant may enforce a right of contribution.

Real Property Law

5. Alienability, descendibility, devisability

Both tenants in common and joint tenants may **alienate** their co-tenancy interest, meaning sell or otherwise *transfer* it away. By contrast, tenants by the entireties cannot transfer their co-tenant interest. Tenants in common convey whatever fractional interest they hold, whereas joint tenants convey their equal interest. The interest of a tenant in common is also **descendible**, meaning that an heir can inherit the interest, and **devisable**, meaning that the tenant in common can pass the interest to another by will, on the co-tenant's death. By contrast, a joint tenancy is *not* descendible or devisable because of the right of survivorship attendant on a joint tenancy. When a joint tenancy dies, the tenancy interest passes by operation of law to the surviving joint tenant or joint tenants.

D. The law of landlord and tenant

Owners of real property have rights to lease interests in the land. Those who wish to occupy land without an ownership interest may have the opportunity to form a non-freehold estate that the law recognizes as a **leasehold** or **lease**, making the occupant a **tenant**. Ownership thus needs to address the law of **landlord and tenant**, a landlord being the owner who leases occupancy to a tenant. Landlord/tenant law must address the *types* of leaseholds including how parties create and terminate them. Landlord/tenant law also must address tenant rights of *possession* versus landlord rights of *rent*. Landlords may *assign* their interest, while tenants may be able to *sublet*. The *termination* of tenancies is another subject as are issues of *habitability* and *suitability*, all addressed in the following sections.

1. Types of holdings: creation and termination

The law recognizes several different types of **tenancy**. The following sections address a *term of years*, which is a tenancy for a specific period whether or not measured in years, *tenancies at will*, terminable by either party, *holdovers* and other tenancies *at sufferance*, and *periodic tenancies*, typically measured by the period of the original lease. Landlords and tenants typically create the type of tenancy at least initially by entering into a lease. The conditions for terminating a lease depend on the type of tenancy that the lease or other circumstance has created.

a. Terms for years

A **term of years** is a common leasehold that conveys the right to occupy and use the land *for a specific period*. Although the law calls the leasehold a term of *years*, the landlord and tenant may provide for a period of days, weeks, months, years, or any other period, if the period is specific. The landlord and tenant need only know when the term will end. Thus, a lease that lasts *until the third full moon rises* is a term of years because the parties can calculate the date certain when the third full moon rises. A term of years may be **determinable**, meaning that although the lease provides for a specific period, the occurrence of a condition may shorten the period, terminating the lease. Thus, a lease *for one year, as long as tenant lives alone* is a determinable term of years. A term of years terminates automatically, meaning *without notice*, at the end of its term.

b. Tenancies at will

A **tenancy at will** is a leasehold that either party may terminate at any time, with or without reason. While the common law did not require notice to terminate, the modern rule and many state statutes require *reasonable notice*, particularly as to residential leases. Thus, a residential landlord may have to serve a thirty-day notice to quit. While a landlord may terminate a tenancy at will for any reason or no reason, a landlord must not terminate in violation of **anti-discrimination laws** protecting classes including race, color, national origin, sex, religion, age, disability, family status, meaning with or without children, and in some states marital status or other statuses, meaning with children.

c. Holdovers and other tenancies at sufferance

A **holdover** is a tenant who stays beyond the termination of the lease, whether the lease ends by term of years or at the end of a periodic tenancy. A holdover tenant has only a **tenancy at sufferance** during which the landlord may decide whether to evict the tenant or to hold the tenant to a renewed lease period equal to the original lease period. Thus, if the original lease was month-to-month, then the landlord could only hold the tenant over, meaning require the tenant to commit to and pay for, another month's lease. If, instead, the lease was year-to-year, many jurisdictions permit the landlord to hold the tenant to an additional year, although some states provide for only a month-to-month tenancy, particularly for *residential* leases. If the original lease was for more than one year, many jurisdictions would limit the landlord to holding the tenant over for a shorter period such as one month or one year. The landlord must make the decision within a reasonable time whether to hold over or to evict.

d. Periodic tenancies

A **periodic tenancy** is a tenancy that renews automatically for the initial lease period or other renewal period that the lease provides. Thus, for example, a *month-to-month* lease, providing that the tenant rents by the month, is a periodic tenancy that renews for one month as long as the landlord intends each month that the tenant stay and the tenant intends likewise. Landlord and tenant can also have longer periodic tenancy such as year-to-year or even providing for five-year renewal periods. The landlord or tenant

Real Property Law

may only terminate a periodic tenancy at the end of one of the periods. The lease may require notice a certain number of days before the end of a period.

2. Possession...

A lease grants the tenant the right of **possession** and the landlord the right of **rent**. A lease fundamentally includes the landlord's *duty to deliver* to the tenant the *legal right of possession*. Most jurisdictions hold to the English rule that the landlord also has a duty to deliver *actual* possession, not just the legal right to possess. Thus, in those cases, a landlord who grants legal right of possession to a tenant but leaves the premises occupied by a holdover tenant would have breached duty to deliver actual possession. The tenant's remedies would then be to either withhold rent until the tenant can occupy the premises or void the lease and sue the landlord for any damages due to the lost possession. If the landlord delivers only partial possession, though, the tenant has a right only to reduce the rent for the lost portion. The tenant may alternatively sue to evict the holdover tenant. Jurisdictions following the minority American rule do not require the landlord to deliver actual possession, instead requiring the tenant to sue the holdover to evict and take possession.

Tenants must avoid **waste**, meaning that they must not destroy the property, allow its collapse into disrepair, or make other significant changes to the property. For example, if a tenant discovers a significant plumbing leak, the tenant must act or notify the landlord promptly to do so, rather than ignore the problem as it causes growing damage. Tenants must also not deliberately destroy walls, floors, appliances, and mechanical systems. Tenants do *not*, though, have a duty to renovate or remodel to address normal wear and tear. Tenants also have no duty to repair after catastrophic damages, for instance from hurricane or flood, although they must try to avoid such damage when reasonably able to do so. Tenants must also avoid **illegal uses** such as prostitution, drug sales, and the like. A landlord discovering such uses may terminate the lease or seek to enjoin such uses while enforcing the lease. Tenants must also not interfere with quiet use and enjoyment by *other tenants*.

...and rent

While the landlord owes the duty to provide the tenant with legal and likely also actual possession, the tenant owes the landlord the duty to pay **rent**. While the traditional rule made the tenant's duty to pay rent independent of the landlord's duties, the above section and a following section on habitability and suitability show the widespread abandonment of the traditional rule. The lease states the rent amount, in the absence of which a court will infer a *fair market value*. The lease also states when rent is due, in the absence of which rent is due on the last day of the month in a month-to-month lease or the last day of the term for a tenancy in term of years. A landlord who wishes to eject a non-paying tenant brings an action for

Real Property Law

ejectment also referred to as *eviction*. **Frustration of purpose** can be a rent defense when the basis on which the landlord and tenant agreed to the lease proves incorrect. **Illegal** leases, such as for a residence that fails to meeting housing codes, void the obligation to pay rent. If the law changes, making the use illegal, then the tenant may terminate if the tenant cannot use the property legally. A section well below treats the question of the landlord's right to **fixtures** on the tenant vacating.

3. Assignment and subletting

A tenant may wish to **assign** the tenant's lease rights and obligations to a new tenant. An **assignment** transfers the tenant's *entire* interest to a new tenant. Tenants may also wish to **sublet** a part of the leasehold to a subtenant, keeping the remainder interest. A sublet refers to a conveyance of less than the tenant's full leasehold interest, such as to sublet for three months of a six-month lease. The law generally allows either assignment or sublet of a leasehold interest, unless the lease bars assignment or sublet, which many leases do. The rules for assignment and sublet implicate both *privity of contract*, referring to the agreement between landlord and tenant, and *privity of estate*, referring to the transfer of the leasehold estate from landlord to tenant.

Assignment ends the privity of estate between landlord and tenant but not privity of contract. The tenant continues to owe whatever obligation the lease calls for in the event of assignment, which is typically full right to enforce the lease against the tenant notwithstanding assignment. Assignment *creates* privity of estate between landlord and the tenant's assignee but *not* privity of contract. By contrast, sublease does *not* create any privity, whether of contract or estate, between landlord and the tenant's sublessee. The tenant retains both privity of contract and of estate with the landlord, while creating privity of contract and estate only between tenant and sublessee. The rules, then, are that a landlord can collect rent from anyone with whom the landlord is in privity of contract *or* estate, but a tenant can enforce obligations only of a landlord with whom the tenant is in privity of *estate*. So, in assignments, the landlord can collect rent from *either* the tenant or assignee, while only the assignee can enforce the landlord's obligations. Yet in subleases, the landlord can collect rent *only* from the tenant and the tenant from sublessee, while the tenant can enforce the landlord's obligations, and the sublessee can enforce the tenant's obligations.

4. Termination (surrender, mitigation of damages, and anticipatory breach)

The above sections on the types of tenancies address how each type terminates. The above section on **rent** addresses a landlord's action for ejectment or eviction for nonpayment of rent. The law strongly discourages *self-help evictions*, particularly for residential leases. Landlords must usually instead get a *court order* following appropriate procedures including notice,

Real Property Law

hearing, and in some cases even jury-trial rights. Landlords who resort to self-help such as changing locks and putting personal property out at the curb may have civil liability or criminal responsibility for those actions. On the other hand, states that require judicial proceedings for eviction typically offer streamlined procedures. A tenant may **surrender** a leasehold. The landlord may accept the tenant's surrender without pursuing unpaid rent, accepting partial payment of past due rent, or accepting a lease buyout of future unpaid rent.

A landlord may sue for contract damages in **anticipatory breach** if a tenant makes a positive and unconditional refusal to take possession and fulfill the lease, or becomes unable to perform. Likewise, if a tenant *abandons* a lease after having taken possession for part of the lease term, and does so without the landlord's agreement as to surrender terms, then the landlord may pursue a contract-breach action on the lease for past unpaid rent, future unpaid rent, and other damages as contract law allows. However, in the case of anticipatory breach or breach in abandonment of the lease, landlords have the same contract-law obligation to **mitigate damages** that others enforcing contracts owe. In the case of a lease, the landlord's duty to mitigate means that the landlord must ordinarily promptly and diligently seek to re-lease the premises to another tenant. In practice, tenants may attempt to help the landlord do so by sending prospective tenants to the landlord, which may also help the tenant prove the landlord's failure or refusal to mitigate as a defense to a rent action.

5. Habitability and suitability

The law implies in every lease a **covenant of quiet enjoyment**, not referring solely to peaceful premises but rather to use the property for the purpose that the lease intended including to be free of nuisances that interfere with that use. The common law, followed in most jurisdictions, allows the tenant to withhold rent if the landlord violates the covenant. Landlords can violate the covenant by either wrongfully locking out or evicting the tenant, or allowing another to do so, from all or any part of the premises. The landlord's doing so relieves the tenant of *all* liability to pay rent, unlike the forgoing rule for partial evictions in which the tenant must continue to pay partial rent.

In some jurisdictions, the law also implies in every *residential* lease a **warranty of habitability** that assures the tenant that the premises are fit for the tenant to inhabit the premises safely and sanitarily, even though the common law does not imply the warranty. Where the warranty exists, a tenant can add to the above remedies the option of deducting repairs from the rent. The common law, though, generally imposes no duty on the landlord's part to maintain and repair the premises, which instead becomes the tenant's responsibility on taking possession unless the lease provides otherwise. Many jurisdictions today require a residential landlord to maintain and repair the premises, creating an obligation much like that of the warranty of habitability. Jurisdictions do prohibit landlords from evicting tenants for

Real Property Law

reporting housing-code violations. In commercial leases, the law implies a warranty of **suitability**, which is roughly equivalent to the residential warranty of habitability. Unless the lease provides otherwise, the commercial premises must be suitable for the anticipated commercial use.

A tenant, whose possession nuisances so badly disturb as to frustrate or destroy those uses, has a right of **constructive eviction**. The landlord must have committed such wrongful actions or so neglected the premises as to *substantially interfere* with its uses. The tenant must also have *given notice* of the interference, and the landlord must have failed to remedy the interference. Constructive eviction also requires the tenant to *leave the premises*. Constructive eviction is both an action that the tenant may maintain for damages due to the interference *and* a defense to the landlord's rent action. Non-functioning mechanical systems for heating, cooling, plumbing, electricity, and access, often constitute grounds for constructive eviction. Jurisdictions split on whether landlords must prevent others from interfering if able to do so but do routinely hold landlords responsible for common areas.

E. Special problems

Ownership entails certain **special problems** that the above sections do not treat. The *rule against perpetuities* both in its common-law and modified forms is one special problem. The *alienability*, *descendibility*, and *devisability* of ownership present other special problems. Finally, *fair-housing* and *anti-discrimination* laws present other ownership issues, all addressed in the following sections.

1. Rule Against Perpetuities: common law...

The **rule against perpetuities** provides that *executory interests* and *contingent remainders* must vest, if at all, within twenty-one years of a *life in being* at the time that the grant created the future interest. The rule's purpose is to preserve property's alienability and marketability, while preventing the wishes of persons long dead from controlling the disposition of lands. The rule against perpetuities does *not* limit interests that the grantor *keeps*, like reversions to the grantor or rights of re-entry in the grantor, because a grantor should be able to control the grantor's own property. The rule against perpetuities makes sense to promote alienability and marketability but can produce absurd results, for instance by voiding a conveyance on assumption like a ninety-year-old woman having a child. Some jurisdictions address that absurdity by presuming that women will not bear children after age fifty-five. Policy aside, to apply the rule against perpetuities, simply determine whether a grant creates either a **contingent remainder** or **executory interest**. If not, and instead the grant only creates *vested* remainders, then the rule does not apply, and the conveyance is valid. Thus, a conveyance *to A for life, then to B*, does not violate the rule against perpetuities because the only remainder interest, B's interest, is a *vested* rather than contingent remainder. The interest does not depend on a condition that may not ever occur or that will

Real Property Law

vest more than twenty-one years after a currently living person dies. For another example, a conveyance *to A as long as A does not use the land for a landfill* also reserves only a *vested* rather than contingent remainder, in the form of a possibility of reverter in the grantor. Thus, the conveyance does not implicate the rule against perpetuities, and the conveyance is valid even if A's grandchild or a later descendant misuses the land as a landfill and the land reverts to the grantor or grantor's heirs.

If instead a conveyance *does* create a contingent remainder or executory interest, then determine whether the grant limits the interest's vesting by a condition that *may not ever occur*, in which case the grant violates the rule. For example, a conveyance *to A as long as A does not use the land for a landfill, and then to B*, creates an executory interest in B that may not ever occur, if A and A's heirs never use the land for a landfill. Thus, the rule against perpetuities applies to void the interest. If instead the interest will vest when *currently living persons* die, then determine whether the grant allows vesting more than twenty-one years after the last such person dies. For example, a conveyance *to A, then to A's oldest living male child*, does not violate the rule, even though the remainder is contingent, because the remainder vests or not immediately on the measuring life A's death, rather than more than twenty-one years later. If, on the other hand, the prior conveyance was *to A, then to A's oldest living male child when that child reaches age thirty*, then the contingent remainder would violate the rule against perpetuities because it could vest more than twenty-one years after the measuring life A's death. A could die leaving an oldest male child who was under age nine and whose interest would therefore not vest for more than twenty-one years after A's death.

...and as modified

The modern form of the rule against perpetuities recognizes an exception for **class gifts**. Class gifts are to a group as in *to A's children or grandchildren*. The common-law rule against perpetuities operates under an *all-or-nothing* rule that invalidates the entire conveyance if invalid for even one member of the potential class. Courts, though, have created an exception to the all-or-nothing rule called the *rule of convenience*, closing the class to new members (typically, children born after the conveyance) when at least one member of the class takes possession of the property. For example, in the conveyance *O to A's children when they reach age 25*, the rule against perpetuities may invalidate this interest if A is still alive at the time of the conveyance because A could have after-born children. However, if at the time of the conveyance, A has at least one child who is over twenty-five, that child's interest would vest. The *rule of convenience* would then close the class gift, so that after-born children would share in the gift.

Because of the harshness of the common-law rule against perpetuities, many states have further modified it for results consistent with the grantor's intent. The *Uniform Statutory Rule Against Perpetuities*, adopted in over twenty jurisdictions, provides a waiting period of ninety years to see if the future interest vests. If it does not, then the court may modify the interest. Other states have adopted a similar *wait-and-see approach* that, instead of invalidating all potential future interests that could remain unresolved, waits to see if the circumstances do resolve before invalidating the interest.

2. Alienability, descendibility, and devisability

The above sections on the types of estates in land, including *co-tenancies*, address in detail their rules on **alienability**, meaning the right to sell or otherwise convey the interest, **descendibility**, meaning the right of an heir to inherit under laws of intestacy, and **devisability**, meaning the ability to convey by will on demise. As to co-tenancies, for example, a co-tenant may *alienate* either a tenancy-in-common interest or joint-tenancy interest, although conveying the joint tenancy severs it into a tenancy in common. While tenancies in common are also *descendible* and *devisable*, joint tenancies are *not* descendible or devisable because of the other co-tenant's right of survivorship. A joint tenant may devise the interest, meaning purport to dispose of it in the joint tenant's will, but the devise will be ineffective *unless the other co-tenants die first*, in which case the joint tenant will hold the fee-simple title that the will may then treat. Tenant by the entirety, though, referring to a husband or wife co-tenant, have no ability to alienate or devise the property, which will also not descend by intestacy, the estate's purpose being to preserve the property for the other spouse.

3. Fair housing/discrimination

Federal **fair-housing** laws prohibit discrimination in housing based on race, color, national origin, religion, sex, age, disability, or family status, meaning with or without children. States may include other anti-discrimination protection for marital status and other categories. The protections involve *residential* rather than commercial uses, although other federal law also makes unlawful racial discrimination in contracts and thus commercial sales or leases. The residential protections extend both to *sales* and to *leases*. Thus, a landlord who rejects a tenant because of any of the above protected characteristics, misrepresents the availability of the housing, or changes any term such as charging a higher price, is subject to the tenant's private civil action for damages and an injunction, and may also face federal or state administrative enforcement and sanctions. The protections also extend to advertising to sell or lease housing. For example, a landlord who advertises apartments for *singles* or persons *without children* would implicate federal and may implicate state anti-discrimination laws.

II.   Rights in land

Real-property law addresses and provides for other **rights in land** beyond the ownership estates that the above sections address. Those other

Real Property Law

rights in land include *covenants at law and in equity*, restricting and controlling the use of land, and *easements*, *profits*, and *licenses*, creating rights in others than the owners of the land to use the land, even if inconsistent with the owner's wishes. Covenants differ from easements in that covenants involve *contract* obligations while easements create *ownership* interests in the land. Keep that distinction in mind as you review the law of covenants and easements. Real-property issues also arise around *fixtures* permanently affixed to the land and *zoning* restrictions. The following sections address these other rights in land beyond the ownership issues addressed above.

A. Covenants at law and in equity

Covenants at law involve rights of use that the owner of land grants by *contract* to another that the other may enjoy, even when inconsistent with the owner's current wishes, subject to a damages action for breach. **Covenants in equity**, also called *equitable servitudes*, involve rights of use that the owner grants in a contract obligation, as to which equity grants enforcement by *specific performance*. As indicated above, covenants in land do *not* involve ownership in land, only the contract obligation, although a following section shows that covenants can *run with the land* like ownership interests. The following sections address the *nature* and *type* of these covenants, their *creation*, and their *scope, enforcement*, and *termination*.

1. Nature and type

A **real covenant** is the grantor's contract promise and related obligation to permit the grantee to use and enjoy the grantor's real property without creating a freehold estate in the grantee. Because covenants in land involve *contract obligations* rather than ownership interests in land, covenants typically arise out of *promises* enforceable in contract rather than, for example, easements by implication, necessity, or prior use, although the effect of a covenant is often the same as that of an easement. For example, a resident who lives and owns a home behind another home the property for which the city has just changed to a commercial district, may for consideration contract with the other homeowner not to build a commercial structure that would burden the resident's own home. The resident would then have a *covenant*, not an *easement*, although the resident could enforce the covenant to prevent construction of a commercial structure or for contract-breach damages. Real covenants, though, have a unique quality beyond the typical contract in that **successor owners** of the land that a covenant benefits, called the **dominant land**, may be able to enforce the covenant. The law holds that covenants that successor owners can enforce must *run with the land*, the requirements for which the next section addresses.

The law also recognizes **equitable servitudes**, also called **covenants in equity**. An equitable servitude or covenant in equity is an enforceable promise relating to the use of land that the benefitted promisee enforces through the equitable form of relief *specific performance*. Specific performance involves the court's order that the owner of the servient land comply with the burden to benefit the owner seeking that equitable relief. Unlike covenants at law, equitable servitudes can arise *and run with the land* without horizontal or vertical privity, as the next section addresses.

2. Creation

As indicated briefly above, because **covenants in land** involve *contract obligations* rather than ownership interests in land, covenants typically arise out of *promises* enforceable in contract rather than by implication, necessity, or prior use, although the effect of a covenant is often the same as that of an easement. To create a covenant in land, the parties must satisfy the **statute of frauds**, specifically if the restriction lasts for more than one year. The bigger question, though, is often whether the covenant's creation allows it to *run with the land*, meaning to benefit and burden subsequent owners of the dominant and servient parcels.

To run with the land, a covenant must have been *in a writing* that expresses or implies the *intent that it run*. The courts readily construe that the parties intended a covenant to run when the writing states that the covenant applies to successors, heirs, and assigns. Yet courts will also construe intent from the circumstances. The covenant must also *touch and concern* the **servient land**, meaning the burdened land, such as requiring payment of association maintenance fees. For a covenant's burden to run with the land, the parties must also have formed the covenant when in **horizontal privity**, meaning when sharing some interest in the servient land, such as the sale from one to the other or a lease from one to the other. Thus, in the above example, the neighbors who agreed to a covenant not to build commercial on one neighbor's land would *not* have horizontal privity, meaning that the covenant could *not* run with the land.

For a covenant's burden or benefit to run, the servient land's owner must also have **vertical privity** with the owner with whose activities on the land the covenant interferes, such as the original owner making the covenant conveying the land to the burdened owner. While successor owners will usually have vertical privity with the owner originally covenanting to burden the land, *adverse possession* interrupts vertical privity. Finally, the burdened owner must have had **notice** of the burden, typically through the covenant's recording against the land, although sometimes through constructive notice of the existing burden. Benefitted owners usually enforce covenants at law through monetary-damages actions.

A signed writing satisfying the statute of frauds will also create an equitable servitude or covenant in equity enforceable by specific performance. Unlike covenants at law, though, equitable servitudes can arise and run with the land *without horizontal or vertical privity*. An equitable servitude need only be in a signed writing showing the intent that it run with the land, touch and concern the land, and provide notice to the owner of the burdened land. Equitable servitudes, though, may also arise **by implication**, meaning through notice or constructive notice of a *common plan*. For

Real Property Law

example, if a landowner divides a large parcel to sell lots under a common plan for only single-family residences but mistakenly leaves the written covenant out of some of the later conveyed deeds, then the other written restrictions and construction of only single-family homes will have put on notice lot owners taking those later deeds.

3. Scope

The **scope** of covenants at law or in equity depends primarily on the promise that creates them and the intent of the parties behind that promise. Rules like those that courts apply to any contract interpretation apply to the express promise of a covenant at law or in equity. The courts will give plain meaning to plain terms while resolving ambiguities against the drafter. The court will not generally impose terms to which the parties have not agreed. On the other hand, the scope of a covenant in equity arising by implication depends on the circumstances of the implication. Refer to the section below on the scope and construction of easements for more detailed rules also applicable to covenants at law or in equity.

4. Termination

The law recognizes the **termination** of covenants at law and in equity, or equitable servitudes, in several ways. If the document of grant includes a durational restriction, then the covenant terminates when its term **expires**. Covenants can also terminate if a single owner acquires the dominant and servient parcels, in which case the covenant **merges**. A benefitted owner can also **abandon** a covenant by indicating that intent to give up the rights that it affords. Covenants terminate as easements terminate, covered in greater detail in a following section.

B. Easements, profits, and licenses

An **easement** involves an ownership right in land limited to its use or restriction, in contrast to the freehold estates described in sections above that reflect ownership interests in the full bundle of ownership rights. Easements function like *covenants at law or in equity*, addressed above, except again that an easement is an ownership interest rather than, as in the case of a covenant at law or in equity, only a contract interest. Consider the *nature* and *types* of easements in the following section, followed by sections on their *creation*, *scope*, and *termination*.

1. Nature and type

The law first distinguishes between **affirmative easements**, entitling the holder to use of the servient land, and **negative easements**, *restricting* the *owner* from some use. For example, an easement that permits one neighbor to use the driveway of another neighbor has an *affirmative* easement, while an easement that prohibits one neighbor from building a structure on a portion of that neighbor's *own* land, for the benefit of the other neighbor, is a *negative* easement. The law also distinguishes between **easements appurtenant**, referring to rights that owners of a dominant parcel have relative to the servient parcel, and **easement in gross**, referring to rights that owners hold relative to the servient parcel but *not* attached to any dominant parcel. For example, both above examples involve easements *appurtenant* because they both benefit a specific neighboring parcel of land. By contrast, an easement *in gross* would entail a person's right to enter another's land to, for example, put one's boat in the water, without that person's right benefitting any specific land. The law also labels types of easement by their manner of creation, as the next section addresses.

Easements appurtenant *run with the land*, while easements in gross do *not* run with the land. As indicated above in the sections on covenants at law and in equity, to run with the land means that the easement's restriction benefits the successors in interest to the dominant parcel while burdening successors in interest to the servient parcel. For example, the right to put one's boat in the water in the above example, being merely in gross, would *not* run with the land, while the other rights to driveway use or prevent building of structures, being appurtenant, *would* run with the land. Beneficiaries of easements in gross may *not* generally transfer their rights unless the parties so agree or the rights are for a *commercial purpose*, such as when a company buys the right to maintain a billboard on an owner's servient land. However, the servient land remains subject to an easement in gross on the servient land's conveyance.

The law also recognizes **licenses** in land. A license involves the right to use another's land for a *limited purpose*, such as if a landowner permits a friend to temporarily park the friend's motor home on the landowner's land. Unlike an easement, a license is *not* an interest in land. When the parties are not clear whether they intend a license or an easement in gross, the courts tend to construe a *license* unless the parties clearly intend the restriction to be more than temporary. The grantor of a license who gives oral or written permission to the limited use may generally revoke it at any time. However, under the **doctrine of estoppel**, the grantor must *not* revoke if the grant specifically stated that it would be irrevocable *or* if the license's holder has *substantially and detrimentally relied* on the license, although some jurisdictions refuse to recognize estoppel. Thus, in the above example, if the friend *had* to park the motor home on the owner's land overnight or for another short period to avoid a fine or fee that the friend would incur for having relied on the owner's license, then estoppel could prevent the landowner from objecting. Indeed, an easement that fails due to the statute of frauds or other reason may give rise to an **irrevocable license** of this type. However, an irrevocable license, while like a permanent easement in gross, lasts only until it no longer prevents an injustice.

2. Methods of creation

Real Property Law

Parties create easements in several ways, each addressed in the following sections. Easements arise most easily and obviously by express **grant** of the owner of the servient land. Yet easements also arise by **reservation** of the owner who transfers the then-servient land to another. Easements also arise by **implication** from the circumstances of the conveyance, indicating transferor and transferee intent to recognize an easement. Easements also arise of **necessity** when an owner divides land and leaves one parcel needing an easement across the other to make use of the land. Finally, easements also arise by **prescription**, referring to *adverse possession*, in the manner that freehold estates arise by adverse possession.

a. Express

Parties create easements by **grant**, in which the servient land's owner transfers the right to the easement's grantee, and by **reservation**, in which the owner transfers land to another while reserving the easement right to the transferring owner. The law presumes that an easement by grant intends the easement to be permanent, unless the grant expressly states otherwise. For example, if a landowner agrees in exchange for a neighbor's consideration that the neighbor and successors to the neighbor's land may cross the landowner's property to reach a nearby beach, the landowner may grant the neighbor an easement that the neighbor can record to document the right. Alternatively, if the landowner decided to sell half of the land but reserve a path across the sold portion for the landowner and successors to reach the beach, the landowner could *reserve* the easement in the deed conveying the sold half. If the grant or reservation does not mention duration, then the court will construe the path as a permanent easement.

b. Implied

The law recognizes three types of **implied easement**, each treated in the following sections. Implied easements arise from the circumstances rather than by express grant. The first type of implied easement is a *quasi-use* easement that begins with an owner using the land in an apparent way that, when the owner later divides the land into dominant and servient parcels reflecting the prior use, allows the owner or a purchaser of the dominant parcel to continue the use. A second type of implied easement is an easement *of necessity* that the law implies to ensure that the dominant parcel would not otherwise be without use. A third type of implied covenant arises from the owner recording a *plat* on the land's division, burdening the platted lots with the initial restrictions.

i. Quasi-use

Parties can create an implied easement of **quasi-use** when a landowner begins with a single parcel on which the landowner conducts an apparent use, such as maintaining a driveway or providing for utilities. The owner's uses at that time are not easements, only *quasi* easements, because the owner holds the whole of the land. When the landowner then divides the land into two or more parcels at least one of which requires an easement to *continue the apparent use*, then an easement can arise by implication as necessary to continue the use. For example, if an owner maintains a driveway that the owner's land division subsequently interrupts, and the driveway is necessary to the owner's continued use of the parcel that the owner retains, then an easement by prescription will burden the parcel that the owner sells. Easements by implication, though, require that a single owner have owned the dominant and servient lands, that the use is reasonably necessary to the dominant land, that the use was continuous rather than sporadic before division, that the owner and successor have intended the burden of the continued use, and that the use was apparent to the successor when taking.

ii. Necessity

Easements **of necessity** can arise even when the circumstances do not satisfy all requirements for an easement by implication or prescription. An easement of necessity requires that the land division have deprived a parcel of a right that is *necessary* for the property's use, such as access to a public roadway. Thus, for example, if a landowner divides a property front to back rather than side to side, leaving the back parcel landlocked without public-road access, the law will recognize an easement of necessity even if prior use had not established the access, access use was not apparent, or the parties had not intended access, as a quasi-use easement would have required. Because easements of necessity do not satisfy the conditions for a quasi-use easement or easement by prescription, easements of necessity require *strict necessity*, not just convenience or other general benefit to the dominant land.

iii. Plat

Easements can also arise by implication from a recorded **plat**. A plat is a map of the owner's land divided into new parcels. The plat map may include descriptions of and restrictions on the land's use when divided, such as for single-family housing only. A master deed, master agreement, plat map, or other document recorded or referenced in recordings may include other restrictions, such as subjecting the parcels to control of an association, payment of association fees, and the like, and other benefits, such as use of the land's private streets, parks, and beach or other access. Prudent owners reference plat restrictions when granting deeds to individual lot buyers, including for express easements. However, when an owner neglects to include express easements in a deed, the law may imply those easements from the plat map and apparent uses of other parcels complying with the platted restrictions, under a rule of *beneficial enjoyment*. The plat and circumstances, though, must indicate the owner's intent to create the easement. Just because an easement would benefit all owners does not authorize the court to imply it.

Real Property Law

c. Prescription

An easement by **prescription** can arise when a person adversely possesses the easement right. The use must be open and notorious, continuous, hostile to the owner's use, and under a claim of right, for longer than the state's statutory period for **adverse possession**. Notice that only the exclusive-use requirement of adverse possession is absent among the requirements for a prescriptive easement. When not creating a freehold estate because of the limited nature of the use or the absence of *exclusive* use, the use can give rise instead to an easement by prescription. Thus, for example, if neighbors cross an owner's land to reach a beach satisfying each of the above conditions and do so for the statutory period, then the neighbors acquire an easement by prescription to continue beach access. An easement by prescription grants the holder only the earned adverse right, not greater rights. Thus, the neighbors acquiring the access right would have no right to burden the easement further by, for instance, widening and improving their path, and building a deck for a beach overlook.

3. Scope

An easement's **scope**, meaning what rights it affords and burdens it imposes, depends on how the easement arose. If the easement arose by *express grant or reservation*, then the easement's scope depends on the **terms of the express grant**. The easement's holder must not expand the scope of the grant, such as by widening an area of use, improving the easement beyond the grant, or making a different use than the grant expressed. Likewise, the owner of the servient land must not restrict the grant to less than the rights that it expresses, such as by denying vehicular ingress and egress as the grant expressed while permitting only foot traffic. An easement's right of use should change only when the parties creating the easement intended that it change, such as for vehicular travel rather than horse-and-buggy travel on the advent of the automobile. Easements may also limit or grant use by quantity, such as for only a single person or residents of a single parcel to pass or for residents of multiple parcels or even the public to pass.

If, by contrast, the easement arose *by implication*, then the court must look to the use from which the law implied the easement. *Quasi-use* easements, arising from prior use, would have the scope of the prior use. Thus, if an owner divided the land in a way that one parcel depended on an apparent utilities easement across the other parcel, the dominant parcel would have the right to continue the utilities use but *not* to construct a driveway or otherwise expand the use. The same rule holds for easements *by prescription* that the prescriptive use determines the easement's scope. Thus, if the prescriptive use was beach access, then the users creating the prescriptive easement would have that right but not the right to widen and improve the access, or increase the use to include building decks or other structures, or partying on the servient land.

Real Property Law

4. Termination

Although easements are typically *permanent*, without ending date, easements can nonetheless **terminate** in several ways. An express easement, whether by grant or reservation, may terminate per the *expressed* terms. Thus, if the grant creates an easement across servient land for as long as the dominant land is within a certain family, or used as a vacation home but for no other use, then the easement would terminate on a change in either expressed condition. Easements can also terminate by **merger**, when the easement in gross's holder acquires the servient land or when the owner of the dominant land acquires title also to the servient land, even if the owner later re-divides the land. Easements can also terminate when the easement's holder **releases** the servient land from the burden, often after negotiation and for consideration. A release is effective, though, only when satisfying the *statute of frauds* insofar as the release reflects a transaction in an interest in land.

Easements can also terminate when the holder acts in a way that clearly expresses the holder's intent to **abandon** the easement, such as by building a fence across that part of the path on the holder's dominant land. A holder simply not using an easement is *not* abandonment. Easements can also terminate with **cessation of purpose**, but only if the easement was one *of necessity*. Thus, a landlocked parcel that had an easement of necessity across another parcel would lose the easement if a new public road provided the formerly landlocked parcel with access. Easements for use of a facility may also terminate when the facility suffers **destruction**, if the destruction was *not* at the hands of the servient land's owner. Finally, a servient land's owner may **adversely possess** and thereby terminate an easement, if the owner's possession meets the open, notorious, continuous, hostile, and claim-of-right conditions for the statutory period.

C. Fixtures (including relevant application of Article 9, UCC)

Real-property law must also occasionally deal with the question of what constitutes *real* property versus *personal* property. Land and buildings are obviously real property. The issue arises when personal property such as materials, lighting or furnishings, appliances, and even equipment get incorporated into and affixed to the real property. Things *permanently affixed* to the real property, such that their removal would *damage* the real property, reducing its value, constitute **fixtures**. Fencing attached to posts dug into the ground would ordinarily be a fixture. Custom cabinetry integrated into a building's interior also may be so. Lights installed into ceilings and walls are fixtures, while lighting plugged into a socket is not. Appliances that one can remove without damage to cabinetry, such as a refrigerator on wheels, are generally not fixtures, but appliances built into the cabinetry, such as range hoods, some microwaves, and other cabinet-style refrigerators, are probably fixtures.

Real Property Law

The question as to what is a fixture, and thus real property rather than personal property, becomes important in landlord/tenant law, when a tenant vacates and must take only personal property but not what landlord or tenant have affixed permanently to the real property. Tenants vacating the premises take their personal property with them. Unless the lease provides otherwise, tenants must generally leave behind **fixtures**, even if the tenant was the party who affixed them. In disputes over removal of affixed items, courts look to the parties' intent when constructing or improving the premises and the damage that removal will cause.

The question as to what is a fixture also becomes important when dealing with mortgages of the land and security interests in equipment. For example, a mortgage company may finance a buyer's purchase of commercial property secured by a purchase-money mortgage. A bank may then extend a line of credit secured by a security interest in the buyer's commercial equipment. If both lenders foreclose, then they may dispute whether the buyer has so permanently affixed items like built-in freezers, special sinks, shelving, and even industrial equipment to the real property that the mortgage company rather than the bank should have the benefit of the security. The Uniform Commercial Code's **Article 9** holds that a lender like the bank in the prior example may take a security interest in fixtures *with priority over the property's mortgage* if the security interest arose out of the fixtures' purchase or if the lender perfected the security interest before the borrower incorporated the fixtures into the real property.

D. Zoning (fundamentals other than regulatory taking)

Local governments, whether cities, villages, townships, or other units, may by authorization of state *enabling acts* pass **zoning** laws that regulate land uses within their borders. A typical exclusive-use zoning scheme regulates uses to *residential, commercial, industrial, agricultural,* and other areas, allowing only those uses in those areas. Mutually exclusive zones may also dictate gradations for such as high-density versus low-density or single-family housing. Exclusive-use zoning may also allow from some *mixed-use* areas and *planned unit developments* that enable zoning officials to negotiate with landowners for special mixed or non-compliant uses. Other locales follow *cumulative* zoning, allowing all uses in an area that have less impact than the zoned maximum use, from *highest* use to *lowest* use. Thus, a residential area would allow only residential, but a commercial area would allow both commercial and residential, and an industrial area would allow all uses. Some locales mix exclusive and cumulative zones.

When a locale adopts zoning that creates **non-compliant** existing uses, the laws typically *grandfather* those non-compliant uses to avoid a government **taking**. State and federal constitutions require *just compensation* for government takings including *regulatory takings*, which grandfathering avoids. Grandfather provisions, though, typically include forced phase-out of non-compliant uses. If the non-compliant owner discontinues the use, or fire or other cause destroys the non-compliant structure, then the owner loses

Real Property Law

the grandfathered right to continue the non-compliant use. Forced phase-outs also typically restrict to figures such as *ten percent* of value the extent to which the owner may repair, improve, or expand a non-compliant. Constitutionally suspect forced phase-outs require the owner to desist the non-compliant use after a period such as five years, giving the owner a period within which to depreciate the value. Landowners may challenge **ultra-vires** zoning laws that exceed the state enabling act's authority, such as if a zoning law failed to grandfather non-compliant structures or sought to impose monetary fines or other penalties that the state act did not authorize.

Zoning boards also typically hold authority to grant a **variance** from zoning laws under criteria that the zoning scheme establishes. Common criteria include *undue hardship*, *unique uses* that the zoning scheme did not anticipate, *beneficial uses* that serve the community in unique or important ways, or that the restriction does not make sense for the specific use in the specific location. Local zoning and building schemes often have other restrictions other than use restrictions, for conditions like *setbacks*, *parking*, *height*, and even *exterior finishes*, *window percentage*, and other architectural concerns, to preserve or improve a zone's character. Zoning and building officials may also consider variances for those restrictions, although local officials tend to strictly enforce zoning provisions.

III. Contracts

The law treats **contracts** for the sale of land as it treats other contracts. However, unique practices having to do with the sale of land, such as **real estate brokerage**, implicate other principles, rules, and concerns outside of the ordinary concerns surrounding contracts. Real-estate transactions also follow certain *customs* in the **creation** and **construction** of contracts. Also, unique questions over the **marketability of title** to land arise, given land's permanence and significant value, and the complex relationships and transactions of persons taking interests in the land. The following sections also treat **equitable conversion**, **options** and **rights of first refusal**, **fitness** and **suitability**, and the doctrine of **merger**, all unique issues relating to contracts for the sale of land.

A. Real estate brokerage

Because of land's high value and the complexity of a real-estate transaction, land sales often occur through a **broker**. A broker is the agent who either represents the seller in preparing, listing, and selling the land, or the agent who represents the buyer in locating, evaluating, and buying the land. Agents sometimes act as both the *listing agent* or *seller's agent* and *buyer's agent*. The seller of land forms a **listing agreement** with the listing agent under which the agent assumes the duty to list, show, and sell the land. The seller promises to pay a *commission* reflecting a sale-price percentage, often around six percent, whether the listing agent finds the buyer or not, if the sale occurs during the listing agreement's term. Listing agreements

Real Property Law

typically have a term of around three months to give the buyer the opportunity to list with a more-effective agent if the land doesn't sell. When a seller and buyer agree to terms, the seller and buyer may consult lawyers to prepare, review, and negotiate the land sale contract, although often the broker prepares a standard contract form that includes an attorney-review contingency.

When the land sells, the listing agent typically *divides* the commission with the buyer's agent, unless of course the listing agent has also attracted the buyer. States and listing agreements may follow different rules as to when a commission is due. A traditional rule required the seller to pay the broker a commission if the broker brought a buyer who signed a contract to purchase the land, even if the buyer subsequently refused to perform the contract. While some states and listing agreements still follow this rule, many other states and listing agreements now provide instead that the seller owes the commission only when the sale closes with the buyer's payment of the purchase price. Uniformly, though, if the seller fails or refuses to perform the land sale contract with a willing buyer, then the seller owes the commission for which the listing agreement calls.

B. Creation and construction

Because of their complexity and unique issues around financing and inspections, real-estate transactions follow two steps. The first step involves the seller and buyer forming a contract for the sale of the land, variously called a *purchase contract*, *purchase agreement*, or *land sale contract*, as just mentioned above. A signed purchase contract is necessary to complete or compel the sale of land, which is subject to the **statute of frauds**, as the next section addresses. As is true for other contracts, land sale contracts must include the **essential terms**, treated in a following section. Another following section addresses the **time for performance** of land sale contracts. The second step in the two-step procedure involves a *closing* at which the seller conveys the *deed* and the buyer conveys the sale price. The seller may also execute a *bill of sale* for any personal property transferred in the transaction such as appliances or furnishings. Closings in which the buyer finances the purchase through a mortgage lender involve executing many other documents including the mortgage, promissory note, and statutory disclosure forms. A last following section addresses **remedies for breach** of land sale contracts.

1. Statute of frauds and exceptions

The **statute of frauds** requires that contracts transferring an interest in real estate be *in a writing* and *signed* by the party against whom another seeks to enforce the contract. As indicated in the prior section, the enforceable writing that seller and buyer typically prepare is the *purchase agreement* anticipating a later closing, usually thirty, sixty, or ninety days following the purchase agreement's execution. Usually, the buyer will prepare and present a signed purchase agreement, constituting the buyer's

Real Property Law

offer. If the seller accepts, then the seller countersigns the offer and delivers the completed agreement to the buyer so that the agreement is formed and enforceable. The seller's simply countersigning but not delivering the completed agreement and not notifying the buyer of its countersigning with the intent to deliver would not ordinarily complete the agreement. Delivery completes the agreement. If the seller counteroffers by presenting the countersigned but modified agreement, then the buyer must sign and deliver the seller's counteroffer.

As is true for other contracts, parties may in certain circumstances enforce an agreement for the sale of real estate without a writing signed by the charged party. **Part performance** can take a land sale contract out of the statute of frauds, just as part performance can in other statute-of-frauds restricted transactions. Part performance in land sales typically involves the buyer taking possession of the land while also making part payment that the seller accepts in acknowledgment of the transfer. Where the buyer has not yet made any payment, jurisdictions may instead accept that the buyer *improve* the land, such as by commencing renovations, or otherwise change position in *detrimental reliance* on the sale. Possession alone is not enough to take the transaction out of the statute of frauds.

2. Essential terms

As is true for other contracts, a land sale contract must include the **essential terms** for either party to enforce the contract. A contract missing one or more essential terms is ordinarily unenforceable. Because land sale contracts fall within the statute of frauds, their essential terms must be in a *writing* that the charged party has signed. The essential terms in a land sale contract begin with *identifying the seller and buyer*. A contract may identify a buyer's agent acting for an *unidentified principal*, even a principal unknown to the seller, if the contract adequately identifies the agent and agency role. The next essential term involves a *property description*. Ordinarily, land sale contracts will include the land's metes-and-bounds description, often by reference to an attachment already stating that description. A metes-and-bounds description, though, is not always necessary if identifying the street address, city, and state, or other manner in which others commonly know the property, adequately remove ambiguity as to the parties' intent. If the contract refers to the number of acres sold but includes a metes-and-bounds description that contradicts the acres number, then the metes-and-bounds description controls.

Other essential terms include land's **price**. If the contract does *not* include the price, then it *must* include an objective means of calculating the certain price. Agreements to negotiate a price are *not* sufficient to satisfy the essential price term but are instead merely unenforceable commitments to continue negotiating, sometimes called *agreements to agree*. Again, because of the statute of frauds, a land sale contract must include any other terms and conditions on which either party intends to rely in completing the transaction. Common terms, none of which would necessarily be essential to a complete

Real Property Law

agreement but any of which may be essential to the party's interests, include a *financing contingency* that the contract is not enforceable unless the buyer qualifies for financing, *inspection contingency* that the buildings pass inspection to the buyer's satisfaction including as to environmental contamination, and *attorney-review contingency* that the seller and buyer may consult counsel about the agreement's legal sufficiency. Parties benefitting from contingencies must exercise them in **good faith** rather than manipulate them to change contract terms or avoid the agreement.

3. Time for performance

As briefly indicated above, land sale contracts typically include **time for performance** by setting a *closing date* when the seller will exchange a deed for the buyer's payment of the purchase price. The closing date, constituting time for performance, is ordinarily long enough after the land sale contract's execution, typically thirty, sixty, or even ninety days, for the buyer to accomplish several important tasks. One of those tasks is to confirm that the buyer has the necessary *financing* to complete the purchase. An appraisal satisfactory to the mortgage lender is routinely part of the financing process. The buyer may thus need some weeks to have the buyer's mortgage lender approve the purchase agreement and appraisal, and even confirm or re-confirm the buyer's creditworthiness. Another common buyer task between the land sale contract and time of performance at closing involves exercising the common *inspection* contingency in which the buyer reserves the right to retain a builder or other expert to examine the premises for defects. Scheduling, completing, and reviewing the results of inspections requires some time before closing. Commercial lands in particular may also require *environmental* testing before the closing date.

When contingencies reveal defects, the parties may require additional time to negotiate and accept adjustments to the land sale contract, including adjustments to the sale price. The seller may also require time for performance between the land sale contract and closing date, particularly if the seller must pack and move either residential furnishings and personal property, or business equipment. The **closing date**, though, sets a time limit within which both sides must be ready to perform. Land sale contracts often make the closing date *time of the essence*, where a party's failure to close by the required date voids the contract at the other party's election. In a hot market with land values increasing, the seller may have other buyers ready to perform and thus may hold the buyer to the closing date. In a soft market, the seller may accept extensions of the closing date to ensure a sale to a buyer who may have overpaid. The time for performance, in the form of a hard closing date, gives the parties grounds on which to enforce, modify, renegotiate, or void the contract. A party who fails to perform within the time for performance may also owe the other party contract-breach damages.

4. Remedies for breach

Real Property Law

Remedies for **breach** of land sale contracts follow remedies for breach of other contracts. Buyers may *rescind* and seek *damages*. For example, a buyer whose contract calls for the seller to convey title to a commercial premises for $500,000, when the buyer can prove that the premises have a $750,000 value, may obtain the $250,000 difference in damages on rescission. A buyer may alternatively seek *specific performance*, disfavored in other contracts unless involving a unique subject but common as a remedy in land sales because land is routinely unique. **Specific performance**, the equitable remedy requiring the parties to perform their contract obligations, involves the reluctant seller conveying a deed to the land and possession of the land, or the reluctant buyer to pay the purchase price. Orders for specific performance may require that the seller vacate, unlock locks or provide keys or other access, and remove equipment. If the seller fails or refuses to execute a deed as ordered, then a buyer due specific performance may obtain the court's recordable order conveying title.

Occasions also arise where seller and buyer are willing to transfer the land for the agreed sale price but one party breaches some other term or condition of the transfer. In those cases, the non-breaching party may sue for damages that the other party's breach caused, notwithstanding that the parties followed through with the land transfer. For example, a buyer may not close by the required date, causing the seller to incur additional expense or consequential and foreseeable losses, in which case the buyer could recover those damages in a breach-of-contract action. Likewise, a seller may convey the premises in an unclean or unsafe condition that the sale contract prohibited. Parties often use a closing agreement to attempt to address, resolve, and require release of contract-breach claims, so that litigation does not follow the closing. The land sale contract itself may provide for liquidated damages, particularly as to the seller overstaying, often treated at a charge of $100 per day or a like figure approximating damages. A concluding section below also addresses the doctrine of **merger**, barring certain claims over defects in the transaction predating deed transfer at closing. Closing agreements, releases, and the doctrine of merger may not prevent the buyer from later claiming the seller's fraud in inducing the sale, when the seller has actively concealed and misrepresented the premise's true condition.

C. Marketability of title

Land sale contracts routinely require that the seller convey **marketable title**. Indeed, in the absence of a contrary term, the law *implies* a *promise* or *warranty* of marketable title. *Marketable* title is title that reasonable persons would not doubt as to validity and that third parties would not likely challenge with claims or ownership or encumbrances like mortgages or easements limiting the buyer's rights in the property. When a seller fails to convey marketable title, and instead conveys title that reasonable persons would reject due to impending or actual third-party challenges, then the seller breaches the contract, and the buyer may pursue one of the above remedies including rescission and damages, or specific performance. Specific performance may include that the seller act to clear the title, including by paying the just claims of competitors to the marketable title or otherwise obtaining their release.

Sellers typically convey marketable title by showing the property's good **chain of title** reflecting a history of the property's sale that shows the seller's clear ownership. Real-property records enable either seller or buyer, or a lawyer or title company employed by either seller or buyer, to complete a **title search** revealing and confirming the condition of title. A seller may alternatively prove good title by adverse possession, although doing so would likely require a *court judgment* including a recordable order of title, to constitute marketable title. Buyers are otherwise understandably reluctant to accept the seller's proof of adverse possession, which would not be recordable. Unmarketable title reflects a defect likely to cause a buyer to reject the purchase or to suffer injury in the future from accepting purchase. The buyer having to defend a third party's lawsuit over title may constitute injury due to unmarketable title, even if the proceeding proves that the seller had good title. A later section addresses a land sale contract's common contingency for **title insurance** and the title insurer's obligation to defend and indemnify as to title challenges, and cure title defects.

While sellers have a duty to convey *marketable title*, traditional common law does not require sellers to disclose other defects and conditions. The rule of *buyer beware* would instead require the buyer to exercise the inspection contingency with *due diligence* to discover those conditions. Yet many states today require that the seller disclose certain defects, using *statutory disclosure forms*, particularly in residential sales. Even absent a statutory disclosure requirement, the law today would tend to require that the seller disclose defects about which the seller knew but that would not be apparent to the buyer on reasonable inspection. The law also prohibits the seller from *actively concealing* defects to frustrate the buyer's discovery. Breaches of these duties may give rise to fraud remedies in the buyer's favor, including rescission and damages for lost benefit of the bargain.

D. Equitable conversion (including risk of loss)

Issues can arise when events occur changing the property's condition between the time that the seller and buyer execute the land sale contract and the closing date. In that interim period, the buyer has the right to own the land, but the seller still has possession and legal title. The doctrine of **equitable conversion** holds in its majority form that equitable interest in the property transfers to the buyer *on land-sale-contract execution* rather than later at the closing date. The traditional form of the doctrine passes the risk of interim loss or gain *to the buyer* who, after all, has the equitable ownership. Equity does what is fair and just. Equitable-conversion doctrine enables the court to adjust the rights and responsibilities of the parties to reflect changes occurring between contract execution and closing. For example, if the buyer dies after contract execution but before closing, then the buyer's estate

Real Property Law

remains the equitable owner. Likewise, if fire or flood destroys buildings on the property in interim, then the buyer must still go through with the closing. On the other hand, if the parties discover oil, gas, or minerals on the property in the interim, the seller must still go through with the closing.

Some states alter equitable conversions' *risk-of-loss* rule so that the seller retains the risk until the closing date. In those states, if natural disaster destroys or diminishes the property's value, then the law reduces the land's sale price to reflect the loss, forcing the loss on the seller. If, though, either party was *responsible* through deliberate act or carelessness for the loss, then the law in all jurisdictions places the loss on that party rather than the other. Fire, flood, or other loss insurance may also affect the rights and responsibilities of the parties. If, for instance, the buyer bears the loss risk under the traditional rule, but the seller has insurance that would pay for a structure's damage or other reduction in land value, then the court acting in equity would adjust the parties' rights and responsibilities accordingly for the fairest outcome.

E. Options...

A seller and buyer may form an **option contract** for the sale of land, just as parties may form option contracts for personal property or other goods or services, the same rules applying. An *option contract* is a contract promise, ordinarily supported by consideration, to keep an offer open for a specific period. In land-sale option contracts, the buyer may exercise the option at any time during the option period, while the seller *cannot revoke the offer* during the option period. Land option contracts can be especially beneficial to buyers who need time to obtain financing, sell other property, or, if already a tenant on the land, investigate and confirm the land's suitability for business or other purposes. For example, a tenant intending to lease, improve the premises, and operate a business for the five-year lease term may also negotiate a *purchase option* at the end of the five years or any other time during the lease, at a specific purchase price.

Option contracts relating to land sales must be in a writing signed by the charged party, to satisfy the *statute of frauds*. Like option contracts addressing other subjects, land-sale option contracts also require *consideration*, although the law traditionally accepts nominal consideration to support an option contract. Option contracts must state the *sale price*, or a certain way of establishing the sale price, as an essential term to make the option complete and enforceable. The seller's option-contract breach gives the buyer alternative remedies of specific performance or damages.

...and rights of first refusal

Option contracts within a land *lease* often take the alternative form of a **right of first refusal**. Instead of stating an option sale price, a right-of-first-refusal clause in a lease requires the landlord to present to the tenant any third-party offers to buy the land during the term of the lease. If the tenant chooses to match the offer, then the landlord must sell the premises to the tenant rather than to the third-party offeror. Rights of first refusal solve the option-contract problem of setting a sale price for the land in advance of the date on which the tenant decides to exercise the option. Rights of first refusal also solve the landlord's option-contract problem that an option contract prevents sale of the land. Whenever a landlord presents a third party's good-faith offer under the right of first refusal, the tenant must either buy the land or give up the option. Seller and buyer may contract for a right of first refusal outside of a lease, too, although one typically finds them in leases or other relationships closer than an arm's length sale between unrelated seller and buyer.

F. Fitness and suitability

The law implies a warranty of **fitness** in favor of residential buyers, and warranty of **suitability** in favor of commercial buyers, in the purchase of *new construction* on lands. Thus, if a buyer of a new residence finds defects in the home that make the home unfit for habitation, then the buyer may have warranty-breach remedies including damages or rescission. Settling soil, foundation cracks, significant materials defects exposing occupants to hazards, and defects in the home's plumbing, electrical, and heating/cooling systems are examples of possible warranty breaches. Similarly, if a buyer of a commercial premises finds roof leaks, nonworking electrical, plumbing, or heating/cooling systems, and structural defects that make the premises unsuitable for commercial use, then the buyer will warranty-breach remedies. In most jurisdictions, both the initial purchaser and subsequent purchasers may enforce the implied warranties relating to new construction, if they can trace the defect to the construction rather than subsequent conditions and events, while a minority of jurisdiction limit the rights to the initial purchaser. Buyers, though, must act to enforce the right within a reasonable time from discovery of the defect. The law is generally unwilling to imply warranties of fitness and suitability in the purchase of *established* construction. The parties instead treat the condition of the premises through any statutory disclosure requirements and through inspection contingencies.

G. Merger

The doctrine of **merger** holds that guarantees that either party make, although particularly the seller, in the land sale contract *merge* into the deed at closing. The effect of merger is to eliminate or limit the buyer's right to rely on sale-contract terms once the buyer accepts the seller's deed at closing. In effect, the merger doctrine encourages or requires that all negotiations to resolve disputes over the condition of the premises, the condition of title, and other terms and conditions of the sale, take place before or at the closing, so that the parties can leave the closing without any continuing dispute or subsequent litigation over pre-closing rights. If the deed does not reflect the right that the buyer wishes to claim based on the sale contract, then the buyer has no such right.

Real Property Law

Where recognized and enforced, the merger doctrine can bar post-closing claims not only over the quality of the title that the seller conveys to the buyer, as the deed reflects, and defects in the condition of the premises, but also disputes over unpaid taxes and other charges against the property. The doctrine, though, has fallen into some disfavor so that it many jurisdictions it operate more like a rebuttable presumption against claims than an absolute bar. Decisions are more likely to apply the doctrine and bar the claim when it has to do with the property's *title,* which is at the core of what the deed conveys, but less likely to apply the doctrine when the claims are only incidental to the title that the deed reflects. Courts will also look to the parties' intent as to what rights and claims they may have meant to merge into the deed versus which claims they did not intend to merge. Claims for misrepresentation, in particular, tend to fall outside the doctrine's bar. Indeed, exceptions to the merger doctrine may today be as numerous as applications of its rule.

IV. Mortgages/security devices

Buyers and owners of land use several forms of security, including *mortgages, deeds of trust,* and *land contracts,* to draw on and benefit from the value of the secured land. While lenders make unsecured loans, lenders gain advantages when securing the loan against the borrower's assets. Real property makes peculiarly valuable security because of its permanence, immobility, and value. Thus, mortgages and other forms of security in real property are critical not only to the sale, purchase, and improvement of real property but also to personal and business economics in general. The following sections address the above *types* of security devices in land, security *relationships, transfers* by either the mortgagor or mortgagee, the effect of *payment* of the loan, and *foreclosure* of the security interest.

A. Types of security devices

As just indicated, landowners and lenders to landowners use several types of security device both for the purchase and development of the land, and for other economic interests of the borrower. **Mortgages**, as the next section addresses, are the primary real-property security device, enabling the lender to record a document against the property reflecting the lender's security interest. States also recognize, and convention sometimes prefers, a **deed of trust** operating much like a mortgage but in which the borrower grants the lender a deed to the real property to hold in trust contingent on payment. Sellers of land also sometimes offer a **land contract** as an alternative, particularly when the buyer cannot qualify for a mortgage but also for other purposes. Less common is the **absolute deed**, as the last section on types of security device addresses.

1. Mortgages (including deeds of trust)

Real Property Law

A **mortgage** is a security interest in land that secures the mortgage *loan*. The word *mortgage* at times refers to the entire transaction involving borrower and lender but also has a strict meaning as to the *specific document* that the lender records against the real property. While the lender's purpose in obtaining a mortgage is to have a security interest to protect the loan, the lender's purpose in *recording* the mortgage is ensure that the lender's security interest has *priority* over the interests of others who may obtain second or subsequent mortgages on the land or record liens arising out of other obligations. A later section on foreclosure addresses the relative priority of mortgages. Borrowers use mortgages for different purposes, and mortgages come in different types, as the next sections address.

a. In general

A mortgage transaction typically involves the borrower signing both a *note*, also referred to as a *promissory note*, reflecting the loan *and* signing a *mortgage* instrument that the lender records to show the world that the lender has perfected a priority security interest. The note is the borrower's contract obligation to the lender, including amount, term, payment schedule, interest, and default terms. The mortgage is the lender's security interest against the land, typically referring to the note but not including the note's detailed terms. The mortgage instead includes the grantor's identity, the property description, and the rights to assign, foreclose, or otherwise treat the mortgage, and obligations to discharge it on payment. Recording statutes may require other mortgage terms. Because mortgages are interests in real property, they must ordinarily be in writing signed by the mortgagor (the borrower) to satisfy the **statute of frauds**.

Where the borrower signs no written mortgage, courts may recognize an **equitable mortgage** if, for instance, the borrower conveys a **deed** in trust to the lender. Some jurisdictions expressly recognize a **deed of trust** as a mortgage alternative. With a deed of trust, the borrower executes a deed to the property purporting to convey the land to the lender. The lender, or a trustee agent, then holds the deed according to the terms of the trust, which provide for destroying or returning the deed if the borrower pays the full loan, or releasing and recording the deed if the borrower defaults, so that the lender can then readily execute on the real property, typically without judicial foreclosure. Lenders can typically record a deed-of-trust instrument in the real-property records and transfer a deed of trust by assignment, just as lenders can do with mortgages.

b. Purchase-money mortgages

A **purchase-money** mortgage can mean one of two things. In the conventional sense, a purchase-money mortgage is a security interest that the buyer grants to the lender whose loan pays the purchase price of the property. Yet in the special sense, a purchase-money mortgage can also mean one that the buyer grants *back to the seller*, usually to make up a shortfall in the financing that the buyer can get from other sources. Purchase-money mortgages are generally treated with priority over other encumbrances such as mechanics' liens and judgment liens, even when the holders of those liens recorded them before the seller recorded the purchase-money mortgage. The rationale is that a purchase-money mortgage does not further encumber the property in the way that mortgages taken out of the land's equity for other purposes would encumber the property. Yet no matter the rationale, purchase-money mortgages gain higher priority than other mortgages.

Beyond a purchase-money mortgage, a property owner may also grant a mortgage for a *construction loan* for improvement of the real property or *home-equity loan* or other line of credit for any other purpose. In such cases, particularly as to home-equity loans, the associated mortgages are often second, third, or subsequent mortgages behind the purchase-money mortgage. Mortgage priority can become critical in attempted sales of an *underwater* property, referring to property mortgaged to secure greater debt than the land's value. Mortgage priority can become even more critical in foreclosure, as a later section addresses.

c. Future-advance mortgages

A property owner may alternatively grant a lender a **future-advance mortgage**. An owner grants a future-advance mortgage without yet receiving a loan in return or when receiving only part of the funds that the loan anticipates. A future-advance mortgage enables the owner to draw future advances against the mortgage as the owner's needs arise, operating in effect like a line of credit. The owner's advantages can include to arrange for funds before the owner needs them, for greater speed and flexibility in financing, and to secure interest rates and other mortgage terms when advantageous. The lender's advantage can include to have priority for the security interest as of the date of the mortgage's recording, even if the lender only later advances funds, as law typically provides. State laws vary, though, on the treatment of future advances, some giving retroactive priority only to *obligatory* future advances rather than optional future advances, while others give retroactive priority to *all* future advances but permit the borrower to give the lender a *cut-off notice* so that the borrower can give other new mortgages priority over subsequent advances.

2. Land contracts

A **land contract** is both a means of purchasing real property *and* a means of financing the real-property purchase. Deeds formally convey title to real property, not contracts. By declining to grant a deed to a buyer, and simply signing a contract conveying the land instead, a seller in effect creates a security device. The contract specifies the terms on which the buyer will receive a deed, typically either payment of the full contract price after a long period or, more often, payments for a period of months or a few years until the buyer qualifies for a conventional mortgage, at which time the mortgage proceeds will pay off the land contract. Sellers who offer a land contract expand the market for the property to buyers who cannot obtain mortgage financing. Land contracts are also known as *installment sales contracts*, *contracts for deed*, or *contracts for sale*.

Distinguish a land contract from the *purchase contract* that seller and buyer execute in anticipation of a closing where they would exchange the deed. Even though the buyer does not receive a deed until paying off the land contract, the law considers the buyer to hold **equitable title**, while the **legal title** remains with the seller. Buyers under land contract often record a **memorandum of land contract** to show their land-contract interest in the chain of title, ensure the priority of their equitable title over later-recorded interests, and prevent a devious seller from selling the property again to an unwitting buyer. The memorandum acts in the place of recording a deed, which of course the land-contract buyer does not yet have.

3. Absolute deeds as security

Lenders desire the most-efficient manner of executing on their security. Mortgages are not especially efficient, particularly when the state's law requires judicial foreclosure of mortgage and a lengthy redemption period in the mortgagor delaying the finality of sale for as much as up to a year. Lenders thus sometimes demand an **absolute deed** from the borrower, granting fee-simple title to the lender, as an attempt to avoid restrictions on foreclosure, particularly the right of redemption. The absolute deed appears as if the lender owns the real property, which is the deed's legal effect, although in practice the lender will hold it escrow awaiting the borrower's default. On default, the lender may record the absolute deed to list and sell the real property as security for the defaulted loan. Disputes, though, sometimes arise when the lender records the absolute deed without default or under terms with which the borrower does not agree. The borrower may then prove by parol evidence that the absolute deed was instead an *equitable mortgage*, invalidating the deed so that the court can treat it as a mortgage. The law disfavors absolute deeds as security, which may violate truth-in-lending laws and other restrictions and expose the lender to fines or other penalties.

B. Some security relationships

While the above sections describe *types* of security used in real-property transactions, the following sections address certain **security relationships**. The first section addresses the *necessity* and *nature* of a security obligation. The next section addresses three alternate *theories* of security in land, used in different jurisdictions. Other following sections address rights and duties *before* foreclosure (later sections addressing foreclosure), and the right to *redeem* along with efforts at *clogging the equity of redemption*.

Real Property Law

1. Necessity and nature of obligation

Security interests in land do not arise by implication. Borrower and lender must instead express their agreement, as previously indicated, in a signed writing satisfying the **statute of frauds**. On the other hand, also as previously indicated, mortgages are frankly necessary to transactions in real property, including not only land purchasers but also construction and improvement of buildings, because of the high relative cost of real property. A home is the most-expensive asset that most individuals buy, just as a business premises is the most-expensive business asset that most businesses buy. The value of a home or business real property also serves as capital on which to draw for other personal or commercial economic activity. Thus, mortgages are ubiquitous. Without mortgages or equivalent security devices for land, the economy would not function as it does. Debt financing through real-estate mortgages is critical to many individuals and businesses.

2. Theories: title, lien, and intermediate

States vary in whether they treat a mortgage as a **lien** against the land or instead as passing a special form of **title** to the land. The distinction matters primarily when a *joint tenant* grants a mortgage. In a lien-theory state, the joint tenant granting a mortgage does *not* destroy the unity of title on which a joint tenancy depends. By contrast, in a title-theory state, a joint tenant who conveys a mortgage destroys the unity of title with other joint tenants, thus severing the joint tenancy as to the mortgaging co-tenant, and creating a tenancy in common between that mortgaging co-tenant and other joint tenants. Some states, though, follow an **intermediate** theory that applies the lien theory unless the borrower defaults, giving the parties the relative convenience of dealing only with a lien rather than transfer of title. On default, though, the law applies the title theory, giving the lender greater enforcement rights as a title-holder in the land.

3. Rights and duties prior to foreclosure

Standard forms of mortgages require the borrower to maintain the mortgaged property in good repair, pay taxes, maintain insurance, not conduct illegal activities on the premises such as would forfeit the land, and otherwise protect the mortgagee's security interest. These obligations are contractual, and the mortgagee who identifies their breach can sue for specific performance. The mortgage will also likely grant the mortgagee the right to pay taxes, insurance, and other charges or costs to preserve the value of the land, and then have the borrower's reimbursement, as further described in a section below on subrogation. While contract terms impose the borrower's primary obligations, the law of **waste** may permit a mortgagee to obtain court assistance in ensuring that the borrower does not destroy the property's value. A building without heat in the winter or with a leaky roof can quickly

Real Property Law

depreciate because of natural conditions, as can a building with inadequate lighting, locks, and other security against vandalism.

The borrower's principal right, on the other hand, and the corollary mortgagee restriction, is for the borrower's free use of the mortgaged property if the borrower is not in default. A mortgage may grant the mortgagee a right to **enter for inspection** against waste, but generally, the borrower retains full rights of an owner to use and enjoy the premises, including to exclude others. Mortgagees interfere with those borrower rights at their peril of trespass, breach of contract, or statutory actions for breach of the peace with respect to security interests. A mortgage may, on the other hand, define the terms of default to include a significant change in the use of the premises including its abandonment. Once again, these terms are contract obligations, enforceable in specific performance or damages, like other contracts. While mortgagees properly record a mortgage, borrowers would also have rights not to have a mortgagee place other clouds on the borrower's title.

4. Right to redeem and clogging equity of redemption

The law of mortgages and other security interests in land grants the borrower rights to **redeem** the mortgaged property out of a foreclosure proceeding, meaning to pay off the mortgage obligation either before or a certain statutory period, such as six months, after foreclosure sale. A section below summarizes those redemption rights after foreclosure. Here, though, recognize that the law generally prohibits borrowers from waiving redemption rights in advance and prohibits lenders from demanding or contracting for that waiver. The law also prohibits borrower and lender from fashioning alternative loan arrangements, such as a deed in escrow or an option to purchase on default, treating default in ways intended to skirt redemption rights. The law holds that *clogs on equity are invalid*. Redemption rights can protect homeowners from losing critical housing or losing home equity, if the homeowner is able to redeem, although prospects for doing so are usually poor because the mortgagor could not even meet the original mortgage. Alternatively, the statutory period of redemption simply allows the foreclosed homeowner to accumulate savings and locate other housing, often while living in the premises without making mortgage payments. Public policy judges these redemption rights and their advantages sufficiently important to deny parties the opportunity to alter them in advance.

C. Transfers by mortgagor

Mortgages do not prohibit the borrower from selling or otherwise conveying away the mortgaged land, although seller and buyer must deal with the mortgage. Lenders taking mortgages as security for their loans routinely *record* those mortgages to ensure that the borrower's conveyance of the mortgaged land does not adversely affect the lender's security interest. A recorded mortgage protects the mortgagee's interest on transfer. If, as happens in the typical case, the borrower sells the mortgaged land while realizing sufficient funds to pay off the mortgage lender, then the lender *discharges* the mortgage. A mortgage securing indebtedness greater than the property's value, though, can make transfer difficult as a practical matter. If a sale does not bring sufficient funds to satisfy the mortgage, then the mortgagee will not discharge the mortgage, and the buyer will not buy, unless the buyer is willing to take **subject to** the mortgage or even to **assume** the mortgage as the following section addresses. Other following sections address related issues of the seller's rights and obligations on transfer, and application of **subrogation** and **suretyship** principles, and **due-on-sale** clauses.

1. Distinguishing "subject to" and "assuming"

In some situations, the seller and buyer of land find it either necessary or advantageous *not* to pay and discharge a mortgage on the land. For example, the buyer may not be able to obtain financing or locate financing on the same advantageous terms as the existing mortgage. In such instances, and if the mortgage permits it, the buyer may agree to take the property's title **subject to** the mortgage. The buyer pays a reduced sale price that reflects the mortgage obligation and then makes the mortgage payments to the lender. When a buyer takes *subject to* a mortgage, the buyer does *not* become directly liable to the mortgage lender on the promissory note. Rather, the *seller* remains liable on the note, while the buyer's property remains subject to the mortgage, giving the buyer incentive to make the seller's note payments.

In other instances, a buyer may expressly agree to **assume** an existing mortgage obligation. To *assume* an obligation here means for the buyer to become *directly liable* to the mortgage lender for the indebtedness that the mortgage secures. Direct liability means that the buyer then has personal liability on the seller's promissory note with the mortgage lender, rather than merely having the buyer's property at risk as mortgage security. Ordinarily, buyers would prefer not to accept such direct, personal liability. On the other hand, sellers *would* prefer that buyers assume mortgage indebtedness rather than merely take subject to the mortgage, for the increased incentive that assumption of debt creates. In other words, a seller may in negotiations require a buyer to assume. If, as a following section on *due-on-sale* clauses addresses, the mortgage lender also has a say in the transaction, then the lender may also require the buyer to assume.

2. Rights and obligations of transferor

Just because a borrower manages to sell the mortgaged land subject to the mortgage, or even with the borrower assuming the mortgage obligation, does not mean that the borrower has no further obligations. To the contrary, the borrower *remains obligated* on the promissory note that accompanied the mortgage. The note remains a contract between borrower and lender even after the borrower sells the land. The terms of that contract determine the borrower's obligation, which is routinely that the borrower remains liable notwithstanding the borrower's conveyance of the note's security. If the buyer does not make the mortgage payments reflecting the note obligation, then the lender may look to the borrower to make those payments. In some cases, the mortgage lender may expressly agree to accept the buyer's new commitment to pay the mortgage, including the buyer's *assuming* the note debt, to relieve the borrower from the note's contractual liability. The law calls this action of lender relief of the original borrower a **novation**.

The seller does not necessarily lose all rights when selling to a buyer who takes subject to the mortgage or agrees to assume the mortgage note. If the buyer defaults on payments, leaving the seller exposed to the unpaid mortgage note, then the seller's agreement with the buyer will likely provide the seller with recourse against the buyer. That recourse may include money from the buyer so that the seller can pay the note, in the nature of specific performance, or the seller may recover the property under a right of re-entry on default, extinguishing the buyer's interest. Unless the mortgage lender granted the seller a novation releasing the seller from liability, the seller owes the lender, but the seller has the buyer to whom to look for help in meeting the mortgage-note obligation.

3. Application of subrogation...

The prior section shows that a borrower/mortgagor who sells the real property subject to the mortgage, or with the buyer even assuming the mortgage, retains the risk that the buyer does not pay make the mortgage payments, unless in the unlikely instance the mortgage lender grants the borrower a novation and release from the mortgage-note obligation. The prior section also shows that when the buyer fails to make a mortgage payment, the seller has contract rights against the buyer to make the buyer perform. Yet in those instances, the buyer may also have failed to pay real estate taxes, insurance, or other charges associated with maintaining the property. Because the seller retains an interest, the seller may make those payments for the buyer and then **subrogate** to the rights of the assessor, insurer, or other creditor to recover the payments from the buyer.

To *subrogate* is to take the place or, proverbially, *stand in the shoes* of another to exercise that other's rights. A seller has sound economic reasons to preserve the property's title and value against the destruction or the claims of others. The seller's sale contract with the buyer may provide for subrogation rights, or the law may imply *equitable subrogation*. Even more commonly, the mortgage lender, the financial resources of which are seldom in question and whose economic interest is often greatest, will exercise similar rights to pay taxes and charges related to the property to preserve its value and then *subrogate* to those creditors' rights to obtain reimbursement from the seller or buyer. The mortgage instrument will ordinarily provide contractually for those subrogation rights, while in their absence, the law would likely imply them through *equitable subrogation*.

...and suretyship principles

Real Property Law

Mortgages can also involve the law of **suretyships**, referring generally to the relationship of a *surety* or *guarantor* for the borrower's mortgage obligation to both the borrower and the lender. A surety signs the original contract along with the obligor, while a guarantor signs a separate guarantee, although the distinction is unimportant here. Lenders do sometimes require a surety or guarantor, also loosely referred to as a *co-signer*, for a mortgage note when the borrower's credit is insufficient. The surety or guarantor owes the obligation that the contract or guarantee states, which is typically to pay when the primary obligor fails to do so. Suretyships and guarantees require a *signed writing* satisfying the **statute of frauds**. The surety or guarantor has rights, too, though, including to compel the primary obligor to perform, called *exoneration*, or to *reimburse* the surety or guarantor for performing, in the nature of *subrogation* as the prior section discussed. If the suretyship involves more than one surety, then the paying surety may also obtain *contribution* from other sureties. A surety also has the primary obligor's defenses, if any, when the lender pursues the surety.

4. Due-on-sale clauses

The above sections treat the lender as acquiescing in the borrower's transfer of the land subject to the lender's mortgage, or with the buyer assuming the mortgage. Yet many mortgages include a **due-on-sale** clause. The clauses typically permit the mortgage lender to accelerate the mortgage note and call its entire principal balance due if the buyer sells the land. Due-on-sale clauses typically give the lender the *option* of declaring the note due, enabling the lender to determine which action to choose, whether approval of the sale subject to the mortgage, approval of the sale only with the buyer assuming the debt, or simply acceleration of the debt. Federal law limits the ability of states to frustrate due-on-sale clauses. Due-on-sale clauses typically include a trigger for *land-contract* sales, in other words for efforts at private financing, giving the lender the greatest leverage.

D. Transfers by mortgagee

For their part, lenders may either hold the note and mortgage pending the borrower's payments or, as is commonly the case with residential mortgages, transfer the note and mortgage to an assignee such as an investor or mortgage-servicing company representing investors. Issues can arise, though, when the borrower defaults but raises defenses, such as fraud, against the lender about which the assignee may not have been aware. The rights of a person taking a note and mortgage on assignment can depend on whether the person is a **holder in due course**, meaning one who received the instrument in good faith, without knowing of defects, and having paid value. If the assignee is *not* a holder in due course, then the borrower can raise any defenses against the assignee that the borrower could have raised against the lender.

Real Property Law

If the assignee is a holder in due course, then the assignee takes the borrower's obligation *free of personal defenses*. Personal defenses, addressing conduct surrounding the obligation's formation, include *fraud in the inducement*, *failure of consideration*, and *unconscionability*. Thus, if the lender misrepresented the loan's terms in order to induce the note and mortgage, but the assignee took the assignment as a holder in due course, in good faith for consideration without knowing of the misrepresentation, then the borrower owes the assignee the full obligation. Holders in due course, though, take *subject to real defenses*. Real defenses, addressing the *legality* of the obligation's formation rather than surrounding conduct, include *forgery*, *infancy* or other *incapacity*, *illegality*, and *duress* or *coercion*. Thus, if the lender forged the instruments, or the transaction violated state or federal statutes regulating mortgage loans, then the borrower could raise those defenses to defeat an assignee, even one who was a holder in due course.

E. Payment...

The borrower owes the lender **payment** on the mortgage-note obligation. The note states the total obligation, interest rate, periodic payment amount, and note term over which the borrower pays. A note may amortize the full amount of principal and interest over the full term, or the note may lower payments and require a balloon payment at the end of the note's term. Mortgage notes are often for ten, fifteen, twenty, or even thirty years, although notes with balloon payments may be for terms as short as five, three, or two years, or even one year. Payment is the borrower's primary obligation, although the borrower will have other duties to maintain the property and not to cause its destruction or waste. The mortgage and note will also require the borrower to pay property taxes and assessments, and keep buildings insured, often through an escrow that the lender maintains out of the payments. As indicated in another section, the mortgage instruments will permit the lender to make those payments for the borrower if the borrower fails to do so and to recover the payments from the borrower on foreclosure.

...discharges...

The lender has the contractual and legal obligation to **discharge** the mortgage when the borrower satisfies the note's payment obligations. Cancellation of the note relieves the borrower of further note obligation, while discharge of the mortgage ends the lender's security interest in the land. Discharge may occur at the end of the note's term when the borrower makes the final payment or at an earlier date when the borrower sells the property and pays off the note out of the sale proceeds at close. Notes also typically permit the borrower to prepay the note without sale. Borrowers may do so out of other funds or may do so in a refinancing of the mortgage. The lender's discharge is a signed instrument that the borrower records in the property's chain of title to reflect that the title is clear of the prior mortgage. The lender who fails to promptly discharge a mortgage when payment of the note requires the lender to do so may be liable not only for breach of contract but also for **slander of title**, particularly when the borrower loses an opportunity to sell, mortgage, or otherwise benefit from clear title to the land.

...and defenses

The borrower may have **defenses** to a mortgage and its note obligation. In a judicial foreclosure, the borrower will plead and argue defenses in response to the lender's foreclosure action. If the state permits foreclosure outside of a judicial proceeding, then the borrower may have to bring a civil action to raise mortgage and note defenses. For example, the lender may have *misapplied payments* or made other *mistakes* in calculating amounts due. Alternatively, a lender may not have followed default *notice procedures* in the mortgage or mandated by state or federal law. The lender may have *misrepresented* mortgage terms, fraudulently inducing the borrower into the mortgage transaction without disclosing such things as adjustable interest rates or balloon payments. The lender may not have complied with federal and state truth-in-lending *disclosure requirements* on terms like the annual percentage rate, finance charges, and total interest over the loan term. Also, federal law grants a *servicemember on active duty* a stay against foreclosure. A borrower may also object to *unconscionable* mortgage terms. Defenses may lead to rescission of the mortgage and note obligation, reform of terms, damages, and equitable remedies such as specific performance of terms or correcting credit records.

F. Foreclosure

Foreclosure is the process through which the lender or other mortgage holder executes on the land as security. For a lender to *foreclose* a mortgage requires following the state's mandated procedures and procedures spelled out in the mortgage, to *accelerate* the total mortgage debt beyond overdue payments and then to secure and sell the mortgaged property in satisfaction of the debt. Sale proceeds first go to sale expenses including costs and attorney's fees as provided by statute or mortgage, then to pay the foreclosed debt, then to subordinate mortgage holders, and only then to the debtor if proceeds are sufficient. Any mortgagee may bring a foreclosure action, although who brings the action is of no consequence to priority. A foreclosing mortgagee names subordinate mortgagees whose interests the foreclosure would extinguish. Because the foreclosure does *not* extinguish *superior* mortgages, superior mortgage holders need not participate, although in practice many would simultaneously foreclose, treating the subordinate foreclosure and sale as an event of default.

1. Types

Most states require a court proceeding, known as **judicial foreclosure**, to foreclose on a mortgage in most instances, particularly with

Real Property Law

residential mortgages where concerns for overreaching are greater than in commercial mortgages. Some jurisdictions alternatively allow for **non-judicial foreclosure** in some circumstances, *if* the mortgage or deed of trust expressly permits non-judicial foreclosure. Because of concerns about lender overreach, particularly as to residential mortgages, and to protect the borrower's equity, those states tend to require *public auction* of the foreclosed property rather than private sale through a broker and strict advance personal notice to the mortgagor and other recorded owners. As indicated above, a few jurisdictions also allow borrower to grant and lender or trustee to hold a *deed of trust* as a mortgage substitute, although the law will likely regulate that alternative form closely and may require specific foreclosure procedures as just indicated. The law strongly discourages lender self-help and closely regulates foreclosures to avoid lender overreaching including breaches of the peace.

When seller and buyer form a land contract instead of the buyer obtaining lender financing and granting the lender a mortgage, and the buyer defaults on the land contract, the law may require or seller may desire to pursue a judicial **land-contract forfeiture**. Land contracts typically provide that the buyer *forfeits* payments made to the seller in the forfeiture proceeding. The forfeiture proceeding confirms that the seller has extinguished the buyer's equitable title. After the forfeiture judgment enters, the seller will once again have legal title, which the seller never relinquished under the land contract, and equitable title, restored to the seller from the buyer. The seller can also record the judgment of forfeiture so that the chain of title reflects the extinguishment of the land-contract interest reflected by the recorded memorandum of land contract.

2. Rights of omitted parties

As a prior section suggests, the **first mortgagee** generally has priority over subsequent and thus subordinate mortgagees as to sale proceeds, using *recording* dates and times to establish that priority. The law ordinarily grants an exception for *purchase-money* mortgages, meaning a mortgage that the buyer grants to the lender who finances the purchase *or* back to the seller as seller financing, usually to make up a shortfall in the financing that the buyer can get from other sources. Purchase-money mortgages generally take priority over prior encumbrances. States are especially likely to recognize the exception when the competing security interests are mechanics' liens, judgment liens, and other similar interests. Also as indicated above, a foreclosing mortgage holder need not add superior mortgage holders because the foreclosure would not extinguish those superior mortgages, only *subordinate* mortgages. Superior mortgage holders may, on the other hand, join in a subordinate mortgage holder's action, treating the subordinate foreclosure as a default if the mortgage so permits.

A problem arises when a foreclosing mortgage holder fails to join a subordinate mortgage holder. Subordinate mortgage holders are *necessary parties* to the action because the action affects, indeed *extinguishes*, their

Real Property Law

subordinate rights. A court will require that subordinate parties join when learning about their non-joinder. Yet if the foreclosure proceeds without a subordinate mortgage holder participating, the law does *not* extinguish the subordinate mortgage. The winning bidder at foreclosure auction takes subject not only to any superior mortgages who did not seek foreclosure but also as to the subordinate mortgages that the foreclosing mortgagee did not name. The winning bidder, though, may *re-foreclose* the foreclosed mortgage in a second proceeding that names the subordinate mortgagee, either extinguishing the subordinate mortgage by bidding in the superior mortgage's value or, if the sale realizes more, then paying off the subordinate mortgage.

3. Deficiency and surplus

Foreclosure of the mortgage, execution on the real property, and the real property's sale are not the lender's only rights. The borrower will also have executed the promissory note, constituting a contract for the breach of which the lender may also sue. Thus, judicial foreclosure proceedings typically include a contract-breach count in addition to the foreclosure count. The *judgment of foreclosure* will provide for acceleration of indebtedness, execution on and sale of the real property, and application of proceeds to reduce the debt. Yet the judgment may also include a money judgment against the debtor for the total indebtedness, reduced by the sale amount net of costs. If the sale does not satisfy the judgment debt, then the lender may treat the remaining money obligation as a **deficiency** enforceable by other means such as wage or account garnishment, depending on the borrower's collectability.

If, on the other hand, the sale proceeds produce a **surplus** above the foreclosing mortgagee's costs, attorney's fees, and loan indebtedness, then as previously indicated, the law provides that the proceeds go first to extinguish debt owed to subordinate mortgagees. If the land has no subordinate mortgages, or if any proceeds remain after their payment, then the borrower landowner receives the remaining surplus representing the borrower's equity. Borrowers rarely receive any equity because if the land had any equity value, then the borrower would have sold the land to avoid foreclosure or would have refinanced either with the lender threatening foreclosure or with another lender.

4. Redemption after foreclosure

As introduced well above, foreclosure does not entirely terminate the mortgagor's rights. All states allow the borrower to **redeem** the mortgaged property before foreclosure sale, by paying the mortgage indebtedness. The common law treats the right as the **equity of redemption**, although many states provide for greater *statutory* rights of redemption, especially for residential mortgages. A right of redemption gives the mortgagor additional time, defined differently from state to state but often six months, to raise funds to *redeem* the property, meaning in essence to buy the property out of foreclosure by paying the foreclosed debt. In some states, foreclosure of the mortgage triggers the redemption period, ending with auction sale. In other states, sale triggers the redemption period, during which the buyer waits to see if the foreclosed mortgagor redeems. As indicated above, redemption rights are important because they protect homeowners from losing critical housing or losing home equity, or allow the foreclosed homeowner to accumulate savings and locate other housing, often while living in the premises without making mortgage payments.

5. Deed in lieu of foreclosure

The cost and delay of a foreclosure proceeding, the possibility that the borrower will raise defenses, and the difficulty, cost, and delay of collecting a deficiency judgment from the borrower, all encourage the lender to seek streamlined means of foreclosing. One such means is for the lender to simply take a **deed in lieu of foreclosure** from the borrower. If the borrower voluntarily grants the lender a deed, then the lender may be able to avoid judicial foreclosure entirely, particularly if the property has no subordinate mortgages or all mortgagees can reach terms of agreement as to the property's value and treatment. Borrowers typically demand that the lender *waive* any deficiency in exchange for the borrower's offer of a deed in lieu of foreclosure, evidenced by the lender executing an *estoppel affidavit*. Some states and some federally backed mortgages require deficiency waivers for deeds in lieu of foreclosure, to prevent lender overreaching. A deed in lieu of foreclosure allows the lender to promptly place the property on the private market for sale through a broker, a trusted and flexible process that may obtain a higher value than selling at auction. For similar reasons of efficiency and risk, the lender may alternatively agree to a **short sale** in which the borrower sells to a third party for less than the mortgage debt, the lender receives the sale proceeds, the borrower executes a deed to the buyer, and the lender discharges the mortgage and waives the deficiency.

V.   Titles

The last main area that the Multistate Bar Examination's real-property topics list addresses involves how buyers and occupiers of land acquire **title** to the land. The first section addresses *adverse possession*, a topic that previous sections have only briefly mentioned in the context of other rules. The next section treats the primary way in which sellers transfer title to buyers, which is by *deed*. The following section addresses transfers not by deed but instead by *operation of law or will*. The following section addresses *title assurance systems*, referring to how buyers and others who deal in land ensure that they deal with the owners who hold valid title and can evaluate the integrity of that title. The last section treats a few special title problems.

A. Adverse possession

Real Property Law

Adverse possession is a lawful means by which one who occupies or uses land can acquire title to the land without dealing with the land's owner. To acquire title by adverse possession, a person must possess the property in an *exclusive, open and notorious*, and *continuous* manner for longer the statutory limitations period for ejectment actions, under a *claim of right*. In this context, **possession** means the satisfaction of each of those conditions. If a person can establish each of those conditions either in an action that the person files to gain clear title to the land, or in defense of the owner's ejectment action, then the court may enter a recordable judgment that has the purpose and effect of granting title to the person adversely possessing. The former owner then no longer has any right or title to, or interest in, the land. The adverse possessor's title will be marketable title if the adverse possessor should wish to sell the land.

For adverse possession, the person must first be on the property **exclusively** as an owner would be able to exclude. The person may move onto the property as in residence or may simply use the property exclusively, as an owner would. The person need not use the entire land to gain the entire land by adverse possession, if the limited use of the land that the person makes succeeds in excluding others from the entire land. Conversely, an adverse possessor who occupies only part of the land *without* excluding others from other parts adversely possesses only the used part. *Exclusive* use does not necessarily mean *sole* use. Two or more can simultaneously adversely possess land, as when a married couple or family move onto or continuously use the land, the couple or family then taking title together as adverse possessors when they satisfy the conditions.

The person's possession must then **open and notorious**, meaning that the property's true owner would likely discover the person's possession in inspection's ordinary course. Open and notorious means *visible* to others, particularly the owner. If the owner does not ordinarily visit the property or the occupied part of it for inspection, then the occupiers use of the property may not be sufficiently open and notorious, unless the occupier takes special steps to ensure that the owner knows. The owner's knowledge of the use is sufficient to establish that the use was open and notorious. If the occupier leaves the land each time the owner visits, whether by the owner's request or to avoid detection, then the possession is not open and notorious.

The possession must then be adverse, hostile, or otherwise under a **claim of right**, meaning that the possession is without the owner's consent in conflict with owner interests. Possession is adverse and under a claim of right when the possessor remains on the property intending and appearing to remain so permanently. A *claim of right* in this context does *not* mean a legal claim but instead appearing as if having the right to exclude the owner. Thus, tenants cannot adversely possess their landlord's land, and co-tenants cannot adversely possess their co-tenants' rights, because tenants do not occupy with the intent and appearance of ownership rights. The owner's permission destroys the person's claim of right. The person who concedes the owner's right fails to satisfy the hostility condition. Yet to establish adverse possession, the person need *not* have malicious intent or, in most states, even *know* that the possession was unlawful or against the owner's claim of title.

Finally, the possession must be **continuous**, meaning *uninterrupted*, for longer than the statutory limitations period on ejectment actions, varying from state to state between five and twenty-one years, with ten or fifteen years being particularly common lengths. Continuous does not necessarily mean every hour of every day but instead the use typical of one owning the land, depending on its type. Thus, a person would have to remain in a residence more often and consistently than on vacant lands, to adversely possess the residence. By contrast, even occasional use of a guest house or other property that an owner would only use sporadically may suffice. Abandonment of the property, though, interrupts continuous possession.

Claims of adverse possession sometimes raise the question of **tacking** successive periods of possession by different persons, each of whose possession is shorter than the statutory period. Generally, *voluntary transfer* from one possessor to another supports tacking their periods of possession. Claims of adverse possession also might raise the question of whether changes in ownership of the land interrupts the occupier's adverse possession, except that the rule simply holds that once adverse possession begins, it runs against all successive owners, no matter how many own the land during the statutory period.

B. Transfer by deed

The usual way of transferring land involves the seller executing a **deed** in the buyer's favor. The first section below on *transfers by deed* shows that sellers may offer, and buyers may accept, either *warranty* deed or *non-warranty* deed, including *covenants for title*. The quality of the deed thus varies, some transferors warranting, in the deed itself, more than others. The next section summarizes *deed requirements*, referring to what a transferor must include in a deed for the deed to accomplish the transfer in the manner that transferor and transferee intend, followed by a section on the necessary *delivery* of deeds including the treatment of deeds *in escrow*.

1. Warranty...

The land sale contract usually refers to the *type* of deed that the seller promises to convey at the coming closing. The type of deed determines the **warranties** that the transferor makes in the transfer. Just because the seller or other transferor executes and delivers a certain type of deed, with greater or fewer warranties, does *not* mean that the transferee in fact receives that quality of title that the deed warrants. The transferor has whatever title the transferor has, whether the deed is accurate in its warrants or not. Thus, the effect of transferring a certain type of deed is to give the transferee a breach-of-warranty cause of action if the transferor's title does not match the deed's warrants. Even though deeds in general *merge* the land sale contract's obligations into the deed's warrants, deeds thus serve in their own way,

Real Property Law

somewhat like the land sale contract, of creating or continuing assurances on which the transferee may rely and that the transferee may enforce.

The standard form of land sale contract provides for a **general warranty deed**. When sellers convey under general warranty deed, they covenant that they *own the land* with the *right to convey*, that the land has no *encumbrances* such as mortgages, liens, easements, of covenants, that the seller will *defend* the buyer's *superior title* and *right to enjoy* the land, and that the seller will *cure title defects*. So, if a seller transfers the property to a buyer by executing and delivering a general warranty deed, but the seller instead has defects in the title including mortgages, liens, or easements, then the buyer may look to the seller to cure those defects when the buyer discovers them. If the seller does not cure, then the buyer may sue to enforce those warrants, often joining the title insurer in the suit to have the insurer's resources to cure the defect and indemnity in the event of its failure. Title defects can include the seller's co-tenant, including a spouse or ex-spouse, who failed to sign the deed transferring the co-tenant's interest, predecessor co-tenants who failed to sign a deed transferring to the seller, a lien for unpaid improvements to the property, or other undisclosed defects or encumbrances.

While the general warranty deed offers the transferee the greatest assurance, other deeds offer less. A **special warranty deed** is one in which the transferor warrants and assures only that no defects or encumbrances arose *during the transferor's ownership*. The special warranty deed makes no assurances about the knowledge, experience, or title of prior owners. The only enforcement action that the transferee can thus take is as to defects that arose during the transferor's ownership, a limited remedy that leaves the transferee with the risk that the transferor held that the transferor's own title had defects or was subject to mortgages, liens, easements, covenants, or other encumbrances.

...and non-warranty deeds...

If a transferor wishes to make *no* warrants at all, not even as to what the transferor knows or doesn't know, then the transferor executes and delivers only a **quit-claim deed**, transferring only what the transferor in fact owns without making any assurances. If the transferor owns nothing, then the transferee gets nothing. Quit-claim deeds purport to give no right of recourse to the transferee at all. In theory, the transferee must accept whatever defects the title includes, although given trends away from the *merger doctrine*, especially around misrepresentations inducing the transaction or defects not going to the core of title, quit-claim deeds do not effectively bar all litigation. Yet in an arm's length sale on an open market in which the seller seeks full market value, the seller would typically need to offer a general warranty deed because offering anything less transfers to the buyer greater risk of owning land having title defects and unmarketable title.

...(including covenants for title)

Real Property Law

A similar type of deed to a special warranty deed, in that it provides only limited assurances, is one that makes specific **covenants for title**. Covenants for title warrant only what the deed's recitals state, rather than making the general warrant of fee-simple title against all challengers or special warrant of no defects arising during the transferor's ownership. The specific assurances may include that the transferor has *no knowledge* of title defects, owns the property without *known* co-tenants, or *knows of* no easements or covenants, leaving open whether the title has defects, the owners include co-tenants, or the property has easements and covenants *about which the transferor does not know*. Specific covenants may also include affirmative assurances such as that the transferor received, holds, and transfers the full former rights of a certain co-tenant or predecessor in title. If the transferor's title does not match the special covenants, then the transferee has special recourse as to those defects.

2. Necessity for a grantee and other deed requirements

The transferor's deed must meet two precise **requirements**. The deed must include a **granting clause** that identifies the transferor and transferee together with a statement that the transferor is transferring title to the transferee. The deed usually identifies the transferor and transferee *by name* but need not do so if the deed's identification leaves no ambiguity as to the parties, such as that the transferor is a named person's eldest son or only daughter. The other requirement beyond the granting clause is that the deed must **describe the property** in a way that clearly and precisely identifies what the transferor conveys. The usual means will be by *metes-and-bounds* description, although references to survey maps, natural features, artificial markers or monuments, common name, or a street address, city, and state can do if that description leaves no ambiguity as to the property's contours. Courts will allow external evidence to resolve ambiguities.

A deed need not mention consideration, although some deeds do so to promote that the transferee is a *bona fide purchaser*, having taken for value. Deeds should state what warrants of title the transferor makes. Indeed, deeds typically bear a title *General Warranty Deed*, *Special Warranty Deed*, or *Quit Claim Deed*, indicating the warrants that they include. Yet the text of the deed itself should then refer specifically to the warrants that the transferor makes, such as that *grantor warrants generally that grantor has and transfers fee-simple title free of all defects and encumbrances*, or, conversely for a quit-claim deed, that *grantor transfers in quit claim only that title that grantor holds, making no warrants*. If the deed does not state its type, then the law presumes that the deed is a general warranty deed.

State law determines the requirements for a deed's execution. The transferor must sign the deed, not mistakenly but with the intent of its execution. State law typically requires two adult and competent witnesses to sign, acknowledging the transferor's identity and signature. Most transferees record the deeds that they receive, with the county register of deeds. Recording acts may add other requirements as to the deed's form and execution for recording, such as that a notary public also sign indicating that the transferor signed under oath. The addition of a notary's attestation and signature creates a presumption of the execution's validity. Recording acts may also require the name and address of the deed's preparer, often a lawyer for the transferor, transferee, or title company.

3. Delivery...

As is true to make other contracts and commitments enforceable, when the transferor has executed the deed, the transferor must **deliver** the deed to the transferee with the intent of completing the transaction. Execution alone, without delivery, does not create an enforceable right of title. Nor does delivery without the intent of transferring title. For example, if a seller executes a deed at the office of the seller's lawyer but instructs the lawyer to hold the deed awaiting the buyer's payment or other action, then the deed's execution does not transfer title. Likewise, if the seller executes the deed and then delivers it to the buyer instructing the buyer to hold it until the buyer supplies the payment or satisfies some other condition, then the seller will also not yet have transferred title. The action would still lack the seller's intent to transfer title. But if the seller executes the deed and delivers it to the buyer with acknowledgment of transfer, or in silence without condition, then the actions would complete delivery and effect transfer.

...(including escrows)

As just mentioned, some transfers involve the transferor's execution of a deed and delivery of the deed to a person acting as an **escrow** agent. *Escrow* involves an agent holding an instrument, funds, or other items anticipating exchange, while awaiting satisfaction of the conditions of escrow. Escrow agreements, often in writing but also oral, determine the conditions on which the agent may release the items. An agent, often a title company or one of the parties' lawyers, typically holds the seller's deed awaiting the buyer's funds from the lender financing the transaction. The agent only releases the items out of escrow, directing them to the appropriate party, when the agent can meet all conditions of the escrow. The agent would direct the deed to the buyer for the buyer's recording, the funds to the seller for the seller's deposit, the buyer's executed promissory note and mortgage to the lender, among other items. Escrow facilitates transactions by eliminating the need for contemporaneous exchange. An escrow agent can also bear liability for breaching the escrow agreement, thus insuring the exchange against mistake or wrongdoing.

C. Transfer by operation of law and by will

While acquisition by adverse possession is one way in which title may transfer, and transfer by deed is the routine method of conveying property interests, the law recognizes several other ways in which title may transfer.

Real Property Law

The next section addresses the transfer of property by **will** or the laws of **intestacy**. The following section addresses **ademption**, when although a will purports to transfer, the testator has already transferred to another before the testator's demise. Following sections address other peculiarities in transfers of real property by law rather than by deed, including the principles of **exoneration, lapse**, and **abatement**.

1. In general

The owner of real property may generally pass the owner's interest by **will** to the person whom the owner wishes to receive the property after the owner's death. Real property may also transfer by operation of the laws of **intestacy** when the owner dies without a will. An exception, of course, is when the owner's only interest in the real property is as a *joint tenant*, and the owner dies before other joint tenants who would then receive the dead owner's interest by rights of survivorship. To avoid the cost and delay of probate proceedings, land owners sometimes use joint tenancies, trusts, and other ownership arrangements to transfer or treat title on the death of an owner or beneficial holder of real property. Another example of an interest that could not pass by will would be an *easement in gross* or other covenant that was personal to the holder and would by definition not survive the holder's death. Otherwise, the law permits and upholds the transfer of real-property interests that do not in themselves terminate the right with the death of the owner of the title or beneficial interest. The law of wills and trusts calls the transfer of land by will a **devise** of land. The valid will need only adequately describe the property and identify the devisee for the probate court to approve and sign a recordable order transferring title. The law of intestacy also permits and provides for the transfer of real-property interests when the deceased owner or holder did not execute a valid will, referred to as an **inheritance** of land, subject to the following rules, principles, and exceptions.

2. Ademption

Owners of land may live many years after executing a will devising real property to family members or others. In those years, relationships and circumstances may change, causing or requiring the owner to sell or otherwise transfer the land before death, leaving the will purporting to make a transfer of land that the testator no longer owned at death. The law treats this anomaly under the principle of **ademption** or **ademption by extinction**, in which the law holds the prior transfer to have *adeemed* the property out of the decedent's estate. While in theory the purported devisees might get some equivalent asset out of the estate, the rule of *ademption* holds that the purported devisees instead get nothing. Thus, if an uncle devises his cottage to a niece but sells the cottage before his death, the niece receives nothing, even if uncle had an estate that could have compensated the niece's loss out of other assets. The rule of ademption holds even if the owner had only

Real Property Law

formed a land sale contract but not yet closed, if the buyer has an enforceable contract.

If, on the other hand, something caused the property's destruction in a way that the owner's estate received insurance proceeds after the owner's death, then the common law would pass the proceeds to the property's devisee, although state statutes modify this rule. Ademption can also occur **by satisfaction**, referring to the owner deeding and transferring the property to the devisee before the owner dies. Ademption by satisfaction does not defeat the devise but instead carries it out in advance of the testator's demise.

3. Exoneration

When a testator devises real property, or when an heir inherits real property under the laws of intestacy, a question often arises whether the devisee or heir must take the property subject to mortgages, liens, or similar encumbrances or whether the deceased owner intended that the heir or devisee take the real property free of those encumbrances. The common-law doctrine of **exoneration** holds that the owner's estate must, if able, pay the encumbrances out of personal property so that the heir or devisee take the property clear of those encumbrances. Thus, if an aunt devises her nephew her condominium but with an outstanding mortgage on it when she dies, then the aunt's estate would have to pay off the mortgage out of the aunt's savings or other personal assets, if the estate had the assets to pay.

The doctrine of exoneration, though, has met with such modern disfavor that jurisdictions under the Uniform Probate Code limit its application to instances when the testator's will expressly directs the exoneration. In those jurisdictions, the will's general direction to pay all debts is not sufficient to invoke exoneration of encumbrances on devised real property. Instead, the will must specifically direct such exoneration as to the devised real property. In all jurisdictions, if the testator's will expresses the testators intent that the devisee take *subject to encumbrances*, then the devisee does so notwithstanding the exoneration doctrine. Exoneration does not apply to joint-tenancy interests taken under rights of survivorship. Joint tenants take subject to encumbrances.

4. Lapse

Another anomaly arises in a testator's devise of real property when the person to whom the testator devises dies before the testator dies, without the testator having redirected the devise. The law refers to this occurrence as the **lapse** of the devise. The treatment of lapse depends on whether the testator devised the real property to the devisee by specific term in the will or instead whether the testator simply left the real property in the estate's residuary and bequeathed the residuary estate to the person who predeceased the testator. If the testator made a specific devise of the real property to the person who predeceased the testator, then the devise to the person *lapses*, falling into the estate's residuary, where the real property passes as the

Real Property Law

residuary clause states. The person's heirs at law or by will do *not* receive the property. If, instead, the testator left the real property in the residuary rather than making its specific devise, and the residuary lapsed because of the person's predeceasing the testator, then one looks to the laws of intestacy to determine who receives the real property and other residuary estate. States, though, *disfavor lapse*, instead enacting **anti-lapse** statutes. Anti-lapse statutes *preserve the devise* if the devisee died leaving *issue* who would then receive the real property in devise. The statutes define *issue* differently, some limiting issue to children and others including other lineal descendants or even the devisee's siblings, and in some cases the devisee's siblings' children, who would be the devisee's nieces and nephews.

5. Abatement

Another anomaly arises when the estate lacks the net assets to allow for devises of real property as the will directs. The question then becomes which specifically devised or bequeathed assets, real or personal, the estate must liquidate to pay estate obligations. In this instance, the estate follows the law of **abatement**, the effect of which is to control the allocation of inadequate estate resources. Generally, if the testator has directed the order of abatement in the will, then the estate must follow that order. If the will does not direct an abatement order, then the common law provides that bequests of personal property abate *before* devises of real property. In fact, in the complex order of abatement, devises of real property abate *last*. Devises of real property abate only after the estate has exhausted all other assets. The modern trend, though, is to treat real and personal property the same, destroying the common law's favored treatment of devises of real property, although specific devises and bequests still abate last, even if, under the modern trend, together rather than personal property first and real property last.

D. Title assurance systems

Real-property law and practice offer two systems for assuring that a buyer of land receives the title that the seller should convey in the transaction. The first **title-assurance system** involves the state's *recording act*. As the next section addresses, a recording act establishes a practical system and legal mechanism in which owners of real property can record their deeds or other claims of title, interest, or right, with a local official, the effect of which is to give the recording claimant legal advantages over other claimants who have *not* recorded. The other title-assurance system that real-estate practice offers is *title insurance*. As a following section addresses, title insurers assume the obligation to a policy-holding property owner to litigate and indemnify in efforts secure the owner's title against adverse claims, while also compensating the owner when the owner loses a title challenge, possession, and ownership.

Real Property Law

1. Recording acts...

As just indicated, **recording acts** create systems in each state for real-property buyers, mortgagees, lienholders, and other claimants to interests in land to **record** their interests for the public to see. The act of *recording* involves providing to the local *register of deeds*, usually at the county level, the deed or other instrument that the person wishes to record so that the register can enter the instrument in the system in a manner that others can discover it on search for records relating to the real property. The system allows others, particularly potential buyers or mortgagees, to determine the state of title on the land including such things as who owns the land or has a security interest, easement, or other claim of an interest in it. Buyers of land record deeds promptly to ensure that others know that they are now the rightful titleholders. Once recorded, the register returns the original deed to the buyer, while keeping a copy.

...(race, notice, and race-notice)

Recording acts are significant not just for enabling buyers and lenders to determine who owns and what encumbrances the land's title. Recording acts can also determine which claimant prevails among multiple claimants, particularly when a devious owner purports to transfer title to multiple competing buyers. **Bona-fide purchasers**, referring to those who take *for fair consideration* and record superior title *without knowledge or reason to know* of superior claims, gain the recording act's protection. The conditions, though, under which a bona-fide purchaser gains superior title depend on the recording act's form, either **notice**, **race**, or **race/notice**. A *notice* jurisdiction holds a bona-fide purchaser's title superior to an earlier purchaser's title if the earlier purchaser did not record the deed and the subsequent purchaser did not know of the earlier transfer. By contrast, a *race* jurisdiction looks simply to who recorded first, without considering who had notice of other earlier title. And a *race/notice* jurisdiction grants the subsequent bona-fide purchaser superior title only if the subsequent purchaser did not know of the earlier transfer and records first.

a. Indexes

The key to an effective title search is the **index** that the register maintains showing each instrument's recording and that title searchers use to track recordings. Registers of deeds keep one of two different kinds of indices. A **grantor/grantee** index categorizes and indexes instruments by either grantor name or grantee name, in alphabetical order. Thus, if a buyer wanted to confirm that the seller had title, the title searcher would look up the seller in the *grantee* category because the seller would have previously gained title *as a buyer*. The searcher could then see who *sold* to the seller and look up *that* seller-to-the-seller in the grantee index, and on back to the earliest recording, ensuring a good chain of title *as to buyers*. The searcher must then

Real Property Law

repeat the process *in the grantor* index to see if any buyer sold to anyone other than the next buyer in the chain of title. By contrast, a **tract** index categories and indexes instruments by the land within the county. The tract index divides the county up first by cities, villages, townships, or like divisions, then by sections, then by blocks, and then by lots, or similar divisions. A title searcher can then search the index for any land location in the county, to see what instruments the register of deeds has recorded as to that land.

b. Chain of title

As the prior section suggests, good title depends on establishing a sound chain from the earliest transaction to the most-recent transaction in which the current owner took title. **Chain of title** refers to the continuity of transactions from owner to owner. Good, sound, or marketable title depends on showing that the chain of title leaves no *gaps, missing links, unaccounted-for interests*, or other defects. For example, if A sells to B who sells to C, then the chain of title suggests no defect. Yet if A_1 and A_2 first own as co-tenants, and then only A_1 conveys to B who conveys to C, the chain of title has not accounted for the interest of A_2, and the chain of title thus shows a defect. Similarly, if A conveys to B and then C conveys to D, the chain of title reflects a gap, meaning no conveyance, between B and C, showing a defect in D's title. The primary purpose of title searches through recording indexes is to determine whether the chain of title has defects. A buyer who discovers from a title search before close that the seller does not have sound, recorded title as the land sale contract required, may refuse to close for failure of a material term of the contract. A second significant purpose is to discover and disclose encumbrances.

c. Protected parties

As indicated above, *notice* recording acts **protect** bona-fide purchasers, meaning those who take for value and without notice, no matter who records *after* the bona-fide purchaser takes. By contrast, *race* recording acts protect parties who record first. And *race/notice* recording acts protect only bona-fide purchasers who record first, the bona-fide status of the purchaser satisfying the recording act's notice condition and the first-recording satisfying the recording act's race condition. The type of jurisdiction, whether *notice, race,* or *race/notice,* does not always affect the superiority of title in a dispute over title. Sometimes, the outcome is the same in all three types of jurisdiction. For instance, if neither purchaser records their deed, then the first purchaser has superior title. The seller can only convey good title once, to the first purchaser, unless the law provides otherwise. The recording acts can change the order, encouraging recording. Yet in *all* jurisdictions, a bona-fide purchaser has superior title to an earlier purchaser if the bona-fide purchaser, again meaning one who bought for value without notice of the earlier sale, records first. Similarly, in *all* jurisdictions, if the earlier purchaser records before a later purchase, then the earlier

Real Property Law

purchaser will have superior title because the later purchaser cannot be a bona-fide purchaser, which requires taking without notice. The earlier recording establishes notice.

d. Priorities

The above sections show that one purpose of recording acts is to establish reliable **priorities** for the purchaser who has superior title, so that buyers can follow reliable practices when buying. As shown above, the type of recording act can make a difference in the priority order. The clearest differences among *notice*, *race*, and *race/notice* jurisdictions arise when the earlier purchaser records *after* the later purchase but *before* the later purchaser records. The later purchaser would *not* then have record notice at the time of purchase, but the earlier purchaser would have won the *race* to record. **Notice** jurisdictions favor the later purchaser, if the later purchaser gave value and had no other notice (not having had record notice). **Race** jurisdictions favor the earlier purchaser who, after all, won the race to record. A **race/notice** jurisdiction would change the outcome only if the later purchaser managed to record *before* the earlier purchaser, assuming also that the later purchaser had no notice.

e. Notice

In a *notice* jurisdiction, transferees who take from any transferor who had superior title under the jurisdiction's recording act also have superior title, even if they have notice of a competing claim. The transferor's superior title **shelters** the transferee. Recording acts do not address every situation in which a buyer would have actual or constructive **notice** of a superior title. Specifically, recording acts do *not* resolve how a potential buyer would discover an owner taking by *adverse possession*. Only if the adverse possessor has already received and recorded a court judgment showing that the possessor has taken title from the owner, will the real-property records disclose the adverse possessor's interest to the potential buyer. If, instead, the adverse possessor has the right of adverse possession but has not yet reduced the title to a recorded judgment, then the potential buyer's title search will not disclose the possession. The potential buyer must inspect the property for the adverse possessor, whose possession must, after all, be open and notorious, meaning discoverable on inspection. If the buyer buys without discovering the adverse possessor and then loses title to the adverse possessor, the buyer's recourse is against the seller under the general warranty deed, unless the seller conveyed instead only by quit claim, in which case the buyer may have no recourse.

2. Title insurance

Buyers of land typically purchase **title insurance** to protect against undisclosed defects in title. Title companies insure title. Land sale contracts

Real Property Law

typically include *title-insurance contingencies*, enabling the buyer to inspect and approve the title insurer's commitment, which discloses encumbrances or defects that the title insurer's search discovered. Title defects can include not just adverse third-party claims to title but also *missing links* in the chain of title. Chain of title should show a continuous right of ownership, without unexplained gaps in the record of how the property passed from owner to owner. The title insurer's *title search* would show gaps in ownership, to which the buyer can then object when the title company shares its title-insurance commitment with the buyer before the closing. Title defects can also include encumbrances such as covenants and easements that burden or limit the property's use. The title search should also show recorded covenants and easements. Title insurance pays to resolve title defects that the insurer should have discovered and disclosed but did not do so. If the title insurance cannot cure title and the buyer loses the property, then the title insurer indemnifies the buyer for the loss.

E. Special problems

The following sections address a few remaining **special problems** relating to title to real property. The first section addresses *after-acquired title*, referring to instances when a transferor conveys before acquiring title but then acquires title after the transfer. The law addresses that issue following the doctrine of *estoppel by deed*. The next section addresses how the law deals with *forged instruments* and *undelivered deeds*. *Purchase-money mortgages* also get special treatment, as the following section addresses. Finally, the concluding section addresses *judgment and tax liens*.

1. After-acquired title (including estoppel by deed)

One anomaly that can arise in real-property transactions is that a person who believes in having title or who anticipates soon acquiring title, purports to *transfer* title *before acquiring* title. If the person never acquires title, then of course the transfer remains void. One cannot transfer title that one does not have. Yet if the person who purported to transfer title that the person did not have *subsequently acquires* title, then fairness to the transferee would seem to dictate that the transferee somehow acquires the transferor's **after-acquired title**. Indeed, the law holds under the doctrine of **estoppel by deed** that the transferor who acquires title after having purported to transfer it, cannot deny the transferee's claim to title. The prior transfer of deed *estops* the transferor from denying transfer and refuting title. The transferee has good title as to the transferor's claim, under the estoppel-by-deed doctrine. However, a bona-fide purchaser taking for value and without notice from the same transferor, after the first transfer and after the transferor finally acquired title, may have the superior title over the first transferee, particularly if the bona-fide purchaser records first.

2. Forged instruments...

Real Property Law

Real-property law authorizes practices to discourage forging of deeds and other instruments. A **forged instrument** is one to which the signer has signed someone else's name without that person's authority. The purpose of forgeries is usually nefarious, such as to obtain the forgery victim's funds in purported purchase, although some forgeries, though wrong and damaging, are innocent and done with good intention. One way that states discourage forged real-estate instruments is to require witnesses and notary acknowledgment for recording. The signer must sign in front of witnesses who also sign, and a notary public who attests to the signer's identity and signature. These acknowledgment requirements reduce the incidence of forgeries, although not eliminating them. The law holds that deeds recorded with such facially apparent defects in the acknowledgment that the register should not have recorded them, do *not* give *constructive notice* of the recorded instrument, only notice if the title search reveals the instrument. On the other hand, if the only defects in the acknowledgment are not apparent from the instrument's face, such as that the notary's commission had expired or that a witness was underage, then the recording still satisfies to make the deed superior for a race or race/notice jurisdiction.

...and undelivered deeds

As indicated in an above section, when the transferor has executed the deed, the transferor must **deliver** the deed to the transferee with the intent of completing the transaction for the transaction to be effective. Execution alone, without delivery, does not create an enforceable right of title. For example, if a seller executes a deed at the office of the seller's lawyer but instructs the lawyer to hold the deed awaiting some event or satisfaction of some condition, then the deed's execution does not transfer title. The problem of an **undelivered deed** becomes acute when the owner dies without having delivered. In such cases, the law holds the transfer incomplete. The real property does not pass by deed but instead through rights of survivorship, as the decedent's will directs, or as the laws of intestacy provide, depending on the circumstances. The owner's placing the deed in escrow *to deliver at the owner's death*, a tactic often intended to avoid taxes or probate, is equally problematic. The law in such cases tends to hold either that the deed remains an uncompleted and therefore ineffective gift or treat the escrow as an intended devise, subject to probate. An undelivered deed is generally ineffective in accomplishing anything that the owner may have intended, unless confusion and disappointment were the owner's intent.

3. Purchase-money mortgages

As indicated in an above section, property owners grant a **purchase-money mortgage** when they use the loan's proceeds to buy the real property on which the lender records the mortgage. Purchase-money mortgages are routinely *first* mortgages, lenders typically requiring that all parties, including

Real Property Law

any prior mortgagees, so agree, and law typically so providing. The law generally gives priority to purchase-money mortgages, particularly over mechanics' liens and judgment liens. Yet a purchase-money mortgage can also mean a mortgage that the buyer grants back *to the seller* to make up a shortfall in the buyer's other financing. The special problem that a seller taking back a mortgage from the buyer creates is that the seller only has a *complex*, *expensive*, and *time-consuming* remedy, which is foreclosure under the state's laws, generally protecting the mortgagor landowner, while granting that landowner a right of redemption. A mortgage back to the seller is a creative but disfavored device.

4. Judgment and tax liens

Judgment creditors may record a **judgment lien** against real property that the judgment debtor owes. A money judgment is a court order reducing the debtor's obligation to an obligation that the creditor may enforce against the debtor's non-exempt assets. State laws provide limited exemptions against execution on a judgment. Exemptions relating to real property are for *homesteads*, meaning the home in which the judgment debtor resides. The amount of the homestead exemption varies from state to state, with a few states offering unlimited or high dollar amounts but other states offering lower amounts a fraction of most home values. A judgment creditor may record a judgment lien and await the home's sale, when the debtor must pay the lien to be able to pass good title to the buyer. Alternatively, a judgment creditor may foreclose the lien, seeking the home's sale, although the debtor would realize the exemption amount before the creditor recovered anything. Federal and state tax liens operate similarly. Federal law authorizes the Internal Revenue Service to file a tax lien against the debtor's real property but requires or permits the Service to discharge the lien, subordinate the lien to other encumbrances, or withdraw the lien under some circumstances.

Tort Law

G.   Tort Law

NOTE: The Torts questions should be answered according to principles of general applicability. Examinees are to assume that there is no applicable statute unless otherwise specified; however, survival actions and claims for wrongful death should be assumed to be available where applicable. Examinees should assume that joint and several liability, with pure comparative negligence, is the relevant rule unless otherwise indicated. Approximately half of the Torts questions on the MBE will be based on category II, and approximately half will be based on the remaining categories—I, III, and IV.

The Multistate Bar Examination's topics list gives you a big hint by first instructing you (above) to answer tort-law questions according to **general tort principles**. The two most general of those tort-law principles are that tort law intends to (1) **deter** and (2) **compensate**. At the bottom of nearly every tort-law fact pattern is some form of conduct that society might wish to deter, connected with some form of harm that society might wish to compensate. Thus, in an exam brain freeze, when all memory fails as you face a tort-law question, just **look for the questionable conduct and the harm it caused**, and then choose the answer that most appears to accomplish those twin policies justly and fairly. At root, tort law is the Golden Rule to do to others as you would have them do to you.

The topics list's above instruction to apply general tort principles solves another big problem in national examination on tort law. Tort law, like other state law, has majority rules, minority rules, and rules peculiar to a single jurisdiction. **You need not concern yourself with minority and peculiar rules unless in the unlikely case that a question directs you to them.**

Contributory negligence, still in place in only four states, is an example. A question would clearly alert you to apply contributory negligence as a defense rather than comparative negligence if the answer so required. Indeed, the above topics-list introduction states explicitly that you should **apply the pure form of comparative negligence** unless otherwise instructed. Thus, assume with every question that you are applying the general principle and settled law rather than peculiar interpretations, unless the question clearly says otherwise.

The same is true for statutes modifying the common law. From state to state, tort law has many such statutes modifying the common law. Comparative negligence, just discussed, is a good example. While the great majority of states have adopted comparative rather than contributory negligence, many of those states have statutes that adopt one of the two modified forms of comparative negligence, less-than or not-greater-than. Unless otherwise instructed, you should **assume no such statute**, just as the above instruction explicitly indicates to apply *pure* comparative negligence rather than the less-than or not-greater-than modified forms.

Tort Law

Note, though, that the above instruction says that you *should* assume that **wrongful-death claims** and **survival actions** *are* available. The reason for the instruction is that while you are generally to assume that *no* statute modifies the common law, *all fifty states* have wrongful-death statutes, just as survival statutes are also ubiquitous. A wrongful-death claim is a procedural device allowing tort recovery for death. While the statutes vary, wrongful-death actions are usually in the name of the decedent's estate and controlled by the estate's personal representative. The estate, though, must still have an underlying tort theory such as negligence. Spouses and children are typical beneficiaries under wrongful-death acts, as may be parents and possibly siblings and other lineal descendants, depending on the statute. Wrongful-death acts also differ as to the measure of loss. Some acts limit beneficiary recovery to pecuniary loss while others allow non-economic loss to beneficiaries (loss of the decedent's love, society, and companionship). Other acts allow loss to the estate (what the decedent him- or herself lost in not getting to live a full life). Survival actions permit the estate to recover for losses the decedent suffered before death, particularly pain and suffering but also wage loss and medical expense.

Tort law classifies torts by the actor's state of mind, as either (1) **intentional torts**, (2) **torts of negligence**, or (3) **strict liability**. The significance of this distinction is immediately apparent from the last part of the above instruction. The above instruction says in effect that although the topics list has four parts, your studies should give special attention to the second part that addresses negligence because half of the questions will be negligence questions. The emphasis on negligence claims makes sense because insurance does not ordinarily cover purposeful wrongs. Liability insurance makes tort law work. Negligence is your tort-law bread and butter on both examination and in practice.

I.   Intentional torts

Tort law distinguishes the seven intentional torts (detailed in the following sections) from torts of negligence and strict liability by the wrongdoer's intentional state of mind. *Intent* in its most-common form involves the **purpose or desire to harm**. The intent to harm may be due to the wrongdoer's ill will or malice toward the wronged, although **motive is not necessary to intent**. The purpose or desire to harm suffices even if the claimant cannot prove the wrongdoer's motive or the wrongdoer's motive is ambivalent. Yet to have an intentional-tort claim, the claimant must **connect the intent to the harm** rather than just to the *act* that harms. We intend to drive an automobile, but when we have an accident, the law doesn't call the accident intentional. Only a road-rage incident where the driver intended to ram another vehicle would lead to an intentional-tort claim.

The purpose or desire to harm is just the first of three forms of intent. **Knowledge of substantial certainty of harm** is a second form of intent. The wrongdoer may not desire to harm someone but may be doing an act that will obviously harm someone, such as intentionally setting off an explosive device

Tort Law

to rob a bank or intentionally driving a car into a marketplace in a desperate cry for attention. Those actions qualify as intentional even if the harm, though obvious, is incidental to the wrongdoer's other purpose. One newer intentional tort, **intentional infliction of emotional distress** or IIED, accepts a slightly lower **recklessness** form of intent, defined as **knowledge of high probability of harm**, as satisfying the intent element.

Transferred intent is a third form of intent as to the five traditional intentional torts assault, battery, false imprisonment, trespass to land, and trespass to chattels (but not IIED or conversion). With transferred intent, the wrongdoer intends to harm in one way but ends up harming in another way. The law will use the intent to harm in the first way to satisfy the intent element as to the harm occurring in the other way. For instance, a wrongdoer may intend to scare (commit an assault on) a person but instead ends up striking them (committing a battery). The intent satisfying assault becomes intent satisfying battery. Intent transfers not only among the five traditional intentional torts but also from victim to victim. A wrongdoer may intend to harm one person but ends up harming another person. The intent satisfying battery as to the first person becomes intent satisfying battery as to the second person.

Children, even very young children, and the **mentally ill** are liable for intentional torts if they know the nature of their act, not that the act is wrong but instead what they are doing. The mentally ill person who strikes an aide thinking that the aide is a threat is liable because the actor knew that they were striking another person. The mentally ill person would not be liable if they thought that they were striking at a fly. Parents are generally not liable for a child's tort except by statute, usually limited to a few thousand dollars.

Importantly, **mistake does not negate intent**. If the actor thinks that the actor is cutting a tree on the actor's own land but is cutting a tree on the neighbor's land, then the actor's intent to cut the tree satisfies the intent for trespass. If the actor thinks that the actor is hugging the actor's spouse but is accidentally hugging a stranger, then the actor's intent to hug satisfies the intent for battery (assuming the hug was sufficiently offensive to constitute a battery). If the actor thinks that the actor is shooting a wolf but instead is shooting the neighbor's dog, then the actor's intent to shoot satisfies the intent for conversion.

Finally, the law **presumes damages** for assault, battery, false imprisonment, and trespass to land (four of the five traditional intentional torts, just not trespass to chattels). While the claimant would prove any actual harm to ensure appropriate damages recovery, a jury may award nominal or greater damages for these intentional torts without any supporting damages proofs.

A. Harms to the person, such as assault, battery...

Battery is an **intentional contact harmful or offensive to the reasonable person**. While battery usually involves contact to the person such as a fist to the face or bullet to the gut, contact with anything closely connected with the person satisfies the contact element of battery. Jerking a handbag from a person's shoulder or an object from a person's hand can constitute battery. The contact may be harmful, such as a knifing or shooting, or the contact may be offensive, such as an unconsented sexual touching. The offense, though, must be that of a reasonable person, not someone unusually sensitive to offense such as a hypochondriac or paranoid schizophrenic. A polite tap on the shoulder to get someone's attention or encouraging pat on the back would not be a battery if the reasonable person would consider it acceptable, even if the claimant does not. On the other hand, **good motive or beneficial effect does not excuse a battery**. A physician expanding a surgery beyond the patient's consent, when not in an emergency circumstance, commits a battery even if the expanded surgery has generally good effect.

Assault is the **reasonable apprehension of an imminent battery with the actor's apparent present ability to carry it out**. Although assault involves anticipation of a battery, and assault and battery often occur together, assault may occur without battery when the wrongdoer stops just short of carrying the act out. Battery may also occur without assault when the victim does not see or hear the battery coming, such as when the battery occurs from behind the victim. Learning about an imminent contact after the contact occurs is not assault. The victim must instead anticipate the contact before it occurs, for the proofs to satisfy assault. Words (threats) alone are generally not enough for an assault unless combined with an overt act suggesting imminent harmful contact. For assault, the wrongdoer need not be able to carry out the battery if it reasonably appears that the actor is able. Pointing an unloaded gun or even a toy gun at another while threatening imminent harm can constitute assault, if the reasonable person could believe that the gun is real and loaded.

... false imprisonment...

False imprisonment is **intentional unauthorized restraint against will**. The restraint is ordinarily by force, such as locking or blocking the victim in a room or handcuffing the victim. A known and reasonably safe means of escape, such as an unlocked back door, means no false imprisonment. Yet the restraint can also include subjecting the victim to unreasonable danger on escape, such as requiring the victim to swim an unsafe route from boat to shore to escape. The restraint can also include risking loss of critical property, such as withholding a person's purse containing keys, cash or credit cards, and passport or other identification, making the person effectively unable to leave in reasonable safety. The victim must know of the restraint for it to be false imprisonment. Locking a person in a room while they sleep is not false imprisonment if the room is unlocked again by the time the person awakes. But drugging a person asleep could be false imprisonment if depriving the person of the will to move. False imprisonment can also include arrest without the legal right to do so or refusal to release from confinement when law requires.

Tort Law

... and infliction of mental distress...

Intentional infliction of emotional distress is a newer tort requiring proof of **outrageous conduct beyond all bounds of decency in civil society** together with **severe distress**. As noted above in the section on intent, while the wrongdoer must intend to cause the victim severe distress, the degree of intent may include the lower **recklessness**, meaning knowledge of a high probability of harm. The big issue with intentional-infliction claims tends to be whether the conduct is sufficiently outrageous. Mild to moderate offenses are not enough. The wrongdoer's repeating the conduct may make the conduct more-likely outrageous, as may the conduct's location and duration, and the relationship between perpetrator and victim. For example, a supervisor who holds employment authority over a subordinate and who repeats outrageous acts in the workplace day after day may be more likely to have committed the tort than a stranger who does something reprehensible only once. In any case, the conduct must be **outrageous to the reasonable person**, not to an overly sensitive or mentally ill person. Yet the wrongdoer's knowledge that the victim is unusually susceptible may make the conduct more outrageous, such as when the wrongdoer plays unmercifully on the unreasonable fears of a known paranoid schizophrenic.

... and harms to property interests, such as trespass to land...

Trespass to land is **intentional interference with exclusive possession** of land or, alternatively, **intentional unauthorized physical entry onto another's land**. Once again, as with other intentional torts, mistake does not negate intent. Purposeful but mistaken entries, such as where the trespasser believes that the trespasser is on the trespasser's own land but is instead on adjacent lands, are still trespass. On the other hand, accidental entries, such as where a passing motorist's vehicle slides off the road and onto adjacent lands, are not trespass. The entry must be intentional even if mistaken. Trespass can include an authorized entrant exceeding the scope or duration of consent, such as when a shopper enters an employees-only store backroom or when remains in the store after closing. Trespass can also include entry into immediate reaches above the land, such as low and invasive drone flyovers, or into subsurface areas beneath the land, such as mining or tunneling beneath adjacent lands if the surface owner also owns the subsurface rights.

The law **presumes trespass damages** even if no physical harm to the land occurs. In those cases, the interference with exclusive possession is the damage. In egregious cases, such as when a wrongdoer trespasses to cut and steal timber from the land, law may authorize **punitive damages**. On the other hand, where the interference is only intangible, such as from smoke, vapor, smells, noise, or light, the tort of **nuisance** (addressed in another section well below) is the better theory. Trespass from smoke particles only may require proof of actual damage.

Tort Law

... and [trespass to] chattels and conversion

Trespass to chattels is **intentional impairment of personal property**. A chattel is simply personal property like a motor vehicle or computer rather than real property (land). As the word *impairment* indicates, trespass to chattels is not outright theft or destruction of the personal property but instead some temporary deprivation of the personal property before its return or some partial damage to it that the owner can repair. For instance, to take another's motor vehicle for a joyride without consent, emptying its gas tank and perhaps burning up its tires and even leaving a few dents, would be trespass to chattels. Yet the *impairment* element means that the claimant **must prove some harm** to the personal property. Someone who got in another's motor vehicle simply to back it up a few feet so that it did not block a driveway would not have committed trespass to chattels. The law compensates trespass to chattels for the reduction in the chattel's value or for loss of the chattel's use.

The closely related tort of **conversion** involves **intentional dominion over personal property substantially or totally interfering with the owner's control**. When you think of *conversion,* think of the civil-justice-system remedy for the crimes of *theft* or *robbery.* Note the difference between trespass to chattels and conversion. Conversion involves substantial deprivation or destruction, whereas trespass to chattels involves only temporary deprivation or partial reduction in value. Thus, while joyriding without consent in another's vehicle would only be trespass to chattels, destroying the vehicle in the course of joyriding, or outright stealing the vehicle, would instead be conversion. The law compensates conversion for the chattel's value at conversion. The owner must prove that value (must prove damages). Interestingly, the converted property's owner may recover not only from the original converter (the thief) but also from subsequent holders whether those holders take in either good or bad faith. While the rule may seem unfair to buyers, it simply means *don't buy from thieves* but only from reputable sellers. The owner may, of course, only make one recovery, not a double recovery.

B. Defenses to claims for physical harms

Plaintiffs have the burden to plead, produce evidence of, and prove the claims that they raise. Defendants on the other hand have the burden of pleading, producing evidence of, and proving affirmative defenses. Consider the following defenses to the personal-injury intentional-tort claims of assault, battery, and false-imprisonment.

1. Consent

Consent is a defense to an intentional tort. Take assault as an example. One might consent to have another scare one, such as in a holiday

Tort Law

haunted house. One could also consent to what would otherwise be a battery, such as by stepping into a boxing ring. One could even consent to what would otherwise be false imprisonment, such as to allow a magician in a magic act lock one in a box for a few moments. We usually express consent by words but may also do so by **communicative acts** like affirmative nods of the head or removing one's coat and rolling up one's sleeve to consent to an inoculation.

Importantly, the law determines consent from an **objective standpoint** rather than subjective standpoint, meaning what a reasonable person would have concluded from the words and circumstances. Saying yes but meaning no won't generally work, particularly if the reasonable person would have construed yes to mean yes. To consent, though, a person must understand the authorized conduct and its risks. To say yes to a surgical procedure without reasonable information as to what means and risks the surgery entails may not be to give informed consent.

A person who needs the assistance of another may not be able to give required consent. Thus, parents may ordinarily give **substituted consent** to treat their children, while guardians may give substituted consent to treat the comatose or mentally incompetent. **Emergency medical-care providers** may nonetheless treat those who are unable to give or withhold consent, but only if the reasonable person would have consented to the emergency treatment and guardians are not known or available to give substituted consent. Care providers properly seek court orders for a guardian to provide consent, when time allows the care providers to do so. Consent to an illegal act, such as sex with an underage minor, is invalid. Consent obtained by fraud or duress is also invalid.

2. Privileges and immunities: protection of self and others...

The examiners misplace in part their use above of the phrase *privileges and immunities*. The law generally reserves those words for rights based on the alleged wrongdoer's status or relationship to the claimant, like the employer who has a qualified, good-faith privilege to share information about a former employee, or an agent who has governmental immunity. Here instead, the list that follows the *privileges-and-immunities* topic begins with other traditional *affirmative defenses* much like the consent defense that precedes it.

Self-defense authorizes one to use reasonable force to prevent one's own physical injury. The **force must be reasonable** with respect to the threat, not excessive. The greater is the threat, the greater the force one may use in self-defense, up to and including deadly force in defense of deadly threat. If one uses more force in self-defense than appears reasonably necessary, then self-defense becomes battery. The question, though, is the amount of force that *appears* necessary, not the force that is *actually* necessary. A person who is **reasonably mistaken** about the circumstances, such as when an apparent assailant raises an apparent gun as if to shoot, retains the defense even when the circumstances turn out otherwise. The

Tort Law

mistake, though, must be reasonable. If the reasonable person would have recognized that the seeming assailant was instead a friend or the seeming gun was a toy, then the one who acts otherwise has no right of self-defense.

Unless modified by stand-your-ground statute, the law generally requires retreat before using force likely to cause serious injury or death, in self-defense. One may not, though, have to retreat from one's own home, jurisdictions instead holding that retreat is only necessary *to the wall*. Also, the right of self-defense ends when the threat ends. Self-defense does not authorize retaliation when the threat no longer exists. Provocation plays no role in tort-law self-defense, unlike the criminal law, where provocation may reduce the seriousness of an offense. A person has a right of self-defense only when facing an imminent physical threat, not when provoked, insulted, or offended.

Similar rules apply to **defense of others**. One may defend others using reasonable force. Again, the force must be adjusted to the threat. Excessive force in defense of others becomes battery. The rule for defense of others, though, departs in many jurisdictions from the rule for self-defense, on the **question of mistake**. In those jurisdictions, the defender of others only has the defense if the one whom the defender defends also has the defense. In other words, in many jurisdictions, the defender's mistake as to whether the other needed defense, whether a reasonable mistake or not, destroys the defense-of-others defense. If the defended person knew that the person did not need defense, as for instance if that person was only play-acting with another, then the person intervening has no such defense. The rule in those jurisdictions thus becomes to defend one's self whenever defense is reasonably apparent but to intervene in defense of others only when sure of the need. A question addressed to defense of others and implicating a reasonable mistake would most likely need to alert you to which rule to apply.

...protection of property interests...

One may also use reasonable force to **defend property**. One big distinction, though, between self-defense and defense of property is that with defense of property, **one must not use force likely to cause death or serious injury**. For instance, a shopkeeper could block and passively restrain a shoplifter at the store's exit to recover stolen property. Yet the shopkeeper would have no authority to shoot a shoplifter or likely even to tackle the shoplifter violently and place in a choke hold, to prevent the theft. A second big distinction is that with defense of property, one generally has no room within the defense to make a **mistake** as to who took the property or what right they had to do so. If a property owner intends to block, restrain, or otherwise use force against a person to protect the property, then the owner had better not be mistaken as to the person or their right. In this case, mistake negates the right of defense of property.

On the other hand, the law around a **shopkeeper's right to protect against shoplifting** varies. The law often accords shopkeepers a limited right to make reasonable investigation of a person whom the shopkeeper

Tort Law

reasonably suspects of shoplifting. Where that right of the defense of property exists, the law limits the right to **fresh pursuit** of the person **on or about the shopkeeper's premises**. If the person makes it off the premises with the property, then the shopkeeper's recourse is with the police and courts. The shopkeeper must not restrain the person off the premises or sometime later in an effort to recover the property. Another limitation on the shopkeeper's defense of property is that the shopkeeper must make a demand before using reasonable force to protect the property, unless demand would be futile.

The law allows repossession of personal property from the land of another only without force (**without breach of the peace**) and only by contractual agreement or summary court proceedings. Repossession agents must not use force in recovering repossessed property, although they may use reasonable force in self-defense when threatened with physical injury.

... parental discipline...

Parental discipline can be another defense against assault, battery, and false imprisonment. The right of parental discipline can depend on factors including the child's age, sex, and sensitivity, the reprehensibility of the child's act, the discipline's probability of increasing the child's obedience, and the injurious nature of the discipline. A person who temporarily acts for parents may benefit from the discipline defense. Discipline, as with self-defense and defense of others, must be reasonable.

While the Multistate Bar Examination topics list names only **parental discipline,** other relationships may permit discipline including teachers as to students (often depending on corporal-punishment statutes permitting, limiting, or prohibiting teacher/student physical discipline), military superiors as to subordinates, and ship captain as to crew or even passengers. Authority of law, such as for a police officer to make an arrest or a psychiatric-care facility to confine a suicidal patient, is a related policy defense against false-imprisonment claims that the topics list does not name.

... protection of public interests; necessity; incomplete privilege

Public necessity is a complete defense to a trespass, conversion, or other property-damage claim. Public necessity arises when public health, safety, security, or welfare requires public action destroying or harming private interests. If for instance public officials must destroy one private home in the path of an inferno to save many other homes, or one infected private poultry flock to prevent the infection of many other flocks, then those officials have the right to do so without trespass, conversion, or other tort liability.

On the other hand, **private necessity** is only an incomplete defense or privilege. Private necessity involves the right of a private person, rather than a public official, to protect that person's own private interests, rather

Tort Law

than the public interest. The private person, though, must pay for any harm caused in exercising the private-necessity privilege. If for instance a private livestock owner must turn his herd into a neighbor's crop to save the herd from flood drowning, then the owner may do so, but the owner must pay the neighbor for damage to the crop.

II.   Negligence

The elements of a negligence claim are **duty, breach, causation**, and **damages**. All four elements must be present for the claimant to have a claim. Tort law does not, for instance, presume damages for negligence claims. The claimant must show evidence of damages. Similarly, just because the claimant can show both the defendant's duty and breach of duty on the one hand and damages on the other hand does not satisfy a negligence claim. The claimant must also connect the defendant's fault with the claimant's damages by proving the element of causation. You can see, then, that while negligence questions comprise approximately half of the Multistate Bar Examination's tort-law questions, those negligence questions may address any of the four elements. Consider each element in turn.

A. The duty question...

A duty to others generally arises whenever a person **acts in a way that creates a foreseeable risk of harm**. Most negligence claims begin with the defendant engaging in an affirmative activity that creates a foreseeable risk of harm. Affirmative actions like driving a motor vehicle, hunting game, making and serving food, or manufacturing and selling a product each carry risks of harm. Thus, whenever engaging in those activities, one owes a duty to those whom the activity might foreseeably harm. Driving can harm passengers, other motorists, and pedestrians, not to mention vehicles and structures along the highways. Hunting can harm other hunters or outdoor enthusiasts. Cooking can harm those who eat the food or the kitchen and building the cooking sets afire. The actors owe a duty to those others.

If you cannot identify the risk-creating action within a fact pattern, then you probably have a duty question. Judges, not juries, typically decide whether the law imposes a duty on the defendant, unless the parties dispute facts material to the duty question, like whether the defendant or someone else was in fact driving the car.

...including failure to act...

Generally, tort law imposes **no duty to act**. Tort law is a law of liberty. Tort law does not generally require that you act. Tort law does not require that you drive, hunt, fix food, or make and sell products. Instead, tort law generally imposes a duty only when you decide to act and do so in ways that create foreseeable risks of harm.

Tort Law

For example, one generally does **not have a tort-law duty to come to another's aid or rescue**. Tort law does not require a person to stop along the highway to aid a stranded motorist. For another example, professionals do not generally owe a tort-law duty to volunteer their skills to aid others. Tort law would not require an off-duty doctor enjoying a meal at a restaurant to aid a nearby choking or heart-attack victim, although tort law clearly would require a doctor on duty at an emergency room to do so. If a professional does volunteer aid, then Good Samaritan statutes may protect them, holding them liable only for gross negligence or adjusting the standard of care to the emergency.

The no-duty-to-act rule, though, has several significant exceptions. One exception arises when a person **assumes a duty** where one would not otherwise exist. If someone shouts to call 911 because of emergency, and you say that indeed you will promptly do so, then you must do so or expect liability for any injury that others suffer in reliance on your volunteering. Another exception is when a person **controls the instrumentality** from which another will suffer injury. If your motor vehicle, train, boat, or escalator is about to hurt someone, even if through no fault of your own, and you have the means to prevent it, then you must do so.

Tort law may also impose duties to act within certain **special relationships**. If fire or flood are threatening another person, then you would ordinarily have no duty to act, unless you were that other person's caretaker, guardian, bodyguard, supervisor, or jailer. Indeed, tort law also has an exception to the rule that one has no duty to rescue, for instances where the defendant created the need for rescue. If a driver crashes a motor vehicle into another motor vehicle, then the driver would have a duty to come to the aid or rescue of the other vehicle's injured occupants.

One last exception to the no-duty-to-act rule bears special consideration. Contracts can also impose duties. If an apartment building hires security-guard and snow-removal services, then you might think that the security and snow-removal companies would owe duties to the buildings tenants and their guests. The contract-based duty in tort, though, arises only when the contract promisor performs at least in part (what the law calls **misfeasance**), not when the promisor fails to show up at all (**nonfeasance**). Sure, sue the security or snow-removal companies if they show up and do a poor job, causing your client's injury. Yet don't sue them if they never show up. Sue the building owner instead, who very likely retains a duty for engaging in the affirmative activity of operating an apartment building.

...unforeseeable plaintiffs...

The above introduction to duty indicates that generally, one owes a duty as to those whom one's actions create a foreseeable risk of harm. Sometimes, though, the harm-inducing occurrence is just unpredictable enough to make the person who suffered harmed **unforeseeable**. *Palsgraf* is the representative case in which a conductor negligently pushing a passenger onto a train led to dropped fireworks the explosion from which knocked a

Tort Law

scale over onto a woman some distance away. Some jurisdictions evaluate the unforeseeable-plaintiff question under proximate cause, discussed in that section below. In those jurisdictions, the defendant is liable even if they could not have predicted harm to that person, if the harm is nonetheless the direct, natural, and probable result of the negligent action. Other jurisdictions take a narrower view holding that the defendant owes a duty only to persons who suffer foreseeable harm. In the former case of a proximate-cause analysis, the law relies on hindsight but in the latter case of foreseeable harm on foresight.

The foreseeability-of-harm question also arises in the special case of professional service. Professionals generally owe duties **only to their own clients or patients**, not to third parties. For example, while a physician who diagnoses a patient's venereal disease would owe a duty to tell the patient, the physician would not owe a duty to tell the patient's sexual partners. Tort law would ordinarily leave that duty to the patient, respecting the need for physician-patient confidentiality.

Mental-health providers, though, may owe duties to **warn foreseeable victims** when patients threaten imminent violence. A medical-care provider having charge of a suicidal person may also owe a duty to discourage and avoid that person's suicide. Also, if the professional's service is **for a third party's direct benefit**, then the professional may owe duties to those direct beneficiaries. A lawyer who prepares a will for a client, who intends the will to benefit specific persons or entities, may later be liable to those persons or entities when the client dies, if the lawyer's poor service instead benefits others.

The foreseeability-of-harm question also arises in the case of **rescues**. The rule here is that anyone whose negligence causes the need for rescue owes a duty to those who suffer harm in rescuing. For instance, if a negligent driver causes an accident, and then another motorist strikes a volunteer who had stopped to help at the scene, then the original negligent driver is liable for the volunteer's injury. Danger invites rescue. Rescuers are foreseeable and so within the defendant's duty. In many states, though, the **professional rescuer** (one paid to aid) has no claim.

Accidents involving **unborn children** (injury to a pregnant woman that also injures the unborn child) raise another unforeseeable-plaintiff question. For instance, if a driver's negligence injures a pregnant woman while also injuring her unborn child, then must the driver pay for the unborn child's harm? States vary in their treatment of claims for injuries to children in utero. Some states only allow prenatal-harm claims if the child is **born alive**. Other states recognize claims for children who die in utero if the child was **viable** at the time of injury. The law does not generally allow claims against the mother whose negligence caused her own child in-utero harm, for example by smoking, drinking alcohol, or using illicit drugs.

Unique duty issues also arise around physicians who offer or provide sterilization or abortion procedures to parents. Some states recognize the parents' claim for **wrongful conception** if the physician does not properly perform sterilization, resulting in an unwanted pregnancy, although those

Tort Law

states typically limit the parents' recovery to the cost of pregnancy and delivery rather than requiring the physician to pay for rearing the child. Some states also recognize the parents' claim for **wrongful birth** when a physician or laboratory carelessly fails to inform the parents that their unborn child has identifiable genetic profiles on which the parents would have aborted the child. Again, those states would typically limit the parents' recovery to only the extraordinary expenses associated with the undisclosed genetic condition. States do *not* recognize **wrongful-life** claims by the child carrying the genetic condition. The medical-care providers would not have caused the condition, instead having only prevented the parents from ending the child's life in utero.

...and obligations to control the conduct of third parties

Duties can extend beyond controlling one's own conduct to influencing the conduct of others. The question arises when criminal conduct harms a person who stands in some relationship to another who may have been able to discourage or prevent the crime. For instance, shopkeepers generally **do not owe a duty to prevent crime**. However, a shopkeeper who advertises or provides security may be held to have **voluntarily assumed a duty**, particularly when the shopkeeper knows of prior crimes. Managers of apartments, dormitories, hotels, and other places of public accommodation may similarly owe duties to maintain locks, lights, and other security functions discouraging crime. The frequency and severity of foreseeable crime, and the availability of customary means to protect it, may influence whether duties arise on the part of others to discourage or prevent crime. Tort law also analyzes the question of one's responsibility for the harmful effects of others' crime under the issue of proximate cause.

B. The standard of care

Determining that one has a duty is only a first step toward evaluating negligence liability. Concluding that a duty exists does not yet say what the duty exactly is. Tort law addresses the specific contours of a person's duty as a question of the **standard of care**. As you articulate a potential standard of care, you begin to focus the broad duty on the particular conduct that led to the claimant's injury. The standard of care thus bridges negligence's first element **duty** and second element **breach**. Once you determine the standard of care, you should have a clear idea of whether the defendant breached the defendant's duty.

Do not underestimate the breadth, subtlety, and significance of standards of care. They form the conceptual heart and soul of negligence practice. To evaluate a negligence question, you must often be able to articulate probable standards of care quickly and sensitively. Most of us know a motor-vehicle driver's standards of care because most of us are frequent drivers. Those standards can include maintaining a reasonably safe speed, keeping a reasonably sharp lookout, obeying traffic lights and signs, and keeping an assured clear distance ahead, among dozens of other similar

Tort Law

driver standards. Your challenge is much greater when projecting probable standards for activities in which you may not frequently engage, like designing or constructing a bridge or building. Multistate Bar Examination fact patterns, though, should make clear enough to you when an actor has done something that falls outside of the probable standard of care. Watch carefully for adjectives, adverbs, and other hints of unusually risky or aberrant conduct.

1. The reasonably prudent person...

At the highest, most-general standard-of-care level, one's duty is to use **reasonable care,** also characterized as the duty of a **reasonably prudent person**. The reasonableness standard of care means that the standard is **objective** rather than subjective. The question is not what the defendant would have done, what someone with the defendant's character and experience would have done, or what any other single person would have done, but instead what the (theoretical) ordinarily prudent person would have done under the same circumstances. The concept of **care** is simply to regard others as one would regard one's self, much like the Golden Rule or, if you prefer, Kant's categorical imperative.

The standard of care, though objective rather than subjective, focuses on the specific accident circumstances. Thus, the standard of care for a motor-vehicle driver allegedly causing an accident is not what *any* reasonable person would have done but instead what the **reasonably prudent driver** would have done under those circumstances. The standard of care for a store owner allegedly contributing to a slip and fall is what the **reasonably prudent store owner** would have done under those circumstances, and so on.

In the same way, the weather, daylight or dark, traffic, and other conditions also focus the standard of care to what the reasonably prudent person would have done **under those circumstances. Emergencies not of the actor's own making** also alter the standard of care. For instance, if a property manager faces a sudden flood not due to the manager's own fault, then the manager need only act as a reasonably prudent manager would act **in that emergency** to protect affected tenants. On the other hand, if the manager carelessly caused the flood, then the manager would not be able to point to the emergency to excuse the manager from caring adequately for affected tenants and their personal property.

Learned Hand's formula, although generally not capable of precise application, can nonetheless inform judgments of what conduct the standard of care should require. The Hand formula provides that liability should exist when the burden of the precautions necessary to avoid the harm is less than the probability of loss in the absence of those precautions times the magnitude (severity) of that loss. For instance, if adding a five-dollar pressure-escape valve could prevent a boiler from exploding, and boilers explode frequently without the valve, causing catastrophic loss, then the Hand formula (and common sense) would suggest adding the valve and holding liable the one who doesn't.

Tort Law

...including children...

Children sometimes cause harm, leading to the question of the standard of care for their negligence liability. Children generally owe the care that we expect of **reasonably prudent children of like age and experience**. Very young children are generally not capable of negligence because they cannot yet appreciate objective (community) judgments of reasonable safety. Some jurisdictions favor a Rule of Sevens that children under seven are incapable of negligence, children seven to fourteen owe the care of a reasonably prudent child of that age, and children over fourteen owe the care of an adult reasonably prudent person. However, tort law is consistent that children who engage in **adult activities**, such as driving a car, shooting a gun, or operating motorized mechanical equipment, owe the standard of care of an adult reasonably prudent person, no matter the child's young age.

...physically and mentally impaired individuals...

Physically or mentally impaired individuals also sometimes cause harm, leading to the question of standard of care for their negligence liability. Tort law is clear that in determining the standard of care, the reasonably prudent person **assumes the actor's physical characteristics**. For instance, if the person who caused another's injury was too short to see over an obstacle and too weak to remove it, then the standard of care will not require that they have been tall and strong. On the other hand, the reasonably prudent person **does not assume the actor's mental characteristics**. If a motor-vehicle driver was young and inexperienced, or even psychotic, then tort law holds them to the standard of care of a reasonably prudent driver without regard to youth, inexperience, or psychosis. An exception exists that if a person has **superior knowledge**, then they must generally use it. For instance, an expert mechanic who carelessly disregards the wisdom of his expertise, causing another's injury in doing so, cannot defend based on a reasonably prudent person not being so expert.

...professional people, and other special classes

Tort law identifies as **malpractice** or **professional negligence**, claims against professionals who provide service to patients or clients based on a **specialized body of knowledge**. Professionals who breach the standard of care causing injury are liable in tort for malpractice, not in breach of contract, unless they promise (guarantee) a specific result. Because malpractice is simply a special form of negligence claim, one against a professional, malpractice claims require proof of the same four elements duty, breach, causation, and damages.

Malpractice claims, though, evaluate professional conduct under a different standard of care that refers to the **custom** or **customary practice** in the professional's field rather than to the reasonably prudent person. Jurors

Tort Law

generally do not have the specialized knowledge of a professional on which to judge a professional's performance. Thus the custom of other competent professionals determines the professional's standard of care. For example, medical malpractice includes **failure to obtain the patient's informed consent** to a risk that the custom required disclosing, about which a reasonable patient would have wanted to know, and to which the patient would not have consented if the patient had known. Medical-care providers must also disclose **conflicts of interest** that may affect their judgment and about which the reasonable patient would want to know. A medical-care provider's failure to obtain any consent at all may be **battery** in addition to malpractice.

2. Rules of conduct derived from statutes and custom

Specific standards of care vary widely from activity to activity depending on factors like the custom, safety statutes, safety regulations, and industry standards. **Custom**, though not determinative, influences the specific standard of care. For example, if all carpenters follow certain customs in erecting a stud wall, then the carpenter who follows those customs has probably satisfied the negligence standard of care, even if the wall falls. On the other hand, a custom can in itself fail to meet the standard of care, if the reasonably prudent person would have done differently. Carpenters may too often be taking unsafe shortcuts in their customs. Jurors may draw an inference of breach from a defendant's failure to follow custom, although jurors need not do so.

Safety statutes also influence the standard of care, in some states more powerfully than custom. Not all statutes are safety statutes. A safety statute is one that protects a specific **class** against a specific **risk**. For example, a traffic-code provision not to follow another vehicle too closely protects the class of motorists against a rear-end-collision risk, and so is obviously a safety statute. Yet a statute requiring motor-vehicle registration has more to do with identifying vehicle ownership and raising road-repair revenue than with safety because one cannot easily articulate a protected class or discouraged risk.

Most states treat violation of a safety statute as **negligence per se**, meaning that the defendant is negligent unless able to come forward with a special excuse, like the ambulance driver who excuses speeding for having rushed to the scene of an accident. Other states, though, draw only a presumption or inference of negligence from a safety-statute violation. A **presumption** requires the defendant to produce at least some evidence of non-negligence, like the driver who, while admitting speeding, testifies that everyone else was also speeding making it safer to speed than not (not the best defense but perhaps a plausible one). An **inference** means that the defendant need produce no evidence of non-negligence, leaving the jury to decide whether to find the defendant negligent or not from the safety-statute violation.

Tort Law

Government regulations, when protecting a specific class against a specific safety risk, can also influence the standard of care, although only to the extent of allowing a jury inference for their violation, not a presumption or negligence per se. Violation of **industry standards** may also give rise to an inference of negligence. If shower-door manufacturers publish standards to use only tempered, shatter-resistant glass, then the manufacturer failing to do so and causing injury as a result has likely been negligent.

C. Problems relating to proof of fault, including res ipsa loquitur

Determining whether a duty exists and, if so, what is the appropriate standard of care, are preludes to proving **breach** of the standard of care, a negligence claim's second element. The negligence plaintiff has the **burdens of pleading** breach, **producing evidence** of breach, and **proving** breach by a preponderance of the evidence. While pleading involves stating the claim in the complaint that the plaintiff files with the court, the plaintiff typically satisfies the latter two burdens of production and proof by offering **direct or circumstantial evidence** of the injury-causing behavior. For example, once the plaintiff testifies to the defendant driver's excessive speed, and then offers an expert opinion on excessive speed based on skid marks, the jury may infer the defendant's breach from that direct and circumstantial evidence.

In special cases, though, the plaintiff may satisfy the plaintiff's burdens by other means, when neither direct nor circumstantial evidence of breach is available to the plaintiff. **Res ipsa loquitur** permits an inference of negligence on the three conditions that (1) the injury-causing event speaks of negligence, (2) plaintiff cannot obtain negligence evidence, and (3) defendant had exclusive control of the circumstances. Res ipsa loquitur thus accounts implicitly for the possibility that the defendant may be concealing negligence evidence. If the plaintiff can alternatively show that the defendant in fact concealed, secreted, or destroyed evidence, misconduct that the law calls **spoliation**, then the law grants the plaintiff a presumption that the evidence would have been adverse to the defendant.

Proving a professional's breach of duty raises another special problem. Because malpractice claims generally require the plaintiff to show that the defendant departed from the customary practice within the defendant's field, establishing the professional's standard of care generally requires the testimony of a **similarly qualified expert**. The law may require an expert testifying in a malpractice case to show knowledge of the customary practice in the **same or similar geographic locale**. Other states apply only a **national standard** rather than local standard. All jurisdictions apply a national standard as to defendant **specialists** who qualify for specialty practice by satisfying national board standards. Only in the rare case of obvious breach, like a surgeon mistakenly leaving a surgical tool inside the patient, would the law not require expert testimony.

D. Problems relating to causation

Tort Law

Causation is the third of the four negligence elements, after duty and breach but before damages. Causation, like duty, is a ripe area for examination because of the subtlety and complexity of causation rules. Causation requires the plaintiff to show *both* a logical or scientific connection between the defendant's breach and plaintiff's damages *and* that the connection is sufficiently close for the law to justly hold the defendant liable as a matter of sound public policy. **Cause in fact** is the logical or scientific connection treated in this section, while **proximate or legal cause** is the policy question of sufficient closeness treated in a latter section.

1. But for and substantial causes

The most-common and easiest test for cause in fact requires the plaintiff to show that **but for** the defendant's breach, the plaintiff's injury would not have happened. Notice the logical connection again: **if not for** the defendant's breach, the plaintiff's injury would not have happened. In positive terms, cause in fact requires the plaintiff to show that the plaintiff's injury **depended on** the defendant's carelessness. Tort law is instrumental in its design, intending to discourage wrongdoing. Making a defendant pay for harm the defendant causes is that deterrent, while making a defendant pay for harm that the defendant did *not* logically cause would be no deterrent.

Cause in fact on medical, legal, technical, and scientific matters may require expert testimony based on valid and reliable scientific methods. Causation in malpractice cases ordinarily requires expert testimony as to what would have happened if the defendant had complied with the standard of care. In lawyer malpractice, the plaintiff proves what would have happened in the underlying case if the defendant had not committed malpractice.

2. Harms traceable to multiple causes

But-for causation does not require that the defendant's carelessness must be the *only* cause of harm. The plaintiff's harm may have resulted from combined events and circumstances, only one of which was the defendant's carelessness. Causation still exists in those instances, as long as the defendant's carelessness was more than a trivial contributing factor and was instead **substantial** in bringing about the harm. For example, you may carelessly fail to set your alarm, making you late on the road, one dependent result of which may be that your vehicle just happens to be lawfully passing through an intersection when another motorist runs a red light. A reasonable mind would not call your prior negligence in failing to set your alarm, though logically necessary to the ensuing collision, a substantial factor in bringing it about.

Events, though, present rare instances where two negligent causes act independently, each to cause the same single harm. For instance, such would be the case if two hunters both shoot what they carelessly imagine to be a deer but is instead the plaintiff's prized horse, and either hunter's bullet would

Tort Law

have caused the horse's death. In those rare instances, neither actor's negligence satisfies cause in fact's but-for test. Remove either negligent act, and the other negligent act would still have caused the single harm. Courts here apply a **substantial-factor test** holding *both* actors liable, even though neither actor's negligence was a but-for cause, as long as one can say that each cause was nonetheless substantial in bringing about the harm.

A slightly different anomaly arises when two actors each act negligently, only one of their actions causes the injury, but the plaintiff is unable to distinguish which actor was the cause because of the similarity of their negligent actions. Consider the same example except that this time one hunter's bullet misses while the other hunter's bullet hits, with investigation unable to determine which. When the plaintiff cannot determine which of two negligent actors' similar actions brought about the harm, the law may shift to defendants the burden of **disproving** causation.

3. Questions of apportionment of responsibility among multiple tortfeasors...

Negligence claims often involve **multiple defendants**. A first problem with apportioning responsibility among multiple defendants arises when a plaintiff **settles** with one defendant but not with other defendants. When parties settle a tort claim, the plaintiff typically signs an agreement **releasing** the defendant from further liability, while preserving rights against non-settling defendants. While modern states follow the parties' intent as the settlement agreement expresses it, some states retain a traditional rule that to release one defendant is to release all defendants. Some of those traditional jurisdictions nonetheless permit a plaintiff to **covenant not to sue** the settling defendant, thus preserving claims against non-settling defendants. Other jurisdictions require that the plaintiff **expressly reserve claims** against non-settling defendants, failing which the plaintiff releases all defendants, settling or not. Many jurisdictions also hold that to release an agent is to release the principal who retains and directs the agent. Courts ordinarily set aside releases only for fraud, duress, undue influence, or mutual mistake, although some states have rush-release statutes permitting a regretful plaintiff to return the settlement and reopen the claim within a defined period.

After the question of release, a second question having to do with settlements against fewer than all defendants has to do with whether and how to **credit** a non-settling defendant with a settling defendant's payment. The law entitles plaintiffs to only a **single satisfaction** of their damages even when a plaintiff is able to name multiple responsible defendants. Adding a second or third or fourth defendant does not double, triple, or quadruple the plaintiff's recoverable damages. Thus, if one defendant pays a plaintiff's entire damage claim, then other defendants should have nothing left to pay. The **partial-satisfaction rule** is corollary to the single-satisfaction rule in that non-settling defendants who share in a settling defendant's liability get credit for partial amounts the settling defendant pays. Thus, if the settling defendant

Tort Law

pays only half of plaintiff's damage claim, then non-settling defendants would get credit for that payment, leaving only the other half remaining.

...including joint and several liability

The traditional rule of **joint-and-several liability** means that the plaintiff may collect all or some of the damages from any liable defendant at the plaintiff's election. Thus, if the jury awards the plaintiff $100,000 jointly and severally against three defendants, the plaintiff may collect all $100,000 from any one of them or any portion less than that amount from any of them, for instance, $50,000 from one and $25,000 from each of the other two.

In that respect, joint-and-several liability may appear to give the plaintiff too much power to pursue deep pockets and give the defendants too little opportunity to ensure their relative fair treatment. The law addresses that unfairness in part through contribution actions. **Contribution** is a defendant's claim that another party, typically a cross-claim defendant whom the plaintiff has already joined but sometimes also a third-party defendant whom the defendant joins in the action, should pay a fair share of the damage for which the defendant is liable. Significantly, a defendant who settles in good faith no longer has contribution liability to remaining, non-settling defendants.

When, though, does joint-and-several liability arise? Joint-and-several liability can arise from **concerted action** of two or more tortfeasors who, in effect, work carelessly together. Perhaps three engineers negligently design a building, or four tradespersons negligently construct it. The engineers would have joint-and-several liability among them, just as would the tradespersons. Joint-and-several liability may also arise from two independent tortfeasors causing an **indivisible injury**. If two motor-vehicle drivers each run a stop sign negligently colliding in the intersection with one another, and in doing so cause a single injury to a pedestrian or passenger, then the drivers share joint-and-several liability even though having acted independently of one another.

Joint-and-several liability may also arise from **failures in a common duty**. For example, an apartment-complex owner may hire a manager who hires a snow-removal service. The owner, manager, and snow-removal service may then all owe a common duty to the tenant to keep the walkways reasonably clear of snow and ice. If the snow-removal company clears the walks carelessly, resulting in the tenant's slip-and-fall injury, then the owner, manager, and service may share joint-and-several liability to the tenant.

The example just given of one defendant potentially paying for another defendant's contractual or managerial responsibility suggests another possible unfairness to joint-and-several liability like the unfairness that arises when the plaintiff collects all or too much from one defendant to the unfair advantage of other liable defendants (the unfairness that contribution actions address). **Indemnity** addresses that unfairness. Indemnity is the common-law or contractual right of one defendant to reimbursement from another who had the primary responsibility to do that about which the plaintiff complains,

Tort Law

creating the defendant's liability in the first place. Thus, in the above example, the owner would have indemnity from the manager who would have indemnity from the snow-removal service. Indemnity effectively passes the liability on to the most-responsible party, assuming that parties have insurance or assets to pay the liability.

Most jurisdictions abolish or alter joint-and-several liability in one way or another. Many jurisdictions require the jury to allocate fault to each defendant, say, seventy-five percent to one defendant and twenty-five percent to the other. The judge then apportions damages seventy-five percent to one and twenty-five percent to the other, each paying only their apportioned share. Because changes to joint-and-several liability are mostly by statute, the Multistate Bar Examination's question would alert you to the statute. Contribution actions are neither necessary nor allowed where law allocates fault and apportions damages among defendants.

Be sure to distinguish joint-and-several liability, where multiple defendants contribute in a single event to the plaintiff's indivisible injury, from situations where a single plaintiff suffers **successive injuries**, at different times and in different places, due to the negligence of independently acting defendants. When the plaintiff suffers successive injuries, then the law separately apportions the damages for each separate injury to each successive defendant. For example, if the negligent driver of a car strikes and injures a pedestrian breaking the pedestrian's leg, and a week later the negligent driver of a bus strikes the same pedestrian breaking the pedestrian's arm, then the car driver pays only for the leg injury while the bus driver pays only for the arm.

Sometimes, though, medical-care providers and other witnesses are unable to entirely distinguish one successive injury from another. For example, if a car driver strikes a pedestrian injuring the pedestrian's neck, and a week later a bus driver strikes the same pedestrian again injuring the pedestrian's neck, one may be unable to distinguish which negligent driver caused what part of the pedestrian's injury. When a plaintiff is unable to prove which defendant caused which successive injury, the law may hold the first defendant liable only for the injury up to the moment of the second injury but then hold the second defendant liable for all of the subsequent injury, even if some of it involved an inseparable part due only to the first injury. The rule effectively shifts to the later defendant the burden to separate the injuries.

E. Limitations on liability and special rules of liability

To ensure the ratability and affordability of liability insurance, and also to promote public acceptance of the tort system, negligence law limits liability to a reasonable scope, through several special rules. The first section below addresses how negligence law uses the element of **proximate or legal cause** to limit liability to sufficiently close and foreseeable effects of negligence, cutting off liability for remote and unforeseeable harm. The next section addresses how certain extraordinary **superseding causes** can also cut off liability. The following section addresses how traditional negligence law

Tort Law

modifies the duties that **landowners** owe in **premises liability**, in ways that limit the class of persons whom landowners owe *reasonable care*. A following section then addresses how negligence law limits and discourages claims for pure **mental and emotional distress** when not accompanied by physical impact. Finally, this part on limits to negligence liability ends with the **economic-loss doctrine** barring claims for pure economic loss without accompanying physical impact to the claimant's property.

1. Problems relating to "remote" or "unforeseeable" causes, "legal" or "proximate" cause...

As introduced well above, **legal or proximate cause** involves the policy question of whether the defendant's breach was closely related enough to the plaintiff's injury to justly hold the defendant liable. Also as noted above, the plaintiff must show both cause in fact and proximate or legal cause. Because proximate cause is a policy question, judges have greater opportunity to decide proximate cause than to decide breach, damages, and other fact-dependent negligence issues reserved for the jury.

Proximate cause has two primary tests. The first test of proximate cause is the traditional **direct-sequence test**. The test simply asks whether events led in direct sequence from breach to damages. The direct-sequence test applies easily, and satisfies proximate cause more readily, when breach and damage are close in time and place, with few or no other events contributing. Motor-vehicle accidents are an example where the breach, like running a red light, usually connects immediately with the damage, a vehicle collision. Indeed, proximate cause is seldom an issue in motor-vehicle accidents. The direct-sequence test can satisfy proximate cause even in unpredictable accidents, if damage follows immediately from breach.

Some cases, though, involve greater time and distance between breach and damage, and more contributing circumstances and events. The traditional direct-sequence test often fails in these cases, even though the predictability of the harm might suggest that the court should find proximate cause. In those cases of remote connections, proximate cause offers an alternative modern **foreseeability test**. The foreseeability test asks whether the defendant could and should have foreseen that harm would eventually result from the negligent action. For example, a ship that carelessly discharges quantities of fuel oil on the surface of port waters might not expect immediate harm but should probably foresee that the fuel oil might soon float to dock or shore where it could cause fire, environmental, poisoning, or other damage. While some states prefer or recognize one test over the other, the two tests tend to work well each in their own class of cases as just described.

Spreading fires present a special proximate-cause problem. When a person carelessly starts an uncontrolled fire, the fire may do little or no harm at all, or it may cause catastrophic loss, with little predictability. The law has addressed and limited liability for spreading fires using adjoining-property, first-building, and other anomalous rules. Under these rules, the negligent fire-starter may pay only for minimal damage to the wild grasses in the

Tort Law

neighbor's vacant lot (under the adjoining-property rule), or for the destruction of a barn or shed several vacant properties away (under the first-building rule), or for harm at greater or lesser distances, depending on traditional direct-sequence or modern foreseeability rules.

...and "superseding" causes

Proximate-cause analysis offers a third test after its two main direct-sequence and modern foreseeability tests. Rather than examining the proximity of damages to breach, or the foreseeability of damages from breach, proximate cause's third test examines the **quality of intervening events** that contributed to the harm between the breach and damage. If those intervening events are natural, probable, ordinary, and foreseeable, then their presence does not affect proximate cause. If on the other hand those intervening events are unnatural, improbable, extraordinary, and unforeseeable, then the law will call them **superseding causes** and treat their presence as cutting off proximate cause from the prior negligence.

Intentional, criminal, and reckless acts are more likely to be superseding causes cutting off proximate cause as to prior negligence. On the other hand, intentional or criminal acts that are foreseeable to someone employed to prevent them, such as a security guard or locksmith, will not cut off proximate cause. Unpredictable and extraordinary forces of nature, such as earthquakes, tornadoes, or hundred-year floods, may cut off proximate cause as to prior negligence, but proximate cause remains where the force was foreseeable. Proximate cause has other special rules for special situations. An intoxicated person's voluntary drinking cuts off proximate cause as to the negligent server. So, for instance, the minor whom a bartender negligently (and illegally) serves has no cause of action against the bar if the minor goes out drunk driving and crashes. Yet dram-shop statutes in many states hold the bar liable to third persons injured because the bar served alcohol to a minor or visibly intoxicated person.

Do not confuse proximate cause evaluating the connection between breach and injury, with the issue of the foreseeability of injury consequences. Proximate cause operates to limit the scope of liability before injury (whether an actor should be liable or not) rather than to limit the scope or extent of damages after injury (for how much of the harm the actor should pay). Thus, an actor whose negligence creates a need for medical care is generally also liable for injury from that medical care. Injury from medical care, even malpractice, is predictable, but even if it were not predictable, proximate cause would not limit the damages. Similarly, the **eggshell-skull rule** requires defendant to pay for all foreseeable *and unforeseeable* harm if at least some harm was direct and foreseeable. The person whose careless kick sets off an unpredictable infection in the victim's leg, resulting in amputation, pays not just for the offense and bruise of the kick but also for the lost leg.

2. Claims against owners and occupiers of land

Tort Law

Claims against landowners for harm from unreasonably dangerous conditions of the land, known as **premises-liability claims**, are negligence claims. The claimant must prove duty, breach (including the standard of care), causation (both cause in fact and proximate cause), and damages. The difference with a premises-liability claim is in the duty element. Following the traditional common law, most states require classifying the plaintiff as an **invitee, licensee,** or **trespasser**. An invitee is one who enters the land for **pecuniary purposes** or accompanies another who does so. Shoppers at a retail store, and family members or friends who join them, are the classic invitees. A licensee is a **social guest** and others, like law-enforcement officers and canvassers, who enter for their own non-pecuniary purposes. Trespassers are those who enter the land without permission. A person's status can change from invitee to licensee to trespasser, as their activities and purposes on the land change, and depending on the scope of permission. The shopper who sneaks into a retail store's employees-only back storeroom becomes a trespasser.

The duty owed to each classification differs. Landowners owe **reasonable care**, the duty of a reasonably prudent landowner, to invitees. Thus, for invitees, premises liability does not change the usual negligence rules. Reasonable care may include the duty to design, construct, maintain, repair, warn, and protect against unreasonably dangerous conditions on the premises. A few states require reasonable care as to all entrants, but follow the traditional classifications unless the question directs otherwise. Landowners owe licensees the lesser duty to **warn of known hidden dangers**. Landowners owe trespassers **no duty**, although the law provides several exceptions. Landowners may owe a duty to reasonably warn or protect a trespasser against active operations and concealed artificial conditions, and when the landowner tolerates the intruder or discovers their peril. Landowners may also owe reasonable care to trespassing **children of tender years**, exposed to unreasonably dangerous **attractive nuisances** that the landowner should know draw children onto the land. The landowner must know of the children, know of the risk that draws them, know that the children are too young to appreciate the risk, be able to reduce or eliminate the risk, and yet no do so.

While landowners generally do not owe a duty to **protect against crime**, landowners may advertise and voluntarily assume those duties. Landowners may also owe those duties by special knowledge of frequent crime or special relationship to the visitor, as for example in the case of hotels, apartments, and daycares. Landowners may also owe limited duties to protect neighboring landowners and passersby from artificial or unreasonable dangers on the premises, like rotting trees that the landowner knows or should know may fall on adjacent lands, buildings, roads, and walkways. While the above rules refer to the duties of the *landowner,* the law assigns the duties to the one who **occupies and controls** the land, which may be a **tenant** rather than the owner. Yet landlords who retain control, contract to repair, repair negligently, or fail to disclose defects, may share the duty with the tenant or retain the sole duty.

Tort Law

3. Claims for mental distress not arising from physical harm; other intangible injuries

To avoid opening a floodgate of small and suspicious claims, negligence law discourages claims that involve no physical injury and instead only **mental or emotional distress**. When negligence causes physical injury, the injured person also recovers for mental and emotional distress. Yet when no physical harm occurs, the general rule is that no negligence claim exists solely for emotional distress. Several exceptions exist, the first for when one contemporaneously witnesses an **immediate family member's severe injury or death**, and as a result suffers severe mental or emotional distress. Some states require physical manifestation of the distress to ensure its legitimacy. Some states also permit recovery when a person suffers severe distress for having been in the **zone of danger** for serious physical injury, in a sort of *near-miss* case.

The common law also allows a pure-distress claim for negligent **mishandling of a corpse**, as when a hospital harvests organs without consent from a parent's child who has just died or a funeral home mistakenly cremates the wrong body. The common law also allows a pure-distress claim for negligent **transmission of death notices**, as when police mistakenly notify a person that a close relative, still living, has died. States may also recognize a pure-distress claim for **fear of illness**, such as when a hospital attendant or other medical-care provider negligently pricks a patient with a used needle, but courts tend to limit those cases only for severe distress and when the potential illness has an actual transmission route, confirming that the fear is reasonable.

4. Claims for pure economic loss

Negligence law is also concerned with keeping property-damage claims, not just emotional-distress claims, to a reasonable number and scope. Thus, the **economic-loss doctrine** limits property-damage, business-loss, and commercial-loss claims to cases involving a **physical impact** to the claimant's property. For example, when ships collide, trains derail, or trucks collide because of an operator's negligence, nearby or distant businesses that depended on the ship, train, or truck delivery, or the clear transportation route, can suffer related business losses. The economic-loss doctrine bars those economic-loss claims unless the claimant's own property had a direct physical impact, in which case the claimant could recover for the physical damage to the property plus the directly related business loss. When someone's negligence causes an accident, the negligent person pays losses only for those claimants whose property had a direct physical impact, not claimants who had only indirect business loss.

F. Liability for acts of others

Tort Law

Vicarious liability can hold one person or entity liable for the negligence of another in certain situations. For example, when two or more persons or entities form a **joint venture**, then each joint venturer shares vicarious liability for the negligent acts of the other in the course and scope of the joint venture. A joint venture arises when two or more share common purpose, agreement, pecuniary interest, and direction or control. So, for instance, if a joint venturer in a mining operation, driving a truck into town to get mining supplies, negligently injures a person, then the negligent joint venturer will have direct liability to the injured person while the other joint venturers will have vicarious liability to also pay for the injured person's harm.

Bailments are another special situation where vicarious or even direct liability can arise for the negligent act of another. A bailment involves one person holding the personal property of another, with the owner's consent, for a limited time. A valet-parking service involves a bailment, with the vehicle owner leaving the vehicle with the valet for a limited time. Ordinarily, the person granting the bailment has no liability if the one holding the property negligent injures someone with the property. Thus, the valet who negligently strikes and injures a pedestrian with the owner's vehicle must pay, while the vehicle owner ordinarily need not. However, **owner-responsibility statutes** commonly change the no-vicarious-liability-for-bailments rule, making vehicle owners vicariously liable for injury negligently caused by a person having their consent to use the vehicle.

When a person does *not* have vicarious liability, like in the case of an owner making a bailment (other than for motor vehicles), **negligent entrustment** can be an alternative theory for the owner's direct liability for the negligent acts of another. The owner who loans a rifle to a friend so that the friend can go hunting owes no liability if the friend negligently shoots someone. Yet if the owner loans the gun to someone the owner should know *not* to entrust the gun, like a child too young to handle the gun properly, then the owner may be liable under the negligent-entrustment theory.

1. Employees and other agents

Employers have vicarious liability for harm caused by the negligent acts of employees within the scope of employment. For example, **employer vicarious liability**, also called **respondeat-superior liability**, would arise when an employee driving a motor vehicle on a work errand negligently injures another. The employer would be vicariously liable even if the employer did not own the vehicle, as long as the employee was carrying out an employment activity. Note, though, commuting to and from work, and running personal errands, are *not* within the scope of employment, so that an employer would *not* have vicarious liability for injury that the negligent employee causes while commuting or on personal errands. Employers also generally have no vicarious liability for **intentional torts** unless the employee's intentional act furthered the employer's mission or the employer authorized or ratified the act. Thus, an employer would ordinarily not have

Tort Law

to pay if an employee suddenly beat up the employer's customer. Yet if the employer hired the employee to, say, eject unruly customers, as in the case of a bar bouncer, and the bouncer used too much force causing the customer's injury, then the employer would likely have vicarious liability.

Employers may also have direct liability for **negligent hiring**. For example, if an employer does a background check and finds that the hired job candidate has no criminal conviction or other history suggesting violent propensity, then the employer would likely not be liable if the employee suddenly beats up a customer. Yet if the employer negligently failed to do a background check or negligently disregarded the candidate's violent-crime convictions or other violent history, then the employer may be liable for negligent hiring if the employee continues that history by beating up a customer.

2. Independent contractors and non-delegable duties

Another form of vicarious liability involves a person or entity paying for the negligence of an **independent contractor**. The general rule is that those who hire independent contractors do *not* have vicarious liability for the contractor's negligent acts. The rule for independent contractors is thus the opposite of the rule for employees. Yet the no-vicarious-liability rule for independent contractors has several common exceptions, making it nearly as likely that you *will* find vicarious liability. One exception is where the one hiring the contractor **retains control** over the contractor, in effect telling the contractor how to do the job in a way that makes the hirer responsible for the contractor's negligence. A second exception is when the one hiring the contractor has nondelegable duties, like when an apartment manager hires a snow-removal service to clear the walks but still owes the tenant a lease duty. Another exception is when one hires a contractor to do an inherently dangerous activity, like using dynamite to demolish a building.

Vicarious-liability issues can also arise over whether one person carrying out another's mission for compensation is an employee, for whom the hirer has vicarious liability, or an independent contractor, where no vicarious liability exists unless you find one of the several exceptions. **Control** is the critical factor for employment. If the hirer tells the worker the time, provides the tools, and prescribes the methods to do the work, and has some process for hiring, firing, and discipline, then the worker is an employee. If on the other hand the person works independently without these factors present, then the worker is an independent contractor.

G. Defenses

While the plaintiff has the burdens of pleading the claim, producing evidence of it, and proving it at trial, the defendant has those same burdens on any affirmative defenses. The Multistate Bar Examination's topics list identifies just two negligence defenses, contributory or comparative negligence and assumption of risk, treated in the following two sections. The

Tort Law

list's exclusion of other defenses like the **statute of limitations, statutes of repose, intra-family immunity**, and **governmental immunity**, suggest that the exam may not test those defenses, perhaps because they often depend on statutes rather than the common law and vary widely from state to state. While you need not study these defenses in detail for the exam, a question could introduce a statute implicating one or another of these defenses.

1. Contributory fault, including common law contributory negligence and last clear chance...

Contributory negligence is the traditional common-law defense that **completely bars** the plaintiff from recovering if the plaintiff was at all at fault in causing the plaintiff's injury. The defendant might have been ninety percent at fault and the plaintiff only ten percent at fault in causing the plaintiff's injury, but the plaintiff would still recover nothing. Because of the defense's all-or-nothing harshness, only four states retain contributory negligence, while all other states have adopted some form of **comparative negligence**. Those states that do retain contributory negligence soften its harsh effect using the **last-clear-chance doctrine**. Under the doctrine, if the plaintiff's contributory negligence had ceased, leaving the plaintiff in a position vulnerable to injury, and the defendant had the last clear chance to avoid the injury by using reasonable care but was negligent in causing the injury nonetheless, then the plaintiff's contributory negligence will *not* bar the plaintiff's recovery.

...and the various forms of comparative negligence

Statutes or appellate decisions have replaced contributory negligence with **comparative negligence** in all but four states. Comparative negligence reduces the plaintiff's recovery by the **percentage of plaintiff's fault**. Thus, if the plaintiff is twenty percent at fault and the defendant eighty percent at fault, the plaintiff recovers eighty percent of the plaintiff's damages. Comparative negligence comes in pure and modified forms. The **pure form** in place in some states allows plaintiff to recover whatever percentage of damages is left after deducting for the plaintiff's comparative fault, even if plaintiff's fault far exceeds defendant's fault. By contrast, the **modified form** reduces the plaintiff's damages if the plaintiff's recovery is either **not greater than** defendant's fault (in some states) or **less than** defendant's fault (in other states), while otherwise barring the plaintiff's recovery completely. Thus, in a modified, not-greater-than jurisdiction, the plaintiff recovers defendant's percentage when plaintiff's fault is up to fifty percent, barring plaintiff from any recovery when plaintiff's fault is greater than fifty percent. In a modified, less-than jurisdiction, the plaintiff recovers defendant's percentage when plaintiff's fault is up to forty-nine percent, barring plaintiff from any recovery when plaintiff's fault is fifty percent or greater.

Because comparative negligence requires comparing plaintiff's fault to defendant's fault, states adopting comparative negligence typically require

Tort Law

allocation of fault among multiple defendants, abolish joint-and-several liability, and have no need for contribution actions. Comparative-negligence states also have no need for the last-clear-chance doctrine. Some states by statute allow the factfinder to allocate fault not just among defendants but also to non-parties, reducing the plaintiff's damages accordingly.

2. Assumption of risk

Assumption of risk is a second common negligence defense. A defendant has the defense when a plaintiff **voluntarily encounters a known risk**, accepting the risks hazards. The assumption-of-risk defense often applies when routine injuries occur during recreational activities that bear obvious hazards, like carnival rides or bungee jumping. One should not complain if a rollercoaster ride gives on vertigo or bungee jumping stresses one's ankles and neck.

The assumption-of-risk defense comes in two forms. **Express** assumption of risk involves statements or writings disclosing the risks that the plaintiff expressly acknowledges, often by signing the disclosure. **Implied** assumption of risk involves circumstances that make the risk apparent while also confirming the plaintiff's implicit acceptance of them. When service providers unfairly attempt to gain the service recipient's express acknowledgment of risks and waiver of liability for them, the law may void the waiver. Waivers in **adhesion contracts**, where the person needs an essential service like education or emergency medical care but must sign a liability waiver to get the service, may be void, as may liability waivers in between parties of **unequal bargaining power**.

III.   Strict liability and products liability:

Strict liability refers to liability without proof of intent or carelessness. Strict liability applies to certain **activities on land**, like impounding waters, storing dynamite, generating toxic waste, or keeping wild animals. With strict liability, if one conducts the activity, then one pays for any harm it causes, whether one intended the harm or not, and whether one was careless in failing to prevent it or instead took all care.

Products liability, on the other hand, involves liability for harm caused by the design, manufacture, distribution and **sale of products**. Although law sometimes refers to products liability as *strict* products liability, products liability differs from strict liability in that it requires proof of something more culpable than simply making or selling a product that causes harm. In that sense, products liability is *not* strict liability. Be sure to distinguish the two. See details about each in the following sections.

...common law strict liability...

A first form of common-law strict liability addresses the liability of one whose **animals** cause harm. The common law recognizes strict liability

Tort Law

when an owner keeps a **wild animal** that causes harm, even if the owner has taken all care to prevent the harm. Thus, if one keeps a wild animal, such as a lion, tiger, or bear, then one must pay for any harm it causes. Some jurisdictions make an exception for zoos, where one expects to encounter wild animals, such that the zoo would be liable for harm only on proof of the zoo's negligence.

The common law also recognizes strict liability for **grazing livestock** causing harm, for instance by invading and destroying another's crops. Strict-liability rules for grazing livestock can vary from region to region, some areas requiring farmers to **fence out** livestock while other areas requiring ranchers to **fence in** livestock.

The common law also provides strict liability when an owner keeps a **domesticated animal** that the owner **knows to have vicious propensities abnormal to its class**. Thus, under the common law, the owner of a dog that the owner believes to be friendly would *not* be strictly liable if the dog suddenly bites and injures someone, but the owner *would* be strictly liable if instead the owner knew that the dog tended to bite. The same would be true for an owner's bucking horse, charging bull, or scratching cat. Dog-bite statutes, though, commonly eliminate the prior-knowledge requirement, instead imposing true strict liability absent any knowledge of the dog's vicious propensities. Because the Multistate Bar Examination's tort questions have you assume that only the common law applies, a question would have to alert you to a dog-bite statute if the examiner intended that you apply the statutory rule.

...including claims arising from abnormally dangerous activities...

The common law recognizes a second form of strict liability for **abnormally dangerous activities**. One who conducts an abnormally dangerous activity on land pays for any resulting harm, whether the actor exercises all possible care or not. The significant issue in strict liability for abnormally dangerous activities is what constitutes such an activity. Most jurisdictions follow a multi-factor test weighing the activity's risk against its value, how common the activity is in the location in which the actor conducted it, and the actor's ability or inability to eliminate the risk. Damming water for a reservoir, and using, storing, or transporting explosives, are two examples of abnormally dangerous activities. Statutes address liability for environmental harm, although common-law strict liability may also exist when abnormally dangerous activities harm the environment.

...and defenses to such claims

Both assumption of risk and comparative negligence can be defenses to strict liability. So, for instance, the owner of a vicious dog must pay for the dog's bite, but the law may bar or reduce the victim's recovery if the victim ignored the dog's growl or owner's warning. The claimant must also prove a peculiar kind of causation for strict liability to arise: the harm must be that which makes the animal vicious or activity abnormally dangerous. So, for instance, if a vicious dog bites, then the owner pays in strict liability, but if the victim instead trips over the dog rather than suffers a bite, the owner does not pay in strict liability. Biting is what makes dogs vicious, not posing a trip obstacle.

...claims against manufacturers and other defendants arising out of the manufacture and distribution of products...

Products liability includes several theories. Products liability includes **negligence** claims, particularly when one can identify a careless action. Negligence-based products liability requires proving the traditional negligence elements of duty, breach, causation, and damages. For example, a manufacturer that is careless in designing, assembling, inspecting, or testing a product may owe negligence liability. A negligence theory may also make the best sense when one can show that the product's design violates safety statutes or industry standards, from which one might draw presumptions or inferences of negligence. A negligence theory also makes sense when one can show that the manufacturer had available to it reasonable alternative designs that would have eliminated or reduced the injury-causing hazard.

Products liability also includes **breach-of-warranty** theories. The breach-of-warranty theory makes sense when one can identify promises, assurance, and representations that accompanied the product but that the product did not meet, resulting in the harm. Warranties can be either **express** or **implied**. Express warranties can arise from any communication accompanying the product including advertising and instructions. For example, if a product's packaging shows persons using the product for a specific purpose, then the manufacturer is likely warranting that the product is reasonably safe for that purpose.

The law also implies warranties from a sale's circumstances. When merchants (those in the business) sell a product, the law implies that the product is **merchantable**, generally meaning fit for its ordinary purpose. When a purchaser asks for a product that can perform a certain function, and in response a retailer supplies a product, the retailer warrants that the product is fit for the purchaser's particular purpose. Merchants may disclaim some warranties but not the warranty of merchantability or warranties protecting against personal injury.

Strict products liability is a third products-liability theory after negligence and breach of warranty. Strict products liability provides that merchants who sell products in **defective condition unreasonably dangerous** to users are liable for resultant injury. The significant issue is what constitutes an unreasonably dangerous and defective condition. A **risk-utility test** can help determine whether a product is defective and unreasonably dangerous. Risk-utility-test factors include the product's risk versus its utility, whether the manufacturer could have offered a substitute product or have eliminated the risk from the product, whether the user was

Tort Law

aware of the risk and could have avoided it, and the cost of additional safety features. Alternatively, strict products liability may depend on a simpler **consumer-expectation test** asking how the consumer would have expected the product to perform.

Another strict-products-liability approach is to classify a product defect as having to do with either design, manufacturing, or warning. A **manufacturing defect** exists when at the time of manufacture the product departs from its design. **Design-defect** claims depend on showing that the product is not reasonably safe as designed, as the risk-utility or consumer-expectation test would determine. Design-defect claims require showing an alternative feasible design at the time of manufacture. **Failure-to-warn** claims depend on showing that the omission of a warning made the product unreasonably dangerous. Warnings must be adequate, alerting to the hazard while describing the injury risk and means of avoiding it. In failure-to-warn cases, courts will consider the user's sophistication and whether there were any learned intermediaries who should have given necessary warnings, and not require warning as to open-and-obvious hazards.

Merchants within the chain of distribution, including both **retailers** and **distributors**, bear the same strict products liability to the injured person as the **manufacturer** bears. On the other hand, strict products liability generally does not extend to **one-time resellers** of used products. Entities in the chain of distribution typically indemnify one another, shifting products liability up the distribution chain to the defendant responsible for introducing the defect. Subsequent remedial changes to correct design defects are generally inadmissible except to prove disputed feasibility. Service providers, like physicians implanting a medical device or hospitals facilitating the surgery, do not have products liability for defective devices. The law instead reserves products liability to entities where the sale of goods predominates over the provision of services.

...and defenses to such claims

Contributory or comparative negligence based on product misuse is a defense to products liability in most jurisdictions, although manufacturers must in their safety designs anticipate foreseeable misuses. **Assumption of risk** is another products-liability defense in some jurisdictions. The **statute of limitations** against late-filed claims, and **statutes of repose** as to very old products, are also products-liability defenses. **Federal preemption** is another defense, as to heavily regulated products like medical devices, pharmaceuticals, and fuels, where state tort liability could contradict federal statute or regulation mandating certain designs, procedures, or warnings.

IV.   Other torts

A. Claims based on nuisance, and defenses

Tort Law

Nuisance relates closely to trespass to land, except that while trespass involves unauthorized physical entries onto another's land, interfering with exclusive possession, nuisance instead involves non-physical **interference with use and enjoyment** of land. Nuisance often arises when the wrongdoer's activity sends loud noise, sooty smoke, bright light, or noxious smell onto another's land. Nuisance actions come in two forms. **Public nuisance** interferes with the public's use and enjoyment of roadways, parks, walks, and other public lands. **Private nuisance** involves a substantial interference with a private owner's use and enjoyment of private lands. While most tort actions involve damages claims, the remedy in nuisance may include both damages and an injunction stopping the interference.

B. Claims based on defamation...

Defamation addresses false statements shared with others about a third person that harm the person's reputation. The statements must be **provably false**, such as that a person embezzled funds, not merely non-quantifiable opinions, such as that a person is not particularly trustworthy. While some would say that truth is a defamation defense, more correctly, the defamation plaintiff must usually prove the statement false. The defamer must **publish** the statements, not necessarily meaning to print them but rather to share them with others who understand the statements. The defamer must **identify** the person, not necessarily by name but so that others who know the person understand that the statement is about that person. Defaming a group defames its individual member if the group is small enough and the member prominent enough. The statements must have the stinging effect of **lowering the reputation** of the person within a respectable community.

Defamation comes in two forms with an important distinction in the elements as to each. Defamation in written form is **libel**, whereas defamation in oral form is **slander**. The law presumes libel damages. The libel plaintiff need not prove any harm. On the other hand, the law does not ordinarily presume slander damages. Instead, the slander plaintiff must usually prove some monetary loss (called **special damage**) such as lost income or the cost of psychological care. The slander plaintiff need not prove special damage, though, if the defendant's statement constituted **slander per se**, which includes a false statement that the plaintiff had a loathsome disease, was incompetent in work, engaged in sexual misconduct, or committed a crime of moral turpitude.

Notice that defamation does *not* require that the defamer *know* that the statement is false. A person who believes that their reputation-lowering statements about another are true still commits defamation. Also, defamation law holds liable both **primary publishers**, those who first speak or write the defamation, and **secondary publishers**, those who repeat or print the defamation, as in media. While content providers who post false statements online can have defamation liability, Congress granted internet service providers immunity from defamation liability. Defamation remedies include nominal damages when the plaintiff suffers insubstantial harm but wishes to

Tort Law

prove the reputational point and compensatory damages for economic and non-economic loss. Some state statutes also authorize punitive damages, particularly when requiring the plaintiff to make a retraction demand, and the defendant refuses to retract.

... and invasion of privacy...

Invasion of privacy takes one of four forms. The form most like the tort's invasion-of-privacy name involves **intrusion on seclusion of persona**, a highly offensive invasion into a place where one has a reasonable expectation of privacy. The invasion may be personal, such as by sneaking or peering into the private place, or by video or audio recording device, or even by examining private medical or financial records. The place may be a traditionally private location like a bedroom or bathroom but could also be a public place like a street or walkway, if a serious injury or other event takes place there, leaving circumstances that a reasonable person would consider private.

Invasion of privacy's second form, **appropriation** or **commercial exploitation**, involves unauthorized use of another's name, likeness, or image for commercial or other advantage. Although the famous, such as entertainers, often suffer appropriation for the illicit gains from their fame, one need not be famous to have an appropriation claim. The right is to control one's image, not simply to prevent others from undue financial advantage. The appropriator's motive is often financial gain, but appropriation for political or social cause, or other advantage, is also actionable. An injunction against further use, together with disgorgement of gain or other damages, are common remedies for the appropriation form of the invasion-of-privacy tort. Jurisdictions routinely recognize both the intrusion and appropriation forms of invasion of privacy.

Not all jurisdictions recognize the last two forms of invasion of privacy. **Public disclosure of private facts**, also known as the **right of publicity**, prohibits the disclosure to more than a few, of true private facts, where the discloser has no legitimate interest in doing so and the disclosure would highly offend the reasonable person. For example, disclosing a mature adult's long-ago juvenile-delinquency commitment could give rise to a right-of-publicity claim. Invasion of privacy's last form, **false light**, involves publicly depicting another in a false manner that would be highly offensive to the reasonable person. False light thus relates closely to defamation, although with false light, the concern is the highly offensive misleading depiction rather than false words that lower reputation.

...defenses...

Common-law **privileges** offer defenses to defamation claims. Defamation law recognizes both **absolute** and **qualified** privileges. Absolute privileges protect the defamer whether the defamer speaks in good faith or not (whether the defamer knows that the statements are false or does not

Tort Law

know). **Absolute privileges** apply to **judicial, legislative**, and **executive** proceedings. Thus, a lawyer or party who publishes a false, reputation-lowering statement in court or a court-like administrative proceeding faces no defamation liability even if knowing that the statement is false. Similarly, a defamer who publishes a false statement in a legislative session or record has absolute protection even when knowing that the published reputation-lowering statements are false. Executive officials, such as governors, mayors, and police chiefs, hold a similar privilege to speak defamation when making statements relating to their executive roles.

By contrast, **qualified privileges** protect the defamer only when the defamer speaks in good faith. If instead the defamer knows the statements to be false, then the defamer loses the qualified privilege. Qualified privileges apply when the defamer has a **legitimate interest** in speaking or speaks on behalf of the legitimate interest of others. For example, the owner of stolen property may incorrectly report a suspect to police, as long as the owner does not know that the owner is making a false report. The common law also offers qualified privileges of **fair reporting**, to make an accurate summary in news context of allegations that others have made in official proceedings, and of **fair comment**, to discuss those allegations to inform the public.

...and constitutional limitations

The **First Amendment** provides significant constitutional protection against defamation claims. The First Amendment permits persons to defame **public officials** and **public figures** if the defamer does so without **actual malice**. To apply this test for First Amendment protection of defamation, you must define *actual malice* as **knowledge of or reckless disregard for** the statement's falsity. You must also know the Supreme Court's definitions for *public officials* and *public figures*. A public official is one who controls government (under one test) or whose qualifications the public would want to know beyond the general interest in the qualifications of all public employees (a second test). A public figure is someone who voluntarily injected him- or herself into a public issue and has media access.

Those who defame private figures also have some First Amendment protection. If the defamatory publication concerns a private figure but addresses a **public issue,** then the private figure must show fault for liability and actual malice for presumed or punitive damages. Moreover, if the publication concerns a private figure but is on a public issue, then the private figure must retain the burden to prove the statement false. Only those who defame a private figure on a private issue have no First Amendment protection.

These constitutional protections also extend to the right-of-publicity and false-light forms of invasion of privacy, if the invasion involves a public official or public figure. Indeed, the Supreme Court has also held that the First Amendment protects the right to intentionally inflict emotional distress when done by parody or for political or social causes.

Tort Law

C. Claims based on misrepresentations, and defenses

Misrepresentation, also known as **fraud** and in plain terms a scam or swindle, involves transactional misconduct as to the information that the defrauding party shares or does not share. The law defines misrepresentation as a **false statement** made **knowingly** to **induce reliance causing loss**. The misrepresentation must be a **verifiably false** statement of fact, such as "this business you are buying from me made $100,000 last year," not merely puffing or opinion, such as "this business is great." The statement must also be as to a current fact rather than a prediction. A prediction or statement of intent is not misrepresentation when the event does not occur, even though it may be breach of contract when the event depended on the promisor's performance.

Bare nondisclosure is generally not actionable as misrepresentation. Instead, the general rule of transactions is **buyer beware**, requiring the buyer's own **due diligence**. Yet a claim for **silent fraud** or (the same thing) **fraudulent omission** can arise where one has a **duty to disclose**, such as by statute or within a special relationship of trust and reliance. A related claim of **fraudulent concealment** involves the defrauder actively hiding a condition so that the victim is unable to discover it.

By focusing on *knowing* false statements, misrepresentation ordinarily requires the bad intent of a corrupt purpose and guilty mind. Yet some states under some circumstances recognize a form of **negligent misrepresentation** that does not depend on knowledge of the falsity and the related corrupt purpose but instead only a careless false statement. In those cases, the law may limit the recovery to the careless misrepresenter's unjust gain rather than the broader benefit-of-the-bargain loss available for knowing misrepresentations. A few states even recognize a form of **innocent misrepresentation** involving a false statement made despite all care but again limiting recovery to the misrepresenter's unjust gain.

The fraud claimant must show that the claimant's reliance on the misrepresentation was **justifiable**. Contract terms that the seller sold the item *as is*, requiring the buyer's due diligence, and disclaiming any contrary representations as to the item's quality is not a complete defense to a fraud claim but may make the claimant's reliance less justifiable. Misrepresentations of law are generally not actionable (in theory, everyone should know the law) unless the law misrepresentation falsely implies underlying facts. Professionals who misrepresent facts in work supplied to their clients are generally liable to third parties only when the professional knows of the third party's reliance and takes some overt action supporting it. Claimants must prove fraud by **clear and convincing evidence**, not merely the usual preponderance-of-the-evidence proof burden.

D. Claims based on intentional interference with business relations, and defenses

Tort Law

Tort law recognizes other forms of business tort in addition to misrepresentation. The **injurious-falsehood** torts form one such category of business torts. The falsehood torts include **slander of title**, defined as a malicious (knowing, bad faith) false publication calculated to harm a property owner's pecuniary interest, causing special damage. For example, to record a false lien or mortgage against real property to prevent its profitable sale to another, when knowing that the recording had no basis, would constitute slander of title if successful in stopping the sale.

Trade disparagement is another form of falsehood business tort, distinguished from slander of title in that it protects an owner's business rather than the owner's property. Trade disparagement involves a knowing or reckless false statement calculated to harm an owner's business, causing special damage. For example, to tell a business's customers the deliberate falsehood that the owner is bankrupt and about to go out of business, to get the customers to buy elsewhere, would be trade disparagement if successful in diverting customers.

A second category of business tort involves interference with various business interests. The first form involves **interference with contract** in which the wrongdoer uses improper or wrongful means to cause another to commit a contract breach with the person whose interest the wrongdoer intends to harm. Competition by fair means is fine. The interference-with-contract tort addresses improper conduct harming a competitor, for example by paying or otherwise secretly inducing a supplier to stop delivering needed supplies to a competitor. **Interference with business relations** is another form of the business-interference tort, addressing wrongful interference not with an existing contract but with a contract expectancy. The interfering conduct need not be illegal so long as it violates generally accepted business standards.

Conclusion

A.   Perspective

What, really, is the bar exam? Lawyers, law students, law professors, and others actually give several different answers. Most practically, the bar exam is a licensing test. You take the bar exam to get a law license. In that sense, the bar exam is not one last awful punishment inflicted on law students before they hit easy street on their way to a rainbow's end pot of gold. The bar exam is simply something you must do first before you practice law. Keeping the bar exam in that perspective can help. The bar exam is certainly not anything even remotely close to facing combat, indeed not even close to fighting fires or patrolling dangerous streets. Not only is your physical safety never at risk, your preparation and the exam itself are both in relative comfort, with no extreme heat or cold like the millions who work outdoors daily face. You will be well fed at all times and have every other modern convenience throughout. In that sense, preparing for the bar exam and even *taking* the bar exam are both positions of rather extraordinary *privilege*. Treat the whole experience for what it truly is, which is a premier if not *the* premier professional-preparation experience, and you will have gained appropriate perspective.

B.   Growth

The bar exam does more than qualify you for licensure for a highly desirable professional career. The bar exam is also probably the single greatest challenge that a person can choose today to promote one's own development of clear thought and sound reason in pursuit of social, economic, and other good. The bar exam itself may not be the greatest fun, but it can be an indispensable spur to profound development. After the bar exam, you will likely feel differently about yourself than you did when you began bar studies because indeed you *are* different after the exam. You will have studied, organized, digested, and integrated your law knowledge into a highly useful whole. You will have also learned new self-management skills and new skills at reading, summarizing, reviewing, recalling, writing, and analyzing. Your new capacities will serve you well not only in a law career but in life. Yet you will also have increased your appetite for personal and professional growth. Passing the bar exam is not all that you will accomplish. As you recover from the bar exam, you may for a while not think about anything big as your next career or life step. Yet soon enough, you will be looking for that next challenge, and then the one after it, and the next one, and beyond to ever greater pursuits. You will have developed such personal and professional capacities that you will soon yearn to entrust them to appropriate ambitions. After the bar exam, you should relax and celebrate but also know that you will have more to achieve and celebrate in the future.

C. Outcomes

The one thing that makes the bar exam so frightful for so many examinees is not arduous bar-exam preparation or the conditions of the test itself. You can study intensely for an extended period, and you can manage a two-day test. The experience is nothing even remotely as risky and arduous as military boot camp. No, the one thing that makes the bar exam so frightful for so many is *not passing*. Examinees have several common reasons for fearing not passing, most of them pretty sensible, like the additional wait and cost of taking it again, the examinee's disappointment and embarrassment, the potential loss of a job or job opportunity, delay in hiring, and the disappointment of family and friends. When one thinks about each of these things, though, one realizes that they are each entirely manageable. They are, if you will, *first-world* problems, not third-world problems. *If they happen, and you have no reason to believe in advance of your earnest preparation that they probably will, you can and will survive them. The other remarkable thing about these concerns, in addition to each of them being not such great concerns in the grand scheme of things, is that with responsible commitment to earnest preparation they are not all that likely. Most examinees who take the bar exam pass the bar exam. Even for those who do not pass on their first try, many examinees who retake the bar exam pass the bar exam on their second or subsequent try.

D. Alternatives

Law practice is a dream career for many of us. Law students routinely get to taste that dream in the clinical part of their law school curriculum. You have heard how special law practice can be, and you have probably already experienced at least some of that allure. While the sound allure is in law practice's meaning, the benefits of practice are also material. Studies continue to show substantial average increases in earnings with licensure for law practice. Yet lawyers who pass the bar exam often move immediately or soon into other careers, for many different reasons. Law practice under licensure is just one of many careers pursued by those who earn a law degree. Many who earn a law degree never take a bar exam because they have no need for doing so. Your decision to take the bar exam is likely a good-to-great decision, the outcome of which you largely control. At least, you control many things influencing whether you will pass the bar exam. Other things you cannot control. Life goes on while you prepare for the bar exam, and life may keep you from preparing adequately or even from taking the bar exam at all. Even with your best effort, circumstances may conspire to lead you down a different path than the bar exam and licensure. Keep the perspective that while you value hugely the challenge of taking and passing the bar exam, you are doing more than taking a licensure exam. No matter the outcome, by giving bar preparation and the exam your best, you are proving once again your deepest commitment and faith. Those of us who have prepared for and taken the bar exam have something special to share, something more special than we would have had if we had *not* taken the bar. But for you, as for any examinee, only the future knows just what that special thing is. Keep the bar exam, and preparing for the bar exam, in perspective. For one last help, consider this concluding humorous but true story, contributed by a noble professional who after passing the bar went on to become both a distinguished judge and international mediator. If he passed the bar exam under the circumstances that he describes, then you too can pass.

Though he had solid plans for his law career, indeed employment already lined up, the young man had decided to return to his parents' house while studying for the bar exam, where he hoped that he would not only save room-and-board costs but also have the peace, comfort, and familiar social support of a warm and welcoming home. That his beloved younger sister would be at home from college was more consolation than distraction, especially when he was able to make the home's quiet basement his bar-exam command center. And indeed, everything went fine as the bar exam approached until a fire suddenly engulfed the first floor of the home. As the family stood safely outside counting their blessings but shocked at the sudden loss, the young man caught the attention of one of the firefighters. Could he possibly, the young man asked, rescue his precious bar-preparation notes and materials, so critical to his career, from the basement? In through the flames, smoke,

and hosed water went the brave firefighter who moments later came back out proudly holding the sodden and blackened bar materials. The family took temporary residence crammed together in a single motel room where the only study solitude the young man could find was to hole up in the tiny bathroom. Uncomfortable sitting on the closed toilet lid to study, the young man instead slumped down in the bathtub for hours at a time poring over his charred, smoke-smelling bar materials, not the perfect way to prepare for the bar but yet, as it turned out, wholly sufficient. He passed, just as you will with due diligence.

Index

impairment of third-party rights, **136**
impartial jurors, right to, 176
impeachment of witnesses, **186**,187-188
impeachment power, Congress's, 73
implead, 39
immunities, of federal branches, **76**
immunity, qualified, 61
immunity, state sovereign, 61
implied easements, **232**
implied-in-fact contract, 103,**109**,110
implied warranties in sale-of-goods contracts, **126**,127
implied warranty of merchantability, 127
impracticability of contract performance, **124**,125
inadequacy of damages, 36
inadvertent disclosure, 44
incapacity to contract, **115**
inchoate crimes, **155**
inchoate offenses, **155**
incidental beneficiaries in contract, 135,**136**
incompetency to stand trial, 165
incomplete privilege, tort defense, **281**
inconsistent statements of witnesses, **186**
incorporation of rights, 81
indefeasibly vested remainders, 214
indefiniteness of terms, **108**
indemnity, 40,292
independent contractor, vicarious liability for, **299**
indexes for recording systems, **267**
indispensable parties, 39
individual rights, **80**
industry standards as standard of care, 289
infancy as defense to crime, 165
inference of negligence, violation of statute, 288
informed consent, lack of, tort theory, 288
inheriting land, 264
injunctions against contract breach, **133**
injunctions, appeal of, 56
injurious falsehood, 309
innocent misrepresentation, 308
insanity defense to crime, 164-165
installment contracts, 126
instruct the jury, 184
insurance coverage, excluding evidence of, **199**
intended beneficiaries in contract, 135,**136**
intended killings, **141**
intent, criminal law, 161
intent in tort law, 274-275
intent to injure, criminal law, **143**
intentional infliction of emotional distress, 275,**277**
intentional interference with business relations, **308**
intentional torts, **274**
inter-branch relationships, federal, **73**
interest of witness, impeachment, **186**,187
interested party, 39,63
interference with business relations, 309
interference with contract, 309

intergovernmental immunities, **77**
interlocutory review, **56**
intermediate scrutiny, 86,94,96
intermediate theory of mortgages, 249
interpleader, 26,40
interrogatories, 42
interstate-commerce power, Congress's, 66
intervention, 40
intoxication as defense to crime, **165**
introduction of evidence, **181**
intrusion, 306
invasion of privacy, 306
invitee, liability to, 296
involuntary dismissal, 48,**52**
involuntary manslaughter, 143
irreparable harm, 36
irrevocable licenses, 231
issue preclusion, **55**

joinder of parties, **38**,54
joint-and-several liability, **292**
joint tenancy, **218**,264
joint venture, vicarious liability in, 298
judge, scope of review, **57**
judgment, final, 54
judgment and tax liens on real property, **272**
judgment on the pleadings, 49
judgments, **51**
judgments of conviction, hearsay exception for, **208**
judicial admission, 37
judicial branch, 65
judicial findings and conclusions, **53**
judicial foreclosure, 255-256
judicial notice, **183**
judicial review, **58**,60,62
judicial review in operation, **62**
jurisdiction, **60**
jurisdiction and venue, 24
jurisdiction, appellate, 60
jurisdiction, class actions, 41
jurisdiction, congressional power over, **60**
jurisdiction, diversity, 26,34,60
jurisdiction, federal-question, 24,25,60
jurisdiction, federal subject-matter, **24**,25
jurisdiction, original, 60,61
jurisdiction over criminal cases, 169
jurisdiction, supplemental, 27,28,40,60
jurors, right to impartial, 176
jury composition, **47**
jury demand, 45
jury instructions, **47**
jury, scope of review, **57**
jury selection, **46**
jury trial right, civil, **46**
jury trial right, criminal, 176
jury trials, **45**

worldwide jurisdiction, 30
writ of certiorari, 61
writ of mandamus, 56
writings, recordings, and photographs, admissibility
    of, **200**
wrongful birth, as tort claim, 285

wrongful conception, as tort claim, 284
wrongful life, as tort claim, 285

zoning, **236**
zoning, ultra vires, 237
zoning, variance from, 237

Acknowledgments

The author thanks Western Michigan University Thomas M. Cooley Law School and its board of directors, President and Dean Don LeDuc, other leaders, and faculty and staff members. The school's practice-access mission serves the nation ably in increasing the law profession's diversity while ensuring public access to markets and public confidence in the quality of justice. The author thanks Auxiliary Deans Tonya Krause-Phelan and Devin Schindler, and Professors Paul Sorensen, Chris Trudeau, Christi Henke, Victoria Vuletich, Chris Hastings, Brendan Beery, and Monica Nuckolls, for contributing questions or commenting on and correcting questions. The author thanks Auxiliary Dean David Tarrien for comments on design. The author thanks Head of Public Service Aletha Honsowitz for library support. Most of all, the author thanks the many students and graduates of the law school's Grand Rapids campus whose ambition, insight, and perseverance informed and inspired the authors in this work. I hope it serves future students and graduates well.

About the Author

Nelson Miller is Professor and Associate Dean at Western Michigan University Thomas M. Cooley Law School. Before coming to the law school, Dean Miller practiced civil litigation for 16 years, representing individuals, corporations, agencies, and public and private universities. He has since published thirty-five books and dozens of book chapters and articles on law, law school, and law practice, and edited other books. The State Bar of Michigan recognized Dean Miller with the John W. Cummiskey Award for pro-bono service, while the law school recognized him with its Great Deeds award for similar service. He was among two dozen law professors recognized nationally in the Harvard University Press study *What the Best Law Teachers Do*. Dean Miller earned his law degree at the University of Michigan where he was on law review and graduated Order of the Coif, before joining the firm that later became Fajen and Miller, PLLC, his practice base before moving full-time into law teaching. At the law school, Dean Miller teaches Torts I, Torts II, Civil Procedure II, Personal & Professional Responsibility, Employment Law, Michigan No-Fault Insurance Law, Law Practice: Business Development, and other courses, while administering the Grand Rapids campus and Western Michigan University affiliation.

CPSIA information can be obtained
at www.ICGtesting.com
Printed in the USA
FFOW04n1743240317
33620FF